man in prehistory

LIBRARY OF EARLY CIVILIZATIONS SERIES
Thames and Hudson, Ltd., London
McGraw-Hill Book Company, New York
General Editor: Professor Stuart Piggott

Aldred: EGYPT TO THE END OF THE OLD KINGDOM

Baldry: ANCIENT GREEK LITERATURE IN ITS LIVING CONTEXT

Bushnell: THE FIRST AMERICANS: THE PRE-COLUMBIAN CIVILIZATION

Clark: THE STONE AGE HUNTERS

Culican: THE FIRST MERCHANT VENTURERS

Hood: THE HOME OF THE HEROES: THE AEGEAN BEFORE THE GREEKS

Lloyd: EARLY HIGHLAND PEOPLES OF ANATOLIA

Mallowan: EARLY MESOPOTAMIA AND IRAN

Mellaart: EARLIEST CIVILIZATIONS OF THE NEAR EAST

Phillips: THE ROYAL HORDES: NOMAD PEOPLES OF THE STEPPES

Watson: EARLY CIVILIZATION IN CHINA

Wheeler: CIVILIZATIONS OF THE INDUS VALLEY AND BEYOND

WORLD UNIVERSITY LIBRARY SERIES
McGraw-Hill Book Company, New York

Bordes: THE OLD STONE AGE

Ucko-Rosenfeld: PALAEOLITHIC CAVE ART

MAN IN PREHISTORY

Chester S. Chard

Professor of Anthropology
University of Wisconsin

McGraw-Hill Book Company
New York   St. Louis   San Francisco   London
Sydney   Toronto   Mexico   Panama

man in prehistory

Library of Congress Catalog Card Number 68-58731

10651

4 5 6 7 8 9 – M A M M – 1 0

Maps designed and drawn
by James J. Harvin.

Cover Photograph:
"The Venus of Brassempouy,"
Courtesy of The Musée des Antiquités Nationales, Paris, France.

A dozen years of teaching an introductory prehistory course, eleven of them at the University of Wisconsin, has provided the basis for the particular approach used in this book. Students, we may expect, approach the study of prehistory with a set of expectations. They will want to see the relevance of the prehistoric human experience to an understanding of cultural processes, human behavior, and human evolution. Stressing problems and trends and attempting always to avoid producing another catalog of artifacts, the author has sought to emphasize interpretation and not to parade facts in a way which tends to stifle interest in all but the most ardent beginner.

Consideration is given to the aims and contributions of the study of prehistory and to the methods of its principal technique, archeology. Some knowledge of how the data of prehistory are recovered and interpreted is essential to any understanding of the subject.

Primarily designed as a text for one-semester or quarter courses in introductory world prehistory at the freshman or sophomore level, or for students at any level who are approaching the subject for the first time, this volume should also prove of interest and use to the general reader who would like to acquire a brief overview of the human background and an introduction to the increasingly popular subject of archeology. Suitable and accessible readings are appended to the chapters for those who are interested in further information or seek more illustrations.

The author owes a special debt of gratitude to those experts who sought to rescue him from grievous error in their special fields of competence: Hansjürgen Müller-Beck, John T. Robinson, Kwang-chih Chang, Marija Gimbutas, and Donald E. Thompson. Stubbornly, he did not always heed their advice. Susan Bennett provided helpful comments from the viewpoint of the prospective audience and strove to improve the literary style. Anne Powers assisted with technical matters and assumed responsibility in the final stages during the author's absence abroad. Jean Reynolds typed the final manuscript with her usual expertise.

Chester S. Chard

contents

man in prehistory

introduction

the laboratory of human history

No understanding of human biology, culture, and behavior can be achieved solely on the basis of the phenomena observable in the world today. It is a basic thesis of this book that the present is quite literally the product of the past and that a grasp of the panorama of human history, however inadequate the picture remains as yet, is a prerequisite in any attempt to understand man. Moreover, human history in any true sense must comprise the whole story of the biological, cultural, and behavioral development of man from the time he ceased being a nonhuman primate and made the first moves in the direction of humanity

Just as modern man, the organism, is a product of evolutionary processes, present-day human culture is the product of cultural processes operating through time in constant interaction with environmental and biological factors. Since these cultural processes and associated cultural phenomena have also played an important role as factors in human biological evolution, it is obvious that the biological and cultural evolution of man is an integrated process that cannot be separated and must be viewed as a whole. Thus, although this book is primarily concerned with *cultural* evolution, we shall strive for an awareness of the concurrent biological processes and factors.

Culture[1] can be understood, then, only in the light of its background and development as revealed by human history. This is especially true

[1] Culture is the learned behavior patterns, ideas, and values acquired by man as a member of a social group.

1

because the basic processes of culture—invention and *diffusion*[2]—operate through time and thus are visible to us only through the perspective of time. The processes that have shaped culture in the past are those still operating today. The study of human history from this point of view can be called *culture history* or, in a very general sense, *cultural evolution*.

It has been well said that in order to see big things whole, we must view them from afar, and it is just this that such a culture history enables us to do. When we immerse ourselves in some particular phase of history, as we do in a conventional academic history course, it often impresses us as being a maze of apparent inconsequences: We cannot see the forest for the trees. It is only when we stand off, viewing in the larger perspective afforded by a history of *man* rather than of particular men, that the broad sweeps and significant trends become readily apparent. This kind of history provides the major laboratory for cultural anthropology, in which we can check our hypotheses and even test fundamental theories about human nature and human progress. An outstanding example of this testing of theories is provided by the culture history of the New World prior to European contact. The Spanish conquerors were amazed by the native civilizations they encountered in Middle America and Peru, which in some ways were the equal of those in the Old World. If it can be definitely established by historical evidence that these civilizations had developed independently without stimulus or borrowing from their Old World counterparts, we would be led to conclude that, given time and favorable environment, man is bound to produce the level of cultural complexity we call civilization through the action of some innate evolutionary process. Hence, if modern civilization were to be destroyed but some humans survive, there would be the probability that eventually the level of modern civilization would once more be attained (though the lack of easily available natural resources, after thousands of years of exploitation, would be a handicap). On the other hand, if it can be demonstrated that at least the ideas for the basic elements and skills of civilization were borrowed from outside the New World, a fundamentally imitative, non-creative nature of man would become apparent, and it would be possible that civilization, once lost, might not be re-created. The chance of solving such basic problems as this is ample justification for the great amount of time, effort and resources that are devoted by anthropologists to the study of aboriginal New World culture history—an undertaking that to many people must seem of dubious value and scant relevance to the problems of today.

To take another example, perhaps the most striking phenomenon revealed by the panorama of man's cultural development is the series of ups and downs which have marked the slow upward curve. Progress has been the net achievement of mankind as a whole, not of any single group. Leading roles have been played at one time or another by many different groups, but never for very long: No matter how brilliant their contribution

---

[2] Diffusion means the spread of ideas and techniques from one group to another.

to the total of human civilization, every leading group has sooner or later fallen, and a new people in some different region has taken over the role. What has caused all earlier civilizations to wither eventually, or their seeds to sprout with greater vigor in some alien soil? Until we gain some understanding of the processes underlying the rise and fall of man's many experiments in civilization, can we glibly assume that ours is immune to a similar fate?

As a final example of the relevance of the past for the present, of the significance of the laboratory of human history, we can cite our present-day concern with the impact on human societies of major, rapid, technological change, epitomized in such terms as Industrial Revolution and Scientific Revolution. When we view this change in the light of past human experience, we come to realize that these problems with which the world is currently grappling are not something new in man's history; on the contrary, this is a repetitive pattern, a recurrent phenomenon which has faced mankind before and which we have every reason to assume will face it again in the unforeseeable future. We shall find that men in earlier times have had to deal with problems broadly similar to those now confronting us: problems resulting from major technological revolutions that had very profound effects on human society, on human culture, on human economy, on human settlement and human population—just as the present-day revolutions will lead to changes and developments that are beyond our comprehension. And it will be worth our while to pay some attention to these earlier revolutions, to see what common elements we may discern, what parallels may exist between them and our own situation, and what we may learn from human experience in the past that will give us broader insights in facing our own problems. It must especially be emphasized that only in long-term historical perspective of this sort can we possibly study the *biological consequences* on man of such technological changes, which may well prove in the long run to be equally profound.

One of our aims, then, is to make the reader aware of the fundamental continuity of the present with the past, to overcome the average student's tendency to think of history as a separate body of chronological details relating to another world that has no connection with the here and now. We shall try to impart some realization of the immense antiquity of human culture, of its initial simplicity, and of the complexity of its growth and diversification, with emphasis on the earlier stages as representing the shared, common tradition of all mankind that underlies and provides the sources for the later experiments in civilization. We shall hope to impart some appreciation of what has gone into the making of the modern world. All too many of us take our present state for granted, not bothering to think about the effort which achieved it, seldom realizing the overwhelming difficulties that mankind has undergone in the course of this long, upward struggle. We shall show, too, that our Western cultural heritage has far deeper roots than the standard textbook presentation of history would suggest, roots running back far beyond the classical world through thousands of years of preceding civilizations which underlay that of Greece. Such a demonstration of the depth and complexity of our own background should enhance our awareness of "one world." And while acknowledging the strong influence still exerted by Judeo-Christian and Greek value systems in our lives, we should consider the possibility that what we like to call our thinking may (as Stuart Piggott suggests) be as much conditioned by the fears and prejudices of the mammoth hunter or of the "Neolithic" peasant as by the religious aspirations of the early Semites or the speculative thoughts of the Greeks. However solid it may appear, civilization is only a very thin veneer over two or more million years of savagery. The vast bulk of the human experience is prehistoric.

But we cannot hope to understand the factors and forces responsible for the development of civilization solely by examining the background of our own. If more space seems to be devoted to the latter in this book, this is primarily a reflection of the greater amount of information available in this area. Only through the comparative study of all civilizations and major traditions can we hope to glimpse the cultural processes involved, which is our basic interest. Actually, isolated regions that may have contributed little or nothing to the main stream may be of the greatest value in this connection since they best approximate controlled experiments. Therefore, the course of development in Africa, in the Far East, or in the Americas is of equal importance for our purposes and will receive, proportionately, as much attention as the state of knowledge permits. The broader our scope, the sounder will be the generalizations that we may eventually be able to make. Finally, we shall try to present the patterns of the growth and diffusion of culture and not simply document the specific events of the human story.

history vs prehistory

The conventional study of history, which is based entirely on written documents, supplies us with some of the data for our panorama of man's cultural development. But the historian, thus limited by the nature of his source materials, can record only a tiny fraction of human history, since in only a very few places does the keeping of historical records go back even as much as 4,500 years. We use the term *prehistory* to designate the preceding 99.9 percent of the story of mankind. In the English-speaking world, the study of prehistory has fallen by default to the lot of anthropology.

When we realize that the New World and the bulk of Africa remained prehistoric until a little over 450 years ago (and most of it until even later), that the northern half of Europe was in the outer darkness until the Christian era, that historical records in the Far East or in India at best take us back 3,000 years in a few areas, we begin to realize how much we must depend on prehistory for our knowledge of man and how little the historian can help us. It has been aptly pointed out that one can no more hope to understand the human story solely from the study of recorded history than one can hope to understand a weighty book from reading only the last few pages. And prehistory was not only immensely long but also profoundly eventful. Except for the Industrial and Scientific Revolutions, all the great breakthroughs in human experience, the basic achievements that made possible all that has happened since, were prehistoric. Indeed, it is doubtful whether any subsequent economic change has affected the potentialities of human life more profoundly than the establishment of food production in prehistoric times through the domestication of plants and animals. With all our modern scientific knowledge, we have been able to add very little of fundamental significance to what these anonymous benefactors bequeathed us. The invention of writing certainly played a comparable role in the intellectual history of man. The basic technological achievements of prehistoric men—the wheel, metallurgy, textiles, pottery, control of fire, and the like—are the essential building blocks of our own technology, the prerequisites of all modern inventions.

In addition to its very limited coverage, conventional history has other drawbacks as a source of data for the study of culture history. In the early civilizations, writing was often used only for limited purposes, such as bookkeeping, and was known only to a small number of professional scribes. Our concept of writing—to record anything and everything which can be put into words—was a much later development. Hence the early civilizations were literate only in a very restricted sense of the word. Their literature, like that of nonliterate peoples everywhere, must still have been an oral literature transmitted by word of mouth. And when we do reach the first conscious written historical records we find them largely limited to chronicling the political maneuverings of a few ruling figures or the cult activities of the priesthood, ignoring the vast bulk of the population and the latter's way of life. Even the voluminous written history of the famous classical historians is mostly military history, giving little attention to culture, technology, commerce, economics, population density, and similar matters. In fact, technology and applied science are virtually ignored in European writings down to the sixteenth century, and what we know has been largely reconstructed in recent years from archeology. In addition to the inadequacy of the information provided by ancient history, its emphasis on individuals makes it difficult to discern trends and processes.

prehistory: its scope and nature

The study of prehistory differs in many respects from that of conventional history. These differences, mostly enforced by the nature of the evidence, offer both handicaps and certain advantages from our point of view. For one thing, prehistory is anonymous, while so much of conventional history is biographical; the familiar "great man" concept of history is thus ruled out. The actors in prehistory, the basic units, are social groups, societies; our concern is with social patterns and problems, not with the moral and psychological problems confronting individuals. We can hope to study the organization, relationships, *ecology*,[3] patterned behavior and history of human groups which were social units, and on this basis aspire to reconstruct the history of man. Anonymity has its advantages: By this merging of the great with the humble, the good with the bad, this universal leveling and averaging (as A. V. Kidder put it), we thus eliminate from the picture the complicating and confusing psychological reactions of numbers of unique human personalities, so that the cultural processes and major trends which are our principal concern stand out more clearly. Indeed, our concern with the individual reflects our own cultural conditioning. We must realize the group nature of the life of early man, the subservience of the individual to his social unit. Our ideal of the free-standing human being was hardly formulated before the Greeks. In this sense, the picture presented by prehistory is not distorted or colorless; even though the actors are societies, the disappearance of the individual need not deprive the drama of human interest.

Like anthropology, prehistory embraces the whole range of human activities and accords them equal attention; it is interested in all men who have ever lived, anywhere in the world—the total record of humanity. Unlike conventional history, it stresses cultural, economic, and scientific development and must concern itself with trends more often than with events. Prehistory reveals the workings of the basic cultural processes which have shaped man's life from the beginning—invention and diffusion—and by emphasizing the rarity of the former and the importance of the latter, makes us realize the tremendous interdependence of human cultures and the essential cultural brotherhood of man. It is not a search for origins as such, which would be a futile and rather pointless quest, but a study of *process*. For instance, we are not so much interested in how, when, or where fire was first tamed by man as we are in examining the impact of fire on man's cultural development.

Another advantage of prehistory is the opportunity it provides to study the interrelationships of men and their societies with the natural environment over long periods of time. Only on the vast scale which prehistory alone can provide may we hope to study such long-range problems as the effects of soil exhaustion, erosion, or long cycles of climatic change on society, or the effects of cultural factors on human biology. In fact prehistory is, in a sense, the study of man's progressive ability to cope with the forces of nature.

As a final comment on the nature of prehistory, we should point out

[3] Ecology deals with the interrelationships of living organisms, or groups thereof, with their environment and with other living things in it.

the very irregular and nebulous nature of the frontiers of conventional history. If we wish to think in terms of "historic" and "prehistoric" eras, we must do so for each locality separately, for the threshold was reached at different times everywhere: the point where a given group either began consistently to maintain written records of an historical nature, or came in contact with some literate people who wrote about them. As examples of the former, Mesopotamia and Egypt entered the realm of history about 2500 B.C., China about 1000 B.C.; in the latter fashion, northwestern Europe became "historical" about the time of Christ, the New World, by degrees, from 1492 on to the present, and parts of interior New Guinea only in the last few years. Thus prehistory has existed side by side with history, though its scope has steadily shrunk until today it has reached the vanishing point. Even though we may accept the commencement of written records as a strict definition of the beginning of the historic era in each place, we must bear in mind that it is usually much later before these records are really adequate; the picture must still be supplemented by data obtained by the methods of prehistory. And of course even a literate civilization whose writing has not yet been deciphered—e.g., the Indus Valley or the Maya—is still prehistoric.

the framework of prehistory

The conventional subdivisions of man's prehistory—Paleolithic, Mesolithic, Neolithic, Bronze Age, Iron Age—are simply an elaboration of the old "Three Ages" concept which we shall discuss in the next chapter. These subdivisions are based on certain technological changes in western Europe (primarily in France), and actually represent classifications of local archeological materials rather than any real attempt to mark off stages in cultural evolution. The system is inadequate for a meaningful presentation of the evidence available today, or for an understanding of the real significance of the various cultural developments, but the terms persist stubbornly in general usage and therefore we must be familiar with them.

The *Paleolithic*, which means literally "Old Stone Age," was originally defined as the era of chipped stone tools. In modern usage it has come to denote human culture during the Pleistocene. So vast a time span of course necessitated further subdivision, and three periods were set up, supposedly representing stages of technological development, as they appeared in France. Following the pattern of geological nomenclature, these were named, from oldest to youngest, Lower, Middle, and Upper Paleolithic. (It should be pointed out that these do not correspond in any way to the geological subdivisions of Lower, Middle, and Upper Pleistocene, with which they are easily confused.) The Lower Paleolithic, originally identified with the presence of the so-called "handax," now simply denotes all cultures prior to the Middle Paleolithic. The latter is equated with the

Mousterian, considered to represent the culture of Neanderthal Man; the Upper Paleolithic comprises the blade-and-burin industries associated in Europe with early Homo sapiens—a concept scarcely applicable elsewhere. The *Mesolithic* ("Middle Stone Age") was originally coined to cover the hiatus between the Paleolithic and the Neolithic in the western European sequence. It is generally used to refer to human cultures in postglacial times which had not attained a level definable as Neolithic. The *Neolithic* or "New Stone Age" was defined as the era of polished stone tools—i.e., as characterized by tools made by the techniques of abrasion (grinding and polishing) rather than by chipping. This concept proved to be of doubtful diagnostic value, and there was an increasing tendency to define Neolithic cultures in terms of the presence of pottery but absence, as yet, of metal. The term is still widely used in this sense in the Soviet Union and in eastern Asia. In recent years, under the influence of the great British pre-historian V. G. Childe, "Neolithic" has come to denote in the Western World a socioeconomic pattern: food production, based on the domestica-tion of plants and animals, and the resultant village community as the social unit. It is therefore generally thought of today as the time from the beginnings of food production to the beginnings of metallurgy. The *Bronze Age* and *Iron Age* were the successive prehistoric stages in western Europe characterized by metallurgy based predominantly on these respec-tive metals. In its later phases the Iron Age emerged into the light of history and brought the prehistoric archeological sequence to a close.

This conventional system is increasingly inadequate as a framework for the study of human cultural evolution. It obscures the really significant developments and makes major divisions where there is actually no break in the continuity; its stages do not correspond to the natural divisions in geological or biological history, or to the stages in human evolution—a major concern now that we realize how closely biological and cultural evolution are interrelated. It is specifically tied to western Europe, does not fit much of the rest of the Old World, and has never been accepted in the New World, where archeologists have shown a strong resistance to any use of this terminology. Moreover, the subdivision names have become largely meaningless and at best they ignore the major events in man's history. The Lower Paleolithic in particular has become too unwieldy, bracketing as it does some 95 percent of the story and having become a palpably artificial concept.

In this book we are going to use the following framework to present the story of human cultural evolution in what we hope is a more mean-ingful fashion. Like any classification it is, of course, not the only frame-work that could be set up based on the available evidence, and we expect to revise it whenever some other arrangement seems to better present the picture. It should be noted that although human history is considered to begin at the point where the hominid line crossed the threshold of hu-manity, which will be discussed presently, this is an arbitrary point, and for a better perspective our scope must extend back a distance into the prehuman past.

I. Food-gathering Stage (Man the Hunter)
    Characterized by slow but continuous evolution with no major breaks
    or changes in the basic pattern
    A. Lower Pleistocene (protoculture)
        Duration perhaps 2 million years
        1. Prehuman
        2. "Human" (after crossing threshold of humanity)
    B. Middle Pleistocene
        Duration perhaps 600,000 years
    C. Upper Pleistocene
        1. Neanderthaloid Phase (Last Interglacial and Early Würm)
            Duration perhaps 100,000 to 150,000 years
        2. Homo sapiens[4] Phase (Aurignacian Oscillations and Last
            Glaciation)
            Duration about 30,000 to 35,000 years
    D. Postglacial (incipient cultivation and survivals of earlier patterns)
        Within the last 10,000 years
II. Food-producing Stage (Man the Farmer)
    Characterized by increasing control over the natural environment and
    by a succession of major shifts or so-called "revolutions" in the basic
    pattern
    Within the last 10,000 years
    A. Village farming
    B. Urbanism ("civilization")
    C. Industrialization

Our two principal stages were initiated by decisive ecological shifts that revolutionized human life by releasing potential and launching cultural (and biological) evolution that resulted in mankind as we know it today. These two decisive ecological shifts are often labeled, respectively, the "Ecological Revolution" and the "Neolithic Revolution" (or "Agricultural," or "Food-producing"). The term "revolution" is a misnomer when applied to prehistoric events and tends to create an erroneous image. Each of these developments had revolutionary consequences, but it required a long time for the potential to be realized. With the accelerated tempo of change in the last 5,000 or 6,000 years, the effects of major shifts become more immediately drastic, and it is thus perfectly proper to speak, for example, of the "Industrial Revolution." However, comparable phenomena in prehistoric times are best thought of as the crossing of a certain threshold—or point of no return in a spectrum of continuous development—often independently in several different parts of the world, as in the case of food production and urbanism.

Further subdivision of these stages is of course necessary in order

---

[4] "Homo sapiens" is used throughout the book in its traditional sense of fully modern forms of man. This is not intended to imply that Neanderthal and related forms do not belong to this same species taxonomically.

conveniently to handle so large a subject. In stage I the primary subdivisions utilize the established geological time system but are also intended to correspond roughly to phases of human evolution. It is not yet feasible to subdivide A and B, despite their size, except in very tentative fashion; C has been further subdivided owing to the greater abundance of information and growing complexity of the picture. Stage II has been subdivided into cultural-economic phases of development resulting from the major breakthroughs that launch each phase. However, it must be borne in mind that these stage II phases do not completely replace one another; populations in some areas have remained in the earlier phases of development down to modern times. Some, in fact, like the Australian aborigines or the Eskimo, never attained stage II at all, because of isolation or environmental factors that prevented the development of food production. Furthermore, the passage from one stage, phase or subdivision to another is never synchronous over the world; each region attained the various levels according to its own historical pattern of development.

General features of the Food-gathering Stage include (1) the achievement of full humanity (in the modern sense) from primate beginnings, with initial continuity from the primate past and no gap or sharp break between "animal" and "man"; (2) the achievement of adaptation to all environments by cultural means to the extent that man, a tropical organism, escaped from his physiological limitations and came to occupy and exploit all the habitable world—i.e., technology, toward the end of the stage, had been brought to the point where it could serve as a screen between man and the natural environment; (3) a continuous process of development throughout this stage with no breaks in the basic pattern or in the continuity; (4) an enormous time span involved with almost imperceptible progress against this background until the final phases when the tempo begins to accelerate—as reflected in the time scale on our framework (mankind, in other words, got off to a very slow start); (5) a close interrelationship at this stage between man and the natural environment, with the influence of environment on human life as a controlling factor (especially in the earlier phases); (6) the general coincidence of this stage with the Pleistocene, with the result that human development during the Food-gathering Stage is intimately bound up with the conditions prevailing during this period in the history of the earth and the history of life; and finally, (7) the limited picture of actual human life at this stage available to us owing to the limited *types* of evidence surviving, even though stone tools are abundant in comparison with remains of fossil men themselves—a situation that will remain a permanent handicap even after much more extensive archeological work has been done. (It should also be borne in mind that much of the record may have been obliterated by rising sea levels in coastal areas doubtless favored by early man, as it was obliterated by erosion and glacial action in many inland areas.)

Any discussion of the general features of the Food-producing Stage will be postponed until later, except to note the radically increased tempo of development and rate of change.

Two important observations should be made on the overall picture as set forth here. First, it reveals graphically that man has been a hunter—a carnivorous predator in the natural world—for virtually all his career. This overriding fact has never been adequately recognized. It not only shaped the entire pattern of human life until what is only yesterday in the human time scale, but must inevitably continue to affect our own behavior in the modern world. It is too unrealistic to expect any species to completely transform its basic nature in so short a time—especially when the instincts of Man the Hunter have been fostered and usually glorified in Man the Warrior.

Second, humanity has never presented a uniform picture at any stage or point in time, any more than it does today. Always it is a mosaic of relatively more or less conservative, more or less changing regional or local populations—these differences reflecting not significant differences in capacity between groups but rather differences in habitat and pressure for adjustment and, increasingly with time, in the ethos shaping each cultural pattern: differences in what each culture selects as the focus of its attention and interest.

Before beginning our survey of man's cultural evolution, we should like to impress upon the reader that any account of human prehistory should be considered as merely a "progress report" of the current state of knowledge, with each page prominently marked "subject to change without notice." In probably no other field of anthropology does the picture change so rapidly—at least with respect to the earlier time periods and the shift from stage I to stage II. It may be assumed that our account of these is likely to have been rendered obsolete by the time it appears in print. This is due to the inadequacy of our knowledge of such crucial periods and to the flimsy nature of the conventional constructs and concepts of human prehistory set forth with such confidence and authority in the average textbook. (The evidence on which these conventional constructs and concepts were based, secured mostly during the early years of archeology, is now known to be inadequate and often unreliable.) As a result, a few new discoveries, or reanalysis of older materials with modern techniques and viewpoints, can produce radical changes in the picture overnight. Furthermore, leading authorities are not always in agreement as to the interpretation of the available evidence. Quite divergent views may be encountered in different publications. This seems to dismay many beginning students, but it must be recognized as commonplace in any field of science. And opinions are subject to change just as is the body of evidence. The progress report that follows represents our interpretation at the moment of the available evidence. Both are equally "subject to change without notice."

archeology

archeology: the primary technique of studying prehistory

"If we are going to study individuals, societies, communities or other groupings of people in the past, we have got to use various techniques which will get around the fact that just because it *is* the past, the people we are studying are dead, and we cannot go and ask them questions or watch their daily life" (Piggott, 1959, p. 2). What, then, are the techniques by which the prehistoric span of man's cultural experience can be studied? The most important is *archeology*, the science that studies the history of culture through its material remains. Archeology rests upon the fact that all human societies unconsciously leave concrete records, not only of their material possessions, but also of their behavior, beliefs, and social institutions; and although these records may be fragmentary and ambiguous, they are capable of recovery and interpretation to a greater or lesser extent by archeological techniques.

Of more limited application, but often providing useful information in particular situations, are a number of other techniques. Historical linguistics, by studying the relationships and distribution of present and past languages, can throw light on the history and movements of the groups speaking them. Comparative studies of the physical and genetic characteristics of living human groups (or of past ones, where skeletal evidence is available) can similarly demonstrate relationships and illuminate past history. The distribution of traits or elements in existing cultures is tangible evidence of former contacts or movements and documents the process of diffusion in past time. And the oral traditions of nonliterate peoples, although they must be used with caution, cannot be disregarded as a source of historical information. Finally, there is the evidence that botanists and zoologists can supply on the history of domesticated plants and animals, which throws light not only on the processes of domestication but also on the movements and contacts of the peoples involved. Naturally, the more types of evidence that can be brought to bear on any problem, the better will be our understanding. And when the findings of several approaches are in agreement, we can enjoy a high confidence in the reliability of the conclusions.

Archeology is thus only one of many disciplines involved in the reconstruction of prehistory, but it is unquestionably the central one. Just as paleontology provides most of our data for the study of human evolution, so archeology has provided most of our knowledge of man's cultural development. As a technique for the recovery of historical information in the absence of documents or to supplement documents, archeology, however, is finding additional uses, so that today one finds archeologists studying western U.S. Army posts of the 1880s as well as the earliest remains left by man. For historic periods it provides a check on the reliability or interpretation of documentary evidence and helps to fill in the many gaps in our information. In the case of the early civilizations, literate in only a restricted sense, archeology is still the mainstay—not to mention the fact that the basic historical documents of these civilizations were all recovered by archeologists in the first place. Whether we are studying the early dynasties of Egypt or Mesopotamia or the period of the Saxon invasion of England, literary evidence alone would afford us only a very sketchy picture of the lives and achievements of the people of those times.

Archeology is a term familiar to almost everyone, far more than is anthropology itself, but the image is generally distorted and the real aims of this discipline rarely appreciated. In the public mind there is the stereotype archeologist of the New Yorker or Satevepost cartoons, an odd character with pith helmet and magnifying glass puttering in Egyptian tombs— blood brother to the stereotype cave man with club and leopard skin. Or, to the reader of Sunday supplements, the archeologist is a romantic figure who devotes his life to one perpetual treasure hunt for lost cities and gold-filled tombs. Unfortunately, the life of the professional archeologist is not one of glamor and adventure but of hard and painstaking work under conditions of frequent discomfort. The refuse of past human activity which is his stock in trade is for the most part monotonous and uninspiring, with little or no aesthetic appeal or monetary value. This is not to say that archeology is devoid of excitement or satisfaction. Obviously, it has great attractions and rewards for its practitioners. There is an element of that universal lure represented by the mystery or detective story—and the archeologist can rightly be considered a scientific detective. But there is equal fascination in what might be called the human touch. The archeologist "handles the actual things which helped men to pass their lives:

the pots from which they ate and drank, the weapons with which they hunted or killed one another, their houses, their hearthstones and their graves. He is concerned with the lives and achievements of countless ordinary, anonymous people" (Hawkes and Hawkes, 1955, p. v). The prehistoric archeologist, in fact, is nothing more or less than an anthropologist—except that the people whose life and culture he is studying happen to be dead.

Even among well-educated people the notion persists that anyone who digs things out of the ground is an archeologist. Persons who turn up fossils often send them hopefully to the nearest department of archeology for identification or preservation; others are surprised or disappointed to discover that dinosaurs are no concern of the archeologist. The recovery and study of fossil animal remains is the task of paleontology, a branch of zoology. Archeology is concerned only with the remains of human activity.

history of modern archeology

Although the study of conventional history—and an interest in it—was well developed in ancient Greece and contemporary China of the Chou dynasty, the study of prehistory is a recent intellectual development. It is not that the techniques for illuminating the distant past were not developed until the nineteenth century—this is true of other sciences as well—it is rather that there was no interest in, or even curiosity about, what people were doing before the first page of the standard historical accounts. Difficult as it is for us to comprehend, there was simply no awareness that man had a prehistoric past until barely a hundred years ago. In the classical world, mythology supplied adequate answers to any questions that might have arisen in even the inquiring Greek mind; the same held true in China. With the eclipse of classical learning during medieval times, the Old Testament became the unquestioned authority on the background of man. But even while the Western mind gradually freed itself from the stifling intellectual bonds, beginning with the Renaissance, and laid the foundations of modern science, the prehistoric past, unlike the wonders of nature, aroused no interest and formed no part of the subject matter of scholarly inquiry. It was not so much that it was actually ruled "off limits"; it simply did not exist in the consciousness of even the men of science. In view of the profusion of evidence of prehistoric human activity brought to light quite accidentally in the past hundred years in the course of everyday activities, it is difficult for us to comprehend this previous total unawareness of the very existence of prehistoric man. Inevitably, then as now, ancient stone tools were stumbled over continually, but they were firmly believed to be thunderbolts or attributed to elves and pixies. Remains that were too obviously human—burials, mounds, earthworks—

were ascribed to semihistorical people such as the ancient Britons immediately prior to the Roman conquest. The Western mind, down to the mid-nineteenth century, could not conceive of any real antiquity for man. In the English-speaking world this situation was compounded by the fact that the Creation had been calculated to have taken place in the year 4004 B.C. This mathematical exercise on the part of a certain Archbishop Ussher had become such an entrenched dogma in Britain that to question it, even in the mid-nineteenth century, was like denouncing the Bible itself. As a result, eminent scientists could examine human remains lying side by side with the bones of admittedly extinct animals and see no association; the human remains were invariably explained as an intrusion of a later historic age. Given the preconceptions of the time, no other explanation was conceivable, even to the scientific mind. There could be no science of prehistory until the mental blocks had been cleared away.

This intellectual revolution occurred in 1859. In large part it can be attributed to the new horizons, the great reorientation in thought, set in motion by the publication of Darwin's book *Origin of Species*. By coincidence, the same year saw the acceptance by an influential segment of the scientific community of the association of tools of human manufacture with Pleistocene deposits and thus, by implication, the acceptance of the Pleistocene antiquity of man. Overnight, the prehistoric past became a reality. The intellectual curiosity set free by the new climate of thinking catalyzed by Darwin made necessary further illumination of the human story. Nor was there any delay in undertaking this: The techniques of archeology were already being developed in other areas, and were ready to be applied.

The first excavations deliberately undertaken for the recovery of ancient remains had been an outgrowth of the revival of interest in classical Greece and Rome that began with the Renaissance. Their purpose was simply to obtain art objects to fill national museums and the cabinets and mansions of private collectors. This type of activity is more accurately termed *antiquarianism*. Since it was motivated entirely by a humanistic approach, this early interest in the past was limited to what was considered to be the background of Western culture—the remains of ancient Greek and Roman civilization. As time went on, a secondary interest also developed in each part of Europe in its own national origins—i.e., in the local "barbarian" peoples such as the Gauls and the Britons, long forgotten but now rediscovered through the accounts of the classical writers. The visible ancient remains of the countryside were now attributed to these peoples.

During the Napoleonic period, antiquarian interest was extended to the spectacular monuments of the Near East, all of which could be connected with the events or nations mentioned in the Bible. The first half of the nineteenth century saw a burst of activity in Egypt and Mesopotamia, much of which was scarcely more than looting, but which produced a growing body of information about the ancient remains of this region. Deciphering of Egyptian hieroglyphics and other early inscriptions led to greater awareness of these civilizations of the ancient East. A little later, work began in Palestine, motivated by a desire to illuminate the background of the Bible. All this embryonic archeology had a humanistic orientation, however, and none of it ventured beyond the familiar area of history or the Old Testament. Even the archeologists of the day, bedazzled by the spectacular remains, were not conscious of the presence of a truly prehistoric past.

The post-Darwinian discovery of prehistory in Britain sparked an entirely different approach to archeology—the beginnings of modern anthropological archeology. The burst of activity in the natural sciences set in motion by Darwin's book stimulated social scientists to view their data in an evolutionary frame of reference. Since the developmental schemes which began to be formulated by social evolutionists purported to reflect historical reality, there was a quest for concrete evidence of past societies as verification. The significance of this development was twofold: First, there now began to be archeologists who treated the remains of the past as evidence of former ways of life and not just as curios or objects of art. The possibility of reconstructing and studying extinct societies in the absence of written records was demonstrated. Secondly, the interests of a number of archeologists were now attracted to the remains of exotic, remote, or primitive cultures outside of the Western tradition or the biblical scene—cultures disdained by the humanists and their kind as of no interest or value, but a major source of significant data for the social scientist. Out of this development has grown the anthropological archeology of today and most of what we now know of prehistory.

The humanistic approach, direct descendant of the original antiquarianism, still survives, represented primarily by the classical archeologists, who are attached to departments of classics or fine arts. "Classical archeology is still suffering from having been established as a field of study at a time when it could only have been conceived as art history, so that works of art became an end in themselves. The dead weight of this tradition is still felt" (Piggott, 1959, p. 119). The result of this preoccupation with art objects and spectacular public buildings is well exemplified by the fact that until as recently as 1935 no one even knew what an ordinary Greek dwelling house of the classical period was really like. The art museums have also perpetuated this approach to the present day by sponsoring excavations aimed largely at acquiring spectacular display objects for their galleries. This has resulted in a great concentration of activity in the Near East and the classical lands and the focusing of attention on spectacular remains, ignoring or discarding the everyday materials, the refuse and the other types of evidence which yield so much knowledge of the past. Unfortunately, it is this type of activity which has so largely shaped the image of archeology in the public mind. Expectably, the unprepossessing *sites*[1] of prehistoric age have also been ignored. All this

---

[1] A site is any location of former human activity of which some trace survives.

explains the paradox that areas which have been the scene of greatest archeological activity are often the ones whose prehistory is the least known.

The disparate interests and viewpoints of these two approaches to archeology have kept them well apart and fostered a certain snobbishness. Only in recent years are the two beginning to get together and show an interest in what each has to offer in the way of techniques and subject matter.

Whole books have been devoted to the fascinating story of the history of archeology. Only a few of the most significant developments can be mentioned here.

The first of these—the influence of which still lingers—is the concept of the Three Ages, formulated sometime around 1830 by Christian Thomsen of what is today the Danish National Museum. Thomsen was faced with the task of arranging the museum collections, which contained a considerable quantity of undocumented antiquarian specimens, into some sort of order for exhibition purposes. He decided to do so on the basis of the material of which these tools, weapons and other objects were made: stone, bronze, and iron. Subsequently, excavations in stratified sites in Denmark—places where there had been successive human occupations at different times—established that these categories had followed one another in time and, at least in Denmark, represented three technological stages characterized by reliance on one or the other of these materials. This was in pre-Darwinian times, and no great antiquity was attributed. But no sooner was the study of prehistory born than the social evolutionists seized upon this ready-made concept of Stone Age, Bronze Age, and Iron Age and easily developed it into an evolutionary sequence for all prehistory. Indeed, given the state of archeological technique at the time, such a technologically based sequence was the most that could be justified on the basis of the evidence of material culture. As knowledge of the prehistory of the rest of the world has increased, however, the applicability of the sequence to all areas has become less convincing, and other schemes, based on different types of data, have been advanced to replace it. Thomsen's terminology still persists in many areas—especially the U.S.S.R.—though in Western Europe it has become merely a classificatory label, and in the Americas it never gained a foothold.

By and large, the early field methods of archeology were highly destructive. At this stage, the data of archeology consisted entirely of objects, and the aim of even the anthropological excavators was to find objects without regard for their context or associations. We now realize that it is precisely these contexts and associations that provide most of the evidence for prehistory. The development of modern scientific techniques and attitudes was a long, slow process.

The recognition that *information* and not just objects could be obtained from an archeological excavation we owe largely to a retired British general, Pitt-Rivers, who has been called "the father of scientific excavation," since he established the standards for excavation technique which are held valid today, although they were slow to be adopted by his contemporaries. Pitt-Rivers inaugurated the practice of total excavation of a site to recover the whole body of evidence, and he insisted on high standards of accuracy and care. Every detail must be recorded, even if it seems trivial at the time, for in the light of later developments it may prove to be important to those who come after you. In an age when attention was still focused on the striking or artistic find, he stressed the importance of common things.

Somewhat different factors affected the development of archeology in the New World. Instead of the classical and biblical background of interest, the initial stimulus stemmed from the keenly felt need to explain the existence, and therefore the origin, of the substantial body of newly found humanity, undreamed of by pre-Columbus Western minds and unmentioned in the Scriptures. Theories of sunken continents or the lost tribes of Israel, among others, gained wide followings and still display amazing vitality even today in uncritical minds. In the early nineteenth century, exploration began to replace armchair theorizing, and the discovery of elaborate earthworks in the Mississippi Valley and "lost cities" in the jungles of Central America, both seemingly divorced from the living aboriginal populations, gave rise to another hardy concept—that of mysterious vanished peoples and civilizations, such as the "Mound Builders," who had supposedly preceded the historic Indians. The realization that New World archeology represents the prehistory of the American Indian is a surprisingly recent phenomenon.

Equally recent is the realization of any time depth for prehistory in the Americas. The establishment of the remote antiquity of man in Europe in the mid-nineteenth century sparked an initial search for comparable remains in the Western Hemisphere, but the failure to produce convincing finds led to general disillusionment, and the pendulum swung to the other extreme. In the first quarter of the present century, leading scholars in America believed that the New World was initially peopled only a few thousand years before the Christian era and that known prehistoric remains represented later descendants of these early peoples. Archeological sites were viewed as reflecting single occupations of no great age. The stratigraphic approach, aimed at recovering a sequence through time and already commonplace in the Old World, was ignored or considered not applicable. As a result, prehistoric remains in the Americas were viewed as if they all represented a single time horizon, being "prehistoric" only in the sense of being pre-European contact. Archeological studies were purely of a descriptive, instead of an historic, nature.

A revolutionary change began in 1927 with the discovery of artifacts of previously unknown type indisputably associated with the bones of extinct animals near Folsom, New Mexico. Early man in America became a reality, and horizons expanded. About this same time, stratigraphy had also been "discovered" in the New World, or at least a stratigraphic approach to excavation began to become fashionable. Some even refer to "the Stratigraphic Revolution." In any event, chronology became the central theme, and American archeology began to supply historical information for the first time. In a sense, the study of prehistory was born in the New World.

Since 1950, new trends are visible. Social-environmental problems have become of as much interest as the purely historical problems. Scholars have begun to ask questions about structure and function in prehistoric societies and to seek for causative factors. They are interested today not just in where and when, but in how and why. The data of prehistory are being viewed as reflections of human activity.

The most significant development of recent years in both hemispheres has been the growth of the interdisciplinary approach in field work. A team of scientists representing different disciplines—geology, botany, zoology, physical anthropology, for instance—cooperate in the actual excavation to recover and interpret data in their respective fields. They thus extract the maximum possible information from a site of former human activity and reconstruct the fullest picture of its environment.

In closing this brief discussion, we should stress that some knowledge of the history and development of any science is essential to an understanding of its current state and is also a valuable antidote to our inevitable smugness and complacency. It should help us realize that we are no more at the height of prehistoric scholarship than were those pioneer workers and remind us that all the secrets of man's prehistory are not going to be revealed to our generation any more than they were to theirs. We should hope that our efforts today will seem as quaint 100 years from now as those of the mid-nineteenth century sometimes seem to us.

nature of the archeological record

We have described archeology as the study of past human cultures as reconstructed from their material remains. With this aim of reconstruction, archeology studies all changes in the material world which are due to human action, insofar as these survive in recognizable or at least detectable forms and can be recovered by the techniques available. Thus, the amount of evidence of the past that the archeologist of today can potentially recover with present techniques is greater than it was a few generations ago, and we may confidently expect that new developments will greatly increase the scope of our studies in the future. These changes in the material world are expressions of past human thoughts and purposes, and the archeological record thus consists (as V. G. Childe aptly puts it) of the fossilized results of human behavior, although we must bear in mind that not all human behavior fossilizes. The archeologist hopes to reconstitute that behavior as far as he can and thus to recapture the thoughts of which that behavior was an expression.

What are these surviving results of past human behavior recorded in the material world? By far the largest category is the things that have been made or altered by deliberate human action. These include *artifacts*—portable objects manufactured or created by man, such as tools, weapons, ornaments, works of art, as well as objects altered by man, such as charcoal, or bones split for marrow. Nonportable things, perhaps best described as structures or features, are equally included: buildings of every sort, refuse pits or heaps, hearths, graves, earthworks, ditches, trails, mines or quarries, felled trees or stumps. A second category consists of those phenomena that are due to human agency but are not strictly speaking things made or altered by man. It includes, for example, (1) changes in the natural environment such as deforestation, extermination of certain animal species, or introduction of others; (2) natural objects removed from their habitat by man and utilized according to cultural patterns: game animal bones in refuse, or seashells traded over long distances for aesthetic or prestige reasons; (3) the positions and relationships of things that are the consequence of deliberate human action, such as the position of a corpse in a grave, or the relative size of houses in a settlement. Finally, it includes the relationships of man's activity to the natural environment when no alteration was involved: the particular location of a settlement, the use of a cave for shelter. All these things are records of past human behavior and provide the subject matter for archeology.

The inherent incompleteness of this archeological record is the archeologist's chief handicap. Only if everything ever made or used by man were preserved intact would the record be complete; but most of it is doomed to perish. It is not the insufficient number of objects surviving; unlike the bones of fossil man himself, we have great quantities of his artifacts. It is rather their onesideness. An extinct culture may be known to us only through its most durable remains, which may actually represent an insignificant portion of its possessions and activities. For example, many groups of living Australian aborigines, with their scanty material equipment and emphasis on elaborating the social and ceremonial aspects of their culture, would leave almost no trace of their existence in the archeological record. We would have small chance, either, of reconstructing the elaborate but perishable material culture of many modern peoples of Southeast Asia, where even cutting tools may be made of bamboo. Or take our own civilization. It has often been pointed out that a Montgomery Ward catalog is an excellent index of our material culture from generation to generation, reflecting the concrete aspects of our civilization as far as the daily life of the average person is concerned. Yet just think for a moment how much of what is depicted in that catalog would survive after only 100 years in the ground. And how well could you reconstruct our total American civilization solely from the items that had managed to survive in some degree? These examples should give some appreciation of the problems facing the archeologist and a better perspective in which to view his findings.

While the archeological record is obviously incomplete, it is not hopelessly so by and large, and the trend is toward greater completeness as new and improved techniques are continually devised. Moreover, this incompleteness is relative and variable, differing in almost every case. A number of factors contribute to this situation.

There is, of course, what might be called the "human factor"—the excavator himself. How much of the record is recovered from any given site will always be determined by the skill of the particular excavator, the techniques known or available to him, and by his preconceptions—which are generally the preconceptions of his time and his scholarly environment. Unless the archeologist asks the right questions, even one with best intentions is apt to overlook potential evidence. (The bulk of existing archeological data could be said to have been gathered by accident rather than by design.) And of course if one has only a narrow objective, like the excavators of the Near East who collect in order to fill museums, large parts of the record are simply ignored.

But even the most skilled and inquiring investigator faces an absolute limitation in any given site, and that is the degree of preservation of what it once contained. This varies with time, with region, and from site to site. Even the habits of the numberless extinct human societies are a significant factor in determining what the archeologist may hope to learn. Obviously, the farther back in time we go, the skimpier will be the archeological record, since the remains of human activity will have had increasing opportunity to undergo destruction or concealment by the omnipresent natural processes of erosion and deposition, by the biological processes of decay, or often by the hand of man. Thus as a general rule we cannot expect to learn as much about earlier periods as about later ones. Regional differences primarily reflect the influence of climate, a major factor in preservation. An extremely dry desert climate like that of Egypt or the coast of Peru may preserve things almost perfectly for thousands of years, even perishable materials. Permanent freezing is an even better preservative; witness the deep-frozen mammoths of Siberia with flesh still edible after ten or more thousands of years. On the other hand, a temperate climate like that of the eastern United States or Europe is highly destructive to anything except stone, well-fired pottery, and certain metals. In most cases we can hope to recover only traces of organic materials such as wood. Tropical forests are the worst of all: Even masonry constructions are subject to destruction, and bone remains rapidly disintegrate.

Within a climatic region, differing soil conditions are also an important factor. For instance, acid soils will not preserve bone; thus any people who used bone extensively as a raw material for their artifacts would leave little trace of their activities if they happened to have lived in such localities. Waterlogged soils may preserve wood for thousands of years, although it will disintegrate in a matter of hours when exposed to the air unless chemically treated. Natural forces also play a role, e.g., by rapidly burying a particular site before too much destruction can occur, as with a volcanic eruption or shifting sand dunes; or conversely, by

destroying a site through erosion and weathering. And there is the differential survival power of the various basic raw materials used by man even
under identical conditions of soil and climate. Gold, for instance, is
indestructible whereas iron will often dissolve into rust in very short order.
Objects made of stone or well-fired pottery have very high survival potential and hence loom large in the archeological record, doubtless out of all
proportion to their original role—a circumstance which must be borne
continually in mind if the investigator is not to conceive a very warped
picture of the culture he is studying. All too often it is probably the trivial
which has survived while the significant has perished. Organic materials
rarely survive except under favorable conditions like those mentioned
above, or unless they have become chemically altered as by fossilization
or by carbonization through fire, in which cases they acquire high survival
powers. And perishable organic substances must always have been the
principal materials used by early man.

Cultural factors—the patterned habits of the extinct group—play a
considerable role. We shall inevitably learn more about people who lived
for extended periods in one spot than we shall about those who habitually
roamed around, and more about groups who had the custom of placing
objects in the grave with the dead than about those who did not.

Finally, it needs to be remembered that even at their best, the records
of archeology are unintentional ones, unlike the deliberate, often self-
conscious nature of so much of the written sources of conventional history.
Archeological records were never intended to convey historical information; only when they are discovered and interpreted by the archeologist do
they become historical evidence.

In a further effort to gain some better understanding of the nature
of the archeological record, studies are being made of the camp sites of
surviving primitive groups such as the Bushmen. Thus the traces and
leavings of the group after it moves on can be compared with the known
pattern of human activities it reflects, and the fate of this fresh archeological record can be observed over subsequent periods of time.

The archeologist, who is compelled by circumstances to rely upon
the material traces of the people he is studying in order to arrive at any
idea of their life and behavior, must often appear to be preoccupied with
things which are in themselves unattractive and uninspiring; but he is
really interested all the time in *people*—in the man behind the artifact, in
other words. And in this and many other ways the archeologist greatly
resembles a detective or criminologist. He has to rely upon circumstantial
evidence, and much of his time is taken up with details which may appear
to be trivial although as clues to human actions they can be of absorbing
interest. The interpretation of archeological evidence is not unlike the
attempt to reconstruct the details of a murder and the identity of a
murderer from a cigarette butt and similar odds and ends found at the
scene of a crime. If the average person finds it difficult to comprehend
the archeologist's enthusiasm over some bit of stone or broken pottery, he
should realize that it differs in no way from the enthusiasm a detective

might exhibit over an even less prepossessing cigarette butt. In each case the interest is not in the object itself but in the clue which it offers to the identity and activities of *people*. And in both cases it requires a trained observer and the aid of scientific techniques to make any object yield this information. Furthermore, it is not so much the object itself as its relationships to its surroundings, its *context*, that yields the most important information. Context involves associations with other objects and with the deposit itself and is an essential part of the archeological record. Much of the work involved in excavation is primarily an attempt to record context. No object, for instance, is ever removed from the ground until its associations have been carefully studied, noted, plotted, and photographed, so that its exact original position and relationships can be reconstructed. Without this information, the artifact or other object is of little value. Just as valuable clues may be unwittingly destroyed at the scene of a crime by untrained meddlers, the most important information contained in an archeological site is easily lost when it is dug into by relic collectors or "pot hunters" who loot it of artifacts to adorn their shelves, in ignorance or callous disregard of the irreplaceable historical record they are destroying. From a scientific standpoint, such collections, devoid of context, are virtually worthless. The relic collector has simply torn pages from the book of human history and thrown them away; the story will never be complete again, the loss can never be made up. Such vandalism is unfortunately on the increase in many parts of the United States, although illegal on federal and many state lands. Persons with a serious interest in archeology as a hobby may join one of the recognized state archeological societies in this country and engage in work of scientific importance under the supervision of professional archeologists.

The archeologist, then, seeks to recover as complete a record as possible of the activities of an extinct human group. An archeological *assemblage*, ideally, would comprise everything made or used by such a group at a particular place. As we have already seen, only a varying portion of such a total assemblage could be expected to survive; we must resign ourselves to working with proportionately incomplete assemblages. All things found associated together in context at one site, so that we know they belong together at one point in time, would form such an assemblage[2] and represent an actual human group, a social unit of some sort. When a similar assemblage recurs repeatedly at a number of sites, we are dealing with a *culture*. Each archeological culture is thought to represent a society and to reflect the patterns of behavior common to the members of such a larger grouping.[3] It is customary to name archeological cultures after the place or site where they were first found or are most typically represented —e.g., Mousterian culture from the type site of Le Moustier in France.

---

[2] The term "component" is often used in this sense by American archeologists.
[3] Culture in this archeological sense could be compared to the concept of the culture of some particular living group, as opposed to the more generalized anthropological concept of culture.

references

Hawkes, Jacquetta, and Christopher Hawkes: *Prehistoric Britain*, Harvard University Press, Cambridge, 1955; Chatto and Windus, London, 1955. (By permission.)

Piggott, Stuart: *Approach to Archaeology*, Harvard University Press, Cambridge, 1959. (With the author's permission.)

suggested readings

Bibby, Geoffrey: *The Testimony of the Spade*, Alfred A. Knopf, Inc., New York, 1956.

Hawkes, Jacquetta: *The World of the Past*, Alfred A. Knopf, Inc., New York, 1963. (Especially pp. 3–104.)

Piggott, Stuart: *Approach to Archaeology*, Harvard University Press, Cambridge, 1959.

Trigger, Bruce G.: *Beyond History: The Methods of Prehistory*, Holt, Rinehart and Winston, Inc., New York, 1968.

methods in archeology: 1

the recovery of data

Like the remains of early man himself, or any evidence of past life, the traces of former human activity have for the most part been buried under the surface of the ground by the natural processes of soil formation. The recovery of archeological data, therefore, is primarily a process of excavation.

It is natural to wonder just how the archeologist secures his data: how, in other words, he sets about unraveling the prehistory of some given area, and studying its extinct societies. In any unknown or little-known area, the first step will generally be a site survey to locate and assess the remains of former human occupancy. All such traces will be located on maps for future reference, described, and sampled by collecting any exposed artifacts or sinking test pits to ascertain what lies beneath the surface. A general idea will thus be obtained of the relative age, cultural affiliation and importance of the site, and of the amount and significance of the information it might be expected to yield. When all identifiable sites in the area have been tabulated in this way, it should be possible to formulate the major problems involved in the local human history and to select for fuller excavation those key sites which would contribute most substantially to their solution. In any area where some previous work had been done, of course, there would be study of all published information and examination of all specimens in museums or other collections. The general procedure outlined above would apply to both types of archeological field work: *salvage* archeology, which seeks to recover as much as possible of the prehistoric record in areas where it is about to be destroyed by construction work or flooded by dam reservoirs; and what might be called *problem-oriented* archeology, which seeks particular kinds of information and may be content to leave much of the evidence of human activity for future workers.

How may a site be recognized as the scene of past human activity? What are the forms, in other words, which an archeological site may assume? Settlements or camps, workshops, and burial places are perhaps the commonest types of sites. In fortunate cases a camp or habitation may have been situated in a protected spot such as a cave and thus have survived virtually intact just as its occupants left it. But the vast majority of human settlements are open sites subject to erosion or burying. Such former settlements generally contain hearths, some trace of habitations such as house floors, and, above all, rubbish. Rubbish has always been an inevitable accompaniment of human living at all times, and is a major source of evidence for the archeologist, since the things that were thrown away or lost are the things most likely to survive. Only graves surpass rubbish heaps as sources of information. Where a settlement has lasted for any length of time, rubbish heaps build up in the same way as our city dumps and have the added value of providing a time sequence, since the lower levels, laid down first, will be older than the successively overlying ones—the basic geological principle of *stratigraphy*. In coastal areas where shellfish are abundant such rubbish heaps or *middens* will often be composed of vast quantities of shells and form conspicuous features. Sometimes industrial or craft activities are not all carried on in the settlement or habitation, and separate workshop sites may be found where stone tools were chipped or metal smelted, these sites being identified by the characteristic debris. Mines and quarries where prehistoric man secured his raw materials could be included under this category.

Burial places of the dead are one of the most important sources of data for the archeologist, not only for the information they provide about the people themselves but also owing to the widespread practice of furnishing the dead with equipment, provisions, or offerings. Such objects are usually preserved intact and just as they were left, so that a grave forms an ideal archeological assemblage of items known to belong together and representing one moment in time. Burials not infrequently occur in the settlement itself, under houses or in the rubbish heaps, but generally there is a definite area or cemetery for the purpose in the vicinity. In more complex societies, members of the ruling group or honored persons may be accorded elaborate burial in tombs or have mounds of earth raised over the grave, sometimes to considerable height. The barrows of England, the kurgans of the nomadic tribes of the Eurasian steppe, or the mounds of many prehistoric Indian groups of the American Middle West are well-known examples.

Other types of sites that should be mentioned are traces of economic activity such as fields, gardens, fish weirs, or places where game animals were killed and butchered ("kill sites"). There are also places which might be labeled "art sites": places not associated with habitations, where prehistoric man left examples of his artistic expression, such as the famous painted caves of France and Spain or the innumerable petroglyphs adorning rocks in the western United States.

Uppermost in the minds of many people is the question: How do archeologists know where to dig? How do they locate these prehistoric sites, the great majority of which have become buried beneath the ground? Generally speaking, sites come to light either through accidental exposure of one sort or another or through deliberate search by the archeologist. Accidental exposure may occur as the result of natural forces, such as erosion of the land surface by wind and water, the cutting action of streams, or the wearing away of seacoasts by the ocean. More commonly today exposure results from human disturbance of the land, especially from the ever-increasing amount of construction activity. Excavations for buildings, grading for highways, trenching for pipelines, quarrying for gravel and fill are important factors in exposing, and all too often destroying, the remains of the human past. The farmer's plow has always been a useful ally of the archeologist in revealing what lies below the surface over large areas of the land, but of course it effectively destroys the context in the process. All these accidental exposures, it must be realized, are lost to science unless some observer is present who is able to recognize remains of human activity for what they are (and they may not be recognized by the average person) and who appreciates their significance sufficiently to report the find to the proper quarters. Thus probably only a small proportion of the sites accidentally exposed ultimately contribute to the archeological record.

Locating sites by deliberate search involves, first, knowing where to look—the likely spots which prehistoric man would have chosen to live, work or bury his dead; and secondly, the ability to recognize surface indications of former human presence. Older sites may be so deeply buried that they can be located only through exposures, but searching for them, again, requires examining exposures in likely places. Some types of remains protrude more or less conspicuously above the surface and present no particular problem. This category includes visible ruins, like the cliff dwellings of the southwestern United States or the hill forts of England; burial mounds; art remains in the open (such as petroglyphs); shell middens; caves and rock shelters (which may or may not have been used by man); and any other man-made features of the landscape. For instance, the sites of early villages in the Near East are often easily located because of the common habit of constructing settlements on the same spot as former ones. The accumulating refuse and the disintegrating mud-brick walls raise the ground level with each succeeding occupation, so that after 2,000 years or so of human living a mound or *tell* has built up with the latest village perched on top. Such tells are often of considerable height and form conspicuous features.

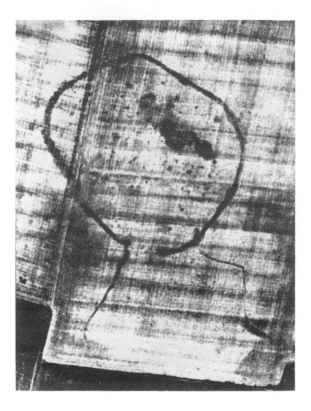

FIGURE 2–1. *Enclosure and structures of prehistoric farmstead at Little Woodbury, England, revealed in air photograph.* (By permission from J. G. D. Clark, *Prehistoric Europe,* copyright © 1952 by Philosophical Library, Inc.)

But in most areas the vast majority of prehistoric remains lie beneath the surface with little or no apparent indication of their presence. Theoretically, some evidence should remain wherever the natural surface of the land has been altered or disturbed in any way by human activity or occupation—although it may require special techniques to detect such traces. Evidence may be the chemical content of the soil or the difference of the vegetation covering it. Often such things as faint surface features or differences in soil reflected in growing crops or showing up on ploughed land can be identified in aerial photographs although invisible to an observer on the ground. In many cases, stray artifacts may have reached the surface in some way and betray the presence of a site. And finally, one can always hopefully sink a test pit in what seems a promising location. The salvage archeology referred to previously is largely a matter of deliberate search in an effort to locate all sites in some threatened area.[1]

[1] The possibility of locating buried structures and features by the use of various types of magnetometers is being explored. New experimental devices can detect such remains as much as 5 meters below the surface.

The archeologist obtains his evidence primarily through excavation, and to a lesser extent (depending on the circumstances) from study of surface features, museum specimens, and pertinent written reports of other archeologists. It would perhaps be more correct to say that he obtains *observations* in these ways and that these observations become historical evidence only through interpretation, which we will consider shortly. Excavation, then, is the fundamental process by which the archeologist recovers under reliable circumstances the basic material for subsequent study. Through his own excavation he is able to control the context, whereas in the case of the numerous specimens that come to light as accidental finds there is no such control; the context will always be questionable, or may be lacking. Archeological excavations should be thought of as elaborate laboratory experiments that, unlike the case in the physical and biological sciences, cannot be repeated or checked, especially if a site has been completely excavated. All excavation is at the same time destruction: The original site will survive only in the records of the excavator. This places an unusually heavy burden of responsibility upon the archeologist. Ideally, he or any other archeologist should be able to reconstruct the site on paper, as it were, solely from these records. This, at least, should be the aim of every excavator in recording his observations. Of course, the observations can be no more complete than the techniques of the time and place permit; modern elaborate techniques are an effort to make this record as complete as possible. But even so, the human factor plays an inevitable role. What any archeologist extracts from his excavation will depend also on his individual qualities and abilities, his experience, and his familiarity with the materal. In reality, therefore, excavation reports are only more or less complete, and we cannot hope that they will actually contain all the evidence that once existed in any site. Since prehistory must be constructed from the records of all available excavations, the reliability and completeness of the archeologists' written reports is thus a crucial factor which must be borne constantly in mind.

How does the archeologist proceed in excavating a site so that the maximum amount of evidence will be recovered? Broadly speaking, his procedures will be of the following types: (1) locating whatever has survived in tangible form, recording its context (position and associations), removing it for later laboratory study (if it is an artifact, bone, or other portable object) or documenting and studying it in position if it is a nonportable feature such as a house floor; (2) recovering the shape of things that have vanished, such as beams, posts, or other wooden objects;[2] (3) collecting ecological samples (e.g., pollen, soil) which may provide

---

[2] Upon decay these will often have been replaced by soil of a different color from the rest of the deposit. Also, surviving metal fittings may provide clues, as with some of the buried Viking ships which were restored on the basis of the nails and fastenings still in their original positions although all the wood had disintegrated. Similarly, clothing worn by a person at burial may often be reconstructed from the ornaments and fastenings once attached to it. Again, the importance of recording the exact position of everything found, no matter how small must be emphasized.

FIGURE 2–2. (Above) *Fine packed soil replacing rotted wood and leather preserves the shape of these Chinese chariots from the eleventh to eighth centuries* B.C. (By permission of *Antiquity,* copyright © 1963, Antiquity Publications, Ltd.); (below) *Form of the buried Anglo-Saxon ship at Sutton Hoo, England, revealed only by iron nails and stains in the sand.* (*Antiquaries Journal,* vol. 20.)

evidence for reconstructing the environment, and studying (done by a geologist if possible) the geological nature and relationships of the deposit and the physiographic surroundings of the site for the same purpose; (4) searching for, recording or collecting any evidence or samples which may serve to date the site by any of the various techniques to be described later; and (5) looking for any evidence of time sequence within the site as revealed by *stratigraphy*, the vertical position of remains in relation to one another within the deposit.

To achieve these goals when excavating a site, the archeologist must proceed with the utmost care. He does not dig things up like someone searching for buried treasure; it would be more correct to say that he *uncovers* a site. Of course, if there is a considerable overburden of sterile soil covering the site, this will be disposed of as rapidly as possible; earth-moving machines may even be employed nowadays where circumstances warrant. But once the culture-bearing deposit has been exposed, the trowel replaces the spade, and whenever remains are located the final exposure will more likely be carried out with whisk broom, paintbrush and jackknife. In order to be able to record the precise position of everything found, the site will be carefully mapped before excavation and often divided into squares on a grid system, the corners of which are marked on the ground by stakes. Finds can then be located horizontally in relation to these. A reference point will also be established from which depth measurements (vertical position) can be ascertained. In this way, everything in the site can be accurately placed in relation to everything else even after the site has been completely destroyed. As the site is uncovered and features of interest located, horizontal plans will be drawn at intervals, supplemented by photographs. When the bottom of the deposit has been reached, vertical plans or *sections* of the walls of the pits or trenches are made to provide a series of cross-section profiles of the site which will record the stratigraphy and structure of the deposit. The objects encountered are removed to the laboratory after they have been uncovered and recorded with their associations, labeled, and cataloged for future identification. Fragile objects may be treated in various ways to preserve them from disintegration or to strengthen them for removal. Sometimes a feature of particular interest, such as a burial, may be removed entire to the laboratory or museum by isolating and undercutting the block of earth containing it and encasing it for transportation. Features that cannot easily be removed are left after study, or may have to be destroyed to reach underlying levels of the deposit. All this involves long hours of arduous and painstaking work. Archeology can be exciting, like any scientific research, but there is also a great deal of sheer drudgery.

If the site has clearly defined stratigraphy—that is, is composed of a succession of readily identified levels differing in the nature of the soil or otherwise distinguished—it may be stripped off level by level, so that each time period is studied as a unit. In other cases, the deposit may be removed in arbitrary levels of, say, 10 centimeters. Or, if excavation of the

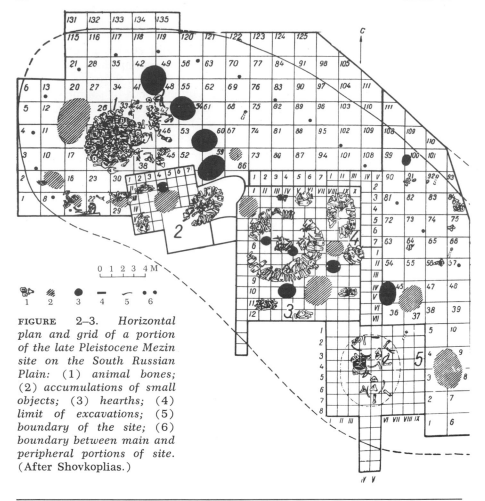

FIGURE 2–3. *Horizontal plan and grid of a portion of the late Pleistocene Mezin site on the South Russian Plain: (1) animal bones; (2) accumulations of small objects; (3) hearths; (4) limit of excavations; (5) boundary of the site; (6) boundary between main and peripheral portions of site.* (After Shovkoplias.)

total area is impractical, a trench may be dug across the middle of the site to provide a cross-section sample of the deposit and reveal any stratigraphy. The precise plan of attack will depend upon the particular circumstances and nature of the site in each case.

Because of the crucial importance of stratigraphy in establishing time sequences and in determining the relative age of remains as compared with others (in terms of their relative vertical position) and because of the supreme value accorded this type of evidence, the utmost care must be exercised in identifying the existence of stratigraphy in a site. Not only individual objects, but even entire layers, may no longer be in their original position and relationship, and thus present a false picture. The site may have been disturbed by subsequent digging or cultivation, so that the original deposit has been mixed up. Pits may have been dug into it, so that much younger material has been introduced into the deepest levels. Objects may work their way downward in a variety of ways. For example, a land surface on which artifacts lie may be eroded by wind so that they settle down to the level of a lower (and earlier) occupation. Or the activities of burrowing animals may create havoc in a site by displacing artifacts. Under arctic conditions (such as periodically prevailed in Ice Age Europe), surface soil on slopes, becoming thawed in summer, often slides downhill over the frozen subsoil and may eventually cover and overlie younger deposits at the foot of the slope—a process known as *solifluction*. In such a case the stratigraphy will be reversed and lead to erroneous conclusions if the two layers contain human remains. Disturbance and displacement of this sort is often difficult to detect. When there is any likelihood of such a situation, the most careful observation and study is called for.

Special types of archeological sites require, of course, special tech-

FIGURE 2-4. *Cross-section profile of the Laugerie-Haute Est rock shelter, Dordogne region, France.* (From *Science,* vol. 142, no. 3590, p. 352; copyright © 1963 by the American Association for the Advancement of Science. By permission of Denise de Sonneville-Bordes and *Science.*)

Laugerie-Haute Est

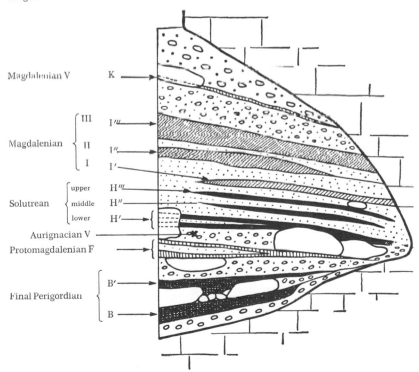

niques. With art sites it is a question of copying the drawing, painting, or engraving as accurately as possible, and for this mere photographs may not be sufficient. Sometimes it may be very difficult to reconstruct the original appearance, or later pictures may be superimposed and the resulting confusion may have to be disentangled. Such contemporary pictorial records may be a very valuable source of information to amplify more strictly archeological types of evidence, although in many cases they are difficult or impossible to date with any certainty.

In the case of features such as former fields, trails, or structures and monuments above the ground it may be largely a case of mapping and describing, perhaps aided by aerial photography.

Underwater sites have been attracting increasing attention in the past few years. These include wrecks of ancient ships, which throw valuable light on early commerce and often yield large assemblages of objects indisputably belonging together; deposits of material thrown in or fallen from settlements on the adjacent shore (these often being preserved intact whereas on land their survival chances would have been slight); and sites formerly on dry land that have been submerged for some reason, such as rising sea levels. A special branch of archeology, underwater archeology, carried out primarily by scuba diving, is developing its own techniques to cope with the peculiar problems involved. The basic aims remain the same, however: namely, the recovery or recording of remains and the fixing of their exact positions for subsequent reconstruction through underwater photography, surveying, and establishment of grids or other reference points wherever possible. Since many areas of importance for early man are now submerged and their human record lost to conventional archeology, underwater techniques have great potential significance.

the analysis of data

After excavation and recording of a site have been completed, the archeologist is in possession of a collection of artifacts and samples and a body of observations which have been incorporated into his notes, drawings, maps, and photographs. To be of practical use and ultimately to yield historical information, these raw data must first be analyzed. Analysis, especially in the case of the artifacts, is primarily a question of classification, as in any science. Only by classification can the bewildering variety of human behavior be reduced to manageable proportions for scientific treatment. Various schemes have been developed for the classification of the products of man's handiwork. They may be based on such objective criteria as composition material (e.g., stone, bone, bronze) or technique of manufacture—the latter presupposing that the archeologist knows something about how they were made, as any good archeologist should. Or they may be based on more subjective criteria such as form or the function they performed—information which may not always be apparent or beyond question. In any case the basic principle is the selection of a *type* to represent a whole class of objects, and these types will subsequently serve as the units of study and comparison for analytic purposes. Such a type is admittedly an abstraction—but in dealing with abstractions, the archeologist differs in no way from other scientists. (For example, a zoologist does not study an animal as an individual, but as a representative of a type, such as a species, which is also an abstraction from reality based on more or less subjective criteria.)

The archeologist, then, classifies his material into types and describes these in order to facilitate comparisons with other types that may reveal significant relationships. He will scrutinize the artifacts of stone, bone, wood, or metal for evidence of the technique employed in making them and the use to which they were put. Sometimes only microscopic examination will reveal such information, such as the characteristic marks resulting from specific ways of use. The type of use indicated by the marks present may be established by experiment. Sometimes the position of a known object (say in relation to a skeleton or to other objects) may reveal its function or indicate what it once formed a part of. Pottery, where it is present, always claims the major share of the archeologist's attention because its sensitivity as a reflector of even slight cultural change makes it the most useful category of archeological remains, and the great variety of possible characteristics (e.g., shape, technique, decoration, composition of clay) make very refined classifications a simple matter. Although entire pots or vessels are very fragile and only rarely are recovered intact, except in certain protected situations, their broken fragments, referred to as potsherds (or simply sherds), are extremely durable and are often the most abundant thing encountered in a site. However, all too many archeologists become so preoccupied with the study of their pottery remains that the other aspects of the extinct culture may receive inadequate attention or be largely ignored, with the result that the history of a series of pottery wares is sometimes mistaken for the human history of a region, and the study of potsherds tends to become an end in itself.

While the archeologist thus busies himself in classifying, describing, and studying the artifacts from the site in terms of the types that he (or some other archeologist) has established, the rest of the collections of specimens and samples will be turned over to specialists in other branches of science best equipped to deal with them. The human skeletal remains will be studied by a physical anthropologist, who will determine the sex, age, and *pathology* (anatomical abnormalities or peculiarities, and evidence of disease or injury) of each individual, and the general characteristics and racial affinities of the prehistoric population of the site as a whole. A zoologist will similarly study the animal remains, in the form of bones and shells, to identify the species represented and calculate the number of individuals of each present, so that the relative abundance of the different species may be worked out. This is an important source of information on the environment and climate as well as on the economic patterns. The zoologist can also furnish information on the habits of these species—e.g., whether they are solitary or gregarious (herd), if they are migratory, if they are restricted to a particular environment such as deep or shallow water, forest or grassland. All this can serve as a valuable basis for inference on human activities, as can information on the age and sex of the animals, the season of the year when death occurred (which can be determined for some species), the cause of death or manner of wounding, and whether the animal is wild or domesticated.

The botanist will study plant remains that have been preserved by becoming carbonized or waterlogged, or which have left accidental impressions in clay. He also will identify species and their degree of domestication, and report on relative abundance and any changes through time. The most abundant plant remains, the microscopic pollen spores which have amazing powers of survival in the soil, will be examined by a pollen analyst or *palynologist*, who can identify them as to species and calculate relative abundance and any changes in this abundance over a span of time. Other specialists will analyze the raw materials used by the prehistoric group, and by chemical, spectographic, and other methods determine in many cases the source from which the stone or metal was obtained.

The above does not exhaust the various types of analysis to which the specimens and samples from a site may be subjected, but suggests the major and commoner categories. The more ways in which the materials may be studied, the more information one may hope to extract.

suggested readings

Bass, George F.: *Archaeology under Water,* Frederick A. Praeger, Inc., New York, 1966.

Brothwell, Don, and Eric Higgs: *Science in Archaeology,* Basic Books, Inc., Publishers, New York, 1963.

Clark, Grahame: *Archaeology and Society,* Barnes & Noble, Inc., New York, 1960.

Deetz, James: *Invitation to Archaeology,* Natural History Press, Garden City, N.Y., 1967.

Heizer, Robert F.: *The Archaeologist at Work,* Harper & Row, Publishers, Incorporated, New York, 1959.

Hole, Frank, and Robert F. Heizer: *An Introduction to Prehistoric Archeology,* Holt, Rinehart and Winston, Inc., New York, 1965.

Rainey, Froelich, and Elizabeth K. Ralph: "Archeology and Its New Technology," *Science,* vol. 153, pp. 1481–1491, 1966.

Wheeler, Mortimer: *Archaeology from the Earth,* Penguin Books, Inc., Baltimore, 1956.

methods in archeology: 2

The vital step through which all these processed data become actual historical evidence, and the past can thereby be reconstructed, is *interpretation*. The nature of archeological evidence demands the use of a whole set of complicated techniques (including the analytical ones already sketched) in order to extract the hidden information—especially when so much of the archeological record is perishable. The essential procedure is to interpret everything that has been observed during excavation and analysis, and to *infer* as much else as possible. One can, for example, infer the whole from a surviving part: Arrowheads imply the presence of the bow, even when no remains of the latter survive; garment fastenings often betray the general type of costume; gouges indicate well-developed woodworking, though none survives; spindle whorls imply the production and use of spun thread.

Nonmaterial aspects of culture present far greater problems of reconstruction, of course, and archeologists, especially in years past, have sometimes been tempted to infer by analogy with living primitive societies. Initially, this was based on the discredited premise that the more primitive cultures of today (such as the Australian aborigines) represent living fossils somehow preserved intact from the distant past—are authentic replicas of our Pleistocene ancestors. But culture is never static; the Australian aborigines have a long history of cultural development behind them, even though it may have taken rather different directions from our own, and we have no right to assume that they display the behavior and thought patterns of the original Homo sapiens. This is not to say that all inference from *ethnography* (the descriptive study of living cultures) should be rejected as worthless. It is reasonable to suppose that where there is a general correspondence between the prehistoric group and a modern one in economic basis, technological level, and environmental resources, certain valid analogies can be drawn regarding, for example, the size of the group that can normally be supported by a given area or can feasibly live together in any one place. Equally valid analogies can often be made between past and present groups with a fairly close historical link, such as late prehistoric and modern folk or peasant culture in some areas of Europe, or prehistoric and living Pueblo Indians in the southwestern United States. In the British Isles, for example, many prehistoric handicrafts have survived unchanged or with very slight modification down to recent times. Much of the material in a typical British Iron Age site could as easily have been made a hundred years ago. And in the Hebrides Islands off Scotland, or some of the remoter parts of Ireland, only a few years ago one could still encounter ways of life basically corresponding to the Early Iron Age and see dwellings and a variety of handicrafts in active use which archeologists elsewhere are laboriously attempting to reconstruct. And in studying the remains of prehistoric pueblos in the American Southwest, archeologists have repeatedly solved puzzling matters by reference to modern Pueblo Indian customs and practices. By and large, the principal value of ethnography to the archeologist is that it will often suggest to him what to look for and will enrich and fortify his interpretation of the past.

The first step in reconstructing an extinct society from archeological evidence should be the reconstruction of its natural environment and ecological setting. Owing to the intimate relationship between man and the natural world in the earlier stages of his cultural development, we can hardly begin to interpret the cultural evidence without the fullest possible knowledge of the setting. Only in the light of the setting will our analyses of cultural data yield their full meaning and an understanding of the cultural, social, and economic abilities of the extinct group become possible.

The physical appearance of the surroundings and location of the site, especially if it differed from the present, should be supplied by the geologist from his observations and studies. For instance, at the time it was occupied, the site might have been located directly on the coast (now some miles away) or on a river which has long since changed its course, or it might have had a good harbor (now silted in).

The vegetation, as reconstructed from pollen and plant remains, is an essential part of the setting, and as well as being an indicator of the plant resources available to the people, is also a valuable indicator of the climate of the time. A sequence of pollen samples from different levels in the deposits will show the changing history of the plant and tree cover of the area, which in turn reflects climatic variations which would have had

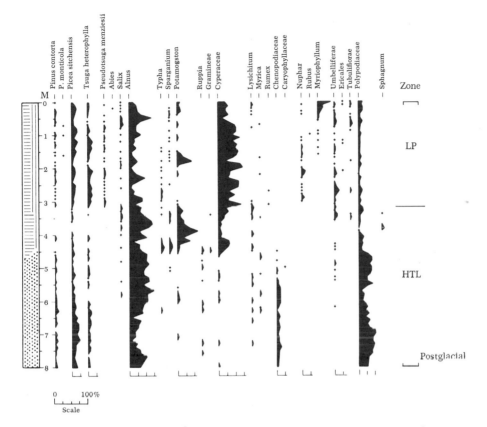

FIGURE 3–1. *Pollen diagram showing fluctuations in quantity of species and genera represented over the time span of the sample.* (From C. J. Heusser, *Late-Pleistocene Environments of North Pacific North America,* American Geographical Society, 1960.)

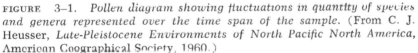

a significant influence on human life. Evidence from pollen analysis will also reveal man-made alterations in the natural landscape. For example, a sudden drop in the proportion of tree pollen with a subsequent increase of grass, weed, and cereal pollen indicates that clearance and cultivation of the land has taken place even if direct archeological evidence of this is lacking.

Pollen, being deposited naturally, provides a random sample and is hence a more reliable indicator of environment than are animal remains, the presence of which in a site is due to deliberate human action and involves considerable selection. Only those animal species in which the particular group was interested for food or other purposes can normally be expected to occur, and while this provides essential economic and dietary information, it is only a portion, and usually a small one, of the local animal kingdom with which man was coexisting. Thus animal remains yield more a history of diet than a history of local climate. In addition to plant and animal evidence, analysis of the soil in which the site lies may also provide information on environment and climate.

Such a reconstruction of the ecological setting of a prehistoric culture makes it possible to study man's effect on environment as well as its effect on him, and there is a mutual interaction. Man alters his environment in such ways as deforestation and overgrazing of plant cover (both of which can lead to significant alteration of the landscape through erosion), extinction of native animal or plant species, and introduction of alien new ones which may markedly upset the former balance of nature.

Once the environment has thus been established, the next important step is to determine the economic basis and subsistence patterns of any prehistoric group. At the simpler levels of culture where little survives, the majority of the evidence will pertain to this aspect of life. Only through an understanding of this aspect can we hope to throw light on the behavioral patterns of those distant times.

The nature of the food remains and of the equipment for economic activities will establish the subsistence basis of the culture and the type of economy: whether based entirely on gathering of food (hunting-fishing-collecting) or on food production (farming and stock breeding), or combinations of both in varying proportions. It will also show the economic resources available to the people, or utilized by them, in the form of game animals and wild plants, or crops and domestic animals. The first appearance of cultivated species in the locality will be revealed by the evidence of pollen. Changes in crops over time will reflect the history of farming in the area. Uses to which domestic animals were put may sometimes be inferred from the zoologist's analysis—e.g., a high proportion of female cattle, sheep, or goats would suggest the practice of dairying. Use of animals for draught purposes or riding may be established through finds of characteristic items of equipment. It should also be determined, if possible, whether the economy had a seasonal nature and was characterized by very different activities at specific times of the year, each requiring special equipment; i.e., during certain months the entire group might have devoted itself to fishing; during certain other months it might have regularly moved some distance to another area for hunting, and at other times moved again to particular localities for the harvesting of some major wild crop, such as acorns or pine nuts. The importance of these shifts in location lies in the fact that campsites of such a group at these different seasons might present very different appearances and contain such different remains that they might be mistaken for sites of several distinct cultures instead of merely seasonal aspects of the same one.

The specific techniques by which economic activities were carried on can also be established. The zoologist's information on the identity and habits of the animal and fish species will suggest whether hunting was of a mass communal nature (as with migratory herd animals) or by single pursuit of more solitary quarry and whether the fishing would have involved deep-sea techniques or could have been carried on from shore or by intercepting the mass upriver movements of species like salmon. Weapons embedded in or associated with animal and fish remains will show the specific means of hunting particular species. These types of associations yield information in addition to what can be inferred from the form and function of the items of hunting and fishing equipment themselves. (For instance, if harpoons and sea-mammal bones are found at opposite ends of a site, the connection between them is obvious even though they are not directly associated.)

The time of year that game were hunted can be ascertained in the case of young animals by their age from a known season of birth or by the condition of the antlers in species that undergo seasonal differences in this respect. Pits of wild fruit in food refuse at a fishing camp indicate fishing activity during the particular month when the fruit would have been edible. Study of animal remains will also often reveal the techniques of butchering employed.

Much can also be learned concerning farming methods and land use. The form and size of the fields and the type of soil cultivated, as well as actual remains of equipment, will indicate whether simple hoe or digging-stick cultivation was practiced, with frequent shifting of plots when the soil became exhausted or the weeds too thick; whether a light plow and larger fields were customary; or whether the people had the heavy equipment to deal with difficult soil and to plant fields of real size.

And finally, we can learn about the food habits and actual diet of the group from the faunal and plant remains in refuse, from analysis of human feces where these have survived, and from chemical analysis of food residues adhering to the insides of pots and containers. In this way we can ascertain what were the staple or preferred foods of the group and what, though readily available, was forbidden or felt to be unfit for some reason. We can trace shifts in diet over time as economic conditions change, as for example, from a predominantly meat diet to one largely of cereal as large areas were brought under cultivation and the supply of wild game dwindled.

The means by which human societies cope with the natural environment, utilize its resources and to an increasing extent modify it to meet their needs is the body of techniques generally referred to as *technology*. Technology has been aptly described as a screen between man and his environment, which has enabled him to become increasingly independent of it and to escape the physiological limitations of the human organism. Where other animals adapt to changing conditions by slowly changing their anatomy, man adapts by changing or improving his technology to cope with the new conditions. We reconstruct the technology of prehistoric societies largely through a study of their *material culture*—that is, of the artifacts that were used for these purposes—supplemented by inferences such as we have described based on other sorts of economic evidence. The remains of material culture always comprise the bulk of the archeological record, and are thus the most abundant type of evidence which the archeologist has at his disposal. Understandably, they receive the major share of his attention.

It is true that archeologists have at times been criticized for their apparent preoccupation with material culture. Yet the study of material culture, equally with the study of human activities and behavior, enables us to abstract the patterns that make up culture itself. Tools are simply direct material manifestations of thinking and as such record and preserve patterned human behavior that is no less significant than that embodied in, say, social or religious practices. Furthermore, as Kroeber pointed out, these "fossils of civilization" are a reflection of the degree of culture or civilization possessed by the people who made them, so that a more advanced type of tool generally suggests a decided development in the use of intelligence.

Still, it cannot too often be reiterated that just because it is the hardware that has survived, we should not automatically regard it as the most significant feature of the culture under study. Even archeologists of repute sometimes fail to appreciate the fallacy inherent in judging prehistoric societies solely in terms of their surviving material culture. As Stuart Piggott says, "Our thinking is controlled by the evidence which has survived, which in its nature stresses the material aspects of the people it now represents. We may be dealing with a society in which myth and song, the dance and ceremonial rites, played an overwhelmingly important part, yet to the prehistorian it may be represented by a type of pottery and little else. What is important and significant to the archeologists may have been supremely irrelevant to the people originally responsible. We have therefore to keep a watchful eye on our own presuppositions and not e.g. equate a lack of well-made pottery with an absolute poverty and degeneracy on the part of the inhabitants of the region which has disappointed the archaeologist in this respect" (Piggott, 1959, p. 79).

We are especially prone to such bias in viewing other cultures because our civilization sets such a high value on material culture and technological progress, whereas in many other societies the reverse is true: Once a satisfactory adaptation to the natural environment has been achieved, technology may have remained virtually stationary and would-be innovators have received little encouragement. Since we tend to view technical development as socially desirable and an unquestioned good, we must guard against unconscious value judgments in categorizing prehistoric cultures whose material equipment may seem deficient to us but may have been perfectly satisfactory to its owners. The simultaneous coexistence of such "innovating" and "conserving" societies is just as typical of all stages of the prehistoric past as it is of the modern world with its "developed" and "underdeveloped" countries, and reflects the normal variability of human societies.

What may we expect to learn about the material culture of an extinct society from archeological evidence? First, we can learn the distribution, favored location, and internal pattern of settlements, and deduce something about the stability of the group and the type of occupation of the area—nomadic, shifting, seasonal, or permanent. We can learn a certain amount about the construction and plan of dwellings from their ground plans and whatever else remains. We can learn in detail about their cutting tools, the key items in any technology down to our own; their weapons and economic equipment for securing and processing food and materials; their containers and methods of transportation; their ornaments and adornments and, it is hoped, infer something about their clothing. All this, of course, also reveals the technological processes and knowledge which they controlled. Any artifact has something to tell us, if we ask the right questions of it.

Data on the sources of raw materials and the relative proportion of foreign imports will establish the trade routes of the time and the importance that trade had in the economy. Similarly one can ascertain the extent of commercial as opposed to individual manufacture of needed items. Information from analysis of metal objects will identify regional centers of metallurgy, their sources of materials, and the range of distribution of their products.

Demographic information, such as population size, population density—what the area can support at different technological levels and population increases, can be computed from analysis of the human remains in burials, from the size and number of contemporary settlements, and from estimates of what the available food resources would support. Much information on what we might term "social biology" can also be derived from the physical anthropologist's report on the skeletal remains. His report would cover such matters as life span (longevity), sex ratio, infant mortality, health problems, malnutrition, and incidence of certain diseases that leave identifiable traces. Medical scientists can learn about the parasites afflicting earlier human populations, as well as details of diet through the study of feces (coprolites) where these have survived.

Works of art are fortunately often on durable materials, so that we know more about this aspect of prehistoric intellectual and aesthetic activity than any other. Owing to the fact that art is often closely associated with religion—as it was in our own civilization until quite recently—works of art are frequently one of the most important sources of information on the religious aspects of extinct cultures. Other surviving items of religious activity include cult objects, remains of shrines, and traces of ritual activity (such as in the postulated "bear cult" of some Neanderthal groups).

Inferences are also made about more philosophical matters. For instance, the placing of food and equipment in the grave with the dead has been widely hailed as proof of an early belief in an afterlife and hence in the immortality of the soul. However, we must guard against interpreting prehistoric beliefs in terms of our own ingrained preconceptions or wishful thinking.

The social life of early man is the aspect about him least known, but inferences as to social distinctions or the lack of them may be made from studying settlement patterns and observing inequalities in dwellings or graves. Something may also be inferred regarding size and nature of the family and other social units as these traits may be reflected in the size and plan of the dwellings. A ruling group of alien conquerors may reveal itself by the difference and foreign nature of its furnishings and equipment. The relative size and importance of religious structures as compared with secular ones may suggest whether the religious or civil authorities held the preponderance of power. And the presence or lack of weapons and fortifications will reflect the warlike or peaceful orientation of the society.

Some social customs leave concrete records. If one finds split and broken human bones scattered through the food refuse, it is hard to escape the suspicion that these people practiced cannibalism. This custom was not unknown in the American Middle West several centuries back, or in parts of Europe such as Denmark only a few thousand years ago.

Evidence of cultural processes such as diffusion and migration, or of relationships between different prehistoric cultures, may be established by demonstrating similarities in the form, appearance, and technique of manufacture of items of material culture possessed by two or more extinct groups—similarities which are close enough to imply identical origin of the items in question or intimate association between the traditions that produced them. This sort of evidence is based on man's tendency to be notoriously tradition-bound, especially on the more primitive levels of culture. Since people learn to do things through instruction and example by the older generation, they inevitably tend to reproduce the same forms. Such changes in form as do occur are more apt to be slow and gradual, unless they are the result of borrowing a rather different trait from another culture. Thus similarities in material forms can be assumed to imply either shared tradition or contact and borrowing between unrelated groups.

As a final word on the extraction of evidence from an archeological site, we must stress again the vital importance of adequate publication of the results. Evidence becomes evidence only when it is made available to other scholars; unreported material might as well have remained in the ground. Proper reporting must include publication of the raw data—that is, full descriptions of the specimens and all observations—as well as giving the methods of analysis and the interpretations and conclusions. This permits others to analyze the data for themselves and to arrive at different interpretations if they so choose.

reference

Piggott, Stuart: *Approach to Archaeology*, Harvard University Press, Cambridge, 1959. (With the author's permission.)

suggested readings

See Chapter 2.

dating the past

time scales

Since the archeologist deals with human activity through *time*, since he is supplying time depth to studies of human culture, time is thus his most important consideration. Only when events can be placed in their proper time relationship to one another can sequences of development or relationships between events in different areas be established and understood. We must therefore say something about the archeologist's time scales and about how he dates his materials—a subject which is called *chronology*.

The names which mystify and confuse any newcomer to the study of prehistory are not intended to be more than labels. Age or period terms like Paleolithic or Bronze Age simply serve to divide up the prehistory of any region into chapters. Culture terms, on the other hand, like Magdalenian culture or Hopewell culture, are meant to distinguish the different societies—often a number of them simultaneously, in different areas— which flourished during a given period. As we have mentioned, a culture is generally named after the site where it was first found or where it is especially well represented. In common practice, an archeological assemblage is usually referred to a culture or period, which establishes its approximate position in the prehistoric time scale. But this sort of time fixation may seem very inadequate to the layman, whose first question is always, "How old is it?"

The archeologist, like the geologist, has two kinds of scales for measuring time: relative chronology and absolute chronology (or chronometric dating, as it is coming to be called). Both are necessary for solving their problems, since they are applicable to different situations. Relative chronology simply places materials in relation to other materials or to some reference point; i.e., it establishes that something is older or younger than something else and makes it possible to arrange a series of things in proper chronological order, although the total span of time involved and the intervals between the things is unknown. In other words, it establishes a *sequence*. Absolute chronology, on the other hand, determines age in terms of years—the sort of dating we are accustomed to in everyday life.

Until very recently, archeologists have had to forego absolute dates for the most part and to rely primarily on relative dating. But in the last 15 years a sensational new development, beyond the wildest dreams of scientists a generation ago, has been literally revolutionizing the science of archeology. This, a beneficial by-product of the atom bomb, is the technique of absolute dating by measurement of residual radiocarbon or C^{14} content of organic substances. It has been called the first major breakthrough since Darwin's theory in the study of man's past. However, it is applicable only where suitable organic material is associated with archeological remains; it cannot take us back much beyond 50,000 years; nor is it by any means foolproof as yet. So we have not yet reached the point where we can dispense with the solid if limited evidence of relative dating—even if only as a check or control on such new methods.

relative chronology

The fact that archeologists have hitherto had to depend to so large an extent upon relative chronology has of course been a drawback, but not as serious a one as might be supposed at first. Basically, the difference between relative and absolute dates is less a difference in kind than one of degree: the degree of precision. Obviously, by using dates in terms of years, months, and days, it is possible to define the time of events far more precisely than is the case with the cruder sort of scale provided by cultural or technological changes, which is the basis for archeological periods. But after all, as Grahame Clark has pointed out, the fineness of the scale we use for measure should bear some relation to what we propose to measure. Thus a month, or even a year, may be of the greatest potential importance to students of modern history, but it is supremely irrelevant when dealing with the history of Pleistocene man. We would not be able to use a year-by-year chronology if we had one.

The more important methods of working out relative chronology include first and foremost the basic geological principle of stratigraphy which has already been mentioned, i.e., the relative vertical position of objects in the ground. Finding a stratified site—the result of repeated or prolonged human occupancy of the same spot—is the hope and goal of every archeologist. In fortunate cases, such as a very deep cave deposit or the tells of the Near East, a single stratified site may provide a sequence of cultures spanning thousands of years and reflecting a significant portion of the prehistory of the region. Or sometimes a number of stratified sites of different ages will be found in the same area, the sequences of which overlap and can be fitted together to build up a master sequence covering a far longer period than that represented in any single site.

In the absence of stratigraphy, a number of other methods may be resorted to, but these yield far less conclusive evidence. Relative dating by *typology* is based on the fact that manufactured objects and art objects tend to undergo evolutionary change over the course of time in their form or style. These changes reflect general cultural change, and it is often possible on this basis to arrange objects of different age in a time sequence. For example, if you had a series of Ford automobiles representing, say, the model of every fifth year since 1900, you would not have much difficulty in arranging these in their proper time sequence without looking at any identifying marks simply on the basis of the steadily changing trend in style. There are, however, many drawbacks and complications encountered in typological dating of this sort, one of the more common being the stubborn persistence of a certain number of archaic forms into much later periods. On the basis of appearance alone, these forms (and the associated assemblage) might be ascribed to a far earlier period than was in fact the case. Or, again, a frequent basis for such typological arrangements of artifacts is the assumption that change proceeds through time from simple forms to more complex ones. This is often the case; but on occasion, just the reverse may be true; i.e., a complex form under certain circumstances may degenerate into a rudimentary one. This may happen, for instance, when some complicated form is borrowed by a simple culture from a more advanced one; subsequent efforts will be made to imitate the superficial appearance of the original item, although the group is unable to duplicate it. Thus the archeologist always prefers to have his typological sequences confirmed or corroborated by other types of evidence—although there are times when he has nothing better to go on.

If typology cannot be utilized in establishing the time relationships of unstratified assemblages, they can sometimes be arranged in a sequence by means of *seriation*. This method is based on the presence or absence, or relative frequency, of elements in a series of assemblages, such as a group of sites or the contents of a number of graves. For example, pottery in many prehistoric cultures was subject to changes in style or fashion, like elements of our own culture, which determined the relative popularity of any particular type at a point in time. It is assumed that new types first appear in small quantities, the result of borrowing or innovation, gradually achieve acceptance and popularity, then fade out of the picture as new types replace them. Suppose you have three sites of unknown age which you are trying to arrange in proper time sequence. You have identified three distinct types of pottery among the remains: We shall call them A, B, and C. In the first site, 10 percent of the sherds are of type A, 70 percent of type B, and 20 percent of type C. In the second site, you find

40 percent A, 50 percent B, and 10 percent C. The third site contains 80 percent type A sherds, 20 percent type B, and none of type C. This could be interpreted as the steady rise of type A, the waning popularity of type B, and the dying out of type C, in which case the first site would be the oldest, the second intermediary in age, and the third the youngest. It could, however, reflect exactly the reverse, i.e., the decline of type A, the rise of B, and the first appearance of C.

FIGURE   4–1.

	Site 1	Site 2	Site 3
Pottery type A	10%	40%	80%
Pottery type B	70%	50%	20%
Pottery type C	20%	10%	

You can be sure, in other words, that your second site is intermediate in age, but some other type of evidence is needed to suggest whether the first or third site should be older or younger and hence to indicate which way the sequence should run. In many cases some such indication can be found through one of the other methods of dating we are discussing.

An important method of relative time placement of archeological remains is *cross dating*, i.e., establishing the similarity of the assemblage, or of some significant elements in it, with others in another locality whose relative age has already been determined—thus tying the new site in with some established time sequence. This is extremely common procedure. For instance, if you find a fragment of a prehistoric Indian pot in a ploughed field, the chances are that it can be assigned to a definite period in the prehistory of your locality (i.e., given a relative date) by comparing it with the known sequence of pottery types in that area and finding where it fits in.

For the dating of older periods of human history we rely heavily on the geologists. That is, we try to tie our archeological finds in with some geological deposit or feature that the geologists can date relatively in terms of their own sequence of earth history. Examples of such geologically datable deposits are those whose formation is connected with the successive advances and retreats of the Pleistocene ice sheets in northern Europe and North America. River terraces also provide an excellent relative sequence for archeological remains associated with them in one locality. Rivers, throughout their history, typically go through alternating sequences of deposition (filling wide valley floors with alluvial deposits) and of erosion or downcutting through these deposits to establish a new bed at a lower level. As they cut new valleys, patches of the alluvial deposits forming the old valley floor will remain as terraces along the sides of the new valley. Thus over a long period of time a deep river valley will have been formed, the sides of which show a series of terraces running like steps from the present bed up to the top. For example, the Thames River has five such terraces on the sides of its valley, the surfaces of which

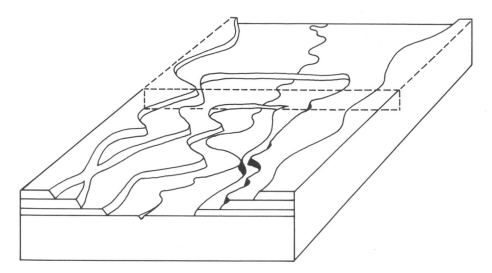

FIGURE 4–2. *Example of river terrace formation. The top part of the diagram, above the dashed lines, illustrates two hypothetical stages of floodplain and terrace formation in a river valley. The lower part illustrates a later stage in the history of the valley with three terraces that are the remnants of former floodplains.* (Diagram by Peter Storck.)

are 10, 25, 50, 100, and 150 feet, respectively, above the present river. In the case of river terraces, the highest one will be the oldest, representing the original valley floor before downcutting began, and the lowest will be the most recent. If archeological remains are buried in the deposits of more than one terrace of any particular river, their time position relative to one another can be firmly established and transferred by cross dating to similar remains elsewhere.

Successive changes in sea level in past time are recorded in many areas by remains of old beaches and shorelines above, or at a distance from, present ones. Archeological sites which were evidently situated on the shore at the time they were inhabited may be relatively dated in areas where the sequence of such old shorelines has been worked out by geologists.

If it is not possible to tie an archeological site to a datable geological deposit of this sort, climatic evidence may help to place it. It may contain, or be associated with, bones of animals that lived at the same time in the area. Animal life in any locality reflects the changing climate, and will differ from period to period. If the remains are predominantly of cold-climate species or of warmth-loving forms, they can often be assigned to a known cold or warm period in climatic history, such as a glacial or interglacial stage. Vegetation is a far more sensitive indicator of climatic change, and for postglacial times in particular we have a remarkably complete record of the changing forest and plant cover preserved in the bog and lake deposits of the temperate zone in the form of microscopic pollen grains. Since this pollen was blown from the surrounding country into the bog or lake deposits as they slowly built up over long periods of time, by analyzing samples from different levels in such deposits it is possible to determine the changing composition of the vegetation at different periods and thus to work out the vegetation history of an area which, again, reflects its climatic history. If pollen samples are present in an archeological site, they may often be fitted into such a sequence and thus place the site in terms of known climatic stages or in relation to other sites.

Paleontologists have worked out the history of past animal life and can often assist the archeologist by placing his animal remains in terms of this. For instance, certain species or genera first appeared or became extinct at known points in time. Major dependence is placed on such paleontological dating in establishing a time scale for the Pleistocene in areas not affected by glaciation or related phenomena, and where the usual geological subdivisions of the Pleistocene consequently cannot be identified.[1]

For determining the relative ages of bone or of bone objects from the same deposit, the *fluorine* method has been of great value in some cases. For example, it played a major role in exposing the famous Piltdown forgery by demonstrating that the jaw of an alleged early specimen of man was of modern age. The fluorine content of bones in the ground increases with time, so that by measuring this content it is possible to tell which bones are older than others, or whether they all belong together. The amount of fluorine that gets into a bone, however, depends upon how much is present in the ground water, and this varies a great deal from place to place. Thus bones of the same age from different areas might show very different fluorine content. The method can therefore only be used to compare bones from the same locality.

A number of other methods of relative dating have been tried in particular circumstances—some very ingenious—but the foregoing are the most important and the ones most commonly employed.

absolute chronology

Relative chronologies constructed by these methods will show succession of events but not duration of time. Archeological techniques by themselves cannot reveal how long a period lasted, how long ago an event occurred,

[1] Chronological correlations between different parts of the world based solely on paleontological evidence encounter a major difficulty in that the history of animal life may vary from region to region. For example, a given species may have survived in the tropics for some time after becoming extinct farther north, as is the case in Africa today.

or how old something is. For this we must enlist the aid of other sciences. The value of an absolute chronology is not just in giving an age to things; even more important is determining the rate of culture processes. The tempo of cultural development is vital to an understanding of it, and this can only be determined by absolute dates. Without an absolute chronology, too, the cultures of different regions cannot accurately be compared or their interrelationships assessed. A crude sort of absolute chronology is provided by the subdivisions of the Pleistocene, which are based ultimately on the fluctuating climatic history of the earth during the last few million years. To be useful for our purposes, these would have to be small enough subdivisions to represent limited segments of time, and with very rare exceptions these are not yet available, and will not be until the climatic history of every part of the world has been worked out in detail. At present we can make worldwide correlations only in terms of the major sub-divisions—i.e., in segments of several hundred thousand years—and even these cannot always be positively identified in every area. Thus it has always been the dream of archeologists to be able to assign absolute dates in years to their finds.

For the very recent periods of prehistory in the Old World there was some hope of being able to do this because these recent periods—the Neolithic, Bronze, and Iron Ages—over most of Europe and Asia were con-temporary with the literate civilizations in Egypt and the Near East. In other words, history was being recorded and calendars were being kept in Egypt and Mesopotamia while the peoples of Europe were still in the Neolithic stage. In the Far East, many prehistoric cultures were similarly contemporary with the earliest historic period in China. Thus until re-cently the efforts of archeologists were concentrated on attempts to tie the late prehistoric record in Eurasia by cross dating to the historic record provided by these literate civilizations. These attempts were based on the occasional occurrence in the later archeological sites of Europe or central Asia of objects which had diffused from the higher civilizations or which had been made locally (e.g., in Europe) in obvious imitation of such foreign models, or, best of all, objects which had been carried rather quickly by trade from Egypt or Mesopotamia to the backwoods areas such as Europe then was. And there was a surprising amount of trade and commerce all over Europe and Asia in these later prehistoric times just before the dawn of history. Often these objects can be fairly well dated in their place of origin in terms of years. Or at least it is possible to say that a certain type of bead was not made before a certain date, which estab-lishes a maximum age—and even this can be a tremendous help to the archeologist. In this way the known age of such foreign objects or trade items can help to date the archeological materials with which they are found associated in another region. However, an unknown time lag is always involved: There is no way of knowing how long it took the object to travel or how long it may have been handed down from generation to generation in its new home before becoming buried in the ground. In many cases, too, certain types of articles were in use for a long time in their homeland, so that it would be hard to determine exactly when any particular specimen was made. Last but not least, the calendars of ancient Egypt or Mesopotamia are not very reliable for any date before 2000 B.C., and their historical records, as already implied, are hardly worthy of the name by our standards. Thus, even when cross dating of this sort has been successfully established, the result is not very exact.

Nevertheless, this was the best that could be hoped for in the way of absolute dating until recent years, and much of what we know of the last 5,000 years of European prehistory was originally worked out in this fashion, based ultimately upon the use of written history. There seemed to be little hope of ever having absolute dates for the remaining 99.5 percent of human history in the Old World or for anything at all in the New World prior to 1492—except for the small area of Middle America covered by the calendar system of the ancient Maya. Archeology, by its own techniques, could never hope to solve the problem. Fortunately, however, some of the physical sciences have come to our rescue, although not intentionally, by developing techniques for their own purposes which have subsequently proved of value to the archeologist, and have been adopted for archeological use. This constitutes an active frontier of research today, and it is impossible to predict what startling new aids to archeological dating may lie just around the corner.

The first method of absolute dating which proved of major importance to archeology is dating by tree rings, or *dendrochronology*, developed by the late Dr. A. E. Douglass of the University of Arizona. Everyone is familiar with the fact that trees form an annual growth ring every year and that by counting the rings in a stump or log it is possible to determine its exact age at the time it was cut. Douglass, an astronomer, was interested in fluctuations in solar radiation and their correlation with changes in climate. Since weather records in Arizona did not go back far enough for his purposes, he turned to trees in the hope of reconstructing some record of the climate over a period of centuries on which to base his studies. The local ponderosa pine has very clear-cut growth rings, and under the arid conditions prevailing in the Southwest, Douglass found them to be unusually sensitive to even minor climatic changes, which made them ideal for his purposes. (Dry years produced very thin rings, wet years relatively thick ones.) Starting out with living trees, he obtained a continuous record of the local climate for the past 500 years, and then decided to extend this record further into the past with the help of timbers from old ruins which are usually very well preserved in these arid conditions. Aided by what archeologists knew of the probable relative ages of various sites, Douglass collected a number of samples from progressively older ruins and translated the ring sequence of each sample into a graph which reproduced the pattern of thick and thin rings. The occurrence of distinctive combinations representing certain definite periods of years that could be identified in different samples and matched up made

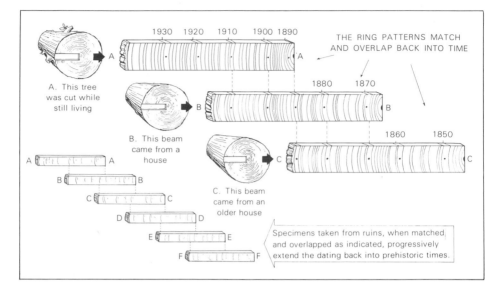

FIGURE 4–3. *Establishing a time scale by dendrochronology.* (From Jesse D. Jennings, *Prehistory of North America* [Figure 1.2], copyright © 1968 by McGraw-Hill, Inc., New York. By permission of the publishers.)

it possible to arrange the progressively older samples in overlapping fashion to create a single overall master graph that ran from the present back to the time of Christ in a continuous record. Archeologists, of course, were not slow to catch on to the possibilities of the method for their own purposes and began to bring in timber samples from sites all over the Southwest to be matched against Dr. Douglass' master graph. By finding the right place where the patterns matched, the exact year in which the timber had been cut could thus be determined. In this way it was possible to tell when an ancient structure had been built or when important alterations or additions to it had been made. Precautions were necessary, of course: An old beam might be reused in a later structure, or the outer part cut away so that the entire ring sequence was not present.

Dendrochronology has been of crucial importance in the southwestern United States, and as a result the prehistory of that area has been on an unusually sound footing for some time. There were hopes that the method could be widely utilized in other areas, but except for a certain amount of work in Alaska, Central Europe, and Anatolia, these have not been borne out. Its particular success in the Southwest is enhanced by the peculiar local conditions. As an archeological technique its usefulness is rather restricted, with its association with prehistoric remains limited to the last few thousand years. But in other ways of indirect benefit to the prehistorian it is assuming great importance, as we shall see presently.

No such limitations apply to the radiocarbon or C^{14} method of absolute dating, which has been revolutionizing archeology in the past fifteen years. Developed by a noted nuclear physicist, Dr. W. F. Libby, this technique is worldwide in its application and can take us back at present 30,000 to 40,000 years. Any piece of organic matter is theoretically susceptible to dating by this method, although some materials have been found to work better than others and to require far smaller samples. Happily, the best substance for the purpose is charcoal, which is one of the commonest types of organic remains in archeological sites since it has great survival powers. An ounce provides an adequate sample.

C^{14} is present in the atmosphere, and plants and animals during their lifetimes contain an amount equal to the atmospheric content, the level being maintained in plants through their processes of oxygen exchange with the atmosphere, while animals obtain it from eating plants or eating other animals that have eaten plants. Although all living organisms are constantly losing C^{14} at a steady rate, they are also taking it in, so that an equilibrium is maintained as long as the organism is alive. After death, however, this intake promptly ceases, and the C^{14} present begins to disintegrate radioactively. Since this disintegration proceeds at a known rate, based on the half life of C^{14}, by measuring the level of radioactivity remaining in a piece of some organic substance it should be possible to calculate the length of time in "radiocarbon years" that has elapsed since that organism was alive. The method is accepted as basically sound, provided that proper precautions are observed in selecting samples which have not been contaminated by the addition of extra radiocarbon from more recent materials, and in protecting samples from any possible contamination before processing in the laboratory.

The dates derived from testing such samples are, however, not absolute in terms of a single year. They simply indicate an interval of time within which the actual age most probably lies. This is expressed in terms of a date which is midway in this interval, with the limits indicated by a plus or minus probable error. Thus a typical C^{14} date might read 7,200 ± 300 years B.P. (before present). This means that the age of the particular sample has two chances out of three of lying somewhere between 6,900 and 7,500 years ago. This lack of precision is not a serious drawback, given the type of materials with which archeologists have to operate and the general nature of the prehistoric time scale, in which a precise year date would be of very little consequence. Generally speaking, the more recent the date, the smaller the probable error and the greater the degree of precision.

Such dates in "radiocarbon years" were initially presumed equivalent to calendar years, on the assumption that C^{14} has been produced in the atmosphere at a constant rate. This is now known not to be the case, with the result that during certain periods of past time radiocarbon dates diverge from the true age of the sample, while in other periods they coincide quite closely. Dendrochronology, by providing wood samples precisely dated in solar years for radiocarbon measurement, has played a major role in revealing this problem, and we may hope that correction factors will be worked out at least for the 7,000 years covered by the tree-ring record. Other problems may also exist. For instance, it is suspected but not yet established that volcanic activity may affect C^{14} dates in some parts of the world.

It must always be borne in mind, however, that even in the best of cases the laboratory can only date the sample; it is up to the archeologist to demonstrate conclusively that the sample of charcoal or other substance was associated in context with whatever cultural remains he is seeking to date. A radiocarbon date should not necessarily be taken at its face value, therefore; one needs always to ask just what was dated. Moreover, any single isolated C^{14} date should be regarded with great caution. The available dates are of varying reliability and are not strictly comparable in every case owing to differences in techniques and basic assumptions on the part of some laboratories at certain times. Some degree of contamination must also be presumed. It is therefore desirable to have a series of dates run by more than one laboratory. If there is general agreement among them, a high degree of reliability is indicated.

Although radiocarbon dating has become a standard tool of the archeologist in the past decade, with laboratories now available in most parts of the world, it is still a very costly procedure and the method cannot be regarded as perfected, although it is steadily being improved. It may never be foolproof, so that it is risky to place blind dependence on it and to ignore the tried and tested methods of relative dating by archeological techniques, which are valuable if only as a cross-check.

We may expect further progress toward greater precision, greater accuracy, and the possibility of measuring still older dates beyond the capacity of present devices. Isotopic enrichment of samples over 40,000 years old extends the possibility of dating to about 70,000 years, although introducing an additional error of up to 800 years. This seems to represent the ultimate limit at present, and only one laboratory is equipped to undertake such long-range dating as yet. No matter how much laboratory procedures are perfected, however, the dates can never be better than their archeological associations, and these will remain the responsibility of the archeologist himself. He must establish what the date really means.

A new experimental technique for dating pottery, thermoluminescence, has the advantage of dating the artifact itself, avoiding such problems as those arising with C^{14} dating, and utilizes the commonest type of archeological find and the one most widely employed as a chronological and cultural indicator. The method seems to have great promise, but its application is limited to the later stage of prehistory when pottery had come into use.

The scope of radiocarbon dating encompasses the most important portion of human history, but it still leaves possibly 95 percent of the story beyond reach. There is now reason to feel, however, that a still newer isotopic method, the so-called "potassium-argon" method, can help to some extent to cover this crucial early period of man's beginnings between 50,000 and 2 million or so years ago. This technique, developed by Drs. J. F. Evernden and G. H. Curtis of the University of California (Berkeley), is designed to ascertain the age of volcanic materials and other igneous rocks and also of *tektites*,[2] and hence, by association, the age of deposits in which these occur freshly formed and which may also contain evidence of man or serve to date geological events which are reference points in human prehistory. It is based on the principle that potassium (K^{40}) decays to argon (Ar^{40}) at a constant rate and that measurement of the argon content of a sample will give the basis for calculating the elapsed time since the material cooled from a molten state. Here again the problem arises of the significance of the date obtained. For example, the age of the lava or other substance may not necessarily date the deposit, since older lavas may be subsequently eroded and deposited along with much younger materials. Problems of contamination also arise. But basically it is a question of establishing the relationship between the sample dated and whatever it is that you are trying to date: This has been the source of most of the trouble. On the whole, the method must still be considered as being in the developmental stage, although it is very promising, and any preliminary results must be viewed with caution.[3] Its major drawback lies in the fact that contemporary igneous material necessary for this dating technique is lacking in most of the situations that badly need dating whether geological, paleontological, or cultural. Thus the geological-climatic time scale is still the backbone of Pleistocene chronology.

suggested readings

See Chapter 2.

[2] Tektites are glasslike objects now thought to have been formed during the impact of large meteorites on the earth's surface and scattered over a considerable area.

[3] For instance, potassium-argon "years," like C^{14} "years," are not necessarily the equivalent of calendar years. Furthermore, the younger the sample, the greater the problems and the chance of error in measuring small amounts of argon. A number of scientists feel that any dates within the range of the Pleistocene are open to question; some even feel the technique is not reliable for ages of less than 30 million years.

the world of the Pleistocene

the setting for Man the Hunter

Man's cultural equipment, his way of life, and the environments in which he lived are all inextricably linked. Thus no human culture can be understood apart from its environment in the natural world. Although no culture is automatically and rigidly determined by environment as some schools of thought used to proclaim, it is always influenced by it in varying degree. This is true even today when we have managed to nullify or even control some of the forces of nature that held our ancestors at their mercy. And at the earlier stages of man's cultural development, when his technology was still too simple to provide a protective screen, the dependence of culture on its natural surroundings and the closeness of the interrelationship between them were at a maximum. Human history, in fact, could be viewed as the story of the gradual emancipation of man from the complete dependence on nature characteristic of his beginnings. But since man himself is a part of nature, he can never expect to escape completely from its influence—something we are all too apt to forget in our self-satisfied, push-button civilization.

No understanding of man's cultural evolution, therefore, is possible without a knowledge of the setting in which it unfolded, since that exerted a major influence on how he lived, where he lived, and what he was able to do. This setting is the Pleistocene—the last geological period in the history of the earth. Evidence of man's cultural evolution is confined to this period, which covers perhaps some 2½ million years, although it

seems obvious that human beginnings must go back at least into the preceding Pliocene. We can think of the Pleistocene, then, as the Age of Man.

From a geological standpoint, as Karl Butzer points out, the Pleistocene is almost as unique an event in the 5 billion years of earth history as
is human existence in the three billion years of biological history. It constitutes a drastic interruption in the otherwise smooth climatic record.
During some 90 percent of preceding time the climate was considerably
warmer, there was no ice (as there is today covering large areas in Greenland and Antarctica), and in particular the climate was less differentiated
than now and more homogeneous over the world, lacking our sharp contrasts of arctic and tropics, and our often marked regional differences
within continents. The Pleistocene brought an abrupt change in this long-
standing environmental picture, substituting alternating spasms of colder
and warmer climate that reached their extreme in the extensive continental
glaciations of the Middle and Upper Pleistocene in the Northern Hemisphere, a pattern that shows no signs of terminating. A number of ingenious theories have been proposed to explain this dramatic shift in the
earth's history, but we are still far from any understanding of the causal
factors. However, we cannot help but be struck by the coincidence between
this period of unprecedented and rapid environmental change and the
time span of human evolution, also unprecedented and rapid in biological
perspective. Is it merely coincidence?

In the mind of the average person the Pleistocene is the "Ice Age."
This is quite understandable, since glaciation was the most dramatic event
characterizing this period and has left the most conspicuous remains,
although ice sheets actually covered portions of the earth's land surface
(never more than one-third of it, usually less) during perhaps one-eighth
of the time span of the Pleistocene. (Ten percent of the world is still
covered by ice, more than was the case during much of the "Ice Age,"
further evidence that the Pleistocene is still with us.) However, glaciation
was only one result of the climatic shift that sets off the Pleistocene from
preceding eras, and it affected only the northern latitudes and higher
mountain areas elsewhere.[1] Of equal importance for human history were
the effects in the rest of the world: the southward depression of environmental zones during colder phases with resultant changes in their relative
extent, the transformation of arid regions into favorable habitats, the
differentiation of regional climates that in some cases created barriers to
the free flow of animals and man, and, not least of all, the worldwide
lowering in sea level that ensued when vast amounts of the earth's water
were locked up in the ice. This last effect meant the emergence of continental shelves nowadays covered by shallow seas so that the map of the

---

[1] Not even all the northern regions were affected. Owing to inadequate precipitation,
glaciers could not form over most of Siberia, which remained largely ice-free during at
least the final or Würm glaciation.

world was altered, quite drastically in some parts, with the addition of large areas of suitable habitat that may have been the home of significant portions of the human population and the establishment of land connections with islands and adjacent continents normally separated by water barriers. Let us consider these effects of the Pleistocene climatic shifts in order.

glaciation

Conventionally, the "Ice Age" was viewed in terms of four major ice advances or glaciations (Günz, Mindel, Riss, and Würm)[2] separated by "interglacial" periods when the ice withdrew and the climate was as warm or warmer than today.[3] This quadruple glaciation concept was based on the pioneering studies of Penck and Brückner of evidence of glaciation in the Alps. On the unwarranted assumption that this represented the definitive picture of Pleistocene climatic history, the sequence has been applied all over the Old World and has tended to become the standard framework of Pleistocene chronology. A great deal of research on glacial geology has been done since the work of Penck and Brückner, and although this "classic" sequence may still be generally valid for the Alps, we now know that Pleistocene chronology and climate are a lot more complicated. A good deal went on in early (Lower) Pleistocene times before the "first" glaciation, though the evidence for the most part was covered or destroyed by later ice action, and is difficult to detect. The "first" (Günz) glaciation itself may be primarily an Alpine phenomenon of local significance only; it has not been positively identified elsewhere. Certainly it is only the last three glaciations of the classic sequence (Mindel, Riss, Würm) that involved extensive continental ice sheets in Europe. And at least the latter two were complex affairs of repeated advances interspersed with partial withdrawals ("interstadials") of temperate climate. Moreover, there is great difficulty in correlating the better-known glacial history of western and central Europe with events elsewhere. We do not know in most cases which evidences of glaciation in other parts of Eurasia coincide with the various European stages, or even whether the same number of ice advances occurred everywhere. Similar problems arise in interpreting and correlating Pleistocene events in North America, although there is a

[2] As an aid to memory, note that the initial letters of these names form an alphabetical sequence.

[3] The earlier notion that the climate of the interglacial periods represented an equally pronounced shift in the opposite direction, with Europe, for instance, enjoying tropical conditions or a markedly warm dry climate, has not been borne out. Available biological evidence from such periods in Europe suggests an ecological picture essentially like that of recent times, although at the maximum warm-up the winter temperatures may have averaged 2° or 3°C higher and the climate may have had a less continental character than today, according to Karl Butzer.

tendency to feel that glaciation was roughly synchronized throughout the Northern Hemisphere. For obvious reasons we know more about the final (Würm) complex of glaciations[4] than about the earlier ones, and fortunately this is also the one that most affected human history. What we have to say about Pleistocene environments is therefore based primarily on Würm data.[5]

For our purposes, the effect of the ice sheets themselves was to periodically remove large areas of northern Eurasia and northern North America from the habitable world, recurrently restricting the human habitat. Local glaciation in many mountain regions also created barriers to the movement of animals and men over accustomed routes, channeling or blocking activity and setting up new conditions, often with significant historical consequences. The record of human history was also directly affected in that any preexisting cultural remains in glaciated areas were in most cases destroyed, concealed, or at the very least redeposited out of context. Our knowledge of prehistory in the northern latitudes is consequently severely handicapped. But by and large popular thinking tends to exaggerate the role of the ice itself upon human history because of the concentration of the glaciation in just those regions—Europe and northeastern North America—which are today the centers of our industrial civilization but which in former times were marginal to the mainstream of cultural evolution. Actually, the other effects of Pleistocene climatic shifts were most important for man and affected a far larger part of the habitable world.

habitat

The Northern Hemisphere today, and as far as we know throughout the Pleistocene as well, is characterized generally speaking by a series of latitudinal environmental zones circling the globe. From north to south these are (1) the Arctic ice, (2) the treeless tundra, (3) the temperate forests, (4) the subtropical forests, (5) the grasslands, (6) the deserts, (7) tropical savannah, and (8) the tropical rain forests. These zones vary in their suitability for human habitat at different technological levels and with different economic patterns. Thus, for example, the tundra is an optimum habitat for groups practicing a hunting economy, but it requires a relatively high level of technology to make human life there possible at all; for hunters with only rudimentary cultural equipment the savannah is optimum. Conversely, the tundra is ruled out completely for groups with a farming economy, and the savannah at best is marginal. Thus the relative extent of these different environmental zones at different stages in

---

[4] Labeled "Wisconsin" in North America.
[5] There is reason to feel that the climate during the earlier Riss glaciation was milder.

human history was the primary factor in determining the habitat of man, his distribution over the world, and the size of his population during the Food-gathering Stage when that depended directly on the natural resources of the environment. The major consequence of the cooler periods during the Pleistocene as far as life on earth (including man) was concerned was the southward depression of these zones, except for the tropics, with a concomitant increase in rainfall in the latter. During the final (Würm) glaciation, the tundra extended down into central Europe, the tropical savannah and rain forest expanded its area northward due to greater rainfall, and the belts of forest, grassland, and desert in between shrank markedly. The results were, first, that more and less of certain habitats became available to man, with direct consequences on his population and development according to his technological ability to exploit them. Secondly, the displacement of certain environmental zones meant that their characteristic plant and animal communities moved with them or were replaced by others. Man in any given locality had either to move with his ecological setting—with all that might entail in the way of competition with other already-established populations, negotiating geographic barriers to movement, etc.—or he had to adapt his technology to a different and presumably more demanding environment. (His ability to do the latter increased markedly toward the end of the Pleistocene, but in earlier times he must have mainly moved with the animals of his ecological community)

As we mentioned, a further effect of these climatic shifts that brought glaciation in the north and markedly lower temperatures to the middle latitudes, was an increase in rainfall in the tropics and contiguous regions, where no real change in temperature would have been discernible. Portions of the present-day arid regions became periodically suitable for human habitat—perhaps highly attractive—with lakes filling now-dry basins and streams flowing in the ancient channels. We have evidence of such former conditions over much of Africa and the arid regions of western North America. In Africa, a direct correlation has been established between the last major rainier period and a phase of the Würm glaciation in Europe. It seems reasonable to assume that previous periods of increased rainfall also correlate with glaciations, but definite correlations with specific earlier European glaciations remain to be worked out. If this can be done, it will provide a valuable geological chronology for many parts of Africa. (The recent scheme of four so-called "pluvials" assumed to coincide with the four glaciations of the Penck-Brückner Alpine scheme has been discredited, but still looms large in the literature on African prehistory.)

The relative homogeneity of climate over the world in pre-Pleistocene times, with its correlate of minimal barriers between regions and free flow of animal populations, seems to have prevailed down to the beginning of the Middle Pleistocene. Perhaps as a consequence of what was probably the first major continental glaciation (Mindel), there seems to be a greater regional differentiation in the Middle Pleistocene faunas of Eurasia and probably in the climates they represent. This suggests the development of barriers there to unrestricted migration of animals and, equally, of man. It is possible that tectonic (crustal) movements may have affected geography in a number of areas. At any rate, there are indications that the primary dispersal of the human stock in Eurasia, at the end of the Lower Pleistocene, was more widespread and unhampered than any subsequent movement for nearly half a million years.

Africa presents a somewhat different picture. Although we have a very limited knowledge of Pleistocene climates in these tropical and subtropical latitudes, as compared with the temperate zone, it would seem that Africa was little affected by the climatic fluctuations except in the form of expansion of favorable environments during periods of increased rainfall. Even so, these ("pluvial" periods were not necessarily very wet, and the older notions of accompanying major changes, with desert becoming forest, are unsubstantiated.) When environmental zones shifted, the absence of geographic barriers here made it relatively simple for the African floras and faunas to move north or south.

In Europe, on the other hand, the Mediterranean and the mountain systems of southern Europe form a barrier that made it much more difficult for the local flora and fauna to follow the climate south, and distinct changes are visible at various points in the Pleistocene record, where species either perished when their environment disappeared or failed to reappear when it was restored. Thus many species no longer found in Europe are still widespread in Africa.

In East Africa, where the Pleistocene fauna is best known, the species present suggest climatic conditions very similar to those of modern times but with somewhat more rainfall. None of the fauna suggest drier conditions, nor do the successive assemblages of different ages provide any evidence for major ecological change of the sort that might bring about large-scale extinctions, etc., elsewhere. In more marginal areas which became favorable habitat only with increased precipitation, a return to drier conditions of course forced the withdrawal of any species that had expanded into them, so that the drier periods in Africa must have been times of migration in these areas, for man as well as flora and fauna. The recurrent wet and dry cycles manifested under the particular conditions of these marginal areas of Africa, with their concomitant population stability and forced migration, might have created a situation of alternate genetic drift and gene flow that could conceivably have accelerated the processes of human evolution. The most extreme, as well as the most important, of these marginal areas was the Sahara, which has formed an insuperable barrier during most of human history, with very important consequences, but which at a few times during the Pleistocene offered suitable habitat and routes for human movement to and from the Mediterranean coast.

sea levels

During the last glaciation, world sea level was lowered approximately 300 feet below the present, adding large areas to the continents in certain regions such as Southeast Asia (see Figure 12-1) and providing a land connection between the Old and New Worlds in the Bering Strait area that was a major factor in the modern distribution of certain animals and in the spread of Homo sapiens. Even greater lowerings of sea level may well have occurred during earlier glaciations, but their extent is difficult to establish with certainty. Present sea level is not a stable norm. Melting of the present ice sheets in Greenland and Antarctica (which are a purely Pleistocene phenomenon and hence are not "normal" in terms of total earth history) would raise the modern sea level by about 200 feet, with disastrous effects upon our major centers of population. Presumably the original Pliocene sea level would have been of this general order. Remains of old beach lines throughout the world at higher levels than the present suggest the existence in the more recent past of higher sea levels—which almost certainly occurred during interglacial periods—and these again would have affected human habitat and activities. However, other geological processes also influence shorelines and thus complicate the picture. For instance, in many parts of the world areas of land are rising or have been uplifted tectonically in the past. Also, areas covered by continental ice sheets sink under their weight and only gradually does the elastic crust return to normal afterwards. Any of these factors can cause the shoreline to stand higher on a steep coast or the sea to inundate low-lying coastal regions ("transgression"), altering the map in areas where this occurs. These constantly changing relationships between land and sea throughout the Pleistocene, as well as the environmental shifts, are what we have in mind when we speak of "the changing world of the Pleistocene." And this overall environmental instability certainly had its effects on the course of human development.

The climate of the past 10,000 years, since the last glaciation, has exhibited a pattern of small-scale cyclical change. It has not, as might be assumed, reflected a steady warming-up from the time of ice withdrawal to the present day. Instead, a peak of warmth was reached approximately 5,000 years ago (the so-called "Altithermal" or "climatic optimum") from which we have receded, with minor variations. Even these smaller fluctuations have played significant roles in human history. For instance, Greenland was settled by the Norsemen during a warm phase in the eleventh century A.D., but their colonists came to grief when the climate turned colder four or five centuries later. Postglacial climatic history suggests that the major warm-cold spasms of the Pleistocene were not the smooth curves so often depicted, but rather jagged lines of continuous minor oscillations which may themselves have affected man in no small way.

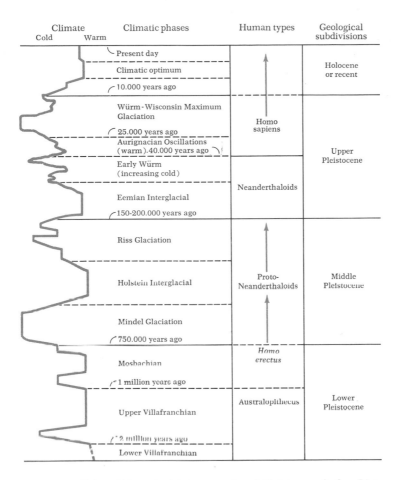

Climate	Climatic phases	Human types	Geological subdivisions
Cold Warm			

	Present day		Holocene or recent
	Climatic optimum		
	10.000 years ago		
	Würm-Wisconsin Maximum Glaciation	Homo sapiens	
	25.000 years ago		
	Aurignacian Oscillations (warm).40.000 years ago		Upper Pleistocene
	Early Würm (increasing cold)	Neanderthaloids	
	Eemian Interglacial		
	150-200.000 years ago		
	Riss Glaciation		
	Holstein Interglacial	Proto-Neanderthaloids	Middle Pleistocene
	Mindel Glaciation		
	750.000 years ago		
	Moshachian	Homo erectus	
	1 million years ago		
	Upper Villafranchian	Australopithecus	Lower Pleistocene
	2 million years ago		
	Lower Villafranchian		

FIGURE 5-1. *Climatic history and subdivisions of the Pleistocene. The basic chronological yardstick is provided by the fluctuating climatic history; the ultimate goal is to tie the events of human prehistory to this. The absolute dates are approximations only, at best suggesting a general order of magnitude. (Note: The Pleistocene is subdivided in different ways by various authors, the disagreements centering mainly on the placement of the boundary between Lower and Middle. This can lead to confusion when the subdivisions are used as time units in dating prehistoric events. It should be borne in mind that they are arbitrary divisions of the course of climatic history; the latter should be the focus of our attention.)*

human environment

We should get over the notion that early man lived in a strange and alien environment. Although the climate at any given point north of the tropics did on occasion change, the resultant conditions can be observed somewhere in the world today, and over large areas there seem to have been little if any significant differences from today. Cartoonists and their ilk to the contrary, the dinosaurs had been dead for many millions of years. The plants and animals of man's natural surroundings would have been mostly familiar. After the Lower Pleistocene, only modern genera of animals are present, although it is true that many of the larger and more spectacular species of these have died out, while others are today restricted mainly to Africa.

In sum, although a changing world has by and large characterized the Age of Man, man has not been subjected to environmental conditions any different from those of today. The Pleistocene changes of geography and climate affected man primarily by forcing him to move: Only in this sense did they pose situations of "challenge and response," of which so much has been made. Subsequent to the initial ecological shift to a carnivorous diet, which started the hominids on the road to humanity, it is difficult to discern occasions on which man was forced to adapt to a different environment until he was technologically ready to do so. When his habitat moved, man generally elected to move with it throughout his early history. Not until 75,000 years ago did the picture change significantly.

suggested reading

Butzer, Karl W.: *Environment and Archeology: An Introduction to Pleistocene Geography,* Aldine Publishing Co., Chicago, 1964, pp. 43–71, 265–334.

protoculture and its antecedents

in the beginning

Prehistorians traditionally begin the story of human history—in the sense of the history of the culture, activities, and behavior of creatures we can call human—at the point where we have the first concrete archeological evidence of culture, indicating that the human stage had by then been attained. We cannot presume that the scant evidence available to us at the moment, such as the earliest remains at Olduvai Gorge in East Africa and the few other sites of Lower Pleistocene age, is representative of the first appearance of culture. In all probability, the human stage had been attained sometime earlier; how much earlier, we do not yet know. Actually, then, human history began at the point where *hominid*[1] progenitors became human, i.e., when they had attained a sufficient development of foresight, communication, and tradition (transmission of acquired skills and knowledge by learning) so we can say that culture exists to a significant extent and, equally important, that this hominid can no longer survive without the assistance of culture (is dependent on *cultural* means of adaptation), and hence is no longer an animal but has crossed the threshold of humanity.[2]

It will be noted that the definition of man is thus not anatomical but functional-behavioral; we can define a hominid in anatomical terms but not distinguish the point at which hominid becomes man. This human

[1] A hominid is a member of the zoological family Hominidae, to which all forms of man, living or extinct, are assigned.
[2] Perhaps we could equally well call this the "threshold of culture."

situation was reached at some stage in the continuing process of biocultural evolution, but even with far more information than we have available we could not expect to pinpoint such a moment and assign a date. For the beginning of humanity was not an *event,* in the sense of a sudden occurrence or change, but simply the passing of a certain point of no return in a spectrum of development.

Thus, although we perforce begin our history with the first available evidence, some consideration of what led up to this purely arbitrary point is essential. Culture did not spring into existence overnight any more than man the organism did. As W. W. Howells remarked, we should not talk about the appearance of man as if he had suddenly been promoted from colonel to brigadier general and had a date of rank. Nor should we any longer, as we have tended to do, talk about the "appearance of culture" as if it too had suddenly leaped into existence. There must have been a previous behavioral evolution corresponding to the anatomical evolution that we all take for granted. Structure and function are inseparable. Yet our standard definitions of man have always tended to emphasize his *differences* from other primates. In our eagerness to place ourselves safely on the side of the angels and to look away from our embarrassing animal past, we have created in our minds an artificial gap, a discontinuity, at this crucial stage of human development, rather than being aware of the continuity that is inherent in the whole evolutionary process itself.

Just as the earliest culture did not appear from nowhere but represents a stage in a long development, so we should not fall into the opposite error of assuming that man thenceforth was endowed with that abstract quality, culture, in the sense that we think of it as an attribute of modern Homo sapiens. On the contrary, there was a very long and very slow development which was more rapid at some times than others and which paralleled the anatomical evolution, before culture as we know it was achieved in modern-type Homo sapiens. We should think of this initial stage of humanity as representing the rudiments of culture, the rudiments of human behavior—as being an intermediate stage in behavioral evolution between the typically primate and the primarily human, as exemplified by the subsequent *Homo erectus* level of the Middle Pleistocene.

For this initial stage of human history when the ground work was laid for the abilities displayed by the full men who follow after, I shall use the term *protoculture,* which has been suggested by Hallowell (1956). Timewise, this period covers the Lower Pleistocene and extends almost certainly back into the preceding Pliocene. We should probably think in terms of something like 2 million years at a minimum for this period, so that it thus represents the major slice of human history. The bearer of this protoculture—the incipient man—seems to have been the genus *Australopithecus.* The area of his activities, in our present knowledge, was primarily Africa, which evidently offered a variety of favorable habitats. However, we must bear in mind that the role of Africa as the cradle of mankind may be overemphasized. Our picture may be biased because of the optimum conditions for finding Lower Pleistocene hominids in Africa. It is quite possible that incipient man may have been equally or more active elsewhere in the tropics and subtropics of the Old World (i.e., in parts of southern Eurasia), but his traces have either not survived or have not yet been found. At any rate we can feel that tropical Africa, outside of the dense rain forests and deserts (i.e., in the more open and grassland regions) was an important arena for protocultural man if not the only one initially.

What can we learn, or infer, concerning this mysterious and shadowy borderland which lies between man and his prehuman past, as it has been called? What sources of information can we draw on? First, there are the very scanty (as yet) actual remains of human activity: things he had made, or used, or altered, or eaten. Second, there are inferences from actual hominid fossils as to behavior and capability: For example, dentition may yield important evidence of diet and hence of ecological pattern. Third, there is our knowledge of the environment in which these hominids lived and which inevitably exerted a major influence on their activities. Fourth, there are inferences from the behavior of living primates. And finally, we may postulate what would have had to happen in order to produce known conditions.

the ecological shift to hunting by hominids

Why did culture develop only in the hominid line and not in other primates? The need to explain this situation has led to the suggestion that there might be certain biological prerequisites for the appearance of culture, certain factors which created the *capacity* for culture in the hominid line, in conjunction with maximum development of those innate primate characteristics such as superior vision, enlarged brain, and adaptation toward adaptability to a variety of ecological niches by *behavioral modification* rather than by the evolution of specialized anatomical structures. These advantages characteristic of primates played major roles in human development, to be sure, but something more was needed. Perhaps by lucky accident, the ancestors of the hominid line retained relatively primitive, unspecialized hands, unlike the apes who became too adapted to brachiation, or the baboons who became too adapted to four-footed walking on the ground. It is doubtful whether the adoption of upright posture by these or any other primate group would have led to the same results as in the case of the hominids.[3] But there is general agreement that bipedalism (upright posture and locomotion) was the basic *anatomical* change that started the ball rolling and eventually enabled some of the hominids to realize these inherent potentialities. Subsequently, *behavioral* changes were

[3] Other possible biological prerequisites for cultural development are discussed in Spuhler, 1959.

to play the major roles, with anatomical changes following after as a consequence of these.

At the moment, we just do not know the cause of this anatomical change that made *habitual* upright posture practical for the first time.[4] It may originally have been a more or less fortuitous structural shift, perpetuated because it conferred some biological advantage. Or cultural factors may have played a role. For instance, there are indications that projecting canines—the defensive weapons of all primates—were already being lost back at prehominid levels; hence, the ability to wield weapons of some sort in free hands might have conferred a definite survival advantage.

However it came about, the initial result was *Paranthropus*, or his direct ancestor: simply an upright, ground-dwelling great ape, otherwise not too different from a gorilla anatomically, mentally, or in his pattern of life.[5] In view of his free and prehensile hands, we may postulate some limited use of objects as tools, though his purely vegetarian diet created little real necessity for them and his powerful molars took care of any food processing. Such a large, awe-inspiring creature would have had little to fear and could have survived without weapons; like the modern gorilla, he would have been able to frighten off potential enemies. But the hominid advance represented by vegetarian *Paranthropus* was a dead end; we find him persisting unchanged and unimproved, with a brain no larger than the apes', from the Pliocene to the beginning of the Middle Pleistocene, where he existed side by side with true men and eventually became extinct.

Thus, erect posture and free hands, although essential preconditions, were not enough to launch the hominids on the road to humanity as represented by *Australopithecus*. The crucial change was not anatomical but a major *behavioral* shift under pressure from natural selection to adapt to markedly changed conditions where survival under the old primate food patterns was no longer possible. This key development has recently been termed the "Ecological Revolution."[6] Since it is typical of primates to adapt to a particular ecological niche by modifying their *behavior* rather than by evolving specialized anatomical structures, such a shift seems entirely natural if environmental conditions underwent significant alteration.

There is abundant geological and related evidence that the entire Pliocene was a time of progressive drought in Africa, with shrinking of forests and increasingly widespread deserts and arid grasslands. Extensive areas became uninhabitable for vegetarian primates, either arboreal or ground dwelling, although the hoofed animals, able to eat grass, continued to thrive. Enough forest remained, of course, probably in the Congo and

[4] We might think of this as the first in the series of thresholds that were crossed in the course of man's biocultural evolution.

[5] For a concise and graphic exposition of these early hominids, the student is strongly urged to consult Howell, 1965, pp. 30–69.

[6] Better visualized as the crossing of another threshold, since it involved the development and intensification of preexisting propensities rather than absolute change.

coastal West Africa, to ensure the survival of the ancestral gorilla and chimpanzee as well as our cousin *Paranthropus* in his original form. But many primate populations in other parts of Africa must inevitably have been isolated and cut off from this refuge area by the spreading desiccation and sooner or later, in many cases, must have seen their normal food supply disappear. Under such circumstances at the present day, baboons have been observed to resort to a meat diet which they obtain by hunting; it is of equal interest that they make no use of readily available carrion left lying around from the kills of their carnivore neighbors, because there is a widespread belief that the earliest hominids would have been incapable of hunting and must have subsisted primarily as scavengers of such carrion. In fact, even under normal conditions baboons have been observed to kill and eat any small creature they happen to encounter although their diet is overwhelmingly vegetarian; so the aptitude for hunting at least small game is clearly always present.

The recent field studies of Jane Goodall[7] have revealed similar unsuspected aptitudes among chimpanzees. There is increasing justification to assume, therefore, that other primates who found themselves in similar straits would likewise turn to hunting, and in particular any Pliocene hominids of *Paranthropus* type whose upright posture, free hands, and possibly rudimentary use of tools would have conferred an advantage in this respect. It would also have led to unique consequences that did not ensue in the case of baboons and other primates lacking these preadaptations. But in the hominid groups that took to hunting, a major behavioral adaptation must have occurred, and in this we may well see the origin of the behavioral system that is unique to man and which above all sets him apart from other animals.

consequences in behavioral patterns

In any organism, behavior must be understood in terms of adaptation. The uniqueness of the human system of behavior must therefore have resulted from some unique complex of factors in hominid history. It is suggested that some of the control factors in this complex developed in connection with this ecological "revolution" whereby a primate living in the typical vegetable food-gathering fashion of present-day primates moved from necessity into a newly opened ecological niche, namely, hunting game in open country, and eventually evolved into a new genus, *Australopithecus*. To make this new mode of adaptation possible, the behavioral system by which primates are adapted to their typical vegetarian mode of life had to be transformed in a number of fundamental ways. The situation can be illustrated by contrasting the behavior system of monkeys, a typical foraging primate, to that of wolves, a typical hunting carnivore.

---

[7] Now Jane van Lawick-Goodall.

The activities involved in securing vegetable food permit very individualistic feeding habits among monkeys: Everyone must fend for himself, including mothers burdened with dependent young. There is social group formation for protection only, with order being maintained within this group by a hierarchy of dominance among males established by aggressive behavior. The dominant male has access to his choice of females, and hence enjoys a reproductive advantage, so that there is selective pressure for the development and fostering of aggressive traits in males. There is a strong sexual dimorphism in the whole behavior pattern: i.e., marked differences between the typical behavior of males and females; in particular, males have nothing to do with their offspring and hence play no role as parent.

Among wolves, on the contrary, there is a minimum of such sexual dimorphism in the behavior pattern, with males fulfilling a definite parental role. Wolves are organized in real family groups rather than large bands, and these groups engage in cooperative hunting, which is the most advantageous way of securing an adequate food supply. The female, burdened with young and unable to participate in these hunts, is not left to fend for herself but is provided by the others with a share of the kill. In many aspects of social and interpersonal behavior wolves seem more akin to us than do our primate relatives.

In view of the apparent crucial relationship between behavior and ecology, what would have been involved in the transition of early hominids from a foraging to a hunting ecology? In other words, what would be the behavioral implications of this ecological shift that started a primate on the road to humanity?

For one thing, a shift in ecology would necessarily involve an economic division of labor between the sexes, since the slow development of primate infants means that the females would be burdened almost continuously and thus be unable to hunt. The males would have to provide for the females for the group to survive, and the females would have to be able to count on such support. This requires a more or less stable, cooperative association of males and females: if the analogy with wolves is valid, a permanent association of the male with one female and her offspring in a cooperative, parental type of relationship, very unlike primates, with the male helping to care for the young and training the male offspring, at least, for their hunting role. Such a socioeconomic relationship would provide the basis for the human pattern of child rearing with its protracted period of helpless infancy that is a requisite for the growth of the human brain. We would expect to see the extreme primate sexual dimorphism reduced except for the necessary division of labor in the subsistence sphere, and cooperation between males replacing the previous characteristic aggression. It is true that not all carnivores hunt cooperatively, so this cannot be represented as an automatic response to such a diet. Nevertheless, for game of any size, cooperative hunting would have been essential in a creature without natural equipment, with no great strength, and with very crude weapons at best.

It is thought that the disappearance of the estrus ("heat") period in females would be essential to the formation and maintenance of such a pattern of social behavior; and this in turn implies a shift in the control of sexual activity from the glands to the brain, so that sexual drives become more readily subject to social control. Among other animals, estrus periods aggravate aggressive competition, disrupt social relationships, and most important of all, are incompatible with the care of a dependent infant and thus would prevent the development of the human pattern of premature birth and a long period of helpless infancy which man's enlarged brain demands.[8] (A female so burdened would simply abandon the infant at the onset of estrus.) On the other hand, continuous sexual receptivity of the female would doubtless function as a socializing mechanism between a mated pair, making a relatively permanent relationship possible, and would reduce sexual competition between males of any group and thus promote cooperation. Consequently we can regard the disappearance of estrus as another essential precondition for the development of the human behavioral system.[9]

The advantages of tool use in hunting by such a small, defenseless creature as *Australopithecus*[10] would have created selection pressures for the type of mentality basic to tool using, i.e., a mind capable of evoking images of things past and in the future in response to signals. In contrast, the animal mind is largely limited to the here and now. This type of mentality is also basic to the formation of symbols, an ability unique in man and the basis of all communication.

Behavioral shifts of the type enumerated, which would be implicit in such an ecological revolution, would actually require very little expansion of the brain over that of higher primates and would have been well within the range of *Australopithecus*, who was clearly, if only slightly, in advance of the level of brain evolution achieved by the great apes. Given their ecological pattern (diet) and survival needs, we can infer, therefore, that *Australopithecus* had achieved a good deal in the way of integrated family organization, a degree of cooperative hunting, and had made some progress

[8] Human infants have to be born before the head is too large to pass through the mother's pelvis. In contrast, a baboon at birth is at a stage of development corresponding to a human infant six months old.

[9] S. L. Washburn has suggested that profound psychological changes must also have accompanied the development of hunting as a way of life. No animal, according to this view, can be a good hunter unless it accepts wholesale killing as natural and to some extent enjoyable, and man differs sharply from the other primates in his brutality—a brutality reflected in the way that he condones slaughter and enjoys spectacles of torture. This is the characteristic behavior of carnivores, and is not typical of apes and monkeys. But man has gone a step further, for even carnivores do not kill, or eat, members of their own species. This psychological pattern persists in modern man; it is easy to teach people to kill and hard to develop customs which avoid killing. These unpleasant tendencies are not our fault; blame them on *Australopithecus*. Only in his case they enabled him to survive, while today they are rushing Homo sapiens toward extinction.

[10] Carnivorous-omniverous *Australopithecus* was much smaller than vegetarian *Paranthropus*. Females are estimated to have weighed around 40 to 50 pounds; males were probably somewhat larger, but lacked the projecting canine teeth which are the effective weapons of all nonhominid primates.

toward vocal communication by symbolizing (though not necessarily language in our sense) and toward toolmaking. We can feel certain that they were at least *using* tools, which is a here and now affair of which apes are capable on occasion; patterned *toolmaking*, on the other hand, implies some communication and a human type of mentality.

What made it possible for this early hominid to achieve an ecological change of such drastic nature by means of cultural adaptation rather than by the usual animal means of genetic alteration of each motor pattern individually? Cultural adaptation is of course vastly superior in many ways to adaptation by genetic change: It is much faster, and provides a greater variety of opportunities to meet needs. What background do we find in the primates which would have constituted a preadaptation for this and have allowed this sort of response to sufficient stress?

Social life is one of the primate's most important adaptations for survival, and in the closely integrated primate societies there is a high development of what has been termed "social sensitivity," and with it many opportunities both for imitative learning from other individuals and, increasingly, for the transmission of this acquired behavior. Such socially learned behavior is a fundamental adaptive determinant of the social life of primates. The behavior patterns thus transmitted in the social context of these earlier primate societies must surely be regarded as the forerunners of what were later manifested as human behavior patterns. Socially learned behavior is the beginning of culture. Thus since the primate subjected to these new selection pressures had already attained a considerable capacity for social learning of new action patterns, the greater efficiency of such cultural transmission over slower genetic change naturally favored subsequent evolution by further development of, and selection for, the capacity for culture.

Out of this behavioral background, this preconditioning, the rudiments of culture emerged, then, under the pressure of natural selection as the most effective and rapid means of coping with the difficult conditions which confronted Pliocene hominids in the large parts of Africa that had become dry, open country.

the role of culture in human evolution

After the basic anatomical shift to upright posture and bipedalism (with its consequent changes in the anatomical structure of the limbs, feet, pelvis, and skull attachment), subsequent major developments in human evolution were behavioral shifts, with anatomical changes following in consequence. The basic anatomical shift to bipedalism took place at a pretty apelike stage, and the rudiments of human culture were apparently achieved by hominids with a brain little bigger than that of apes. Hence, the major anatomical changes that differentiate modern Homo sapiens from his apelike forerunner *Australopithecus* (e.g., brain size, structure of the face, structure of hands) seem to have occurred *after* the development of some degree of culture. These anatomical changes are unique to man and we may therefore assume that they are due to a unique cause. But why should these changes have occurred in only one line of primates and not in any others? Why, for instance, did not vegetarian *Paranthropus*, still persisting into the Middle Pleistocene alongside true men, evolve into a higher form? Obviously, bipedalism and its resulting anatomical changes, or even free hands, are not enough to explain subsequent human evolution; they can take us as far as types like *Paranthropus*, but no further. *Australopithecus* must have had something more.

The only unique factor present in the human line and not in other primates is a significant degree of culture. This—or, more correctly, the natural selection pressures arising from the advantages of culture as a mode of adaptation—must be the responsible factor in specifically *human* evolution as distinct from primate evolution in general. Natural selection continued to be the operating force, as in all forms of life, but if culture had not intervened in the process, natural selection would have gone on producing more and better bipedal ape-men, but not Homo sapiens. Since man has unique attributes, it is to be expected that unique factors were at work in human evolution—factors which have not affected the evolution of other animals. One of these unique attributes is the very rapid rate of human evolution as compared to that of other animals; again, this accelerated tempo requires explanation, and we must seek for a factor not present in other species.

Such recognition of the vital role of culture in human biological evolution is a recent development. Formerly, evolution was considered to be a purely biological problem with only biological factors involved: a process which eventually produced through its own workings an early man anatomically much like ourselves who then began to invent culture. Now there is an increasing tendency to see our distinctive modern anatomical structure as the result of cultural factors. This viewpoint finds expression, for example, in such phrases as the one "tools makyth man" coined by Kenneth Oakley. The manufacture of tools according to traditional patterns is not only the first evidence by which we infer the existence of such a degree of culture, but the tools themselves are also one of the most essential elements of culture. "Man," as Benjamin Franklin remarked, "is a tool-making animal."

Moreover, it has been suggested that the modern human hand is the result of selection pressures fostered by tool use and that the superior advantages of tool using in survival might have contributed to natural selection pressures in favor of increased intelligence. The large part of the modern brain that is devoted to controlling the motor functions of the thumb and index finger also suggests that tool manipulation played a role in developing the brain to its present size. These are some of the things Oakley has in mind. Other large areas of the modern brain are devoted to control of speech, and the large frontal area of our cortex is involved in foresight, planning, and initiative—all these things reflecting cultural activities and complex social life. Thus we can see that changes in the brain since the *Australopithecus* stage represent responses to cultural needs through the operation of natural selection and normal evolutionary processes. It should also be noted that our modern brain is only able to reach its large size and high degree of complexity through growth after birth, during a long period of helpless infancy which has no parallel in other primates and is possible only because of our distinctively human patterns of child care—again, a cultural factor which had to intervene before further brain evolution was possible. Other marked changes have taken place during this same time in facial structure: The modern appearance of the human face as compared with early hominids—our smooth brow, much smaller jaws and teeth, chin, etc.—are largely due to reductions in the jaw muscles and teeth; and this, again, is doubtless related to less need to chew tough foods, which may reflect the development of food preparation—another cultural factor.

But this interplay between culture and biology in human development was most certainly not a one-way process: We must expect that biological factors had an equally strong influence on the development of culture in man. More attention needs to be devoted to this aspect than has hitherto been the case. For instance, the incredibly slow rate of development of culture during the first 90 percent of human history must be due in part to the biological limitations of the early hominids.

references

Hallowell, A. Irving: "The Structural and Functional Dimensions of a Human Existence," *Quarterly Review of Biology,* vol. 31, pp. 88–101, 1956.
Howell, F. Clark: *Early Man,* Life Nature Library, Time, Inc., New York, 1965.
Spuhler, J. N.: "Somatic Paths to Culture," in J. N. Spuhler (ed.), *The Evolution of Man's Capacity for Culture,* Wayne State University Press, Detroit, 1959, pp. 1–13.

suggested readings

Campbell, Bernard G.: *Human Evolution: An Introduction to Man's Adaptations,* Aldine Publishing Co., Chicago, 1966.
Fox, Robin: "In the Beginning: Aspects of Hominid Behavioral Evolution," *Man,* vol. 2, no. 3, pp. 415–433, 1967.
Howells, William: *Mankind in the Making,* Doubleday & Company, Inc., Garden City, N.Y., 1967.
Hulse, Frederick S.: *The Human Species: An Introduction to Physical Anthropology,* Random House, Inc., New York, 1963.
Robinson, John T.: "Australopithecines and the Origin of Man," *Annual Report of the Smithsonian Institution,* 1961, pp. 479–500.

the achievement of humanity

tool use

The product of this ecological revolution, or of the crossing of this threshold to a hunting ecology, is the ancestral *Australopithecus* and the proto-cultural stage of human history, when the rudiments of the human way of life were beginning to develop and to slowly evolve. At some point in this subsequent evolution, the threshold of humanity would be crossed: the point at which hominids could no longer survive without culture and had attained sufficient foresight, communication, and tradition to be reflected in *patterned* ways of *making* tools. Some people have called this the *toolmaking* or cultural revolution, but I would prefer to think of it as the passing of a certain point of no return or the crossing of another threshold in man's long, slow development. It seems generally assumed at the moment that this crossing of the threshold to humanity also occurred in Africa, like the earlier ecological shift. However, this further progress could just as well have occurred, for instance, in the Mediterranean area to the north.

But long before this point was reached, even the earliest forms of *Australopithecus* adapted to a hunting ecology would have needed the aid of artificial objects to supplement their limited natural equipment. Life in open country is dangerous; a biped cannot hope to outrun a pursuing four-legged predator. Lacking any natural equipment for defense, and with only the limited strength of his small body, the mere fact that *Australopithecus* survived at all is sufficient proof that he possessed artificial means of defense enhanced, no doubt, by group action. At any rate, sociocultural attributes made possible his survival, and equally, his ability to subsist as a hunter: He must have had means to despatch creatures too large to kill with the bare hands and, just as important, some means of skinning and dismembering them in the absence of fangs and claws, so that meat on the hoof could become calories in the stomach.

The appearance of such artificial aids is not a surprising development. Examples of employment of artificial objects by apes to facilitate desired activities have been reported often enough to indicate that higher primates possess at least a latent propensity for tool use.[1] But not until a new way of life *demanded* the aid of tools for success and survival did tool using become habitual in the hominid line. When this point was reached, tools came into use readily and naturally.

Tool *use* of this sort means the utilization of natural objects of convenient size and shape in sight at the time needed: sticks, stones, bones. They were probably employed chiefly as clubs, as missiles, or for smashing and cutting purposes. Even such rudimentary implements can confer a tremendous advantage over the bare hands; and many primitive peoples today will on occasion use natural objects for various purposes, as we do ourselves on a camping trip. Efforts to improve on natural objects to secure a more effective implement imply a higher level of mentality, since this generally involves preparation for an imagined future eventuality, a mental process of which only hominids are capable. When we find this preparation adhering to a definite pattern which is evidently accepted by the group as the proper way to make a tool, a pattern transmitted by learning as an image which the maker visualizes in the piece of raw material and then sets about realizing by going through the actions known to bring about this result, then we have reached a level which we can identify as human mentality and human culture. Thus the appearance of *toolmaking*—the production of standardized tools—is generally considered to be the criterion of humanity, albeit in its simplest form.

It is obvious tht we can expect little concrete evidence of this initial tool-*using* stage, though it may have existed for a very long time. Except in rare cases, there is no way of telling which natural objects were actually used by early hominids, although one can find many that could have been.[2] Also, much use must have been made of perishable material. Even the initial efforts to improve on nature defy recognition, since stone, for example, is so frequently fractured by natural forces, often in ways bearing remarkable resemblance to human workmanship.

the achievement of toolmaking

The final stage of protoculture is the result of the attainment of the level of deliberate manufacture of tools according to traditional patterns, by

[1] The recent field observations of Jane Goodall indicate a greater use of tools by at least some groups of chimpanzees in the wild than had been suspected.

[2] For possible examples, see Tobias, 1968.

some hominid group or groups, and the spread of this new behavior pattern to all others capable of adopting it. In terms of human history, it covers the span of time between the crossing of the threshold of humanity, as we have defined it, and the replacement of these first semihuman beings by true men of the *Homo erectus* type at the end of the Lower Pleistocene. Culturally, it is the era of primitive, generalized tools, made both on pebbles and flakes; and, we must assume, only the rudiments of culture and humanity as we think of them. In terms of the geological time scale, it probably corresponds to the Late Villafranchian and most of the Mosbachian (see Figure 5–1). And we are now at the point where archeology can take over.

Before discussing what we know of this stage, it must be emphasized that our present picture is based on a very limited amount of reliable data, many guesses and (all too often) unfounded assumptions, and a tremendous amount of sheer ignorance. Much of what is currently accepted lacks any firm foundation. Plausible hypotheses set forth repeatedly by authoritative sources assume the role of facts. Under the circumstances, we must expect the likelihood of radical changes in the picture as research proceeds. The uncertainty and confusion is not only due to the limited amount of evidence discovered so far, but to the problems and pitfalls of interpreting it.

Thus, although we have relative sequences within given areas, it is impossible to correlate these with one another so that we can say with certainty what was happening all over the world at a given time, or what the relationship between these various developments was. As a result, we do not know where tools first appeared or where true men first appeared, nor can we trace the spread of either or point to centers of progress—because we cannot place the occurrences in relation to one another with any real confidence in our present state of knowledge. For instance, fauna has been the basis of most of the attempted dating between different regions, but we have no idea to what extent such similar faunas are actually contemporary. The other mainstay, correlation of geological or climatic events in different (and often distant) regions, is fraught with pitfalls. Which event matches which—and can we assume they match completely? (For instance, glaciations may correlate in a very general way with tropical rainy periods, but not precisely or fully.)

Another problem is in even identifying early archeological remains. Virtually every type of flake can be produced by natural forces. Standard rules-of-thumb like flaking angles are not conclusive in establishing human workmanship. Thus the greatest care must be exercised in accepting evidence of man in early deposits. Conversely, we must assume that a good deal of acceptable evidence has gone unnoticed over the years. (The tools of Peking Man might never have been recognized had they not been found with his remains.) A further complication is that some very crude tool types continued in use into relatively recent times; or, again, that unfinished tools, quarry blanks, and waste flakes may be mistaken for early implements. Thus the context of the find must be unimpeachable as well as the workmanship, in order to qualify as valid evidence of the earliest period of human history.

archeological evidence of Lower Pleistocene culture

There seems to be general agreement at the moment that all Lower Pleistocene occurrences of tools bear enough resemblance to one another so that one can speak of a single technological tradition existing at this time which is generally called the Oldowan, after the famous site at Olduvai Gorge in East Africa. Others prefer to speak simply of "pebble tool industries." It is also clear that this is the foundation from which all the traditions of the next stage in human history developed: Some of them, in fact, remained only more or less evolved versions of the original, well through the Middle Pleistocene when considerable advances, in stone technology at least, had already been scored elsewhere. The Oldowan may therefore represent the common heritage of all mankind.

The principal diagnostic Oldowan tool type is the pebble chopper,[4] always associated with a more amorphous assortment of flakes and pounders. All these tools are of the most rudimentary sort. We can only guess that wooden implements of equal simplicity were also in use, doubtless clubs and digging sticks. But there are those who maintain that efficient hunting requires wooden spears which must be made of green wood, and that the need to work green wood was a major stimulus to the development of stone cutting and scraping tools. Certainly this is the case by the beginning of the next stage.

The known finds of tools of unquestioned human manufacture that are reliably dated to the Lower Pleistocene are still relatively few in number. There are five localities in East Africa, comprising a number of sites, one in Ethiopia, three sites in Romania, four in France, two in Germany, and one each in South Africa, Algeria, Chad, possibly in Israel and Turkey and (doubtfully) in China. A number of sites in Morocco may also very well be of this age, but better evidence is needed. These occurrences of early tools are not all contemporary, but cover a considerable span of time (Figure 7–1). The preponderance of African and circum-Mediterranean occurrences of early tools, as with the remains of early fossil hominids

---

[3] The possibility that toolmaking developed independently in Southeast Asia cannot be ruled out.

[4] See Figure 7–2. As used by prehistorians, "pebble" refers to a water-worn cobblestone the size of a large potato or large orange.

FIGURE   7–1.   Lower Pleistocene archeological sites.

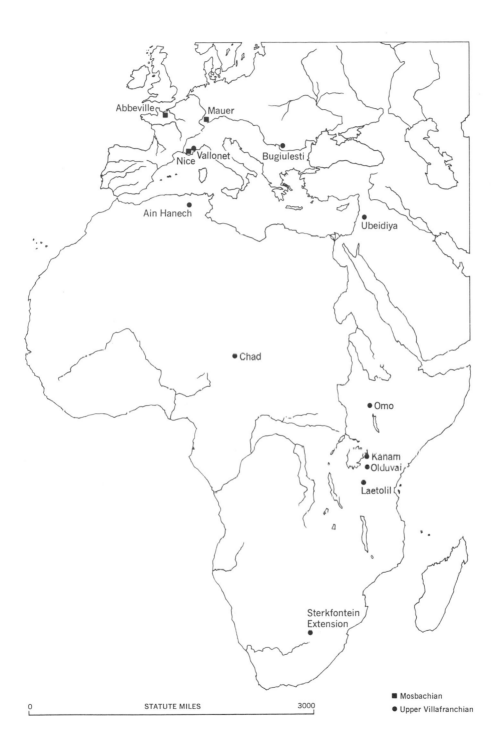

Abbeville

Mauer

Nice Vallonet

Bugiulesti

Ain Hanech

Ubeidiya

Chad

Omo

Kanam
Olduvai

Laetolil

Sterkfontein
Extension

0   STATUTE MILES   3000

■ Mosbachian
● Upper Villafranchian

themselves, may be the result of optimum conditions for discovery and does not necessarily reflect, at this stage of knowledge, the actual relative distribution of human activity in the Lower Pleistocene.

The group of sites in Olduvai Gorge brought to light through the extensive work of Dr. and Mrs. L. S. B. Leakey is currently regarded as providing the oldest archeological materials of undoubted human manufacture and as yielding the most information to date about earliest man. The unique importance of Olduvai for our purposes lies in the presence of a number of actual living floors preserved intact just as their occupants left them; in the excellent preservation of bone which affords a complete picture of the fauna as well as food remains; in the continuous sequence of associated human fossils (thus making it possible to study directly the interrelationship of biological and cultural evolution); and in the occurrence of materials suitable for dating by the potassium-argon method. However, there is no proof that even the earliest remains at Olduvai necessarily antedate Late Villafranchian finds in Europe and the Mediterranean area. The relative temporal position of the spectacular hominid finds here and their relation to the total picture of human history will have to await absolute dating of the earliest human sites elsewhere in the world, if this can be done, as well as careful evaluation of the present very early Olduvai dates themselves, the validity of which is questioned by a number of scientists. We will also have to await adequate scientific publication of the investigations, on which only fragmentary reports and news items have yet appeared. Only then will the historical role of Olduvai be understandable.

But to thus cast doubt on the popular image of Olduvai as the cradle of mankind is not to deny its unique importance as our major source of information on Lower Pleistocene human activity.

Olduvai Gorge is situated in northwestern Tanzania, a remote, waterless area of very difficult access which presents considerable problems for field work. The gorge, which resembles a miniature Grand Canyon, cuts through some 300 feet of old lake sediments and volcanic deposits of Lower and Middle Pleistocene age, exposing them in cross section with their embedded fossils and other remains—a veritable archeologist's dream. Bed I (at the bottom) and the lower part of the overlying Bed II are now known to belong together and to represent a continuous segment of time which is claimed to cover the span from 1.8 million years ago down to the end of the Lower Pleistocene, perhaps 500,000 or 600,000 years ago.

Geologically, this part of the deposits seems to correspond to very Late Villafranchian and the Mosbachian, although there are still great difficulties in definitely establishing the correlation, and the whole question is likely to remain in dispute for some time to come.

Evidence of activity that is clearly human, however rudimentary, has been discovered at various levels throughout these deposits from bottom to top. Small groups of these early humans seem to have camped on what were then the shallow margins of small lakes, or on mud flats exposed by

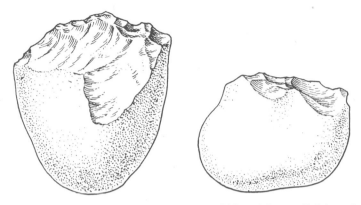

FIGURE 7–2. *Pebble choppers from Olduvai Gorge* (left) *and Grotte du Vallonet* (right). (From François Bordes, *The Old Stone Age,* copyright © 1968 by World University Library, McGraw-Hill, Inc., New York. By permission of François Bordes and the publishers.)

seasonally fluctuating lake levels. The surfaces on which the remains were left appear to have been covered fairly rapidly by deposited materials, a circumstance to which we owe their excellent preservation in undisturbed condition from this distant time. The living floors consist of concentrations of stones and bones; many of the latter are artificially broken to extract the marrow, and the fractures resemble similar remains left by later and even by modern hunters. Many of the stones have been intentionally flaked, and even those with no trace of working have been brought to the sites deliberately, since they could not occur naturally in such a situation. The stone tools consist of choppers, cores, pounding stones, and flakes. Although many of the latter were undoubtedly knocked off accidentally or represent debris from the shaping of other tools, some were intentionally struck off and show definite signs of having been used, and a very few were actually retouched to increase their effectiveness for cutting or scraping. The raw material for these tools was primarily pebbles. Naturally sharp stones do not occur in this area, and intentional fractures are necessary to secure a cutting edge.

The most famous of these early Olduvai campsites or living floors is the one which included the remains of "Zinjanthropus," who was initially credited with being responsible for making the tools and killing the animals whose remains are represented. Now we know that he was an example of the nonhuman vegetarian *Paranthropus,* who may well have formed part of the meat supply of the hominid who lived here, presumably some type of *Australopithecus.* The food remains comprise portions of a number of species of animals, the great majority reportedly being small mammals or immature young of larger species, along with such "slow" game as lizards and frogs. Almost every bone that could have contained marrow has been broken, indicating the importance of this item in the diet from the earliest times.

The cultural remains indicate that this campsite was the temporary home base of a small group of hunters—perhaps of only a few individuals—who habitually carried back to this place during their brief occupancy the smaller animals, or portions of the larger ones, that they had secured in the course of their hunting activities. Presumably this was done in order to share the food with other members of the group who did not accompany the hunters. And here it was then reduced to meat and marrow through the necessary agency of stone tools either made for the purpose on the spot or deliberately brought in from elsewhere with the same aim. The actual means of securing game, however, is not revealed by these remains. If wooden spears were not yet in use, we have only to remember the addiction for throwing missiles exhibited by most higher primates, which makes throwing stones a likely candidate for the earliest offensive weapon of our hominid ancestors. We should also remember that until quite recent times Man the Hunter, in the pattern of other carnivores, focused his efforts and skill on getting as close as possible to his prey by stalking or running it down, so that even the crudest equipment could make its mark. All in all, there seems to be nothing in the activity reflected at this site that would be beyond the capabilities of at least the more evolved forms of *Australopithecus*.

The other living floors in Bed I are also temporary camps generally similar to the "Zinjanthropus" one. Two feet lower in another section is the so-called "Pre-Zinjanthropus" site containing the remains of a juvenile *Australopithecus* who seems to have met his end from a violent blow on the head, suggesting cannibalism.[5] This is the site dated at 1.75 million years by potassium-argon. A bone tool, polished from use perhaps on hides, and remains of tortoise and catfish were also associated. Of particular interest, however, is the lowest site of all, only a foot or so above the lava on which the bed rests. Here the stone tools are, on the average, a good deal smaller (the designation "Micro-Oldowan" has been suggested), and are described by Leakey as "beautifully made." They are associated with accumulations of natural stones. It is very difficult to see how these stones could have got to their present position except by having been carried there. In at least one case the stones are reported to be concentrated in rough semicircles, with several stones resting upon one another as if they had been purposely piled up, perhaps as a sort of windbreak. Unfortunately, no more specific information has yet been divulged about these important sites.

[5] Leakey and others feel that this specimen was sufficiently evolved anatomically to be included in the genus of true men, Homo, as its earliest form, and have given it the name *Homo habilis*. The matter is still in dispute.

The only other certain undisturbed living site of this age is the recent discovery by Professor Nicolaescu-Plopsor near Bugiulesti in Romania, where bones of Late Villafranchian animals had been broken on a lakeshore by hominids. Excavations are continuing here. A group of sites of similar age near Craiova in the same region has yielded about twenty acceptable pebble tools.

Near Menton on the southern coast of France, a small number of artifacts, including pebble choppers, associated with bones of Villafranchian animals, occur in the Grotte du Vallonnet, which had evidently been used as a temporary shelter by some form of toolmaking hominid. The site is important because it is the oldest trace of man in Europe, dating from a somewhat earlier phase of the Late Villafranchian than any other. It is also at least as old as anything at Olduvai Gorge.

Two other important sites are somewhat later in age. At Mauer, near Heidelberg in Germany, we have the oldest firmly dated specimen of a *Homo erectus* type of man (the famous "Mauer jaw") as well as about thirty-five genuine tools of human manufacture along with a quantity of stones sometimes claimed to be artifacts but certainly of natural origin. The occurrence of this man and his very crude industry was during the warm phase in the middle of the Mosbachian, and he had a forest environment. At least of late Mosbachian age is the extraordinary living site recently discovered at Nice on the French Riviera, with apparent remains of artificial structures and the oldest known use of fire—considerably earlier than hitherto supposed. Unfortunately, further details are not yet available. The site may be a million years old.

We must also recall that early forms of *Homo erectus* occur in the Djetis beds in Java which may be of Mosbachian age, although no trace of tools has yet come to light at this level. The comparable form recently found in China, Lantian Man, could be of approximately the same age. The dating is very tenuous but not improbable. Except for one very doubtful site in China (Hsi-hou-tu), there are as yet no tools of Lower Pleistocene age known from East Asia.

reference

Tobias, Philip: "Cultural Hominization among the Earliest African Pleistocene Hominids," *Proceedings of the Prehistoric Society*, vol. 33, pp. 367–376, 1968.

suggested readings

Bordes, François: *The Old Stone Age*, McGraw-Hill Book Company, New York, 1968, pp. 32–50.
Howell, F. Clark: *Early Man*, Life Nature Library, Time, Inc., New York, 1965, pp. 70–75.

man in the Lower Pleistocene

the primary dispersal of man

What inferences can we draw from this body of archeological evidence regarding human history in the latter part of the Lower Pleistocene, after the attainment of toolmaking?

First, the initial general similarity of the technological pattern would seem to suggest a single origin for this toolmaking and its subsequent diffusion from one area, wherever that may have been. Although Olduvai Gorge is the fashionable contender at the moment for the honor, there are some who believe that the earliest tools in southern Europe antedate anything at Olduvai. The Mediterranean area might equally be proposed as the hearth of toolmaking. Although this is a sheer guess, its claims are as good as any.

Second, the wide distribution of Oldowan and related finds by the close of the Lower Pleistocene suggests the spread either of toolmaking or of man himself at this time, throughout the tropics and much of the temperate zone. There seems to be a common impression that toolmaking was so obviously a superior way of life or conferred such an advantage in terms of survival that the idea would have spread like wildfire among the less enlightened hominid groups, or else that the superior toolmakers would soon have expanded at the expense of the rest and supplanted them. I think that such a view greatly exaggerates the efficiency of these earliest tool kits. We know that the hominids must have been tool *users* for quite a long time prior to this point, and that the natural objects utilized must

have been entirely adequate to ensure their survival. An examination of
the Oldowan living areas yields no item of equipment that is markedly
and intrinsically superior to natural objects to the extent that it would
have conferred an immediate advantage, as is so often implied. I think
that the true significance of toolmaking is not in the tools themselves but
rather as evidence of the attainment of a human level of mentality, however rudimentary.[1] This *would* represent something superior and more
effective than anything hitherto existing; this *would* confer an immediate
advantage. It would enable groups so endowed (as reflected in their toolmaking) to expand at the expense of others, to spread into regions hitherto
unoccupied, to cope with new types of environment. The supposed advantages of crude tools over natural objects are not sufficient to account for
all of these dramatic developments that now occur.

It is for these reasons that I see the wide distribution of Oldowan
tools not as the diffusion of an idea but as the primary expansion of man
himself to his ecological limits, in response to biological laws affecting all
species. I do not think that the earlier hominid populations occupied nearly
as extensive a range; and not because they lacked real tools, but because
they lacked the intelligence to cope with the differing environments. If
their way of life arose in the African savannah as a response to this particular ecological setting, then it is highly probable that the range of the
prehuman hominids coincided with the boundaries of this and comparable
environmental zones. Not until the human threshold of mentality was
reached could certain hominid groups spread into different habitats; when
they did so, they spread widely, and their tools document this movement.
That is why I see in this the primary expansion of man.

There has been a general belief that mankind was confined entirely
to the tropics, his supposed natural habitat, until the Middle Pleistocene,
when a few groups of *Homo erectus*, aided by such cultural assistance as
fire, finally ventured into colder climates. In particular, it has been firmly
held that Europe was not occupied until this time. But the new evidence
clearly indicates that this was not the case, and that considerable parts of
the temperate zone were also involved in this primary spread during the
Lower Pleistocene. Only cold grasslands, deserts, and rain forests seem to
have been avoided.

It should be stressed that we do not yet know for sure the physical
type of the first toolmakers, or even of those who made the tools in Bed 1
at Olduvai. The associations of hominids with artifacts here are not conclusive. *Paranthropus* ("Zinjanthropus") is now generally felt to have been

---

[1] Toolmaking requires a higher order of intelligence than mere tool using: It involves the
power of conceptual thought, which is only incipient at lower primate levels. Whereas a
chimpanzee cannot see the separate boards in the smooth surface of an unbroken box
when he needs a stick, early man could see a tool in a formless lump of stone. Foresight—an imaginative realization of the future—is required for the shaping of even the
crudest tool in advance of any particular need or for the manufacture of tools with
which to make tools, present even in very early assemblages.

the victim of the tools that lay with him; the *Australopithecus* ("Pre-Zinjanthropus") child had met a violent end at the hands of parties unknown who wielded the tools. (Some feel that a more advanced hominid was already present whose remains have not yet been found, either a more highly evolved *Australopithecus* or perhaps even a very early form of the subsequent *Homo erectus*.[2])Certainly by the last phase of the Lower Pleistocene (Mosbachian) all finds of fossil men are of general *Homo erectus* type—Mauer, Java, Lantian, and the new individual from lower Bed II at Olduvai called "George." How much further back in time this type may go, we don't know at present. But it is not impossible that it goes back to the first toolmaking. And some respected authorities feel that most of the early pebble tool finds are probably the work of *Homo erectus*. Should this prove to be the case, it would actually fit the facts better. The great break comes with the first toolmakers, the first hominids intelligent enough to adapt to new environments. It seems logical that such a major threshold should coincide with the appearance of the first true men. The primary expansion of man would thus be the spread of true Homo rather than the half-man *Australopithecus*.

Otherwise we are left with the paradox that the appearance of true men brought no visible advance in technology or economy: The great achievements had been made by his half-brained predecessor.

life in the Lower Pleistocene

The protocultural stage in the history of the human stock was probably launched in Africa in the late Pliocene by a major ecological shift that has been called the Ecological Revolution with its necessary accompanying behavioral shifts, including tool using. The new species resulting would then have spread to the limits of its habitat, which I see as the African savannah, and any adjoining areas of possibly similar environment such as southern Europe.

Gradual evolution, both biological and sociobehavioral (cultural) throughout this range in response to the new selection pressures brought some hominid group or groups to the point of humanity (human level of mentality) as reflected in toolmaking, apparently some time in the Villafranchian. During the Late Villafranchian these mentally superior groups spread beyond the original savannah habitat, adapting to somewhat different environments and then expanding rapidly to fill new territory in Eurasia opened up to them for the first time. The center of further cultural development may well have moved north—perhaps to the Mediterranean region where sites are widespread. There is no reason to suppose that East

---

[2] Or that the existing specimens classified by Leakey and others as *Homo habilis* are sufficiently advanced to fill this role.

Africa remained the hearth of human progress. The process of evolution was completed toward the close of the Lower Pleistocene, so that by the beginning of the next period there are true men (*Homo erectus*), and true culture in place of protoculture.

We may summarize the characteristics of the protocultural stage as follows: It is intermediate between primate and man, representing a continuous gradual development from tendencies already present in the primate group. Its bearer was probably a small creature well suited for existence as a predator (females approximately 4 feet high and weighing 40 to 50 pounds, males presumed to be somewhat larger), in process of evolution toward *Homo erectus*. Cultural techniques gave an initial advantage but made them increasingly dependent on these for survival, putting a premium on intelligence and tool use. Hence—at least in those lines that led to man—there was a steady increase throughout this period in manual skill, mentality, and learned behavior, which was reflected in brain development. The development of a distinctively human type of social organization, which must have been achieved by the end of the period, would have demanded an accelerated development of the frontal lobes of the brain so that emotional and instinctive impulses could be more effectively subordinated to the good of the community as a whole. This process must have been taking place in the human line at this time.

Along with this biocultural evolution there was probably a parallel gradual development in vocal communication during the protocultural stage, involving the shift from a closed animal call system to an open system and opening the way to symbolic language.[3]

As for social organization at this time, we may assume the existence of structured groups and a two-parent family with a division of labor between the sexes, with the male as provider, and sharing of food. The crucial social customs are those that guarantee the services of a hunter to a female and her offspring, since the most important rules in the evolution of society are those that guarantee economic survival to the dependent young. The resultant bonds are much more than sexual, though aided by the continuous receptivity of the female without which a lasting male-female relationship doubtless could not exist. We can probably see in this the beginnings of marriage. A great change in mother-child relations would have been necessitated by the expansion of the brain toward the end of the period, since selection for bigger brains must have also involved selection for premature birth, and hence helpless infants.

The ecological pattern was hunting, probably not yet for really big game but rather for creatures the size of baboons and antelopes. This would have involved cooperative action among males of the group; it is hard to see how it could have been accomplished otherwise. Though "slow" game (smaller crawling creatures such as lizards, turtles, catfish) was

---

[3] See Hockett and Ascher 1964 for a discussion of the origins of language at this time.

doubtless utilized to some extent, there is no need to consider that proto-cultural man was incapable of full-scale hunting, as some have main-tained. Nor is there any real basis for another popular view: that car-nivorous man started out as a scavenger of carrion. (Observations of hunt-ing among other primates do not bear this out.) At any rate, we may assume that protocultural man was already displaying the behavior pat-terns of a typical carnivore—of Man the Hunter and Killer—with the psychological and behavioral consequences already suggested.

From the fact that man's primate relatives have a definite home range beyond which they do not stray, plus the fact that the simplest modern food gatherers (e.g., the Australian aborigines) are enabled to survive by reason of their intimate knowledge of a specific area to which they feel themselves inseparably linked, we may assume that earliest man was not free-wandering, as some have postulated, but had a degree of stability in the sense of occupying and exploiting a definite range. The extent of such a range can only be guessed at. When man became a hunter, his relation to the land changed from one in which a small range was adequate to one that demanded a large territory. However, until earliest man became a full-fledged big-game hunter (which level he had reached by the *Homo erectus* stage), his range was perhaps smaller than that of the large carnivorous predators but certainly much more extensive than that of grazing animals. Hominids are dependent on the ready availability of adequate supplies of water, and they probably stayed within 4 or 5 miles of water, although doubtless each range contained a number of such sources. The settlement pattern already involved a definite home base, the remains of which we see in the early Olduvai sites, but these were evidently not occupied for very long, which suggests that groups shifted their base, and hence their sleeping place, frequently within their territory. The Olduvai sites suggest that the size of these bands was quite small. This does not confirm the common hypothesis that early hominids found safety in sheer numbers, (a theory based on the rather overworked analogy with baboons)

The correlation between a canivorous diet and the use of tools bears reemphasis: It is easy enough to kill a creature; the real problem lies in how to get through the skin and divide up the meat without the natural equipment that is available to other meat-eating animals or even to our primate relatives. Sharp bits of stone would have solved the problem, and where these do not occur naturally, a sufficient level of intelligence would have doubtless led to breaking pebbles to get a sharp edge. We can safely postulate the use of some sort of tools as soon as hominids took to hunting; but not all of them were capable of taking the further step of toolmaking. Those that did developed the Oldowan tradition of pebble choppers and associated simple flakes, certainly as rudimentary as one could conceive. It seems possible that the crudeness of this early toolmaking, which can-not represent any very great improvement over what had gone on before, technologically, may be attributable at least in part to the form and pro-

portions of the hands that made them. Since toolmaking is believed to
have developed in close interrelationship with that of the brain and hands,
it would be at a comparable level and no more advanced at any point. The
hand of *Australopithecus* is considered adequate to produce these early
Oldowan tools—but perhaps nothing better.

reference

Hockett, Charles F., and Robert Ascher: "The Human Revolution," *Current
    Anthropology*, vol. 5, no. 3, pp. 135–168, 1964.

the Middle Pleistocene: 1

introduction

We move from a situation still largely guesswork, conjecture, and postulate to firmer ground in the next phase of human history. There is still much that we do not know and even more that we can never hope to know at this distance, but the picture now is based on more concrete evidence. The Middle Pleistocene, which in our definition embraces the Mindel and Riss glaciations and the intervening Holstein interglacial and may span a period of time from roughly 750,000 to around 150,000 to 200,000 years ago, more or less brackets the stage of human evolution represented by the later types of the *Homo erectus* group of men and their more evolved successors whom we have called proto-Neanderthaloid (e.g., Swanscombe Man, Steinheim Man). We are now dealing with true men, though initially with brains averaging three-quarters the size of our own, who are steadily evolving in the direction of Homo sapiens and have probably attained this level by the latter part of this period.

In terms of technology, we can think of it as the time of the so-called "handax" tradition (Acheulean) in the western part of the inhabited world (see Figure 9–1), but no comparable cultural definition applies in the East where evolved forms of the earlier pebble and flake tradition with no equally striking diagnostic features continued through and beyond the Middle Pleistocene. There were thus two major facies of technology

FIGURE   9–1.   *The human world of the Middle Pleistocene.*

92

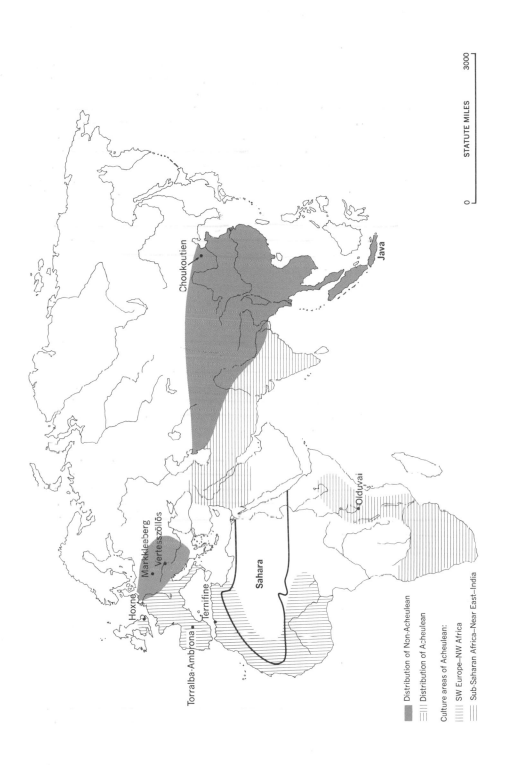

Choukoutien

Java

Markkleeberg

Vertesszöllös

Torralba-Ambrona

Ternifine

Hoxne

Sahara

Olduvai

Distribution of Non-Acheulean

Distribution of Acheulean

Culture areas of Acheulean:

SW Europe–NW Africa

Sub-Saharan Africa–Near East–India

0   STATUTE MILES   3000

and presumably of human activity at this time. In terms of ecology, full-fledged hunting was now the prevailing pattern, with the capability being present of taking really big game as occasion offered.

The primary distribution of the human stock had been completed quite early in this period, and the boundaries that were to define the "known world" of early man and the arena of history down to perhaps 50,000 years ago were now set. These boundaries were formed in part by natural barriers such as the seas and high mountain ranges and in part by climate which, by determining the location of environmental zones, established the limits of favorable habitat at any particular time. Thus the human world fluctuated to a greater or lesser extent, but within certain fixed limits. In addition to all of Africa (except for the rain forest, and the desert in dry periods) the human world now stretched over a narrow crescent-shaped zone along the southerly shores of the Eurasian land mass from Britain to north China, with evidence of human activity appearing suddenly in previously unoccupied regions in the early Middle Pleistocene. Evidently the human species, like any other mammal, had undergone relatively rapid expansion out to the limits of its habitat. But this habitat was no longer restricted to the tropics and subtropics to which the human organism is physiologically adapted. Man's technology, simple as it still seems to us, had reached a level at which it could begin to serve as a screen between himself and the natural environment. As a consequence we see man extending his range well into the temperate zone both in Europe and northern China not only during warm phases but even during periods of cold climate. And the ability to do this implies, as the evidence supports, the regular use of fire—the first instance of human control over the forces of nature. But there was no expansion beyond the boundaries reached in the early Middle Pleistocene: Available evidence indicates that the vast heartland of the Eurasian land mass—and along with it any access to the New World—was off limits until very late in human history.

We should think of the Middle Pleistocene as a period of steady though slow evolution in man's anatomy, brain, behavior, ability to communicate, and technology. In terms of the latter we can characterize it as the very slow progress through time of a few basic themes rather than as the appearance of any changes or new developments.

nature of the evidence

It is important to appreciate the nature and types of evidence on which our picture of human culture in the Middle Pleistocene is based and especially the limitations on it. We have as yet only a few undisturbed living sites with remains in their original context that can provide any real idea of the life of the times. (To reconstruct behavior from archeology, actual living sites are needed.) For the earliest part of the period we have only the living floors in the upper part of Bed II and lower Bed III at

Olduvai Gorge—thought to equate with the Mindel glaciation. Somewhat later, during the close of the Mindel, there are in addition the cave of Peking Man at Choukoutien, the new open site at Vertesszöllös in Hungary, and the recently studied sites of Torralba and Ambrona in Spain. However, very little information is yet available on these sites, and only Olduvai Gorge provides undisturbed contexts that may span the entire period. In a few other cases we have remains in "geological context," as for instance in deposits representing the bottom of an ancient lake into which artifacts and refuse from an adjacent camp had been thrown or had fallen and were not subsequently disturbed. Examples would be such sites as Ternifine in Algeria and Hoxne in England. Here we know that the finds belong together and can be firmly dated by association with the geological deposit, though they yield far less information.

But the majority of the sites of human activity from this time, especially in Europe, were subsequently destroyed by erosion or glacial action and the surviving objects redeposited often some distance away in new deposits in process of formation. Thus all context has been lost: We do not know what belongs together, what may be missing, nor can we tell the location or nature of the original site or its time placement, other than to say that it is older than the deposit in which it has been reincorporated. The bulk of remains of this type in Europe have been recovered from gravel pits in the course of commercial working of such deposits, and all too often the finds have been made by workmen who recognize and preserve only the most distinctive and conspicuous artifacts, in so far as they recognize and preserve anything at all. Most European Middle Pleistocene collections in particular have been highly selected in this fashion, with the result that the standard picture of these early human cultures in Europe has been very distorted, and thus our attempts to understand the life and behavior of men of the time are severely limited.

Similarly, a large number of artifacts of types characteristic for this period, sometimes incorporated in Middle Pleistocene deposits, have been found all over Africa and in southern Asia, but lack adequate or any context and can tell us only about the distribution of certain tool types and nothing about the life of their makers. The evidence from eastern Asia is the scantiest and poorest of all, and hence we know least about human cultural history in this important part of the world although, paradoxically, we know more about the people themselves than anywhere else. Except for the single habitation site of Peking Man, all archeological remains in East Asia down to the last glaciation are redeposited in river gravels.

Since stone cutting tools comprise the major body of evidence from the Middle Pleistocene, prehistorians must devote a great deal of attention to seemingly trifling differences in the forms and techniques of manufacturing of these tools in order to exploit this evidence to its utmost limit.[1] Only in this way can historical development be traced and cultural differ-

[1] For an excellent illustrated explanation of early stone working, see Howell, 1965, pp. 100–121.

ences between groups be assessed. Next in importance are food remains in the form of animal bones. A small amount of worked or utilized bone has also been recovered, but few standardized bone artifacts. Despite its abundance, bone could not be exploited effectively as a raw material at this stage of technology. It could not be worked by the techniques and with the tools that were successfully employed on wood (you cannot carve bone with a flint knife); and attempts to treat it like stone proved unsatisfactory. Not until the development of suitable engraving tools in the Homo sapiens phase were effective techniques of bone working devised.

Wood remains from this time are naturally extremely rare, although sufficient to indicate its importance as a material. The predominance of flake tools, assumed to be used primarily for woodworking, in the tool kits points in the same direction. Fossil human remains are an important source of information as in the previous period but are still scanty; as far as we know man did not yet bury his dead and their preservation is therefore accidental. The fragmentary nature of these finds and the fact that they are scattered and individual also limit the amount of information they can yield. The only actual human *population* of the Middle Pleistocene available to us is Peking Man.

Lastly, the utilization of this archeological evidence is limited by the serious problems encountered in dating remains so that they may be placed in proper relationship with one another. A rather detailed relative time scale, based on geology and paleontology, has been worked out for western and central Europe; the difficulty lies in correlating with this the remains in Africa and Asia where both geological events and faunas were different. In time the situation may be improved by potassium-argon dating of deposits in all these areas so that a uniform chronology can be set up against which archeological materials can be placed. Only then will it be possible to make meaningful comparative studies between different parts of the world as well as to see the tempo of development within any area.

general characteristics of the period

What are the general characteristics of the Middle Pleistocene period of human cultural evolution? Technologically, this period has always been thought of as the era of generalized, all-purpose tools, with few if any really specialized implements designed and used for only certain specific purposes. However, evidence is coming to light (particularly at the site of Torralba) that specialization and proliferation of tool types was already well under way at this time. There is still a minimum of standardization, however, the major standardized forms with wide distribution being the handax and cleaver.

Stone tools were expendable, being made when needed and left behind when the group moved on; they were probably never carried about, except for immediate use. Considering how quickly and easily they could be manufactured, this is understandable in view of the more important things that must be carried by people traveling light. For example, wooden implements, requiring considerable time and labor to fashion, were probably the prized items of equipment. This expendable nature of stone tools also accounts for the large numbers of them found in certain areas which cannot have supported more than a scant population. Throughout the period we see a growing mastery of stoneworking technique leading to complete control of the raw materials, whatever these might be, as well as progressively more economical use of raw material.

Perhaps the outstanding impression of Middle Pleistocene culture one gets is that of stagnation, which it inevitably creates because of the incredible slowness of technological change during a time span of perhaps 600,000 years. Yet we are dealing here with true men, far more intelligent and capable than their protocultural ancestors. The latter's slow progress need occasion no particular surprise since they were taking the first few

FIGURE 9–2. *Acheulean handax* (left) *and cleaver* (right). (From François Bordes, *The Old Stone Age*, copyright © 1968 by World University Library, McGraw-Hill, Inc., New York. By permission of François Bordes and the publishers.)

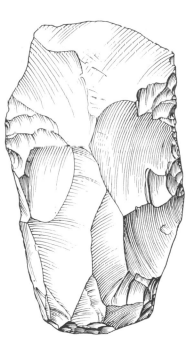

faltering steps. But man should now have been well on his way; the fact that he got off to such a slow start raises problems regarding culture process that demand explanation.

Culturally—as reflected in technology—the inhabited world was divided as we said into two realms or two facies of technical tradition: a western one (Acheulean) characterized superficially by the handax (and, later, by the prepared-platform techniques for producing superior flake tools) which included all of Africa, southwestern Europe, and southwestern Asia as far as India; and another, discontinuous, comprising eastern Asia and eastern Europe, representing the marginal areas of the human habitat into which handaxes and prepared-platform techniques never spread during the Middle Pleistocene, for reasons unknown, and in which the original pebble and flake tradition continued to slowly evolve. On present evidence there seems to have been no connection between eastern Europe and eastern Asia; these nonhandax regions were simply the outer margins, somehow insulated from western developments, where despite sporadic local occurrences of handaxes, this distinctive tool of the west never took hold.

The homogeneity of handaxes all over the west has created an erroneous impression of the cultural uniformity of the western world during the Middle Pleistocene. Actually, what we call Acheulean is simply a basic technical tradition, perhaps correlated with some broad ecological pattern, which was shared by many different groups of people over a large area who had developed otherwise distinctive local cultures. Other than the handaxes, which we may emphasize more than they ever did, and the prepared-platform techniques, they may have little in common. One can see at least two major culture areas in the west at this time, one comprising north Africa and southwestern Europe, which share much in common from the beginning, and the other including Africa south of the Sahara, the Near East and India, which share certain elements among themselves. Within each of these there would have been many local varieties. Similarly, east-central Europe and eastern Asia would be comparable culture areas with distinctive local traditions within the latter at least.

The men of the Middle Pleistocene were able to cope with a wide variety of habitats with equal success: not only the original savannah and open woodland of Africa, with extensions into the desert (presumably during periods of greater moisture and vegetation), but also the very different temperate woodland of Europe and north China and even, apparently, the more severe conditions of an environment transitional from forest to tundra. We also find them occupying what must have been the tropical rain forests of southeastern Asia, although not, it seems, the comparable zone of Africa. In general, they seem to have avoided mountainous areas and to have favored the neighborhood of rivers and lakes. Since all our evidence is from interior regions, there may have been considerable exploitation of sea coasts of which we know nothing. We do not know to what extent any given human population moved readily between these habitats, although some groups obviously must have done so initially, whatever the reason, in order to effect such a distribution of man. More probably, once adapted to a particular ecological habitat, they tended to remain with it, moving as it shifted with climatic changes. Despite this demonstrated ability to cope with these varied conditions, large accessible areas of quite similar habitat remained unoccupied, such as the steppes of central Eurasia. Since these must have been teeming with game animals, we can speculate that some other essential factor was missing—perhaps an adequate supply of wood.

Human occupation of the more northerly environments, especially under the rigorous climatic conditions which now challenged man as a result of the Mindel glaciation, must have been greatly facilitated by, if not in fact dependent on, the use of fire, which now seems widespread in these parts of Eurasia—having been found at a number of European sites and in north China. By analogy with such modern primitives as the Australian aborigines, fire probably preceded clothing as a means of keeping warm. Heat, however, is only one of many useful functions that fire can perform: Protection from animals after dark would seem an equally compelling incentive for initial adoption. Once in regular use, the many secondary functions would eventually become apparent: illumination, so that activities did not have to cease at sundown; aid in woodworking (charring renders wood easy to scrape down with simple tools); driving game; cooking—probably a later development, but one with very important consequences, both in terms of shortening the time that had to be spent in eating (reducing mastication) and in the reductions in size of teeth, jaws and facial musculature that must have followed from less need for habitual chewing of tough foods. Cooking also renders many substances edible, or at least more palatable, and would thus have considerably expanded man's sources of food. There is no actual evidence of cooking, however, before Neanderthaloid times, and even here the matter is in dispute.

It is generally assumed that means of making fire artificially at will did not exist until the Upper Pleistocene although this is an assumption based on negative evidence and open to question. The apparent regular use of fire in northern regions during the Middle Pleistocene is thought to represent the capture and preservation of fire of natural origin. Indeed, before man would have been able to take advantage of some accidental discovery that this or that action led to producing fire, he would have needed some experience in handling it, and an opportunity to appreciate its useful qualities, and this he could only have gained through having isolated and controlled fire of natural origin (e.g., caused by lightning or volcanic activity). Once obtained, it could have been preserved for long periods with any sort of care, just as is commonly done by simpler peoples all over the world today, who much prefer to keep a fire smoldering all the time rather than going to the bother of kindling a new one. Even groups who roam around constantly, as the Australian aborigines do and as we assume men of the Middle Pleistocene did also, will very often carry their fire with them in the form of smoldering sticks of slow-burning material. Early man may thus have used fire, and even used it continually in some regions, long before he had any idea of how to make it artificially.

culture history

From a common basic Lower Pleistocene technological tradition of pebble tools and utilized flakes, certain human groups even before the start of the Middle Pleistocene have begun to specialize their tool kits in the direction of a heavy *pointed* tool which we commonly label "handax." The widespread and enduring popularity of the handax, and the craftsmanship often evident in its manufacture, indicate that this implement must have been regarded as indispensable. Yet we really have no idea just what it was used for. Obviously it could have served a variety of useful functions— almost anything *except* chopping, so that the term "handax" is understandably rejected by many scholars as an inappropriate misnomer. Majority opinion has favored the idea that it was a general purpose tool. But at undisturbed sites handaxes seem to be confined to certain activity areas only, suggesting their use for specific purposes. We may surmise that they filled a specific economic need in the subsistence patterns of these particular groups. What this was, we do not know. It was apparently not a universal need, and it was fading out at the end of the Middle Pleistocene or else was being met by new and better types of tools.

While this development was taking place in Africa and southwestern Europe, populations elsewhere continued the original Lower Pleistocene technology and progressed slowly, in parallel fashion, within the framework of its traditional patterns. Either they felt no need for a specialized pointed tool, or the idea never reached them for one reason or another. This technological dichotomy during the Middle Pleistocene should be thought of as reflecting two different facies of human activity rather than as being two distinct cultures. If the handaxes are subtracted, the tool kits of both are very much the same at least in the earlier Middle Pleistocene. There are large numbers of flake tools in a variety of forms, and choppers continued in use almost everywhere. In fact, a few handaxlike (or at least pointed) tools occur sporadically in many so-called "nonhandax industries," but seem never to have achieved importance.

Initially confined to Africa and southwestern Europe, the idea of handaxes, or groups using them, spread from East Africa through the Near East and into India during the Holstein interglacial if not before. But any further eastward spread of this idea was halted, perhaps by the rain forests of Southeast Asia. Mountain barriers evidently discouraged any attempt to penetrate eastern Europe through the Balkans from the Near East, although the Dardanelles were readily crossed as far as Greece, or by eastward spread from Italy or southern France. Apparently the ecological pattern in which the handax functioned was not suited either to tropical forests or highland areas. There were no such natural barriers farther north in Europe, however, and it remains one of the enigmas of early prehistory why handaxes never spread very far east of the Rhine after having achieved such a wide distribution elsewhere in the human world. Again, some ecological factor is presumed to have been responsible.

The Acheulean groups in western Europe were evidently sensitive to climate; their northern limits fluctuate with changing conditions, and in the coldest periods they withdrew southward. Perhaps their economy was geared to the Mediterranean-type fauna, which prefers a warmer climate, and they reflect the changing range of the latter. The nonhandax groups of central and eastern Europe, on the other hand (perhaps descendants of the first settlers), seem to have been better able to endure the cold, or else they had nowhere comparable to which to retreat. At least there is evidence of their existence under more severe conditions than those the Acheuleans chose to cope with, which suggests a more generalized economy and a technology capable of adapting to change in contrast to that of the perhaps already overspecialized Acheuleans.

At the end of the Holstein or early in the Riss glaciation, increasing emphasis on standardized tools made of flakes led to the development of greatly improved methods for obtaining flakes of the desired size, thickness, and shape rather than the reliance on what might be available among the waste material dislodged during the manufacture of heavy implements. These new methods are known as the *prepared-core, prepared-platform* or Levallois technique, since they involve advanced preparation of the core before the flake is removed: In particular, there is the creation of a striking platform at one end of the future flake on which the dislodging blow will be delivered. The highest development of this technique is the *prepared-flake* or *tortoise-core* variety. Here the idea is to shape the desired tool on the surface of the core and then to dislodge it with a single skillful blow, it then being ready for use with little or no further trimming. The cores from which such preshaped tools were removed somewhat resemble the carapace of a tortoise (Figure 9–3).

These methods, which are evidence of a considerable degree of intelligence, foresight, and technical skill, became widespread at this time throughout the Acheulean world and are as much a diagnostic Acheulean trait as the handax. In most regions they became increasingly important as handaxes faded out of the picture, and toward the end of Riss times began to spread to some of the nonhandax groups of central and eastern Europe.

Turning now to the other facies of Middle Pleistocene human activity, the groups with non-Acheulean industries representing technological evolution out of the "Oldowan" tradition or something similar, they are now firmly established in eastern Europe at the new site of Vertesszöllös in Hungary and are dated somewhere in the latter part of Mindel times.

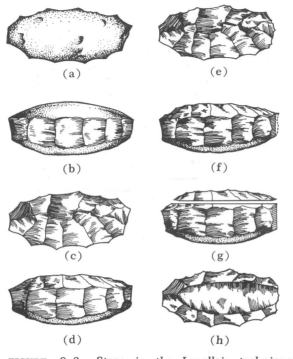

FIGURE 9–3. *Steps in the Levallois technique:* (a) *edges of a nodule are trimmed* (top view); (b) *side view of same;* (c) *top surface is then trimmed* (top view); (d) *side view of same;* (e) *striking platform is now made at right end* (top view); (f) *side view of same;* (g) *preshaped flake is detached by blow on this platform;* (h) *top view of core after removal of flake.* (Modified from drawings by Jean Zallinger; reproduced by permission.)

Pending fuller reports, little can be said as yet other than that these people were living successfully in a fairly severe climate with the aid of fire. Presumably we can see them as at least the cultural descendants of the Villafranchian pebble toolmakers of Europe.

The population of East Asia was isolated from these non-Acheulean people of Europe as well as from the Acheulean world. The Eurasian plain lying in between seems to have been uninhabited until well into the Upper Pleistocene, and there is no evidence of any contact whatever between India, the outpost of the West, and neighboring Burma, the closest of the Eastern peoples. The first tools in East Asia (Trinil beds of Java) probably date from the very beginning of the Middle Pleistocene, although early types of *Homo erectus* from the underlying Djetis beds, as well as Lantian

Man in China, are older still (probably of Mosbachian age). Nothing is known as yet about the nature of these tools. They are younger than early tools in the West, and it would seem logical to derive them from that source, although there is no indubitable evidence and we must at least consider the possibility of an independent hearth of toolmaking among the *Homo erectus* populations of Java. The earliest remains at Choukoutien (the cave of Peking Man) date from the end of Mindel and the early part of the Holstein interglacial. The extremely primitive nature of the industry here (the flake tools are mostly utilized waste flakes, rarely retouched and many unrecognizable as artifacts if found outside the cave) contrasts strongly with contemporary industries in the West. The changelessness of the cultural remains over the long span of time represented by the deposits (over 50 meters deep) in the cave is also puzzling.

Other rather crude local industries have been found in Burma, Java, Malaya, Thailand, and Vietnam. Once started, all these regional traditions seem to continue through the Middle Pleistocene and probably the Upper as well. We may hypothesize that they all derive ultimately from the early Trinil tools (whatever the source of these) and represent the spread of populations related to Java Man.

reference

Howell, F. Clark: *Early Man*, Life Nature Library, Time, Inc., New York, 1965.

suggested readings

Bordes, François: *The Old Stone Age*, McGraw-Hill Book Company, New York, 1968, pp. 51–97.

Butzer, Karl W.: *Environment and Archeology*, Aldine Publishing Co., Chicago, 1964, pp. 350–372.

Cole, Sonia: *The Prehistory of East Africa*, Mentor Books, New York, 1965, pp. 125–160.

Howell, F. Clark: "Isimila: A Paleolithic Site in Africa," *Scientific American*, vol. 205, no. 4, pp. 119–129, 1961.

Howell, F. Clark: *Early Man*, Life Nature Library, Time, Inc., New York, 1965, pp. 76–121.

the Middle Pleistocene: 2

economy

Judging by the available evidence of economic activities, the Middle Pleistocene economy centered on meat animals of medium size such as deer and horse—the typical prey of carnivores—but exploited any opportunity to secure big-game animals. Obviously, the latter would offer the greatest return in food for effort expended, once man was able to cope with them, and by the beginning of the Middle Pleistocene this level of hunting ability had evidently been achieved. But just how it was managed has not been clear. The favorite prize in many areas was not only large but often thick-skinned and sometimes dangerous. Yet, in contrast to the later big-game hunters of the Upper Pleistocene, there is nothing in the assemblages of *stone* implements at this stage that could be called an offensive weapon —with the possible exception of rounded stones that may have been used as missiles, perhaps simply thrown by hand, as some primitive groups still do. In fact, the tool kits seem to have been designed for two purposes: cutting up animals *after* they had been killed, and working wood. This, plus the find of a sharpened spear of yew wood in Middle Pleistocene deposits at Clacton in England, and new discoveries at the Torralba site in Spain, suggests that major dependence was placed on wooden piercing weapons, though there may have been clubs as well. Modern examples show that plain wooden spears can be very effective at close quarters, though less so in the case of thick-skinned beasts. The absence of any sign of improvement in hunting equipment throughout this long period is doubtless due to the fact that the attention and efforts of the hunters centered on getting close to the prey, in good carnivore fashion, so that even a mediocre weapon could effect the actual kill. It was animal behavior, rather than technology, that was the focus of attention of Man the Hunter at this stage of his development; it was the easier and the more natural course for him to have taken.

Ordinary game was doubtless hunted by essentially carnivore techniques of stalking, ambush at water holes or along game trails, and, when the game was within reach, stabbing from behind or from the side. Generally, with these techniques the victim is only wounded and must be tracked down until it succumbs or can be dispatched by further attack. In Europe, sites like Torralba[1] and Markkleeberg suggest the ambushing of seasonally migrating game herds at strategic points. In such cases the hunters can expect the game to come to them in considerable numbers and under conditions where it can be surprised and attacked at close quarters. This suggests awareness of the seasonal calendar as well as detailed knowledge of animal habits.

In Africa, where animal life follows a different pattern of permanent residence in any given locality, the intended victim had to be singled out and immobilized. One way in which we know this was done was by driving large, heavy beasts into swampy ground where they became mired down and could be dispatched at leisure with even the simplest weapons such as stones. Near the earliest site of Middle Pleistocene age at Olduvai Gorge are the remains of three animals who met such a fate: a giant buffalo (*Bularchus*), a cousin of the giraffe with antlers (*Sivatherium*), and a huge sheeplike creature (*Pelorovis*) larger than a buffalo whose horns may have had a span of 12 feet. Their lower limb bones were still in place, standing patiently upright in the clay of a former swamp; everything else had been hacked off and dragged to the site, where the meat was cut up, the bones were smashed for marrow, and the tools used were left scattered around when the feast was over and the group moved on.

[1] For a reconstruction of the hunting activities at Torralba and nearby Ambrona see Howell, 1965, pp. 85–99.

FIGURE 10–1. *Middle Pleistocene wooden spear from Clacton-on-Sea, England, with concave scraper probably used in shaping such implements.* (By permission from Kenneth P. Oakley, *Man the Toolmaker,* copyright © 1959 by the Trustees of the British Museum–Natural History.)

Elephants, despite their size, were well within the capabilities of early hunters. Having no enemies, they do not fear man and can thus be approached more readily; if they run, they do not go fast or very far, and when frightened, they head for the nearest body of water.

Obviously, the ability to cope with larger animals by any such methods is dependent upon cooperation and organization more than anything else, and this would have involved cooperative action among adults outside of the immediate family, thus placing a heavy premium on socializing factors in human behavior which must have had important consequences for the development of human social life. Communication must also have been fostered. The fact that early man in the formative stages of Homo sapiens went through a very long period as a big-game hunter thus had a lot to do with what emerged as the end product. Hunting has well been termed "the master behavior pattern of the human species."

In areas where such big game was not continuously available or the major hunt was unsuccessful, there must have been considerable use of smaller game. Peking Man seems to have lived primarily on venison, but here again considerable cooperative effort would be required to stalk, surround, and dispatch such fleet creatures with the available equipment, although we must remember that man as an animal does possess the endowments of superior vision and running ability to supplement his cultural attributes. On modern analogies, it is doubtful that the diet of these early hunters was ever 100 percent meat, but it is impossible to estimate the proportion or nature of vegetable food since only the animal remains survive. Some authorities believe that plants might still have supplied up to 75 percent of the diet. In addition to hunting, there must have been utilization of small game: nestlings, birds' eggs, and crawling creatures (lizards, various insects, etc.)—again on modern analogy and ease of securing. Quite generally women collect food of this nature, along with plants, while the men are out hunting.

Among his other unique and supposedly superior attributes, man has the distinction of being the only higher animal who eats his own kind. This achievement, already suspected of him in the Lower Pleistocene, is clearly evidenced now, especially by the remains of Peking Man from Choukoutien. The scarcity of human remains elsewhere from the Middle Pleistocene and their fragmentary nature makes it impossible to determine whether this habit was typical of mankind as a whole. But in view of the number of instances reported from the succeeding Upper Pleistocene, one cannot escape the suspicion that throughout most of human history persons outside of one's own group were regarded more as game animals than as fellow men. Doubtless such attitudes would have retarded the spread and exchange of ideas and inventions and may have contributed to the snail's pace of human progress during these times. The possibility sometimes suggested that this early cannibalism was of a ritual rather than a gustatory nature implies a level of intellectual sophistication that seems hardly credible.

social life

Inferences as to social life in the Middle Pleistocene must be drawn from the few living sites available, with cautious analogies from modern hunters. The necessity of protection and cooperative hunting would have required men either to live in groups of a size adequate for the purpose— perhaps something on the order of twenty or thirty people—or to combine smaller groups together whenever needed; but the nature of the economic base and the general pattern of life would impose a definite ceiling on the number who could live together in any one locality, though this would doubtless vary according to the resources of the area. In localities where big game was the exception, smaller groups of single extended families might be expected. We would expect such a larger band to be composed of a number of small biparental nuclear families, and these families would probably be closely related. By now the awareness and recognition of kinship had doubtless developed to the point where the concept of incest existed and already played its dominant role as a determinant of sexual behavior patterns. From this we could also infer the presence now of *exogamy*[2] as a social institution. Bernard Campbell has made the interesting suggestion that the fast evolution of the Hominidae may prove to be correlated with the appearance of exogamy and the resultant increase in genetic variability—in contrast to inbreeding primates with their slow evolutionary change over millions of years.

Such leadership as existed would probably have been accorded to the best hunter on modern analogy and some sexual division of labor may be assumed. It has been hypothesized that the human life span was short, perhaps averaging forty years. It is also likely that infant and child mortality was heavy, especially during the first year of life. Two of the individuals at Choukoutien were over fifty years of age, which clearly indicates that social life had developed to the point where old people were cared for. This is an important consideration, since old people are the repositories of the sum total of knowledge and wisdom in any nonliterate society and also have the leisure to transmit it to the younger generation. When man becomes dependent on learned behavior for survival, old people become socially valuable beyond their active or reproductive years.

The settlement pattern continued to be one of transitory campsites, briefly occupied and then abandoned for another as the requirements of hunting dictated. Most of the available living sites are simply places where animals happen to have been killed and where the band consequently camped to cut them up and eat them. When everything had been eaten up, they started out on the hunt again. A favorable hunting spot was, of course, often periodically reoccupied over a period of time, accounting for stratified concentrations of finds at such localities as Olduvai Gorge and

[2] The rule that one must marry outside one's social group to avoid incest.

Torralba. The cave of Peking Man at Choukoutien gives the impression of more stable occupation, but at the most this was seasonal, the cave having provided an attractive cold weather refuge. At least we can say that during the winter months Peking Man brought his game home instead of camping beside it; in summer, however, his pattern of life may have been no different from that observed elsewhere. Generally speaking, then, Middle Pleistocene man was always on the move, traveling light, and, hence, readily discarding his heavy stone tools and preferring to make new ones as needed. But he was almost certainly not a "free wanderer," as sometimes theorized. By analogy both with the animal world and modern primitive hunters, we must assume that his movements were within a definite territory whose resources he knew intimately and could thus exploit with maximum effectiveness.

intellectual life

About intellectual life at this time, little can be said. The fact that Peking Man collected rock crystals has been cited as an indication of esthetic sensibilities, as has the evident pride in craftsmanship displayed by the Acheulean handax makers toward the end of the period, who sometimes lavished more care and skill on their products than would be necessary to produce an efficient implement. Scant as they are, these hints of the beginnings of human sensibilities are highly significant as reflections of the emerging mind and psyche.

Some reflection of intellectual capacity may be seen in the planning and organization of group hunting activities, especially those involving knowledge of the seasonal habits of animals and the ability to time them accordingly; in the knowledge of animal anatomy required for most effective killing and subsequent butchering; in the production of specialized tools for particular purposes, and especially of tools with which to make tools (i.e., machine tools). The Levallois tortoise-core technique in particular implies a considerable level of forethought and conceptualization.

Closely related is the question of the level of communication ability that had been attained by this time. Obviously the amount of cooperative activity and the increasing body of tradition and technical knowledge implies a development of language adequate for these purposes. It has been suggested that the evolution of the brain mechanism for speech may well have been correlated with the rapid increase in cranial capacity that took place just at this time and perhaps also with the slower maturation of the brain which would inevitably be associated with this increase. On the other hand, it has been argued that the extreme cultural conservatism or even stagnation of the Middle Pleistocene may have been caused at least in part by the limitations imposed by insufficient development of symbolic speech.)

retrospect

The overall picture is of the coexistence at this time of developed and underdeveloped groups (technologically speaking) in different parts of the world, which reaches an extreme in the contrast between the roughly contemporary sites of Torralba and Choukoutien, at opposite ends of the inhabited world but probably representing essentially similar human populations. However, in assessing the underdeveloped status of technology in East Asia we must bear in mind that these people may have stressed the nonmaterial side of their culture, which could have been the major focus of their interest, just as it is with the modern Australian aborigines; or they may also have had a technology based largely on perishable materials. Again, the Australians do extensive woodworking with only the crudest of stone tools, and the important items of their material culture are almost all of wood, so that Australian culture is scarcely reflected in its archeological remains.

In any event, before making value judgments on the capabilities of the Middle Pleistocene population of East Asia, we cannot stress too heavily that their culture, however it may appear to us, was an equally successful adjustment to a difficult environment and to the problems of life at the time, as was the culture of the West. And even in the West, technology varied greatly in development. The highly developed technology of the Acheulean groups of southwestern Europe seems not to be paralleled elsewhere; At least the stone industries of other Acheulean peoples never attained this level. Occupying what must have been a prime habitat, the Atlantic Coastal Plain of western Europe, these European Acheuleans became specialized hunters and skilled stoneworkers and constituted what seems to have been the center of technical progress at that time. Even as early as late Mindel times at Torralba, we can see the prototypes of tools that were to be of major importance hundreds of thousands of years later and the beginnings of regular use of bone as raw material.

The coexistence of developed and underdeveloped groups is nowhere more striking than in Europe itself where, all through the Middle Pleistocene, there is the sharp dichotomy between the Acheuleans of the Atlantic Plain in the west and the conservative population of the highlands of central and eastern Europe who cling to the old pebble and flake tradition of the first settlers. Perhaps they were pushed back into this marginal environment; only in the absence of the Acheuleans do they seem to appear anywhere in the western plain. They were not necessarily a dead end for further progress, however; their technology slowly evolves, and subsequently, in the Upper Pleistocene, with stimulus and borrowings from the West, central Europe becomes the scene of major developments in cultural evolution.

The Middle Pleistocene was the period that produced full-brained men from an original population of well-developed *Homo erectus* type, evolving through the intermediate stage we have labeled "Proto-Neanderthaloid." It is the time, then, of the final evolution of the human brain. But this evolution of the brain to full size was not reflected in any change in material culture, in technical traditions, or in ability to extend the previous range of man. The technical breakthroughs and cultural efflorescence toward the end of the Pleistocene came long after full-sized brains had been achieved.

some problems

Now to turn, in conclusion, to the major problems posed by our picture of human history during the Middle Pleistocene. The overriding impression is one of stagnation or else of extreme conservatism and stability—raising the question of whether people tend to stay put unless forced to change or whether change is really inherent in the processes of culture. Assuming, as we do, that change is natural and inevitable, we feel the need to seek causes for the apparent stagnation over this long span of time.

An underlying one was certainly the well-known phenomenon that cultural development is a cumulative process in which inventions and innovations take place only when the necessary antecedents already exist. The more inventions, the more will occur in the future—a "snowballing" effect. We live in an age when invention is commonplace—not because of a plethora of gifted men or because each inventor makes a major contribution, but because so much has been laid down, especially in the last few centuries, on which they can build. An equally gifted man of 500 years ago was severely limited in what he could do given the technological level of his time. Equally, there must be acceptance of an innovation by the group, or it is lost; and to be accepted, a need must be felt. When a group has achieved a satisfactory adjustment to its environment, sanctified by tradition, there is little interest in doing things a different way.

Thus it is inevitable that the initial stage of the building of culture should have been a long, slow one of almost imperceptible change, until the point was reached where enough inventions existed to provide antecedents for technical progress on a larger scale. In this initial stage change would occur only if some need were felt or overwhelming advantage seen. As well, man has always been more prone to borrow than to invent, and real enrichment of man's stock of culture has come through the sharing of advances and additions via the mechanism of diffusion—the spread of ideas and elements of culture from one group to another, often over great distances. (The bow and arrow, for instance, may have been a single invention that spread from one area over almost all the Old and New Worlds in a very short space of time, simply as a borrowing from group to group.)

Many other factors contributing to the lengthy initial stage of culture development have been suggested. They include biological ones: We do not know what limits might have been imposed by the brain and structure of these early men, and although it seems plausible that there would be at least some correlation with events, we must point to the paradox just mentioned that the final evolution of the brain seems to have had no reflection in cultural development.

Other suggestions have been: probable intergroup hostility, acting to reduce peaceful contact and promote isolation; the possibility that symbolic language was still in a rudimentary stage, thus hindering thought, invention, and interaction (some would explain the cultural efflorescence of the Late Pleistocene, for instance, as the result of the attainment of real language in the modern sense, thus releasing at last the latent potentialities of fully evolved Homo sapiens); and also the good possibility, given the very incomplete survival of evidence from this distant time, that culture was a lot richer than we think, and that the stagnation is thus more apparent than real.

In view of the well-documented stagnation of isolated marginal primitive groups like the Tasmanians in modern times, which has no other satisfactory cause besides isolation, we can certainly point to isolation as a major factor producing such a situation. But isolation that produces such stagnation must be actual geographical isolation or marginality. East Asia, at least, does seem to have been isolated in this sense.

Some or all of these factors may have operated to produce the picture in the Middle Pleistocene. Certainly there was no one cause.

Demanding explanation, too, is the whole question of the implications and meaning of the two facies of human activity that seem to have existed during the Middle Pleistocene—the Acheulean and non-Acheulean. Even if isolated East Asia is written off as a separate world, reflecting survivals of very early ways of life, the striking dichotomy in Europe still remains. Doubtless the explanation is basically an ecological one, but it is not yet apparent. Although there is some difference in habitat, it is not a major one. And we are still left to wonder why such an apparently useful item as the handax never penetrated central and eastern Europe after being universally accepted everywhere else in the West. Neither ecology nor innate human conservatism seems to provide a satisfactory answer to this puzzle.

---

reference

Howell, F. Clark: *Early Man*, Life Nature Library, Time, Inc., New York, 1965.

the Neanderthaloid phase

the Eemian interglacial

The Upper Pleistocene begins with the Eemian interglacial, which is followed by the first of two major fluctuating cold phases, collectively known as the Würm glaciations, which terminate the conventional Pleistocene. The Eemian and the first major cold phase, which we will call Early Würm, bracket the stage of human evolution which may be termed Neanderthaloid. Actually, we don't know when the first humans who would fit this classification appeared; the oldest known find that is securely dated, that from Ehringsdorf, falls in the middle of the Eemian. But in the light of present knowledge, it seems reasonable to place the beginning of the Neanderthaloid stage at the start of the Upper Pleistocene, i.e., the start of the Eemian. Its end can be fixed with much more assurance at the point where all human remains quite suddenly are completely of Homo sapiens type, in the conventional sense; and this occurs at the close of the Early Würm or the start of the subsequent short phase of warm climate which we will call the Aurignacian Oscillations. The span of time involved is probably somewhere between 100,000 and 150,000 years long, and it ended approximately 40,000 years ago.

The Eemian, which opens the Neanderthaloid phase, was slightly warmer than today for the most part and represented a marked environmental change from the preceding Riss glaciation in many regions. Europe was an inviting human habitat, and the limits of human occupation spread north again, especially in the case of the late handax users on the Atlantic lowland of western Europe. On the other hand, conditions in

Africa deteriorated: There was a marked reduction in the area available
for man, with subsequent effects upon population, and the Sahara developed into a major barrier with the increasingly drier conditions. From this
time onward, Africa south of the Sahara became a world apart, developing
along its own lines in relative isolation, while North Africa in the eastern
part found its closest relationships with the Near East, and northwestern
Africa continued its links with Spain.

Despite the relative recency of the Eemian as compared with preceding geological periods, we actually know very little about human history and human life at this time—which is unfortunate, because significant developments were getting underway in several parts of the world at
least. Our very poor picture occurs because there is very little archeological
material securely dated to this period, particularly in Eurasia, although
it may well be that considerable amounts of existing material belong here.

Technologically, this is a time of further development and elaboration of existing traditions in stone technology in the direction of a greater
number of more specialized tools, the great majority of which are made
on flakes. The various techniques for producing better flakes naturally
play a conspicuous role. Parallel developments in stone technology seem
to have been going on not only in basically related areas like Europe and
southern Africa, but also in East Asia, where the important site of
Tingts'un in the Yellow River Basin shows an active development out of
the old chopper tradition that includes some forms and techniques surprisingly reminiscent of the West but, so far as we can tell, unrelated. It
is in marked contrast to the extreme conservatism that characterizes
Southeast Asia. Industries all over Africa at this time can still be loosely
referred to as Acheulean, and (we may assume the same would probably
be true of India) In western Europe the final, highly evolved Acheulean
industries are often termed Micoquian; these presumably are of Eemian
age. The same area probably also saw the beginning now of the various
flake industries which go under the label of "Mousterian" and which have
been commonly associated with populations of Neanderthaloid type. The so
called "Mousterian industries" represent no break or major development
but are simply another reflection of the general technological elaboration
and diversification going on at this time.

An important event that must have taken place early in the Eemian
was an eastward spread of some Acheulean techniques and ideas for the
first time from the Atlantic lowland of western Europe into central Europe
at least and later into the Balkans and eastern Europe, where they are
present by the beginning of the succeeding Early Würm. This involved
particularly the idea of making bifacially worked tools, the technique
evolved by the Acheuleans in connection with their handaxes (which are
sometimes alternatively called "bifaces"), and also the Levallois technique
of superior flake tool production. Neither had been used previously in
central or eastern Europe, but now we see certain groups here and there
adopting them, grafting them on to their own traditions to produce new

and somewhat better tool kits. At the same time, other groups in the same areas cling stubbornly to the local traditions of unifacial flake tools which evolved from the old non-Acheulean pebble and flake technology of central Europe, with the result that the archeological picture in this region becomes increasingly a sort of mosaic, differing from site to site. These Acheulean influences never spread to Southeast Asia, however, where bifacially worked tools are only accidental, and the Levallois tortoise-core technique is unknown—indicating continued isolation.

By and large, there is no really basic change in economy or in the pattern of human life over the Middle Pleistocene. Hunting techniques seem to have remained essentially the same, judging from the wooden spear from Lehringen in Germany which had been thrust into the side of an elephant from the rear. Aside from the more elaborate tool kits everywhere, which suggest increasingly efficient exploitation of all available resources, there is evidence to suggest the beginnings of a new economic specialization, of improved hunting, and, with this, the first move in half a million years in the direction of expanding the frontiers of the human world by venturing onto the vast northern plain of Eurasia—a move that ultimately was to have tremendous consequences.

This evidence is provided by a unique industry called the Weimarian, represented at the site of Ehringsdorf near Weimar in Germany on the edge of the northern plain and dating from the middle of the Eemian. The technology of this group was far ahead of its time: a blend of late Acheulean (Micoquian) ideas with the earliest appearance of a number of tool types (true backed blades, burins) that are characteristic of the cultures of Homo sapiens at the end of the Pleistocene. Most significant of all, this group was specialized for hunting on the plains and possessed the first known projectile weapons as evidenced by their stone points—the oldest definite projectile points known. These were doubtless hand-thrown spears.

Since it seems desirable to have a broad term comparable to our usage of Acheulean to designate the flake industries of the Neanderthaloid phase in the stretch of contiguous territory (see Figure 11–2) from western Europe to Mongolia and south to the Near East and North Africa, which all share certain common features in greater or lesser degree while retaining their individuality, the label "Mousteroid" (Mousterian-like) would probably be acceptable and convey the right idea. We must emphasize that Mousteroid is not synonymous with the culture of Neanderthaloid man: Neanderthaloid populations over large areas, such as eastern Asia and southern Africa, isolated from the Mousteroid world, had industries sufficiently different that the term cannot be applied; similarly, there are in some places later industries related to or resembling Mousteroid, and hence deserving the label, which were the handiwork of conservative groups of Homo sapiens. As for the old term Mousterian itself, there are now so many varieties of Mousterian, no one of which is any more typical than the others or ancestral to the rest, that the word seems to have little

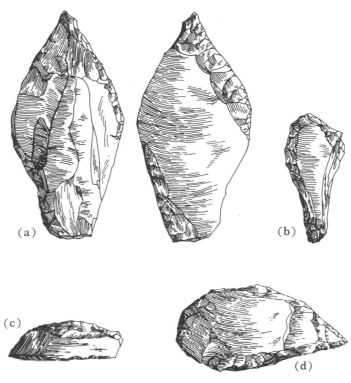

FIGURE 11–1. *Weimarian implements from Ehringsdorf:* (a) *projectile point;* (b) *endscraper;* (c) *backed knife;* (d) *bifacial knife.* (Modified from *Science*, vol. 152, no. 3726, p. 1195; copyright © 1966 by the American Association for the Advancement of Science. By permission of Hansjürgen Müller-Beck and *Science*.)

real meaning. It is used today almost entirely in compound names such as "Levalloiso-Mousterian," or occasionally in the names of certain tool types ("Mousterian point") of long-established usage.

the Early Würm

A great deal more is known about human history during the latter part of the Neanderthaloid stage—the Early Würm—than about the Eemian. Not only is a far greater quantity of archeological material available, but more important, it can be securely dated to this period in a considerable number of cases. Furthermore, the majority of these sites are in caves and

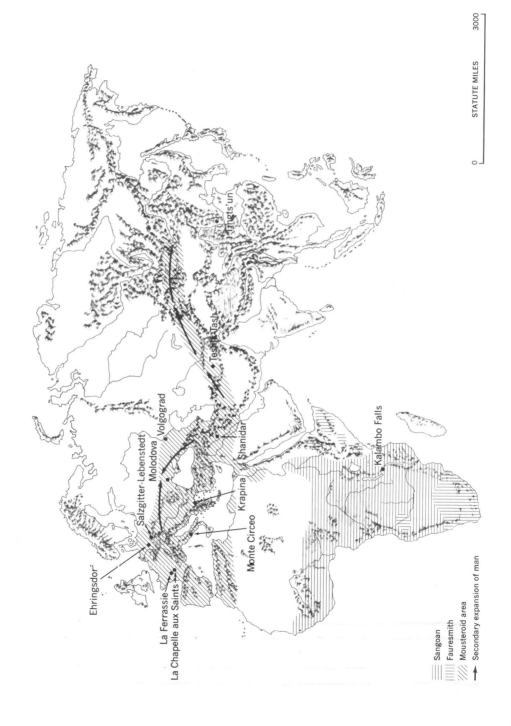

Ehringsdorf

Salzgitter-Lebenstedt
Molodova Volgograd

La Ferrassie
La Chapelle aux Saints

Krapina Shanidar

Monte Circeo

Teshik-Tash

Tangts'un

Kalambo Falls

Sangoan
Fauresmith
Mousteroid area
Secondary expansion of man

STATUTE MILES

0   3000

thus represent relatively undisturbed living sites. However, this preponderance of cave sites may give us a somewhat distorted view of life at the time since most people were doubtless not living in caves, or only did so on occasion. This improved picture, it must be added, applies to the Mousteroid world as just defined. Elsewhere, problems of dating are just beginning to be solved, as in southern Africa, or cannot yet be dealt with, as in India, where we don't know what remains belong to this period. East Asia is practically a blank so far.

The Early Würm is a time of fluctuating climate (see chart of Pleistocene climate, Figure 5–1), which in the Northern Hemisphere deteriorated to a cold maximum late in the period. This climate brought glaciation to northern Europe and mountain regions elsewhere, with the usual environmental changes: southward depression of habitat zones and increased rainfall in arid regions, so that the Mediterranean shores and the Near East doubtless became more inviting. The status of the Sahara at this particular time is uncertain; certainly southern Africa remained essentially isolated. In Europe at least people seem no longer to have moved with the environment but to have stayed put and adapted themselves to the new conditions: They were encouraged no doubt by the abundance of game in a Europe now largely tundra and cold steppe and were facilitated certainly by a technology adequate for these conditions. The glaciation late in the Early Würm also meant lowered sea levels: The Old World was again connected with the New, and Indonesia was once more a continuous land mass. Although the general climate at this time was colder than during the earlier Riss glaciation, it was not as rigorous as that of the later final Würm glaciation. Following the cold maximum, the climate warmed up rapidly, bringing the Early Würm to a close with the succeeding warm phase we have called the Aurignacian Oscillations and which is already in the time of Homo sapiens.

Perhaps the most important historical development in this later part of the Neanderthaloid phase is the expansion of the human stock beyond the limits of its primary dispersal half a million years earlier, a process foreshadowed in the Weimarian industry of the Eemian. This was the beginning of the secondary expansion of mankind, continued and concluded by Homo sapiens in the following phase, which brought about the occupation of all the rest of the habitable world except for the distant oceanic islands whose discovery had to await the development of seafaring. This expansion took two forms (see Figure 11–2): the northward crossing of the mountain barriers in western Asia, presumably by highland peoples living just to the south of them, who then proceeded to follow the slopes of the ranges and the foothills into areas of familiar habitat such as the

FIGURE   11–2.   The Neanderthaloid world.

Crimea, parts of Russian Turkestan, the Altai mountains, and Mongolia, where their accustomed and presumably rather generalized economy and Mousteroid technology could function without essential change; and the spread apparently eastward from central Europe across the great northern plain of groups who had developed a specialized hunting economy adapted to this environment which had earlier lain beyond the capabilities of man. Among other things, this meant the ability to cope with cold without recourse to the cozy caves so prized by their highland cousins; also the development of equipment made of bone to replace the hardwood on which man had for so long relied and which the plains could not supply. The earliest cold-adapted groups living on the plain of which we have knowledge are those at Salzgitter-Lebenstedt in Germany (with the first really standardized bone tools in the form of points and a picklike antler ax later to become famous in postglacial times as the Lyngby ax) and at Volgograd (formerly Stalingrad) in Russia (apparently the first inhabitants of European Russia). The latter is characterized by bifacially worked stone projectile points as well. Salzgitter-Lebenstedt represents a summer camp of a band of perhaps twenty to thirty persons, apparently occupied for

---

FIGURE   11–3.   *Bone implements from Salzgitter-Lebenstedt:* left: *pick or club of reindeer antler;* right: *projectile point.* (Modified from *Science,* vol. 152, no. 3726, p. 1197; copyright © 1966 by the American Association for the Advancement of Science. By permission of Hansjürgen Müller-Beck and *Science.*)

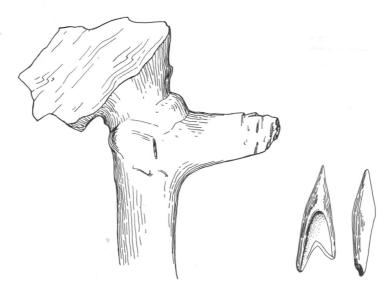

several seasons. Eighty-eight percent of the diet is tundra animals—mostly reindeer, with some mammoth—reflecting their economic specialization.

Perhaps a third type of human expansion should also be included here: what appears to be the first occupation of the tropical rain forests of central and west Africa late in the Early Würm by people who seem to have specialized their technology for exploitation of a forest environment, which in this wetter time covered extensive areas. Instead of withdrawing from a changing environment, as heretofore, the inhabitants along the former forest edge adapted to it as it expanded. Their new culture, called Sangoan, stressed heavy tools such as core axes for woodworking and picks, and it is in marked contrast to the trend elsewhere toward smaller and lighter tools. The Acheulean descendants who remained in the old open habitat of sub-Saharan Africa evolved a culture known as Fauresmith, which is generally comparable to Mousteroid. Like the plains specialization in northern Europe, the Sangoan is one of the first examples of adaptation resulting in exploitation of a specific environment, hitherto off limits. Thus equipped, the Sangoans seem gradually to have settled all the tropical forest area of Africa.

In Europe there is a basic dichotomy between the peoples practicing this new way of life on the plains and the more conservative groups sticking to older ways in the highlands, being not so cold-adapted and typically

---

FIGURE 11 4. *Sangoan implements:* left: *pick.* (From François Bordes, *The Old Stone Age,* copyright © 1968 by World University Library, McGraw-Hill, Inc., New York. By permission of François Bordes and the publishers); right: *core-ax.* (Modified from *Science,* vol. 150, no. 3698, p. 843; copyright © 1965 by the American Association for the Advancement of Science. By permission of J. Desmond Clark and *Science.*)

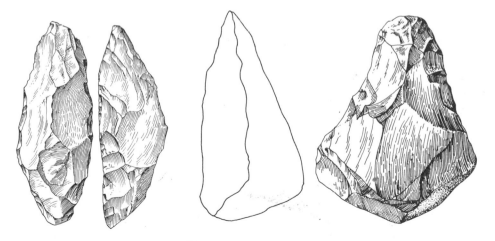

living in caves and rock shelters. This conservative highland area includes the classic cave sites of south-central France with their various "Mousterian" industries. There is no cultural uniformity within these two divisions, however, but rather a variety of distinctive local complexes in each, characterized by differing technical traditions: Some continue to use handaxes, others develop other bifacial tool types such as handsome leaf-shaped points or daggers as a refinement of the basic bifacial technique; still others cling to the old-fashioned flake tools worked on one side only, some producing them by the Levallois technique and some not—so that Europe, as we said earlier, becomes a veritable mosaic of local industries whose details need not concern us here. North Africa also reveals a number of Mousteroid industries, some using bifacial techniques inherited from the Acheulean and producing bifacial projectile points.

Over the Old World in general the picture is one of wide-scale cultural evolution but expressed in the form of many local traditions with the heartland of Eurasia now an important area of progress for the first time— along with the coexistence of areas of extreme conservatism such as southern Africa (where the local version of Acheulean survived after its disappearance elsewhere as at the famous site of Kalambo Falls), presumably India, and certainly Southeast Asia from what we know. Apparently isolation from the ferment of the Mousteroid area is the likely explanation. But it is possible that the dynamic expansion evident all along the northern human frontier affected north China as well: The route to the New World was open during the Early Würm, and there are suggestions that the first Americans used a tool kit remarkably reminiscent of types found at Tingts'un slightly earlier. This would carry the implication that the first Americans may have been of general Neanderthaloid type.

life in Neanderthaloid times

As mentioned, the ability to live on the plains in a time of cold climate implies construction of artificial shelters. There had been no actual evidence of man's ability to do this until the Homo sapiens phase—although we must bear in mind that the sort of shelters erected by Bushmen and Australians (presumably within the capabilities of early man) could not be expected to leave any trace in the archeological record. But in 1958 to 1959 Soviet archeologists uncovered at the Molodova I site in the Dnestr River valley of European Russia (Ukraine) what they consider to be the remains of a dwelling of Early Würm Age, consisting of a ring of mammoth bones enclosing an area 8 by 5 meters, within which is concentrated all the evidence of human activity in the vicinity: a number of hearths, a great quantity of worked flint (548 cores, 4,105 flake blades, 14,457 flakes, 140 shaped tools, plus debris), and fragments of bones of various game animals assumed to be food remains. Presumably this was covered over with poles and brush or skins. If the interpretation is correct, and it seems convincing, this is the oldest dwelling known.

In highland areas where caves were available they were extensively used at this time, giving the impression that cave dwelling suddenly became the typical human pattern wherever possible. (The first known cave sites in Africa also date from this time.) It should be noted that no one ever lived *inside* a cave—in the dark inner recesses. Habitation was in the mouths of caves, or at the base of overhanging cliffs (so-called "rock shelters"). It is hypothesized that windbreaks of poles and skins or brush may have been erected on the outer side for greater warmth and protection from weather, and evidence of a post driven into the ground perhaps for this purpose was found at Combe-Grenal in France.

Fire was of course in general use now, as shown by the first positive evidence from southern Africa. The regularity with which hearths now accompany human dwelling sites leaves no doubt that the Neanderthaloids were capable of artificially producing fire, although no indubitable fire-making equipment has yet come to light. However, even in the succeeding Homo sapiens phase such finds are extremely rare.

All accidental discoveries of how fire could be produced artificially must have occurred in the course of the use or manufacturing of tools. Fire can be produced in two main ways: (1) by percussion of a siliceous stone (like flint) on a sulphureous stone (or of stone on steel); and (2) by long-sustained friction between pieces of wood. The fact that sparks are often produced by striking stones together must have been very evident to even the earlier toolmakers, who spent a fair part of their lives banging one piece of stone against another. But the sparks produced by flint hitting flint or quartz hitting quartz have no incendiary qualities since they are too cold. However, when a nodule of iron sulphide (pyrites) happens to be used as a hammerstone in flaking flint, this will produce hot sparks which will easily ignite any sufficiently dry tinder they may fall on—and such a coincidence would readily lead to the discovery of the percussion method of making fire: provided, of course, that you wanted fire and knew what to do with it once you had gotten it— which leads back to our earlier statement that prior acquaintance and experience with fire would be a prerequisite before any such accidental discovery would lead to anything.

It is probable that the friction methods were also dependent on experiences from toolmaking, but of a different sort that would depend on technology having reached a stage at which bone, antler, ivory, and wood were being sawed and shaped by grinding, and where holes were bored in such materials by the rapid rotation of a drill. As far as we know, these techniques of sawing, drilling, and grinding were not practiced before the Homo sapiens phase. It is thus very unlikely that any of the friction devices for fire making (fire drill, fire saw, fire plough) were invented before this later time—which is only yesterday as human history goes. These methods of fire making require that the friction on a surface of wood be sufficiently sustained to rub off fine particles that are hot enough to smolder.

It is unanimously agreed that the Neanderthaloids must have had adequate clothing in order to survive European winters during the Early Würm and to expand their range northward, but of its nature we know nothing. It must still have been of a rudimentary sort since there is no sewing equipment in evidence as later. The Mousterian side scraper, so typical of many tool kits at this time, is widely viewed as a skin-working tool, and at least one Neanderthaloid skull shows teeth worn down like those of modern peoples who habitually chew animal skins to soften them.

It is obvious that the Neanderthaloids were successful hunters, but they followed in the path of their predecessors and introduced no real improvements as far as we can tell except for the progressive groups on the north European plain with the first projectile spears. Evidently technique rather than equipment was still the focus of attention for the majority of hunters. By and large all available game resources were utilized impartially, but some groups display marked preferences for this or that animal which cannot always be explained in terms of environment and availability.

The absence of any art or ornament, which we could expect to survive in the well-preserved sites from this phase unless it was confined to perishable materials, is perhaps evidence of the intellectual limits of the Neanderthaloids. A few scratches on a piece of bone or an example of a fossil probably collected and prized seem scarcely to merit being called signs of artistic appreciation, however faint. Red ochre is, however, found in many sites, and shows evidence of use both powdered and as a sort of pencil. Since no trace of it appears on the walls of any occupied cave or shelter, it is possible that this was employed to decorate the human skin.

The main reason that we know so much more about Neanderthaloid Man himself as compared with earlier forms is that he was the first (so far as we know) to dispose of his dead, perhaps the most striking evidence of his increasing humanity. In some cases, as at La Ferrassie in France, considerable care was expended. At Shanidar cave in Iraq, pollen analysis indicates that the body of one individual had been laid down on a bed of pine boughs and bright-colored flowers. Typical is the interment of the deceased in a flexed position: perhaps to save the labor of digging a larger grave than necessary, or perhaps, as some suggest, because the corpse was tied in this position to keep it from wandering around and bothering the living. The deliberate placing of objects with the dead was not common, and some supposed instances have been challenged. Wishful thinkers eager to give early man a spiritual life akin to their own have perhaps read more significance into the evidence than it merits.

That Neanderthaloid Man within his own group was living in a human type of social structure involving ethical considerations and humane sensibilities is indicated by the Shanidar cripple, who had been cared for from infancy until his accidental death at age forty. The arthritic old man from La Chapelle aux Saints is another case in point, though here we may suppose that the wisdom of age endowed him with a social value. Such charity evidently did not extend to outsiders. At least two Neanderthaloids display serious wounds from weapons, and the evidence for cannibalism cannot be overlooked. Some writers approach this evidence with embarrassment, as if with Neanderthaloid Man we are getting too close to home, and attempt to clothe this evidence in the relative respectability of religious ritual. And while it is true that the skull found at Monte Circeo, which had been carefully placed on a sort of platform after removal (and consumption?) of the brains and surrounded with a circle of stones, does suggest some sort of skull cult or ritualism, it is stretching credulity to apply the same explanation to the Krapina Cave in Yugoslavia where the bones of more than twenty Neanderthaloids of both sexes and all ages were found intermingled with discarded animal remains. These bones had evidently been broken open for the extraction of brain and marrow; some show traces of fire, and one skull fragment bears definite cuts.[1] One cannot escape the impression that strangers were still apt to be viewed as game animals at this time.

This is not to say that the men of Early Würm times were incapable of ritual with its concomitant belief in magic and awareness of the supernatural. As Howell has pointed out, it is necessary to postulate a good degree of intellectual and fantasy life at this stage in order to account for the appearance of what we see along these lines very soon afterwards. Whether or not it is valid to deduce any concept of life after death from the disputed evidence of grave offerings, the ring of ibex horns around the child's grave at Teshik-Tash must certainly be interpreted as ritualism of some sort. And there are also the reported cases of headless burials and separate burials of skulls.

Much has been made of supposed evidence of ritual practices with cave bear remains at a number of caves in central Europe, which have some resemblance to aspects of the "animal ceremonialism" of northern hunting peoples in modern times. Often cited as the oldest known beginnings of magic and religion, the validity of this "bear cult" remains at best only a possibility, according to authoritative opinion.

From what we can discern, the behavior of the men of the Neanderthaloid phase was sufficiently complex to indicate that it must have been motivated by quite abstract ideas, and the repetitive pattern of this behavior implies that these ideas must have been communicated by the use of conventional symbols—suggesting the existence now of vocal communication at least approaching our concept of language.

---

[1] For an artist's reconstruction of this grisly banquet, see Howell, 1965, p. 134. The atmosphere seems anything but religious.

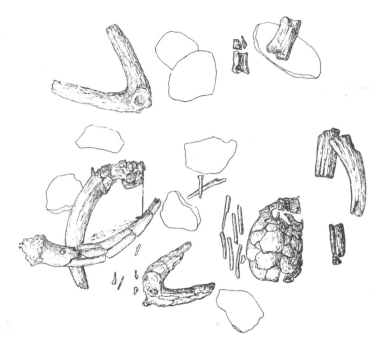

FIGURE   11–5.   *Circle of ibex horns around the Neanderthaloid*
child's grave in the cave of Teshik-Tash, Uzbekistan. (After
Okladnikov.)

---

reference

Howell, F. Clark: *Early Man,* Life Nature Library, Time, Inc., New York, 1965.

suggested readings

Bordes, François: *The Old Stone Age,* McGraw-Hill Book Company, New York,
        1968, pp. 98–146.
Butzer, Karl W.: *Environment and Archeology,* Aldine Publishing Co., Chicago,
        1964, pp. 373–383.
Howell, F. Clark: *Early Man,* Life Nature Library, Time, Inc., New York, 1965,
        pp. 122–143.

the Homo sapiens phase: 1

introduction

It is not yet known where or when the first men of fully modern type—traditional Homo sapiens—appeared. It is more probable that this evolutionary stage was reached at roughly the same time by populations in different parts of the world than that there was some single point of origin from which modern man spread with lightning speed over the earth, exterminating all his predecessors, as used to be the standard textbook picture. Early specimens of Homo sapiens type have been dated at about 40,000 years by radiocarbon in such widely separated localities as South Africa and Borneo, though such dates at the extreme range of the method are subject to a wide margin of error. At any rate, the change must have taken place in Europe during the latter part of the Early Würm at the latest, and perhaps somewhat earlier elsewhere since by the beginning of the warmer Aurignacian Oscillations following the Early Würm, all human remains are exclusively of modern type.

Taking this borderline as a beginning point and terminating arbitrarily at the end of the conventional Pleistocene 10,000 years ago, our Homo sapiens phase has a time span of approximately 30,000 years and in climatic-geological terms covers the Aurignacian Oscillations and the following main, maximum, or final Würm glaciation (Wisconsin in North America).

The phase opens with a period of fluctuating milder climate in the Northern Hemisphere that we have called the Aurignacian Oscillations. It may have lasted something like 15,000 years before deteriorating rapidly to the frigid conditions of the main Würm glaciation. Farther south, conditions would presumably have been like those of today, with aridity in the Near East and North Africa outside of highland regions where there is at least seasonal rainfall. Sea levels would also have risen to the point that the connection with the New World was broken, Japan was isolated, and Indonesia reverted to an archipelago.

The succeeding final glaciation was underway about 25,000 years ago, with sea levels already lowered sufficiently to have reestablished the land connections. The maximum cold was reached about 20,000 years ago and created the most severe climate to which man had been exposed, at least since the time of the Mindel glaciation half a million years earlier, which may possibly have been equally or more severe. This cold was accompanied by extensive glaciation in northern Europe and northern North America and in the higher mountain areas elsewhere. However, the lowlands of northern Asia were largely ice-free since precipitation was not sufficient for the formation of ice sheets. The tropics and subtropics were scarcely affected except for the increased rainfall in arid regions.

As compared with earlier stages of man's prehistory, our evidence for the Homo sapiens phase is abundant, fairly well dated in many areas (we are now within the range of radiocarbon dating), and provides an increasingly better picture of actual life and behavior due to the greater number of undisturbed living sites. However, we still know very little of what was going on in Southeast Asia and in China; and the picture in India is confused owing to the difficulty of dating the materials which may belong in this time range. In the New World the lack of well-dated finds older than around 14,000 years (which must exist) also hampers understanding. But elsewhere the outlines, at least, are clear, and the picture in Europe is known in considerable detail, allowing us to reconstruct long local sequences of development in certain places and also to trace the diffusion of technological traits over quite extensive areas.

It is possible now to be more specific than ever before about the cultural processes taking place. However, this better understanding of the Homo sapiens phase has only recently come about as a consequence of better information from central and eastern Europe. We must remember that the classic textbook picture of this phase (traditionally labeled "Upper Paleolithic") had always been based solely on France, and despite the undeniable wealth of the French materials they were nevertheless very poorly dated due to traditional overemphasis for this purpose on typology; moreover, the provenience of much of the material recovered in earlier excavations is uncertain and unreliable. François Bordes, a leading French prehistorian of today, has pointed out that many of these early data, on which so much of the prehistory of western Europe has been based, are nearly useless in modern comparative studies. It is not surprising, there-

FIGURE   12–1.   *The Old World during the Würm maximum.*

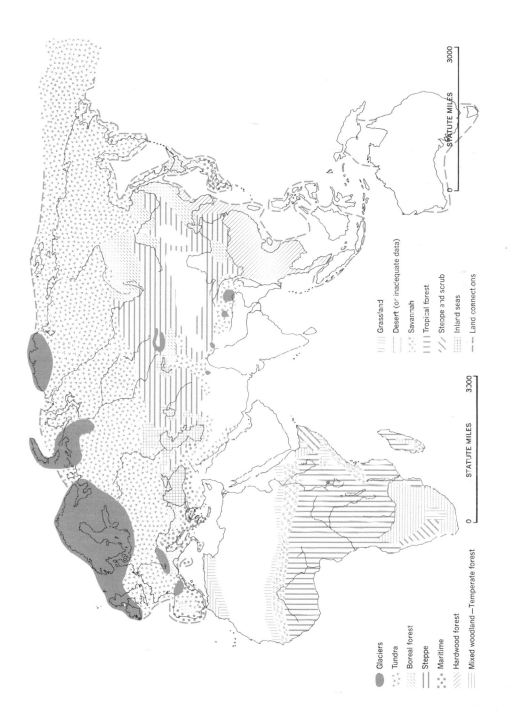

Glaciers

Tundra

Boreal forest

Steppe

Maritime

Hardwood forest

Mixed woodland—Temperate forest

Grassland

Desert (or inadequate data)

Savannah

Tropical forest

Steppe and scrub

Inland seas

Land connections

STATUTE MILES

0   3300

STATUTE MILES

0   3000

fore, that the standard textbook picture, with so narrow a focus, tends to be distorted and misleading.

Culturally, as reflected in technology, this time is characterized by a greatly accelerated rate of change over preceding eras and by many local traditions within such general trends as increased standardization of a great variety of specialized tools. In northern and western Eurasia, the production of blades and fine tools made on blades becomes increasingly conspicuous, with a later trend toward smaller sizes in both. The blade technique is the ultimate refinement in stoneworking. A blade is a long, thin, relatively narrow flake with more or less parallel sharp edges, admirably suited for making into these types of artifacts. Efficient blade production required preliminary shaping of the core so that scores of blades could be struck from it in rapid succession. Most commonly this involved transforming the lump of flint or other very fine-grained material into a core of conical or cylindro-conical shape (resembling an artillery shell) by trimming off the irregular outer surface and breaking the lump cleanly in two to produce a smooth, flat surface to serve as the striking platform. This requires considerable skill. The finished core is then placed point-down and blades are detached around the edge with the aid of a bone or wood punch struck by a hammerstone, producing a fluted effect on the core (Figure 12–2). Such a core will be used until only a remnant remains; the resultant blades, ideally, would be virtually identical. The technique is highly economical of raw material, since 10 to 40 feet of cutting edge can be obtained from a single pound of stone.

The burin for engraving also rises to prominence in this same region as a key item in the tool kit (Figure 12–3). But the classical stereotype of the "Upper Paleolithic" as the "blade and burin" period does not apply in the rest of the world. Moreover, the blade technique does not represent a major technical breakthrough at this moment in human history, as has been the conventional view. Blades occur sporadically in earlier times, even in the Acheulean. And the ultimate blade technique is basically a refinement of the prepared-platform method which could be, and probably was, evolved in a number of different places rather than representing a startling unitary invention.

the Aurignacoid tradition

The main center of technical progress, at least in the earlier part of the Homo sapiens stage, is the great plain of northern and eastern Europe, where the beginnings of specialized adaptation for a hunting life on the open plain were visible during the preceding period. Now there is a great development and wide spreading of projectile hunting cultures, along with a corresponding development and spread of bone technology (equipment made of bone)—a major new departure prompted by the need for a material to replace the essential hardwood, lacking on the plains, and made

FIGURE   12–2.   *Blade   technique   illustrated.*
(Modified from drawing by Jean Zallinger; reproduced by permission.)

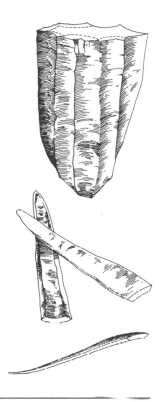

possible on a large scale by the wide use of the burin, the first tool which
made fine working of bone feasible.[1] Both of these developments seem to
center in the northern portion of eastern and central Europe and to spread
out from there in all directions, but chiefly over the plains, although strong
influence was ultimately exerted even on the cultures of the conservative
highland populations. These developments were taking place all through
the Aurignacian Oscillations: Most of these earlier plains hunters still
used stone projectile points (good examples being the groups who lived
at Kostienki on the south Russian plain, or the Jerzmanowice culture in
Poland), but emphasis on bone technology and bone points is clearly
present at sites like Vogelherd in Germany. By the start of the last Würm
glaciation stone points virtually disappear from the Eurasian plain and

[1] As pointed out earlier, the edge of a flint knife is not strong enough to cut bone. The
burin, which occurs in many different types, is essentially an engraving tool with a
chisellike cutting edge backed up by the maximum thickness of the blade from which
it is made. This edge is created by a special technique, the "burin blow," which removes
a corner of the blade. As an engraving tool, its basic function is the cutting of grooves.
It was equally useful on stone, and as might be imagined, played an important part in
the development of art where carving or engraving was involved.

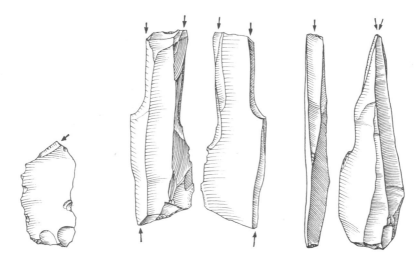

FIGURE 12–3. *Examples of burins. Arrows indicate direction of "burin blow" that created the working edge.* (From François Bordes, *The Old Stone Age,* copyright © 1968 by World University Library, McGraw-Hill, Inc., New York. By permission of François Bordes and the publishers.)

survive only here and there mostly among conservative highland groups retaining the older Mousteroid technical traditions. The puzzling Solutrean of France may represent such a conservative group still clinging at a very late date to the large bifacial leaf-shaped points which, handsome as they are, had gone out of style elsewhere in Europe.

The end product of these developments is the specialized hunters of the Eurasian plain during the last glaciation with their bone-pointed projectile weapons which may already have been propelled by spear-throwers. A spear-thrower is the first artificial propulsive device invented by man and has the effect of increasing the leverage of the human arm. Certainly these were in use, as shown by archeological specimens, during the latter part of the final glaciation, and there is good reason to postulate their appearance somewhat earlier. Despite the harsh environment of the vast wind-swept plain, in terms of tons of meat per square mile it provided a rich living for those who were equipped to exploit it and to survive comfortably in it: rich enough that there was likely leisure to elaborate aspects of life and culture other than economic.

The specialized plains hunters are typified by the Pavlovian culture of central Europe or the Aurignacian of France (which has long been acknowledged as an alien intrusion there from farther east). Many local

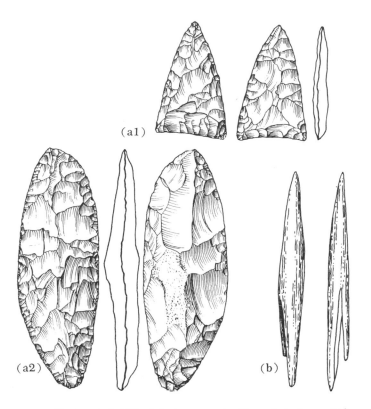

FIGURE 12–4. (a) *Bifacial stone projectile points from* (1) *Kostienki, and* (2) *Jerzmanowice.* (From François Bordes, *The Old Stone Age,* copyright © 1968 by World University Library, McGraw-Hill, Inc., New York. By permission of François Bordes and the publishers.); (b) *typical Aurignacoid split-base bone projectile point from Vogelherd, southern Germany.* (Modified from *Science,* vol. 152, no. 3726, p. 1201; copyright © 1966 by the American Association for the Advancement of Science. By permission of Hansjürgen Müller-Beck and *Science.*)

groups, going under their own names in each area, shared in this general tradition which we will call Aurignacoid ("Aurignacian-like") in the same sense as we previously used Mousteroid. Every local group, of course, had its own distinctive features, so that the common textbook concept of a continent-wide "Aurignacian" or "Gravettian" culture is misleading and best avoided. Even the survivals of older technical traditions (e.g., bifacial stone points) in conservative or highland areas of Europe and northern

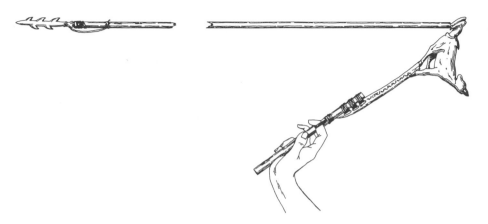

FIGURE   12–5. *Spear-thrower in use.* (Modified from drawing by Peter Storck.)

Asia became strongly influenced by the Aurignacoid tradition and hence differ sufficiently from their ancestral form to be considered as simply still other regional cultures within the range of variation of the Aurignacoid. Eventually, in the last half of the Würm maximum, the area occupied by these Aurignacoid cultures or strongly influenced by them embraced all Europe and northern Asia eastward as far as northern Japan and southward to the Ordos region of Inner Mongolia. Some Siberian Aurignacoid groups may have reached Alaska at this time; at any rate, they were living at Anangula on what is now Umnak Island in the Aleutians some 8,000 years ago, soon after the close of the Pleistocene. They never moved farther into the New World, however, although certain individual Aurignacoid traits were borrowed by the already existing population and spread widely in North America by diffusion.

In certain local areas on which we have detailed information, such as southwestern France (Dordogne), the history of this stage presents a very complex picture, and we can only assume that innumerable other local areas will prove to be equally complex and distinctive when they are

FIGURE   12–6.   *The Old World in the Homo sapiens phase.*

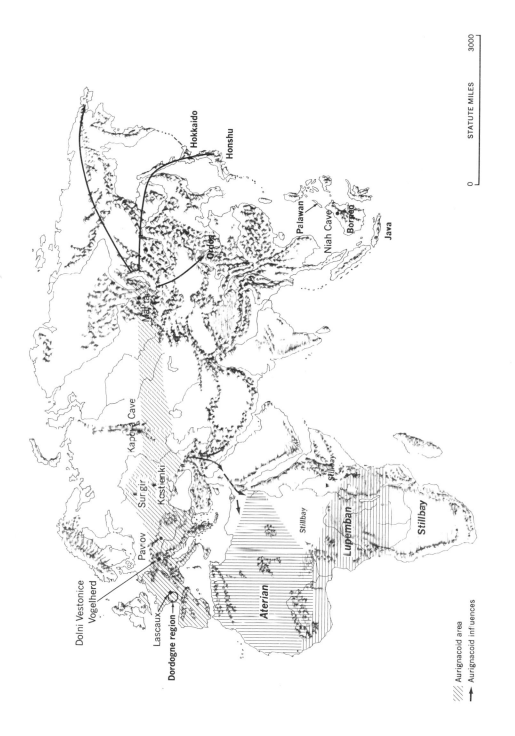

Dolni Vestonice
Vogelherd
Lascaux
Dordogne region
Pavlov
Sungir
Kostenki
Kapova Cave
Mal'ta
Ordos
Hokkaido
Honshu
Palawan
Niah Cave
Borneo
Java

Aterian
Stillbay
Lupemban
Stillbay
Stillbay
Stillbay

//// Aurignacoid area
——▶ Aurignacoid influences

0   STATUTE MILES   3000

better known. Traditionally, the Dordogne "Upper Paleolithic" is presented in textbooks as typifying, if not embodying, the story of man at this time; it is no more typical than any other locality: It is simply better known, but it can be cited as an example of the complexity of culture history now.[2] With respect to developments in eastern Europe, the Dordogne was initially "backward," showing a steady technological evolution, out of the preceding local Mousteroid industries, that is referred to as Early Perigordian (Perigordian O, I, II). This evolution was then abruptly interrupted by an incursion of alien Aurignacoid culture (and perhaps population as well) from central Europe: This is the classic French Aurignacian. After considerable change and development this was eventually replaced by later phases of the Perigordian tradition (III, IV—the "Upper Perigordian," a unique local culture with no counterpart elsewhere). Following this a different industry labeled "Proto-Magdalenian" appeared at two sites; its relationships are unclear as yet. At one site there was a Late Aurignacian, differing from the earlier.

The famous Solutrean (with its beautiful bifacial flintworking) now appeared on the scene—perhaps a conservative group from some neighboring area still practicing earlier techniques, as previously suggested. This vanished completely, replaced by a long developmental sequence of the Magdalenian, a brilliant and very distinctive culture characterized by an abundance of elaborate bone tools, some very small stone tools, and the richest efflorescence of art of any hunting people yet known. The high esteem enjoyed by this culture is primarily based on the art, and must be ascribed in large extent to the accidents of survival. We can never know how many other hunting peoples may have been equally talented but failed to leave their masterpieces for posterity in underground sanctuaries.

The Magdalenian spread over a considerable area of western Europe but seems to have had its center in southwestern France and immediately adjacent portions of Spain. At the close of the Pleistocene the Magdalenian of this area degenerated (perhaps because of the collapse of its affluent economic basis) into a simplified successor, known as Azilian, which retains no trace of the magnificent art tradition. Despite their wide variety, all of these cultural manifestations except the initial Early Perigordian can be considered as falling within the Aurignacoid tradition in the broad sense in which we are using the term.

adjacent areas

Outside of Europe and northern Asia, however, Aurignacoid influence was very limited, and old ways persisted much more strongly. In the Near East

---

[2] A considerable portion of this sequence is reflected in the cross section of the site of Laugerie-Haute Est shown in Figure 2–4.

there are industries that could be called partially Aurignacoid but which show considerable survivals of the old Mousteroid traditions. North Africa felt even less influence from these developments in Europe. The Nile Valley during most of the Upper Pleistocene seems to have been a very conservative area that clung to older ways of doing things as reflected in a technology based on prepared-platform flakes. Only with the Würm maximum does some Aurignacoid influence in the form of blade industries appear in this general region.

Northwestern Africa (Morocco, Algeria) was a stronghold of the Mousteroid tradition. By 30,000 years ago this local Mousteroid had evolved into a distinctive culture known as Aterian, characterized by artifacts with tangs to facilitate hafting—initially bifacial scrapers and knives. The Aterian developed into a more specialized plains hunting culture which apparently spread over most of the Sahara when it became game-rich grassland during the maximum of the last glaciation. In the closing stages of the Pleistocene the Aterians developed smaller bifacial tanged stone projectile points which are widely assumed to have been arrow points. There is thus the possibility that we have here the first (and perhaps only) invention of the bow—but this problem is far from settled. At least it seems certain that the bow was not one of the achievements of the major center of technical progress on the European plain.

Owing to the fact that the bow *may* have been a unitary invention that spread with great rapidity over almost the entire world, it is of very great interest as an example of culture process. However, tracing the history of such a perishable item is a difficult problem. Except in the rarest cases, only the points of the arrows survive in the archeological record, and their positive identification as such is not a foregone conclusion since very similar points were used on projectile spears. Arrow points are generally smaller, it is true, but this is not invariably the case, and where to draw the line is a perpetual problem. The conventional criteria of size and weight are arbitrary classifications and may or may not reflect reality. Moreover, plain, untipped, wooden arrows may often have been used: The oldest presently known find of actual bows and arrows (Stellmoor near Hamburg) contained 25 percent untipped arrows. Except in the few localities where wood may have survived, the only conclusive evidence of the presence of the bow and arrow would be its depiction in works of art, but the known examples of this are all of postglacial age. The best we can do at the moment is to hypothesize an origin in the general western Mediterranean area during the final phase of the Würm maximum and a spread in probably no more than 10,000 years over the entire world with the exception of Australia, reaching the Americas only in postglacial times.

Blade technique reached only a limited area of the coast of northwestern Africa at the close of the Pleistocene (Oranian culture)—presumably from Spain. Much more conspicuous all over northern Africa at this time is the widespread technical trend toward small stone tools.

FIGURE 12–7. *Rock paintings from Spain documenting use of bow and arrow.* (By permission from Hugo Obermaier, *Fossil Man in Spain,* copyright © 1924 by Hispanic Society of America.)

developments elsewhere in the Old World

The various regions of the rest of the world—sub-Saharan Africa, India, Southeast and East Asia, Australia, the Americas—were worlds apart, following their own paths, and old ways persisted in these areas down to quite recent times, albeit with significant local modifications in the course of time that were of importance to their own populations. It has been traditional to stress that from the viewpoint of world history these regions were bypassed by the main currents of change, though most were affected at the close of the Pleistocene or soon afterwards by the widespread technical trend toward small tools, and as we have mentioned, all except Australia ultimately shared in the bow and arrow. However, in spite of their isolation, these regional developments are of very great potential interest

for the study of culture process and human adaptation—the basic goals
of prehistory—and include many of the very best "test tubes" for such
studies. Furthermore, they represent the historical background of the bulk
of the world's present population, and for this reason alone can scarcely
be dismissed as inconsequential.

Africa south of the Sahara showed little change from the uniform
patterns of the Middle Pleistocene until the Early Würm, when, with the
first settlement of the forest regions, a dichotomy developed between the
hunters of the open grasslands (Fauresmith) and the forest-adapted
hunters and gatherers (Sangoan). From the beginning of the Homo
sapiens phase increasing regional adaptation is visible, causing the rise of
many local cultures. There was a general trend toward more specialized
tools and, except in the forests, toward lighter equipment. But the basic
division between life in the wetter forests and on the drier plains is still
clear. The former is reflected in various regional specializations (e.g.,
Lupemban) descended from the basic Sangoan of the preceding period and
characterized by bifacial core axes and other woodworking tools, lanceolate points for thrusting spears (the typical weapon of the hunter in dense
vegetation), and picks. Life on the plains is reflected in a number of regional variants evolved from the earlier Fauresmith that go under the
general label of Stillbay. Their technology was based on lightweight flake
tools from prepared cores, of which the leaf-shaped points, both bifacial
and unifacial, are most characteristic. However, there is no evidence of
projectile weapons until late in the phase, when the bow came into use.
The economy of the Stillbay cultures specialized in the hunting of certain
species of animals in each area.

Thus in the African continent during the Homo sapiens phase there
were two widespread specialized plains hunting cultures, Aterian and
Stillbay, which toward the close of the Pleistocene were both using projectiles. Both seem to represent local evolutions out of traditions of general
Mousteroid or similar type but were historically unrelated and hence somewhat different. And neither had any connection with the plains-adapted
hunting tradition of northern Eurasia. The African hunters were technologically much more conservative than the latter, perhaps because of
fewer pressures under the more comfortable African climate. For instance,
there seems to be no use of bone as a raw material anywhere in sub-
Saharan Africa, hardwood continuing to serve all needs.

In eastern Africa a few blade complexes (e.g., "Kenya Capsian")
appear quite late and evidently represent intruding groups from the north.
From these, the technique of blade making spread south at the close of
the Pleistocene and influenced local technology in many areas. Except for
blade making, the spread of the bow, and the limited contacts along the
southern edge of the Sahara between peoples occupying very different
ecological habitats (the Aterians and the forest dwellers), sub-Saharan
Africa was an isolated world.

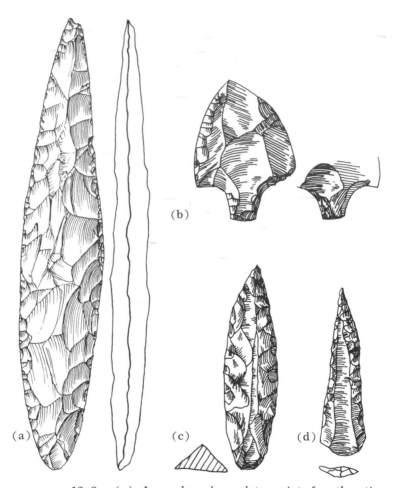

FIGURE 12–8. (a) *Lupemban lanceolate point for thrusting spear;* (b) *Aterian tanged point.* (From François Bordes, *The Old Stone Age,* copyright © 1968 by World University Library, McGraw-Hill, Inc., New York. By permission of François Bordes and the publishers.); (c) *Stillbay projectile point, partly bifacial;* (d) *Stillbay unifacial point.* (Modified from *Science,* vol. 150, no. 3698, p. 844; copyright © 1965 by the American Association for the Advancement of Science. By permission of J. Desmond Clark and *Science.*)

In contrast to the increasingly better-known picture of this time in Africa, the Indian subcontinent remains almost a blank. Very little archeological material is available that may reflect the period, and none of this is securely dated. Evidence has recently been offered for a flake culture with some prepared platforms labeled Middle Stone Age, which occurs stratigraphically between Acheulean and microlithic industries, and thus must belong somewhere in the Upper Pleistocene. Technologically, it corresponds to what we might expect to find at that time. The general trend in India is assumed to be broadly analogous to the situation in Africa: late survival of older flake technologies based on prepared platforms, a small amount of Aurignacoid influence very late in the Pleistocene, and a development of small tool (microlithic) industries at the end which may actually be post-Pleistocene. There has been some speculation as to whether the broad parallels between Africa and India represent mere convergence or actual historical relationships of some sort.

Even less is known about mainland Southeast Asia, which is assumed to be a very conservative area with the strongest persistence of old technical traditions, these presumably connected with a lack of stimulus for change in a stable and comfortable environment. The pebble chopper tradition seems to have persisted here right into postglacial times. The gap in our knowledge is unfortunate since some important movements of people may have been taking place in the area at this time, thought to be the homeland of the Australoid racial group. In island Southeast Asia, one remarkable site at Niah Cave, Borneo, has yielded a Homo sapiens skull radiocarbon dated at 40,000 years, but the artifacts in the site are too amorphous to tell us much or to point to any historical relationships. It would seem that the Upper Pleistocene people of this part of the world got along with a minimum of lithic technology and focused their attention on other matters. Early cave sites are now coming to light on the adjacent Philippine island of Palawan, with flake industries radiocarbon dated to at least 30,000 years; there is also the Sangiran flake industry associated with Solo Man in Java and dated at about 20,000 years ago.

In China, although we have specimens of the incipient Mongoloid population, this is perhaps the least-known prehistoric period and potentially one of the most important. For instance, it may have provided the source for one of the two major early traditions in the New World. But very few archeological remains are known (or thought) to come from this time, and the problems of dating them are, as always in China, difficult. Although some influences from the Aurignacoid sphere in northern Asia penetrated as far south as the Ordos region, China remained primarily an isolated world of its own, with strong persistence of older technological traditions, though probably not as conservative in this respect as Southeast Asia. Some use of blades appears, and south of the Ordos these may represent a local development out of older prepared-platform traditions. In an area like China considerable regional diversification may be expected with fuller evidence. Of the life and ecology of the time we can unfortunately say nothing.

The island world of Japan presents fascinating problems. Until 1949, despite extensive archeological work, there was no evidence that Japan had been occupied by man during the Pleistocene. In the few years since this first discovery at the Iwajuku site, some 500 other sites have come to light. However, it is still difficult to interpret this mass of material, and no coherent picture has yet emerged. The northern island of Hokkaido was connected to the continent throughout the last glaciation, and brief connections of the main island (Honshu) at Tsushima and Tsugaru Straits seem probable. Whether Japan was settled at a still earlier time is not yet clear but is not improbable. From the beginning the islands show the effects of isolation and developed distinctive flake cultures. They are not just a reflection of the adjacent mainland. For example, the ubiquitous East Asian chopper seemed absent entirely until the excavation in 1967 of the lower levels at the Hoshino site where an actual industry of general Choukoutien type is reported. However, it is not necessarily of equivalent age. Aurignacoid blade technique did diffuse to Hokkaido and thence into northern Honshu, but it is only one feature of local technology. And toward the close of the Pleistocene the familiar trend toward microlithic tool kits is apparent. But to a large extent Japan is *sui generis* now as later and has the potential for being an ideal laboratory for the study of cultural development under relatively controlled conditions.

human migrations

In addition to these technological and economic developments which took place in both the Aurignacoid and non-Aurignacoid world, the most important event in human history during the Homo sapiens phase was the essential completion of the secondary dispersal of mankind, with the occupation of the northern plain of Eurasia, the New World, and Australia–New Guinea. Only the oceanic islands of the Pacific and such offshore islands elsewhere as Madagascar or Crete remained unsettled for a short while longer until man became a true seafarer.

During times of lowered sea level, Australia and New Guinea formed a single land mass but always remained separated by deep water channels from adjacent Southeast Asia; (this accounts for their unique biological isolation over millions of years) Available evidence indicates that the first human settlement was by groups from Southeast Asia, probably around 25,000 years ago. This involved the ability to cross water barriers, though not necessarily very wide ones, the opposite shore being visible at least by the midpoint. No elaborate watercraft need to have been involved, although the geography of the region would have favored early experiments in water transportation. And water barriers were subsequently sufficient to keep

Australia free of many later influences (e.g., the bow and arrow) and to foster a state of relative isolation throughout its human history.

The first settlers, who were certainly the ancestors of the present aborigines, found a habitat considerably more inviting than at present over much of the island continent during the time of the Würm maximum. It was also in many ways a unique human habitat: There were no competing predatory animals, no hoofed game that was man's mainstay everywhere else (and hence no antler, horn, or ivory as raw materials), and for the most part only poor quality stone. They brought with them an extremely simple technology of unhafted flake tools that provides very monotonous archeological remains and showed no change whatever until about 5,000 years ago. Main dependence must have been on wooden spears and clubs, and the basic economy and pattern of life was essentially like that of the historic aborigines: one of generalized hunting and gathering. It is generally thought that the Pleistocene culture of the first settlers survived in Tasmania until European contact, perhaps isolated there for 8,000 or 9,000 years by the rising waters of Bass Strait and unaffected by postglacial developments in Australia itself. The Tasmanians are traditionally classed as the most primitive living group discovered by science, although their subsequent extinction was rapid. They were apparently the only humans still using unhafted tools.

We have previously noted that Asia and North America were joined by a land connection during the Riss and Early Würm glaciations, at which times animals crossed freely in both directions. However, we are not sure that man had as yet extended his range sufficiently northward to participate in such movements. The possibility of participation existed, but there is so far no satisfactory evidence that it occurred. There is an interesting broad comparability between the industries at Tingts'un in North China at the end of the Eemian and finds in western North America that suggest considerable antiquity but as yet cannot be dated.

During the Homo sapiens phase, free movement between Asia and Alaska was possible during the final glaciation (roughly 28,000 to 10,000 years ago) over the exposed continental shelf ("Bering Platform"), a level plain stretching up to 1,300 miles from north to south that doubtless offered an appealing habitat for herd animals and those that preyed upon them. This plain was unglaciated, and contemporary remains in Alaska indicate an abundant fauna at this general time despite the glacial climate, which may have been no worse than, say, that of France. Man was by now well able to thrive in such a habitat, on the strength of European evidence, provided the adaptation had been achieved, and there is no reason to believe that he was not exploiting this rich living here as elsewhere despite lack as yet of archeological traces. This lack is not so surprising when it is realized that virtually all the areas most attractive to men of that time, i.e., the level plains, are now submerged beneath the rising sea levels. The rugged highlands that comprise so much of today's dry land area (especially on the Asiatic side) would have had much less appeal. Also, it must be appreciated that Pleistocene archeology in this part of the world is in its infancy and that field work presents many difficulties.

For some 13,000 or more years during this final glaciation (from roughly 23,000 to 10,000 years ago or perhaps even later) the junction of the two Canadian ice sheets formed an impenetrable barrier to the east of Alaska, effectively sealing off further movement into interior North America. During this span of time Alaska should be thought of as actually forming part of Asia for all practical purposes. Access to interior North America would have been available during the times just before and just after this ice barrier. The 13,000 or so years of enforced isolation intervening were of equal importance for the course of New World history, both cultural and biological.

It may be said at the outset that there is no direct archeological evidence whatever in the Old World of this Pleistocene expansion into the New. Owing to the racial affinities of the American Indians and the indubitable evidence of the existence of the land connection, it is accepted as fact that the New World population came from Asia by this route. But many scholars have felt that this did not take place until the very end of the Pleistocene, i.e., not more than 13,000 years ago. However, American cultures of this date are very distinctive, and had they been carried directly from Asia at that time we would expect to find Asiatic ancestors closely resembling them. No such cultures exist in Asia, and any resemblances between Old and New World archeological materials are very distant and general. Thus such a theory of late migration is untenable. Moreover, the American Indians are genetically distinct both from modern Asian populations and from the Eskimos, and this situation would have required a longer period of isolation. The ice barrier provides a mechanism for just the amount of isolation needed to develop the distinctive features of the American cultures and populations. To clinch the matter there are now radiocarbon dates of 15,000 years for the human occupation of Wilson Butte Cave in Idaho, and 23,000 years for the Tlapacoya site near Mexico City, showing that man was demonstrably present during the time of the ice barrier and hence at the very latest must have entered interior North America at the beginning of the final glaciation, 28,000 to 23,000 years ago.

The complete isolation of the New World for 13,000 or more years, sealed off from the rest of mankind, provides a unique laboratory for the study of both cultural and genetic processes. Not only do we have the possibility of examining what took place, but also of comparing the picture at various stages with that in Alaska which was open to continuing Asiatic contact and with contemporary developments in the Old World. The major variable in studying man, the degree of cultural and biological interaction, is in this instance under control.

New World traditions

Archeological evidence of the settling of the Americas must be deduced from New World materials. The Pleistocene archeological remains represent two distinct major technological traditions: one characterized by bifacial stone projectile points and one characterized mainly by crude, often heavy, unhafted stone implements and initially lacking any projectile points. It is obvious that the two traditions must have had very different origins and histories. The crudity of the nonpoint tradition suggests considerable age, and its nearest affinities would seem to lie in such East Asian industries as Tingts'un. (However, none of its manifestations have as yet been securely dated, and we know from the late survival of crude technologies elsewhere that purely typological dating is unreliable.) Although the growing quantity of material of this tradition, often from situations that are possibly of considerable age, makes it increasingly probable that it does in fact represent very old, if not the oldest, settlements, just what age range is involved, and what the actual history of this tradition may be, cannot be determined on the basis of available data.

No less mystery surrounds the bifacial projectile-point tradition, which is well known and firmly dated back to 13,000 years ago. Beyond that its history is a blank in the archeological record. Yet it must have been developing in isolation in the New World for some time to reach its distinctive form when we first see it, and we may infer on geological grounds, as explained above, that its arrival in North America could have been no later than 23,000 years ago. Even at this time horizon its Asiatic roots are not evident, a situation that has baffled scholars for many years and has led to some unnecessarily unbridled theorizing. It is unrelated to the Aurignacoid tradition and must thus have sprung from some still earlier cultural background in Siberia, perhaps with Mousteroid affinities.[3]

The earliest well-dated projectile-point industries in the New World we will label Older Llano; they belong to a period approximately 13,000 to 11,000 years ago and seem restricted to the southwestern United States and northern Mexico. Their characteristic feature is a distinctive fluted point (the so-called "Clovis point") for spears presumably propelled by a spear-thrower, and they were specialized hunters of mammoth, horse, and camel. Our knowledge of their culture is limited, for with one exception (Blackwater Draw) the remains are all kill sites, not living places.

At the very close of the Pleistocene, the descendants of the Older Llano expanded widely into other areas. On the high plains we find the Folsom industry with its very distinctive fluted Folsom point, whose bearers specialized in hunting an extinct species of bison by mass methods. The abrupt disappearance of the favorite quarry of their immediate predecessors, especially the mammoth, makes one wonder if the Older Llano

[3] For a possible solution recently advanced, see Müller-Beck, 1966.

hunters had not had a deadly effect on their chosen species, at least in this part of North America. Groups of industries classified as Younger Llano, with Clovis-type points, spread over eastern North America at this time, including formerly glaciated regions, while the Toldense of southern South America represents the first documented human migration into this continent, presumably following the Cordillera down through Central America. All the fluted point industries died out about 9,000 years ago. Again, little is known about their life and culture outside the hunting aspect, nor, in marked contrast to all other continents, do we yet have any undisputed remains of the people themselves.

In the region west of the Rocky Mountains, groups representing the non-projectile-point tradition were undoubtedly present at this same time if not far earlier, presumably practicing a more generalized economy. In wetter Late Pleistocene times, the entire Great Basin with its numerous lakes may have been a focus of human activity, with a considerable exodus as conditions deteriorated at the close of the Pleistocene. The earliest dated sites in the general area are from this time and are forerunners of the so-called "desert cultures" of the early postglacial period. The archeological evidence now available has led E. L. Davis to postulate the existence at this time of a western lithic cotradition of considerable time depth, stretching from Wyoming to Baja California, whose characteristic heavy tools reflect a predominantly woodworking technology. Its settlements were largely associated with now-vanished lakes.

With improved climatic conditions in the far north toward the end of the Pleistocene, groups descended from or influenced by the Aurignacoid tradition of Siberia crossed the Bering Platform, at the edge of which we find their descendants not long afterwards at the Anangula site in the Aleutians. These groups evidently penetrated no farther into the New World than Alaska, but individual Aurignacoid traits and ideas diffused southward, e.g., burins, previously unknown in America. They therefore constitute a third major tradition entering the New World, but one of very limited distribution. Presumably they represent the ancestors of the Arctic Mongoloids, a racial group including the Eskimo which differs genetically from the American Indians. They would reflect the northeastern Siberian population at a time 10,000 to 15,000 years later than that from which the Indians had been drawn. This third, terminal Pleistocene tradition of Aurignacoid affinities formed the basis for the subsequent development of Eskimo culture.

Perhaps the major enigma of early New World prehistory is the 10,000 to 15,000 year gap between the arrival of the bearers of the projectile-point tradition and their first appearance in the archeological record with well-developed fluted points unlike anything elsewhere in the world. The quantity and variety of fluted points that have been found in the southeastern United States suggests a possible developmental area here— but not one of these has been dated. One might also hypothesize that the sudden appearance archeologically of big-game hunters on the plains about

Anangula

Wilson Butte
Cave

Folsom
Clovis &
Blackwater
Draw

Tlapacoya

Approximate extent of Würm
glaciation ca. 13,000 B.P.
Dotted llnes indicate interpolated
boundaries and solid lines indicate
known boundaries as of 13,000 B.P.

Shaded area indicates approximate extent of
Bering Land Bridge during The Würm Maximum
(ca. 18,000-20,000 B.P.).

FIGURE   12–9.   *North America in the terminal Pleistocene.*

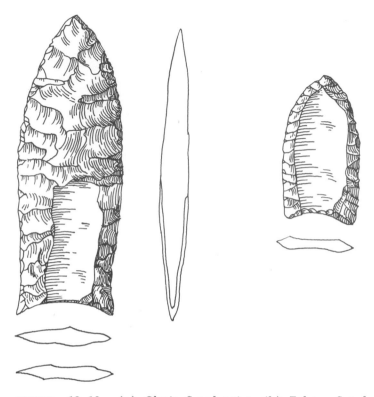

FIGURE 12–10. (a) *Clovis fluted point;* (b) *Folsom fluted point.* (Modified from *Science,* vol. 152, no. 3726, pp. 1202, 1205; copyright © 1966 by the American Association for the Advancement of Science. By permission of Hansjürgen Müller-Beck and *Science.*)

13,000 years ago was in fact their first appearance and that their ancestors had pursued a more generalized type of economy in a different area of North America.

reference

Müller-Beck, Hansjürgen: "Paleohunters in America: Origins and Diffusion," *Science,* vol. 152, pp. 1191–1210, 1966.

suggested readings

Bordes, François: *The Old Stone Age*, McGraw-Hill Book Company, New York, 1968, pp. 147–241.

Clark, J. Desmond: "The Late Pleistocene Cultures of Africa," *Science*, vol. 150, pp. 833–847, 1965.

Cole, Sonia: *The Prehistory of East Africa*, Mentor Books, New York, 1965, pp. 161–219.

Mulvaney, D. J.: "The Prehistory of the Australian Aborigine," *Scientific American*, vol. 214, no. 3, pp. 84–93, 1966.

Willey, Gordon R.: *An Introduction to American Archaeology*, vol. 1, Prentice-Hall, Inc., Englewood Cliffs, N.J., 1966, pp. 26–77.

the Homo sapiens phase: 2

Aurignacoid technology

Available information makes it possible to picture to some extent the life of the Aurignacoid, specialized big-game hunters of Europe and northern Asia, but it must continually be borne in mind that this was not the pattern of life in the rest of the world.[1] Even the Mediterranean shores of southern Europe would have provided quite a different ecological setting with a temperate fauna and a correspondingly different pattern of life. On the other hand, we must assume that intellectual capabilities and "humanity" were at least *potentially* at an equal level elsewhere and thus that culture may have reached the heights revealed in France in other areas where it has not been preserved or discovered. Western Europeans of this time can hardly have been the unique supermen so often depicted.[2] At the same time, cultures of the Aurignacoid tradition may be representative of the most highly developed end of the cultural spectrum of those times, and we know that others must have been less complicated ("underdeveloped"), since this is the normal picture at any stage in human history.

During the final Würm glaciation, an active hunting life on the plains

[1] At the very end of this period (13,000 to 10,000 years ago) there were big-game hunters on the North American plains, as we have seen, but they were the product of a different tradition unrelated to the Aurignacoid, and we know very little as yet about their actual life. The same could be said about the hunters of the African plains.

[2] "[After Neanderthal] we are so grateful to encounter somebody like Cro-Magnon man— somebody who looks like us—that we tend to endow him with more than his share of virtues. . . . He is all too often depicted as a kindly, philosophical fellow with pure motives and noble thoughts, who spent a good deal of his time gently instructing bright-eyed boys in the arts of tool-making and cave painting" (Howell, 1965, p. 170).

of northern Eurasia presupposes skin clothing, and the appearance of real eyed needles during at least the latter half shows that the capability for making efficient tailored garments existed. It was postulated that these might have resembled the costume of modern northern hunters like the Eskimo, which is presumed to have some antiquity. Possible representation of such a costume on Aurignacoid figurines from Siberia lent support, and confirmation now seems provided by a Cro-Magnon burial recently excavated at the Sungir site near the city of Vladimir in European Russia. Because the garments of the deceased had been richly decorated with ivory beads, it was possible to reconstruct their form as a pullover shirt with round neck and a pair of trousers with boots. There was also trace of some other upper garment or head covering. Since the find predates the final glacial advance, conditions may not have been severe enough for a hood or parka-type head protection such as seems depicted on the Siberian figurines of somewhat later age. In addition to the decorated garments, numerous bracelets and necklaces of ivory, fox teeth, shells, etc., have been found on this and other burials of the Homo sapiens phase. Adornment was evidently now an important part of costume as well as an aesthetic expression.

The dead of this time were buried within the settlement or rock shelter; at least the known examples are so situated. The deceased was laid out in all his finery—either extended on the back or flexed (fashions varied with area and period in such matters then and later). A few items of equipment were usually provided, and very characteristically the corpse was heavily sprinkled with red ochre—a custom that has a wide distribution in later prehistoric times. The purpose—whether aesthetic (perhaps to restore a more lifelike hue) or more supernatural—is unknown, but it was obviously considered of vital importance to early Homo sapiens, as placing flowers on a grave is to us.

Although we are dealing with the classic "cave men" of grade-school books, the great majority did not live in caves, although in areas where natural shelter was available it was utilized at least seasonally (winter), as has been done by people of later times, though no one sees fit to dub them "cave men" also. As pointed out before, the vast majority of such refuges were overhanging rock shelters rather than actual caves. Although direct evidence is lacking, it is widely assumed that skin or brush windbreaks were erected on the open side. Stone partitions in caves have been found in at least one case. But open settlements and artificial shelters must have been the more usual pattern. The best examples of these have been excavated in Czechoslovakia, in southern European Russia, and near Irkutsk in Siberia. Although there is no question that these floor plans represent habitations, it is extremely difficult to reconstruct them with any confidence. In most cases they seem to have been small round one-family habitations 12 to 18 feet in diameter, partly sunk into the ground and perhaps roofed over with skins supported on some sort of framework. Large bones or tusks might be used for various purposes in construc-

FIGURE 13–1. *Early Homo sapiens burial from Sungir, European Russia, showing remains of clothing.* (Photo courtesy of O. Bader, Institute of Archaeology, Moscow.)

tion. At Mal'ta in Siberia and at Dolni Vestonice in Czechoslovakia there is some evidence for separate summer dwellings nearby. Two or three such single-family dwellings were in some cases combined into a larger structure, but still preserving the identity of the component units. A three-family combination might be almost 40 feet long and 15 feet wide. Examples of still larger structures—real "long houses"—are known in southern Russia, and in one case one is almost 450 feet long but still maintains a width of no more than 17 feet. It contains ten hearths which are considered to represent as many families. What the superstructure may have looked like it is impossible to say, although a gable roof has been postulated. However, many scholars find it difficult to believe that an area this size could have been covered over. Perhaps they may have been simply fenced enclosures containing separate family huts. Such dwellings seem to have been occupied for a great many years, judging by the debris, but we do not know whether occupancy was year-round or only in winter. Settlements consisted of two to five dwellings, and most of them seem to represent a band of five to ten families, which may be the typical social group at this time. (Sometimes settlements contained up to twenty families, however.)

The Aurignacoid economy seems to have been based on specialized, systematic exploitation of a particular species of gregarious (herd) animal, most often horse or mammoth, or, during the Magdalenian in western Europe, reindeer—(an all-purpose animal providing not only food but raw materials such as skins, sinews, bone, and antler.) Over 80 percent of the animal bones in any site tend to be from one such species. Much of this must represent steady predation (e.g., the remains of 100 young mammoths at Dolni Vestonice), with the really big mass kills occurring only seasonally during semiannual migrations, on analogy with historic arctic reindeer hunters. The hunting of large herd animals by any method presupposes cooperative activity, which must have been highly developed by this time. With mammoths, attention focused on young animals, presumably more tasty and less wary. It is possible that people followed the game herds in summer: There is evidence of this pattern of life toward the close of the Pleistocene in northern Germany at least, and the Magdalenians of France remained in their caves only during the coldest months of winter. On the other hand, some settlements in central and eastern Europe seem to have been occupied the year around.

Hunting equipment had remained rather crude and unimproved throughout human history, we will recall, with attention focused on techniques of coming to grips with the prey. Now we see the first major breakthrough in the widespread employment of projectile weapons, and by the

FIGURE 13–2. *Reconstruction of dwelling at Pushkari on the Russian plain. (After Boriskovskii.)*

end of the Pleistocene a variety of composite weapons is available to the hunter—spears (some with detachable heads), barbed harpoons, arrows—all involving the principle of *hafting*. During the Magdalenian it became customary to hunt reindeer with barbed harpoons whose heads were almost surely detachable though perhaps fastened by a cord to the shaft. Presumably the dragging shaft would impede escape and bring the animal down much faster. Mechanical devices for propulsion were the spear-thrower—the typical Aurignacoid device—and, much later, the bow. But even when equipped with projectiles, getting close to the animal—usually within 30 feet—represents the major investment of the primitive hunter.

Large numbers of ptarmigan and hares in some sites imply extensive use of snares, and fish remains indicate techniques for fishing had been developed. Lack of any deep sea fish in European sites argues against the existence of adequate watercraft as yet.

Food-grinding equipment at some sites for the processing of plant

FIGURE 13–3. *Magdalenian bone tools:* (a) *spear-thrower;* (b) *bone point with beveled base;* (c–f) *harpoons;* (g) *wand;* (h) *shaft straightener.* (Modified from *Science*, vol. 142, no. 3590, p. 351; copyright © 1963 by the American Association for the Advancement of Science. By permission of Denise de Sonneville-Bordes and *Science*.)

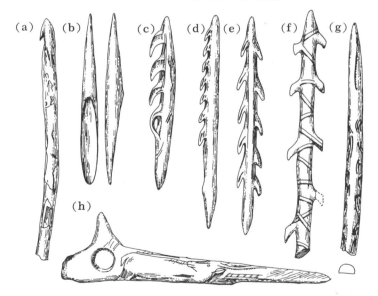

foods such as seeds indicates that the diet did not entirely consist of meat. Until recently, such grinding equipment had been regarded as unknown before postglacial times, where it was viewed as a first step toward food production and the farming life. On the northern tundra, however, with its limited vegetation, plant foods were probably of minor importance.

The rise to prominence of bone as a raw material is one of the most conspicuous features of Aurignacoid technology. And under bone we include horn, ivory, and antler—the latter especially widely used. Bone has advantages over stone: It is possible to make much larger implements such as hoes and shovels, or things that could not be made of stone such as needles, fishhooks, barbed fish spears, flutes, or whistles. Bone has elastic properties: Bone points do not break as easily as stone ones and detach more readily from the shaft where this is desired. Many indirect conse- quences flowed from the development of bone technology, such as more effective hunting, productive fishing for the first time, efficient tailored clothing through sewing, and the ability to live in and expand into new areas where hardwood was not available. As mentioned previously, the ability to work bone effectively depended on wide use and development of the burin. Most bone artifacts were worked down from splinters or small strips cut from larger, heavy bones or antlers by gouging two parallel

---

FIGURE   13–4.   *Groove and splinter technique of working bone.* (Modified from drawing by Peter Storck.)

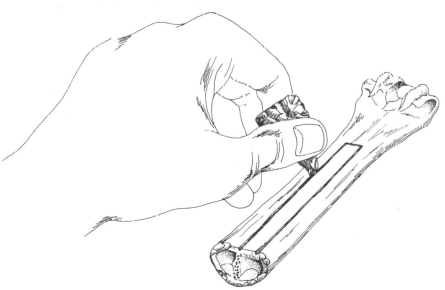

grooves with a burin through to the hollow or spongy center and dislodging the piece between—the so-called "groove and splinter technique."

There are also a number of other interesting technological advances, such as the first musical instruments (flutes and whistles), the use of coal as fuel at Petrkovice, and the firing of clay figurines at Pavlov and Dolni Vestonice—an achievement until recently assumed to be beyond the capabilities of Pleistocene man. The presence of marine shells in Czechoslovakia and Atlantic salmon vertebrae as ornaments on the Riviera suggests the beginnings of long-distance trade.

intellectual life

The appearance and development of recognizable art is our best barometer that early Homo sapiens had already evolved to an intellectual and psychic level comparable to modern man. There are occasional glimmerings of aesthetic sensibilities earlier, it is true, such as evident pride in craftsmanship for its own sake and prizing of unusual objects perhaps for the pleasure they provided (although there may have been other reasons for this). Nor can we entirely discount the possibility that artistic expression may have been developing in perishable media, such as wood carving or body decoration. But now the aesthetic aspect of human life is firmly documented.

Occurrences of art are sufficiently widespread throughout the area of the Aurignacoid tradition to indicate that this is an essential element of it. We must assume that people elsewhere in the world at this time had some sort of artistic expression, but we would expect it to assume different forms, as reflecting different cultural traditions. As yet, we have no certain examples. Even our information on Aurignacoid art is spotty, reflecting the accidents of survival and recovery. The available evidence suggests certain centers of efflorescence rather than widespread uniform development. The highest achievements were reached in only limited areas. Yet these areas are known to us precisely because the art was executed on materials or in locations with maximum survival potential. We have no way of knowing what percentage of the total output this represents. The people who painted on cave walls may also have painted on skins—as may people who had no caves available. Those who carved in stone and ivory may also have carved in wood. (Thus our present picture of restricted achievement may be more apparent than real:) Genius was not necessarily restricted to France and vicinity. We can feel sure of the development of this new achievement throughout the phase with the finest expressions toward the end and an amazing continuity of the basic styles over this long span of time, further validating the continuity and broad relationship of the Aurignacoid tradition itself. No other artistic tradition has so long a history, suggesting the conservatism of attitude and outlook at this stage of human history.

It has been the traditional view that this art vanished abruptly at the end of the Pleistocene, with no reawakening of aesthetic skill or interest until many thousands of years later. This unlikely situation has been exaggerated. But it is true that the finest developments had no visible effect on the future and were a dead end just as the highly specialized Aurignacoid tradition was itself a dead end in terms of the subsequent evolution of human culture. In any case, it presents an interesting problem in culture process.

Aurignacoid art took many forms: paintings in outline or in flat wash that might be a single color or polychrome; crude finger tracings in soft clay; engravings of varying depth, crude or delicate; carvings and sculptures in low relief or in the round; and modeling in clay. In size they range from tiny figurines and engraved decoration on artifacts to imposing paintings life size or larger. The smaller art forms utilized ivory, antler, bone, fired clay, and suitable stone; larger forms are found on limestone slabs, on stream pebbles, or in soft clay; the largest are on walls and ceilings of caves and rock shelters. For engraving and carving, flint burins of various types and sizes were employed. For painting, their pigments were red and yellow ochre, oxide of manganese, and kaolin, applied with the fingers and perhaps with a spatula, a crude brush such as the frayed end of a twig, or a pad of fur. Some effects seem to have been produced by spraying pigment through a tube. Most of the powdered pigments must have been made into paint by the addition of a liquid binder whose identity has not been established.

The drawings and paintings involve a major intellectual breakthrough: the epoch-making discovery of how to represent in two dimensions what is perceived in three. It is hard for us to realize the significance of this discovery because you and I take this for granted, forgetting that we have to be taught to understand a two-dimensional picture, which bears much the same relation to reality as a map does to the landscape it represents.

Despite the considerable variety of artistic expression, there is a definite homogeneity in subject matter, composition, and the realism with which this is portrayed. This is essentially an animal art; regardless of size or medium, it is nearly always inspired by the animal world. Vegetation is almost never depicted. Portrayals of human figures are a small minority: Most of them occur as figurines or as relief or carving on rock slabs or rock shelter walls. Only in rare cases are they realistic, such as the sculptured head from Brassempouy shown on the cover and from Dolni Vestonice (Figure 13–5). Commonly they are stylized, exaggerated, or clumsily executed, sometimes by the same artists, probably, who were capable of superb portrayals of animals. There are also a certain number of signs and geometrical figures whose significance is unknown, as well as decorative patterns on artifacts.

But it is the animals that are the obvious concern of the Aurignacoid artists, and not all the animals with which they must have been familiar,

FIGURE 13–5. *Sculptured head from Dolni Vestonice.* (After Absolon.)

but precisely those that were hunted and around which their lives revolved: wild cattle, bison, horse, deer, boar, ibex, mammoth, rhinoceros, bear, reindeer, muskox. Smaller food items such as birds, fish, or seals are portrayed only rarely. Predators such as lions and wolves with which man had to contend on occasion appear sparingly. This preoccupation is hardly surprising since it is the product of a specialized big-game hunting pattern of life exemplified in other aspects of culture as well.

Aurignacoid art is basically realistic, and the animals are shown in their customary attitudes. Poses are often rigid, and execution is sometimes clumsy, but the subjects are also depicted running, leaping, and grazing. The aim was to represent the animals as they really looked; only rarely do they appear in a stylized or schematic fashion. Realistic portrayal, however, usually took the form not so much of producing images as close as possible to the real objects, but rather in portraying a characteristic attitude or a distinguishing feature of the species, with the rest of the details mostly ignored.

In the presentation of this subject matter, no attempt was made to

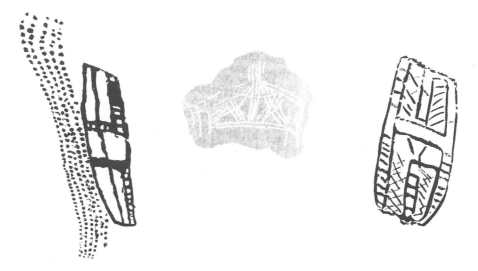

FIGURE 13–6. *Examples of painted signs and tectiforms.* (From P. J. Ucko and Andrée Rosenfeld, *Palaeolithic Cave Art,* copyright © 1967 by World University Library, McGraw-Hill, Inc., New York. By permission of the authors and the publishers.)

FIGURE 13–7. *Geometric design on bracelet of mammoth ivory from Mezin.* (After Shovkoplias.)

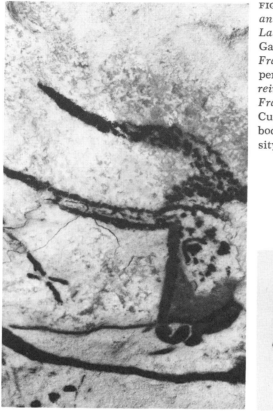

FIGURE 13–8. *Cave paintings of animals:* left: *bull's head from Lascaux, France.* (From Ann and Gale Sieveking, *The Caves of France and Northern Spain.* By permission of the authors.); right: *reindeer from Font-de-Gaume, France.* (After George G. Mac-Curdy, by permission of the Peabody Museum, Harvard University.)

indicate scenery or background, and the animal figures are almost invariably scattered about in total disregard of proportion. Large and small animals may be shown in identical size, or a bison be reduced to fit between the legs of a horse. Animals of the most diverse species appear mixed together in seeming confusion. Superimposition is common.

There is a continuing debate over the purpose of Pleistocene art: Were these first artists inspired by the same motives as those of modern times? Was this art purely aesthetic in nature? From the fact that some of it is so located in perpetual darkness and inconvenient positions that it could scarcely have been readily enjoyed for its own sake, some have argued that the concept of art for art's sake did not yet exist and that the motivation could only have been magical and religious. But art could serve many purposes here as elsewhere, and the primitive artist of today does not draw the distinctions we do. The argument over the "purpose" of prehistoric art is a conflict that exists only in the minds of modern

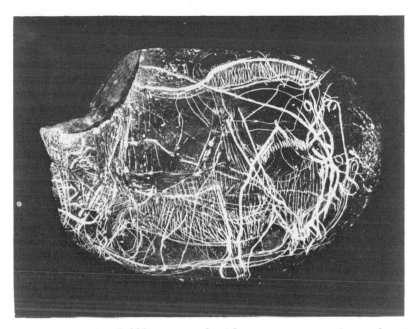

FIGURE 13–9. *Pebble engraved with numerous superimposed animals, from La Colombiere rock shelter, France.* (Courtesy of H. L. Movius, Jr., and Hugh Hencken.)

scholars. As Jacquetta Hawkes has said, our attempt to separate art and magic and religion in the unified life of early man merely shows the folly of the overanalytical mind. The Pleistocene artists could work in the service of magic, if need be, and still remain artists.

categories of art

Aurignacoid art falls into three categories reflecting different patterns of thought and behavior. We will call these portable art, rock art, and cave art. Portable art (*Art mobilier*, or home art, as it is sometimes called) consists of small objects always found in living sites and hence associated with everyday life. This is the earliest expression of art, appearing at the beginning of the Homo sapiens phase and persisting all through it. It is also by far the commonest and most widespread category. Portable art takes the form of engravings, carvings, and some modeling; paint is never used, although people may well have been painting decorations on their

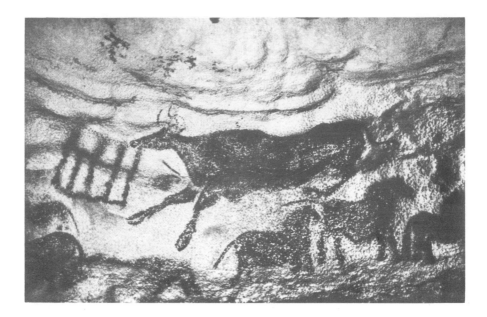

FIGURE 13–10. *Portion of the cave wall at Lascaux, showing grouping of animals and geometric figure.* (Courtesy of Paolo Graziosi, *Palaeolithic Art,* copyright © 1960 by Casa Editrice G. C. Sansoni, Florence, Italy.)

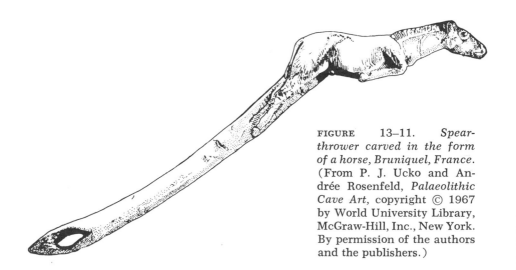

FIGURE 13–11. *Spearthrower carved in the form of a horse, Bruniquel, France.* (From P. J. Ucko and Andrée Rosenfeld, *Palaeolithic Cave Art,* copyright © 1967 by World University Library, McGraw-Hill, Inc., New York. By permission of the authors and the publishers.)

bodies and, for all we know, on perishable items. The most abundant examples are decorations applied to various items of equipment (e.g., spear-throwers) or to objects intended to be worn as ornaments.

Closely related to this home art and inspired by the same motivations would be the assembling (construction) of tasteful and artistic necklaces, etc., of shells and other attractive materials for personal adornment, and the decoration of clothing, both of which were evidently widespread. In addition to engravings on artifacts, there are a small number of animal figures in the round. Insofar as purpose can be isolated, the motivation of all of this would seem to be aesthetic—art for art's sake, or the satisfaction of the owner.

By far the most interesting and distinctive form of home art, however, are the human female figurines, traditionally if somewhat ironically called "Venuses." Many of these figures are fat and emphasize female characteristics such as breasts and hips or buttocks, with limbs and face largely ignored. Some may be intended to represent pregnancy. There has been a strong temptation to see these as reflecting a fertility cult and to liken them to the "mother goddess" figurines of early farming peoples; some even postulate a direct continuity. But the ideological requirements of farmers are very different from those of hunters, and such extrapolations are shaky. Hunting peoples are not concerned with fertility: The abundance of game is controlled by supernatural forces, not by reproduc-

FIGURE 13–12. *Bison carving, La Madeleine, France.* (From André Leroi-Gourhan, *Treasures of Prehistoric Art,* copyright © 1967 by Editions d'Art Lucien Mazenod. By permission of the publishers and Jean Vertut.)

tion, and human families are small. To our minds, perhaps, a fat woman may symbolize fertility: But it has been remarked that fat women are no more fertile than skinny ones—just softer, warmer, and more conspicuously well fed. If the "Venus" figurines did serve any magico-religious function, it was strictly a family affair, in contrast to the sanctuaries to be discussed presently which doubtless represent a group activity. But they may represent nothing more than gratification of the erotic senses—being Pleistocene pinup girls, reflecting the ideal beauty of that far-off time.

The category we have labeled rock art is also found in living sites and is thus associated with everyday life. There is no evidence of its use for magical practices, it is readily visible, and we therefore suppose that the aesthetic impulse was paramount in the eyes of its creators. It appears in the record almost as early as the portable art and may not be basically

FIGURE 13–13. *Baked clay "Venus" from Dolni Vestonice.* (From E. and J. Neustupny, *Czechoslovakia,* copyright © 1961 by Thames and Hudson Limited, London. By permission of the publishers.)

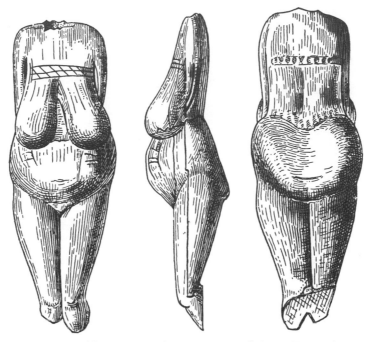

FIGURE   13–14.   *Mammoth ivory "Venus" from Kostienki on the Russian plain.* (After Efimenko.)

---

separable from the latter except that it is mostly nonportable. Rock art consists of bas reliefs, engravings, and drawings on the walls and ceilings of rock shelters and cave mouths, or on slabs of rock or large stream pebbles. Most of the realistic depictions of human beings occur here, although the emphasis again is primarily sexual. Stylistic kinship to the "Venus" figurines is obvious, and the function, whatever it may have been, reflects the same ideas. Though a distinctive feature of rock art, portrayals of human figures (often only portions) are still in the minority; most portrayals are of the animal world.

Cave art is not associated with living sites and hence its dating and cultural attribution are difficult. However, it seems to have been a later development, and the vast majority of known examples are assigned to the Magdalenian culture of southwestern France and adjacent northern Spain toward the close of the Pleistocene.[3] Since it occurs in concentra-

[3] Of great interest is the recent discovery by Soviet scientists of cave paintings in Kapova Cave in the southern Ural Mountains. Many thousands of miles separate these from the Magdalenian center, and the numerous central European caves in between have revealed no trace of paintings.

FIGURE   13–15.   *Low relief of reclining woman on cave wall at La Mag-delaine, France.* (From P. J. Ucko and Andrée Rosenfeld, *Palaeolithic Cave Art,* copyright © 1967 by World University Library, McGraw-Hill, Inc., New York. By permission of the authors and the publishers.)

---

tions in the innermost galleries of caves, always in total darkness, and often difficult of access, a magico-religious purpose is widely assumed and the locations are often termed sanctuaries. The numerous superimposed figures contribute to the impression of nonaesthetic motives. This category contains the highest achievements of Pleistocene art: the often life-sized paintings and engravings on cave walls and ceilings, along with many smaller ones. There are also a very few animals modeled in the round in plastic clay. Most of the enigmatic geometric and other signs and figures accompany these paintings. Portrayals of human figures (here all males, incidentally) occur only rarely and are unrealistic or at best clumsily executed in contrast to the animals. Some of the most famous human figures are disguised as animals. They have conventionally been termed shamans or sorcerers, as if the presence of these seemed called for in a sanctuary. But masks and disguises are almost universal among primitive peoples and serve many purposes, some symbolic and some as utilitarian as stalking game within close range.

What went on in these sanctuaries and what function the art played in any such proceedings are matters of conjecture in which many fertile

FIGURE 13–16. *Low relief sculptures of cattle from Bourdeilles, France.* (Courtesy of Jean Vertut.)

FIGURE 13-17. *Wall engravings from Teyjat, France.* (From Ann and Gale Sieveking, *The Caves of France and Northern Spain.* By permission of the authors.)

imaginations have enjoyed free rein. Turning for insights to ethnography, we know that preoccupation with the supernatural and the practice of sympathetic magic are universal among primitive peoples everywhere, and we may reasonably assume that they were also characteristic of Homo sapiens at the end of the Pleistocene, not so long ago. Also widespread is a feeling that the supernatural aspect of hunting is the most important and that if this is properly attended to, the game will fall readily into the hands of the hunter; if not, no amount of skill will succeed. Beyond such basic attitudes, there is such tremendous variation among living primitives that we can infer nothing further about the beliefs of prehistoric man on ethnographic evidence.

Certainly the preoccupation of cave art with food animals suggests a connection with hunting, and the location and nature of the sanctuaries suggest magical or religious motivation. The use of these sanctuaries for sympathetic magic has been widely assumed: To pierce the picture of an animal with your weapon, or even to depict an animal pierced with weapons, will bring about the desired result in actuality. Yet except for a clay bear pierced by holes made with spears, there are very few examples of the former; and while at Lascaux, for instance, there are pictures that have been claimed to depict wounded animals and weapons, these are a small minority and other interpretations can be suggested. Nor can the portrayal of some pregnant or copulating animals be cited as fertility magic, as mentioned before. More likely, it simply reflects the well-known fact that animals heavy with young or preoccupied with sexual activity are easy to kill.

It is possible that careful excavation of the floor of an undisturbed sanctuary might reveal clues as to the activity carried on there, but this has never been done and is probably impossible now unless new sanctuaries come to light in the future, untrampled by modern feet. If the paintings themselves were intended to convey meaning, some better understanding may result from careful study of groups of figures and their interrelationships and of the puzzling signs and nonanimal figures. This is the direction now being taken by the most promising research.[4] For the present, the sanctuaries—if that is indeed what they are—retain their mystery.

Great interest has recently been aroused by a number of examples of rows of markings on bone that are interpreted by some as representing the recording of a crude lunar calendar. This further possible evidence of man's awareness and intellectual activity—and efforts at recording—is now undergoing further study.

summary and conclusions

In our story of man's development we have now reached a point where we can begin to imagine a fellow feeling with these prehistoric men for the

[4] See for instance Leroi-Gourhan, 1968.

first time. As Jacquetta Hawkes so deftly puts it, we should certainly still have felt ill at ease with the Neanderthalers. In their successors we can more easily see our own ancestors, and the evidence of their intellectual life in the form of art gives us the first opportunity to enter into communion with their minds, emotions, and imaginations. At this stage also it first becomes possible to recognize actual human societies rather than just traditions in stone technology.

The major developments at this stage of human history were the sudden acceleration of the rate of change as compared with the two million or so years preceding; the appearance of economic specialization which made possible adaptation to new environments hitherto unexploited as well as more effective use of old ones; and the resultant secondary expansion of the human stock to occupy virtually all of the habitable world.

The rather sudden acceleration of cultural evolution at this time is an enigma without ready explanation. There is no major technological "revolution" to account for it (as with later changes of tempo) Nor is there clear evidence of significant improvement in man himself. A full-sized brain had been achieved long before with no concomitant change in material culture, toolmaking traditions, or geographical distribution. Perhaps through some physiological change the Homo sapiens brain was more efficient than its predecessors. The sudden increase in tempo at this time is as much of a problem as is the long stagnation of the Middle Pleistocene. But it must be emphasized that this did not represent a break with the past, as so often portrayed in the older literature, but rather a direct evolution out of what had gone before, culturally as well as biologically. Also, the significance of the acceleration is perhaps exaggerated, due to our almost exclusive focusing on Europe where most of the changes occurred.

The most striking economic differentiation is seen in the specialized hunters of the game-rich open country: the tundra, steppe, plains, and savannah. The key item in their economy was projectile weapons—the first real change and improvement in hunting technique since the Lower Pleistocene: first javelins propelled by spear throwers, later arrows shot from bows. The older view that the Homo sapiens phase marked the shift to big-game hunting is misleading; what we see now is more efficient big-game hunting providing a richer living, due both to better equipment and also to the new ability to live in areas where big game was the thickest and hence tons of meat per square mile were at the maximum.

At the same time, the forests, deserts, seashores, and mountainous regions of the world were occupied by more generalized gathering economies, perpetuating the old Mousteroid or East Asian pebble tool technical traditions, reflecting a much more stable pattern of life and perhaps a trend toward settled existence. At any rate, it was out of some of these generalized economies that the first food producers were to emerge at the close of the Pleistocene. The specialized hunters seem to have had no potentiality for further development, and in terms of cultural evolution they were a dead end. Those of Eurasia—the bearers of the Aurignacoid tradition—may have become overspecialized and, like the large mammals on which they based their life, have come to grief when their particular habitat disappeared.

Seen in the perspective of total human history, these Aurignacoid hunters have been idealized and overemphasized as the standard bearers of human progress, the wave of the future, and our cultural ancestors. We should instead view them as reflecting man's capability at this time, but contributing little to the future. We must assume that the seemingly more conservative generalized economies reflect populations of equal capability, because it was from them that the true standard bearers were to emerge. If they seem stagnant and backward at the moment, it is probably because they felt no need to change under existing conditions.

But it is an oversimplification to see the world at this time simply as divided into two distinct economic and cultural traditions. Rather, the picture is one of considerable cultural differentiation everywhere, reflecting many patterns of life and many different variations on the hunting-gathering theme basic to all men.[5] These represent specific adaptations to different habitats replacing the more generalized response visible hitherto. Other factors important in shaping the many distinct local cultures at this time were varying kinds and amounts of outside influences or, at the other extreme but equally significant, isolation.

The possibilities of such cultural differentiation were of course greatly increased by the spread of man to every corner of the globe, providing new habitats, new challenges, and new potential resources out of which grew the rich mosaic of human history of the last 10,000 years.

references

Howell, F. Clark: *Early Man*, Life Nature Library, Time, Inc., New York, 1965.
Leroi-Gourhan, André: "The Evolution of Paleolithic Art," *Scientific American*, February, 1968, pp. 59–70.

suggested readings

Butzer, Karl W.: *Environment and Archaeology: An Introduction to Pleistocene Geography*, Aldine Publishing Co., Chicago, 1964, pp. 384–401.

[5] For example, the specialized hunters of the African grasslands are more conservative technologically than the Aurignacoid hunters of the north—perhaps because their environment was less demanding. Or, as another example, in north China we see the pebble tradition progressing into a much more complex and specialized stone technology, whereas in Southeast Asia it remains much as before: Presumably it was adequate for the habitat.

Clark, Grahame: *The Stone Age Hunters,* McGraw-Hill Book Company, New York, 1967, pp. 43–90.

Howell, F. Clark: *Early Man,* Life Nature Library, Time, Inc., New York, 1965, pp. 144–191.

Maringer, Johannes, and Hans-Georg Bandi: *Art in the Ice Age,* Frederick A. Praeger, Inc., New York, 1953.

Ucko, Peter J., and Andrée Rosenfeld: *Palaeolithic Cave Art,* McGraw-Hill Book Company, New York, 1967.

postglacial survivals of the hunting pattern

the postglacial period

We come now to the final phase of Stage I (Man the Hunter), a phase
that has survived to the present day in areas where the shift to Stage II
never occurred because of environment (e.g., the arctic regions) or isolation (e.g., Australia). It begins with the conventional termination of the
Pleistocene 10,000 years ago and is of varying duration in each area, lasting until the shift to food production occurred or the impact of a higher
civilization put an end to the old pattern of life. The question is beginning
to arise as to whether such a phase even existed in certain places where
major changes seem already to have been under way at the end of the
Pleistocene. By and large, archeological and environmental evidence is
now relatively abundant and better preserved than heretofore, as we might
expect from a time so close to the present. The archeological record is far
more complete both in quantity and types of data; it is also more accessible
and less subject than before to concealment and destruction. Potentially,
therefore, we can expect to find the evidence for quite a full picture of life
at this time. At present, however, quite insufficient study has been made
in most areas, and of some we know virtually nothing—including certain
of the most crucial ones.

The best picture comes from regions where special conditions have
preserved normally perishable materials: peat bogs and other waterlogged
situations of northern Europe and dry caves in arid regions of the New
World. In a few other areas, perishable aspects of culture and behavior
are preserved in the form of narrative pictures painted or engraved on
rocks—the first examples of narrative art. Among more ordinary sites, a

FIGURE 14–1. *Hunting scene, Cueva de los Caballos, Spain.* (By permission from J. G. D. Clark, *Prehistoric Europe,* copyright © 1952 by Philosophical Library, Inc.)

substantial number are undisturbed living areas, giving an opportunity for the study of behavior. Problems of dating are greatly simplified, since the period falls well within the optimal operating range of C^{14} counters, and the necessary organic samples may normally be expected. In some areas, the history of changing land forms, climate, and vegetation is known in some detail and provides supplementary chronological data. On the other side of the ledger, this was in certain areas a time of rising sea levels, and here much of the history of coastal settlement has been lost to us, in contrast to later periods.

The continental ice sheets of the last glaciation in the Northern Hemisphere are considered to have disappeared 10,000 years ago, and this point is conventionally regarded as marking the end of the Pleistocene. Many of the large mammal species so typical of the Pleistocene, such as the mammoth, also become extinct quite suddenly at this same time, for reasons that are not entirely clear since others equally typical, such as the reindeer, have managed to survive in the remaining tundra zone. It is argued by some scholars that the hand of man was the decisive factor in the extinction of slow-breeding species like the mammoth or of other

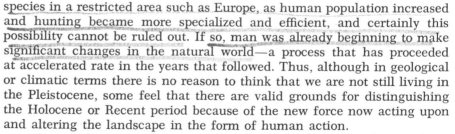

FIGURE 14–2. *Gathering wild honey, Cuevas de la Araña, Spain.* (By permission from Hugo Obermaier, *Fossil Man in Spain,* copyright © 1924 by Hispanic Society of America.)

species in a restricted area such as Europe, as human population increased and hunting became more specialized and efficient, and certainly this possibility cannot be ruled out. If so, man was already beginning to make significant changes in the natural world—a process that has proceeded at accelerated rate in the years that followed. Thus, although in geological or climatic terms there is no reason to think that we are not still living in the Pleistocene, some feel that there are valid grounds for distinguishing the Holocene or Recent period because of the new force now acting upon and altering the landscape in the form of human action.

As stated earlier, the environment of postglacial times has not been necessarily a stable one. In the northern areas, it took a while for the climate to warm up after the end of the Würm maximum and for the forests to become reestablished on the grasslands and tundra and to achieve their present composition. This warming reached a peak (Altithermal or Climatic Optimum) about 7,000 to 5,000 years ago from which it has since receded, with minor fluctuations, to the cooler climate of today. This Altithermal was "optimum" in northern regions, where there is evidence that the tree line extended farther north than today, but is thought to have been a time of increased aridity in areas like western North America, which became relatively unfavorable human habitat as compared with the Pleistocene. Strangely enough, this same time in the Sahara seems to have been one of increased rainfall and favorable habitat. For much of the world, information is not available, but we may expect the tropics in particular to show little change. Many parts of the world even in the Upper Pleistocene did not differ essentially from modern conditions.

Rising sea levels resulting from melting of the final ice sheets had already inundated the continental shelves by the close of the Pleistocene, severing intercontinental connections and depriving man of large areas of former level coastal plain that must have been the locus of considerable human settlement. This must therefore have been a time of population readjustment. The map of the world in early postglacial times was not entirely that of today, however, for in the north the earth's crust was still depressed from the weight of the ice, and some areas of present land were at times under water, while the shallowest parts of the North Sea were not filled until the last hundred feet of rising sea level, so that a dry plain stretched from England through Denmark to Russia during early post-glacial times, and the Baltic Sea went through a series of fluctuating stages before reaching its present form.

In addition to population adjustments caused by flooding of coastal plains and the effects of isolation on offshore islands (e.g., Britain, Indonesia, Hokkaido) and continents, the major change in human distribution was the general northward movement as climate improved and the permanent settlement of northern Eurasia and northern North America for (as far as we know) the first time.

A number of major cultural developments and technological achievements either occurred now or else became very widespread at this time. The universal adoption (except in Australia) of the bow and arrow as the standard means of hunting is especially noteworthy. The stone technology associated with this over much of the Old World featured or included very small geometric forms ("microliths") intended for use as barbs and tips, or to be set in rows in a slot to form a continuous sharp cutting edge (so-called "composite tools"). This implies the use now of adhesive substances for hafting, such as pitch and vegetable gums. The first examples of real watercraft are dated to early postglacial times in northern Europe, and it seems obvious from a variety of considerations that this must have become an almost universal element of culture at this general time, although the details of this process are lost to us. The development of a variety of effective fishing equipment is also evidenced now. Ecological adaptation to the boreal forest environment was a conspicuous postglacial achievement, and comparable adaptation to a desert environment may well be equally unique to this time.

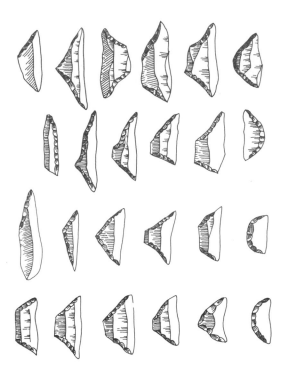

FIGURE 14–3. *Microliths used to barb and tip projectile weapons in western Eurasia.* (Modified from Grahame Clark, *The Stone Age Hunters,* copyright © 1967 by Thames and Hudson Limited, London; U.S. edition by McGraw-Hill, Inc., New York. By permission of the publishers.)

FIGURE 14–4. *Example of microliths set in slots.* (After a photo courtesy of National Museum, Copenhagen.)

cultural patterns

Human cultures of the postglacial phase could be classified into three categories:

1. Pleistocene survivals in areas where no change, or at least no initial change, occurred in the cultural pattern with the onset of postglacial times. Cultures of this type have sometimes been given the label "Epi-Paleolithic." Usually they are short-lived, and everywhere they have been

either replaced by cultures of the next type or swamped by the spread of food production.

2. Distinctive hunting-gathering cultures representing adaptations to changed conditions or else increased complexity and enrichment over their Pleistocene counterparts, often as the result of borrowings. Eventually nearly all these were swamped by the expansion of food production except in the few areas where they have been able to survive to the present day. Not even the richest and most talented of these later hunting-gathering cultures was able by its own efforts to advance to a higher level. In the overall picture these are dead-end cultural developments, although in Europe at least they did make a noticeable contribution to the succeeding farming patterns, and the same probably occurred elsewhere as well where the hunting population was numerous enough and the incoming farming pattern required adaptation to local conditions. And even though they are dead-end in this sense, they are of interest as examples of culture process and adaptation, of viable and successful ways of life, and thus contribute significantly to our goal of a better understanding of man and his behavior.

3. Cultures in nuclear areas where significant changes were under way leading up to the major ecological shift to Stage II, and which presumably played crucial roles in this process. The currently popular label "incipient" might be applied to them. But it must be emphasized that all are still basically hunting and gathering in their way of life.

It might be said that the human ecological pattern of early postglacial times was the last one universal for all mankind, and the last which all men could achieve by their own efforts. Subsequent advance to a new way of life was confined to a few nuclear areas, and advance anywhere else was dependent on diffusion from these areas. We may see this process finally achieved in our time if all of mankind is brought within the system of Western industrialization. Only then will all men once again live under a universal economy and share a way of life familiar to all.

1. PLEISTOCENE SURVIVALS

In the category of Pleistocene survivals we can place the so-called "Plano tradition" of North America east of the Rockies, focusing especially in the plains, which continued the big-game hunting economy of the earlier Llano for many thousands of years with different types of nonfluted projectile points. Some of these groups spread northward with improving climate and even penetrated Alaska briefly. A succession of different industries is recognized, as well as regional groupings, in every case identified almost entirely by a distinctive type of point.

In Australia the previous monotonous archeological record continued until 5,000 years ago, when the art of hafting stone tools made its appearance as probably did other introduced ideas. This sparked a great efflorescence in stone technology, continuing to modern times, and forming the second of the two major stages visible in Australian prehistory. Isolated Tasmania was unaffected by these new developments, however.

3) In Africa south of the Sahara, the pattern of life and technology visible at the close of the Pleistocene continued, marked only by the trend to microliths. The microlithic industries of the plains hunters—the former Stillbay area—go under the label "Wilton," and are generally identified with the direct ancestors of the Bushmen. Some Wilton groups (the so-called "strandloopers") were still living in the Cape area at the time of first European contact. Elsewhere this pattern succumbed to the southward-moving wave of iron-using herders and farmers, and its Bushmen descendants survive only in a few refuge areas like the Kalahari Desert. In this relatively isolated part of the world one can see in effect a direct succession from "Paleolithic" to "Iron Age." The situation presents a rather loose parallel to that in Australia, and both afford an opportunity to study the life of the Pleistocene at relatively close range.

4) The Mediterranean shores of southern Europe and northern Africa also show little essential change from the end of the Pleistocene except for intensification of microlithic tendencies in the stone technology. The bow-hunting population continued its way of life until farmer colonists from the eastern Mediterranean settled the region.

5) In Siberia and adjacent areas of Asia, although some of the larger game animals became extinct, there was no drastic environmental change and Pleistocene patterns persisted initially into the early postglacial, evolving gradually into the forest-adapted Siberian "Neolithic."

2. POSTGLACIAL ADAPTATIONS

Best known of the distinctive adaptations to postglacial conditions is the Maglemosian culture of northern Europe—a highly successful exploitation of the forests and swamps of the area, with development of an extensive new tool kit in wood, bone-antler, and stone to deal with the situation. Much of this has survived through accidents of preservation in swampy areas where many sites were situated, and it has been remarked that this differential survival as compared with other European groups of the time probably makes the Maglemosian culture seem more impressive than it really was, and others undeservedly poorer. The Maglemosians hunted the solitary game animals of the thick forests with bow and arrow, a very different pattern from the big-game herd hunters of the Pleistocene; exploited the masses of migratory waterfowl that breed in northern swamps; and fished extensively for pike and other freshwater fish with traps, fish spears (leisters), and other devices. No better set of equipment and techniques for exploiting the northern forests has ever been devised, and their descendants, moving northward, settled or equipped the settlers of the whole boreal forest of northern Eurasia, even contributing to the technology of the American Arctic.

Much of the folk culture of northern Eurasia in recent times, in the

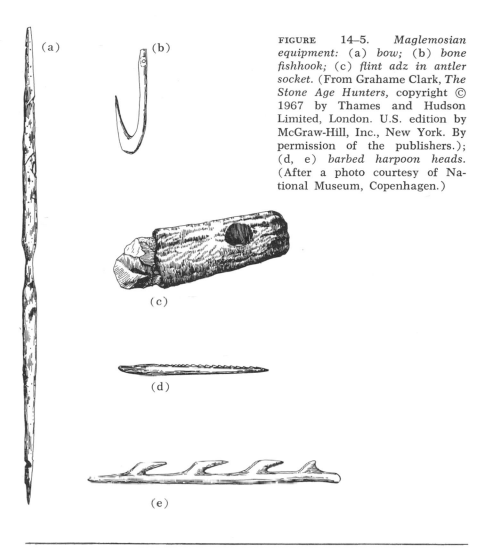

(a)

(b)

(c)

(d)

(e)

FIGURE 14–5. *Maglemosian equipment:* (a) *bow;* (b) *bone fishhook;* (c) *flint adz in antler socket.* (From Grahame Clark, *The Stone Age Hunters,* copyright © 1967 by Thames and Hudson Limited, London. U.S. edition by McGraw-Hill, Inc., New York. By permission of the publishers.); (d, e) *barbed harpoon heads.* (After a photo courtesy of National Museum, Copenhagen.)

material and economic sense, is directly inherited from this source, handed down among local populations over more than 300 generations. Modern Eskimo lcisters from Greenland, for instance, are almost indistinguishable from their Danish counterparts of 7,000 or 8,000 years ago. Although in later times certain items such as pottery and ground stone tools were borrowed from outside the area and added to the pattern, no more efficient pattern of life could be developed for the boreal zone. Beyond the practicable limits of food production, the pattern continued into historic times in northernmost Europe and Siberia. Among other contributions of these northern peoples to modern civilization we may mention skis and sleds, essential for winter hunting.

The Sahara experienced a period of increased rainfall between 8,000 and 4,500 years ago, and in the southern half there appeared a pattern of large, stable settlements along rivers and lakes, representing the first large-scale exploitation of water resources in Africa. So efficient were these regionally adapted groups of hunter-gatherers that farming failed to spread south or southwest beyond the Nile Valley into this area for some 2,000 years. The living patterns are reflected in many rock paintings in the modern Sahara.

Japan, located on the outermost limits of the Old World and isolated for long periods from the main currents of cultural development, has long been regarded as a quiet backwater where technical progress came late. Nothing has been more startling than the recent demonstration that the advanced art of manufacturing pottery is far older in Japan than anywhere else in the world, dating back to the close of the Pleistocene and antedating by some 10,000 years the beginnings of farming with which it has always been confidently associated. During this long period Japan was occupied by groups of hunter-gatherers nicely adapted to local conditions and exploiting the resources of land and sea. Many sites are shell middens, and settlement gives the impression of stability with houses of semiunderground type. The increasingly rich and elaborate pottery tradition, which goes under the label Jomon, attests to aesthetic sensibilities and a high level of craftsmanship. Because of its relative isolation and the large body of archeological evidence (no part of Asia has been more thoroughly studied), Japan provides one of the best potential laboratories for the study of cultural processes and cultural development through time.

Eastern North America provides a postglacial situation roughly like Europe, having been exposed to similar conditions. The forest gradually extended northward once more to reclaim what had been cold steppe, tundra, and glaciated area, and the large Pleistocene herd animals died out (doubtless with a boost from their human predators) as their habitat disappeared or (on the plains) became too arid. In the eastern woodlands the hunters had to turn to the more solitary forest animals that must be stalked individually in thick cover, plus the other usual resources of the forest and waterside. West of the Rockies, the Great Basin and the southwest turned into their modern desert form. As a result, we see the Plano big-game hunting pattern and the lakeside western lithic (nonpoint) tradition fading out and being replaced by adaptations to the new environments: patterns of specialized exploitation of specific regional environments with maximum efficiency which developed effective equipment for the purpose. But in contrast to Europe, these successor postglacial cultures are in nearly all cases richer and more complex than anything hitherto existing in the New World, if we except areas of meager resources where life became harder. There is a trend toward larger groups and more stable settlement.

The pattern in the eastern woodlands of North America is commonly labeled Archaic, and represents an adaptation to forest and riverside conditions of hunting, fishing, shellfish gathering, and utilizing wild plants. This pattern had begun in some places 9,000 years ago, and a whole series of regional adaptations to local conditions developed over the next few thousand years. Along the many rivers and the Atlantic coasts, settlements are often represented by large shell middens, indicating an economy able to support a fairly sedentary existence. By some 5,000 years ago, this group of Archaic cultures was characterized by specialized projectile points and by a large inventory of ground stone artifacts in which heavy woodworking tools are especially prominent: axes, gouges, weights for spear-throwers, net sinkers, stone vessels, and many elaborate ornamental or ceremonial forms. It is of particular interest that the technique of working stone by abrasion seems to have arisen independently in the New World, despite many broad similarities in the products of the two hemispheres, though in both cases it may well stem from earlier treatment of wood and bone. This new way of handling stone resulted in a great increase in the variety and complexity of stone tools and a corresponding decline of stone working by the old flaking techniques, which had reached its peak among the earlier big-game hunters of the Llano and Plano traditions.

A pattern of desert cultures arose in the arid regions of the west with a major emphasis on gathering and processing wild seeds, and special equipment was developed, mainly of basketry, for the purpose. Thanks to preservation in dry caves, we have a rather full picture of the life and material culture of some of these groups. Presumably from contacts with the big-game hunters, these peoples had acquired projectile points, although most of them are relatively crude and the nature of the game supply in the desert made hunting only an adjunct to the basic economy. Rabbits, taken with nets, clubs, and snares, were the major quarry, and their skins, in strips, were woven into blankets and robes. These, plus sandals woven of plant fibers, were essential equipment.

In California outside the desert areas, we find another group of semi-sedentary cultures based on fishing and acorns, supplemented by hunting. The densest aboriginal populations north of Mexico at the time of European contact were to be found here, where the pattern of life still persisted, unaffected by developments elsewhere. A similar isolated area of even richer sedentary culture, based on exploitation of the salmon runs plus salt water fishing and hunting, developed on the northwest coast of North America and lasted into modern times.

Probably the most ingenious adaptation to a special environment was achieved in the far north by the Eskimo population. As far as we know, the Eskimo pattern of utilization of the resources of land and sea developed in Alaska out of the tradition brought by the Aurignacoid settlers at the close of the Pleistocene, plus periodic subsequent additions and influences from Asia. This is the only part of the New World that has been subject to

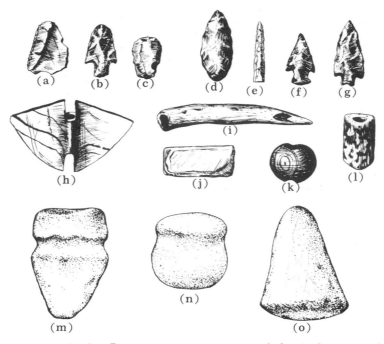

FIGURE 14–6. *Representative equipment of the Archaic period in eastern North America: (a–c)scrapers; (d)knife; (e)drill; (f, g) projectile points; (h, j, k, l) weights for spear-throwers; (i) antler hook for spear-thrower; (m)ax; (n) hammer; (o)pestle.* (Reprinted from *Archeology of Eastern United States*, edited by James B. Griffin, by permission of The University of Chicago Press. Copyright © 1952 by The University of Chicago.)

---

any significant influence from the Old since the end of the Pleistocene. From Alaska, cultures of the general Eskimo tradition spread periodically across the American arctic to Greenland and Newfoundland.

3. "INCIPIENT" CULTURES

At this general time we know or can postulate that the first steps in developments which were to culminate in effective food production and the major ecological shift to Stage II were under way in a number of different parts of the world, which we will call nuclear areas. The fact that these developments occurred at roughly the same time in the broad prehistoric time scale and independent of one another presents a phenomenon demanding serious attention and poses one of the major problems of pre-history. For those who advocate a universal pattern of cultural evolution it provides a telling argument. The factors that sparked these developments are still obscure. Factors of climatic change and environmental pressures, once popular, are generally discredited. The accident of the occurrence of suitable plants and animals in these areas is not sufficient: Animals were ignored in the New World, with few and limited exceptions, and suitable plants in many places did not inspire domestication. One begins to wonder whether sociocultural factors were responsible, and whether certain particular cultures were in effect "preadapted" for the new way of life. All this lends particular interest to the category of cultures we have called "incipient."

Some at least of the nuclear areas within which farming arose in-dependently can be pinpointed either by evidence from the natural sciences pointing to the original source of domesticated crops (cultigens) or ani-mals, or by archeological evidence of very early farming complexes un-related to others—or by both. Within such nuclear areas we can postulate the previous existence, prior to this ecological shift, of incipient food-producing cultures, even though in most cases we cannot positively iden-tify the latter archeologically at present. In the Old World we only know some who, like the Natufians of Palestine, were apparently in the right area at the right time and whose descendants ultimately turn up as indubitable food producers; though for all we know the latter may have borrowed and adopted the new economy rather than invented it them-selves. We must appreciate that incipient cultivation or domestication had only a minor subsistence role, and in no case seems to have had any marked effect on culture change. The new economy was established so gradually and with such little disruption to established patterns that we can expect it to be scarcely visible in the archeological record. Some Natufians, for example, were hunters of wild game and lived in caves like their Pleistocene forbears, though others were erecting more sophisticated settlements. The only hint of something new, and it might already be an old trait for all we know, is the presence of reaping tools which are be lieved to have been used to cut wild grasses; and some at least of the latter may have been future domesticates like wild wheat. This is the only direct evidence at present qualifying the Natufians as "incipient," and it is rather tenuous. Again, the argument seems to rest as much on what their apparent descendants were later doing.

With no evidence as yet we postulate the necessity at this time of incipient cultures in China, another at least probable nuclear area, to ac-count for what was to happen subsequently. The possibility of others in Southeast Asia must be taken into account: Botanists feel that rice was developed in this region, and there is also the necessity to account for the later pattern of cultivation involving tropical root and fruit crops which is basically quite different from the cereal crop pattern of China or the Near East.

In the New World, on the other hand, we can see examples of real incipient cultures, brought to light in recent years by archeologists. In dry caves of the states of Tamaulipas in northeastern Mexico and Puebla southeast of Mexico City, as well as in the Chicama Valley of Peru, there is evidence of a few species of domesticated plants having been cultivated over a very long period of time without any change in the basic economic pattern. In addition, we must postulate an incipient hearth of root crop cultivation somewhere in the tropical forests of the Amazon basin.

suggested readings

Butzer, Karl W.: *Environment and Archaeology: An Introduction to Pleistocene Geography*, Aldine Publishing Co., Chicago, 1964, pp. 402–415.

Clark, Grahame: *The Stone Age Hunters*, McGraw-Hill Book Company, New York, 1967, pp. 91–108.

Mellaart, James: *Earliest Civilizations of the Near East*, McGraw-Hill Book Company, New York, 1966, pp. 11–38.

Willey, Gordon: *An Introduction to American Archaeology*, vol. 1, Prentice-Hall, Inc., Englewood Cliffs, N.J., 1966, pp. 55–83.

the shift to food production

After a million or more years of little change and no potential for anything more advanced than the hunting societies at the close of the Pleistocene, a shift occurred, both to a new economic base and to a new social unit, which within 5,000 years led to the appearance of urban civilization in at least a few nuclear areas. This shift was the dawn of the day in which we ourselves are living, since the farming pattern of life established at that time is still the basis of our existence today and has undergone no fundamental change. Some feel that only from that time did man become fully human in the sense of leading a distinctively human way of life: Until then he had been only another part of the natural world, a hunter among hunters. His emancipation is reflected in his increasing control *over* environment, as contrasted with the increasing ability to cope *with* environment which characterized Stage I (Man the Hunter).

The decisive ecological shift which marks the beginning of Stage II (Man the Farmer) was as significant in its consequences as was the original ecological shift that started the hominids on the road to humanity. It has been termed the greatest single cultural change in human history; yet it was not sudden or dramatic to those involved, as if a light were being switched on, as William Howells put it. Rather, it was dramatic in its consequences long afterward because everything else we have achieved grew out of it. This major change in man's relationship to his environment has been variously called the food-producing revolution, the Neolithic revolution, or the agricultural revolution. The term "revolution" was originally applied to it by the eminent British prehistorian V. Gordon Childe

183

because the major social consequences of the technological changes impressed him as being comparable to the effects of the well-known Industrial Revolution. Whatever we choose to call it (and the term "revolution" is perhaps less fashionable today than it was ten years ago), this was not just an economic shift with consequent technological change but rather a major alteration in the whole pattern of human society, behavior, and psychological outlook arising from the new way of life.

For convenience, Stage II may be subdivided into three socioeconomic phases: (1) village farming, (2) urbanism (or "civilization"), and (3) industrialization. The latter phase, which coincides with modern times, is the concern of the cultural anthropologist rather than the prehistorian, and will not be discussed here.

Stage II, the food-producing stage, seems to have had its beginnings in some areas around 10,000 years ago, in others a few thousand years later. Once an effective level of food production had been attained in these nuclear areas, it spread out from these far and wide over the subsequent years. As a result, the time span of Stage II in different parts of the world is highly variable: It is a developmental stage, not a chronological unit. It should also be pointed out that the stage is not universal for mankind: In some parts of the world, for instance Australia, the arctic regions, or the Kalahari Desert of South Africa, the native peoples remained in the food-gathering stage into modern times. The urban and industrial phases have a much more restricted distribution, large areas of the world having remained in the village farming phase down to the present, either as primitive farmers living in tribal societies outside of the pale of civilization or as peasant communities within it.

This new village farming way of life was an end in itself, a stable system that could persist indefinitely and was not bound to evolve into anything more complex. On this foundation, civilization soon afterwards arose in a few places as an accidental phenomenon or as the result of some combination of circumstances. Village farming was certainly a necessary prerequisite for the appearance of civilization, but it was not the cause of its appearance.

Dramatic as the change seems to us in the perspective of human history, the potentialities of the new economy would not have been immediately apparent to the men of that time. In some areas, as in much of North America, they were not realized; in others, such as Mexico, it was evidently a long gradual process. Apparently there was a certain threshold of effectiveness that had to be crossed before what had initially been a supplement to, or an aspect of, the economy became a self-sufficient way of life; but once this point was reached, the new pattern seems to have jelled and almost immediately began to spread in a snowballing fashion.

Once established by gradual development in the nuclear regions where domestication of plants and animals took place, the subsequent propagation and expansion of farming life was a process of relative and explosive suddenness, even though both farming and food preparation techniques had to undergo change and adaptation to the new and different environments encountered, as did the plants and animals themselves. This spread of farming proved irresistible in the Old World, being blocked only by environmental barriers (as in the Arctic) or natural barriers (as in the case of Australia). Everywhere, contact with farming groups meant either conversion of the former hunting populations to the new way of life, or their swamping by the expanding food producers. Only in the less densely populated areas of the New World, such as North America north of Mexico, did farming become merely a supplement to hunting and not a total commitment, so that under certain circumstances a reversion to a purely hunting life could take place, as on the North American plains after the acquisition of horses. Such reversions seem to be unknown in the Old World, where adoption of farming or herding meant total dependence.

The cause of this explosive expansion in the Old World remains to be determined. It is reminiscent of the spread of an animal species to the limits of its habitat. Small-scale and parochial though the village farming pattern seems to have been, something in it was inherently expansionist. The stock argument of quest for new land seems unconvincing, nor does a population explosion of sufficient magnitude seem likely. In the New World, on the other hand, it was simply crop plants and the techniques of raising them that spread like wildfire, with no comparable overall transformation of the cultural scene or movement of population.

At any rate, over most of the world the shift to the new way of life, where it occurred, was the result of the borrowing or introduction of the full-fledged farming pattern from outside and was a relatively sudden process. This was the real revolution. In the nuclear areas where farming was invented, which were few and widely separated, the shift was a gradual process over thousands of years until the effective level was attained.

The village farming stage is also characterized by a tremendous overall growth of human population over the preceding period. Hunters, like any animal group, can maintain only a limited population in any region, which remains stable through time, in balance with the environment, and will in general increase or decrease only in response to some environmental change. Now man was freed from these environmental limits and his numbers were theoretically controlled only by his ability to produce food to support them. Naturally this ability was restricted in some habitats, but in favorable areas like the great river valleys the potential for population growth was almost unlimited, and only disease and recurrent natural catastrophes like drought or flood have kept human fertility in check. The teeming populations of India and China today reflect a village farming level of development: They are not the consequence of urbanism or industrialization as in the West.

This population expansion led very soon to a complete alteration of the racial map of the Old World at least—that is, to major changes in the relative proportions and distribution of the original races of Homo sapiens.

Those races that early became food producers in favorable areas expanded their distributions as well as their numbers and ultimately came to occupy vast territories at the expense of other races, initially of equal size, which clung to older ways of life and were absorbed, displaced, or restricted to limited areas.[1]

Finally, it is characteristic of the food-producing stage that man increasingly interferes with and alters the natural world through such activities as land clearance, reclamation, and overgrazing, which promote erosion and soil loss, lead to floods, and generally upset the balance of nature. Marked changes in the natural world are also brought about through man's introduction of plant and animal species into regions where they are not native, as well as through extinctions of species as a result of human activity.

explaining the shift

The basic ecological shift which initiates the food-producing stage seems to have occurred independently in a number of places: certainly in the Near East, perhaps in China, possibly in Southeast Asia, as well as in the New World (probably here in at least three different areas). Each developed its own distinctive cultivated plants and in some cases domesticated animals as well. Subsequently these centers influenced and were influenced by one or more of the others as well as creating by example and stimulus at least one additional center (tropical Africa). And all have made contributions of varying importance to the total pool of food resources available to mankind today.

These different cases of ecological shift all occurred at roughly the same time horizon, and thus have all the earmarks of an evolutionary development. Just *why* such a development should have occurred at this time we don't know. It happens to coincide with the end of the Pleistocene, but there is no certain evidence at present that climatic factors were responsible, although this was until recently the fashionable view. In some cases we can deduce, in very broad terms, *how* this shift was taking place, although many vital details are certainly a complete mystery. But *why* should certain human groups have made the experiments that eventually led to such a major shift, and why did this take place more or less simultaneously in widely separated parts of the world? How can we explain the extensive experimentation and selection that are involved in effective domestication when there could have been no real realization of the ultimate potential? Was this simply more or less accidental and not

---

[1] For instance, it has been suggested that at the end of the Pleistocene when the Bushman racial stock is believed to have ranged widely over large parts of Africa, there may have been as many Bushmen as Europeans in the world. Today the former are reduced to a tiny remnant, their former range appropriated by proliferating farmers and herdsmen.

the result of deliberate planning and foresight? It is true that there is little evidence of such experimentation and deliberate selection in later times *after* the potential had been achieved and appreciated, just when we might most reasonably expect conscious effort in such matters.

The whole picture thus seems irrational, and raises the question of whether mutation and natural hybridization may not have played the major roles in the process. If so, we may well wonder why there should have been so much mutation taking place all over the world in one relatively short segment of time, and not thereafter. It is also pertinent to inquire whether there is any documented case of a primitive group in modern times making any effort to improve their crops? It seems implausible to attribute abilities to early human groups which are beyond the awareness of their descendants. Had the art of domestication and selective breeding been lost, or had some limit been reached in the initial shift beyond which crops could not be improved, just as no additional animals could successfully be domesticated?

No existing explanation of the cause for this crucial shift to food production is satisfactory. Environment seems ruled out. The mere presence of suitable species for domestication is not in itself sufficient to bring it about. And the profound psychological shift which would have to take place from the short-term viewpoint of the hunter to the long-term outlook of the farmer and herdsman makes the shift even more difficult to explain.

In only one of the Old World centers, the Near East–Aegean Sea region, is there any real archeological evidence that can be brought to bear on the problem. Here there has been a good deal of recent field work, but much of it has not yet been reported. Even so, the state of knowledge has been in constant flux: The picture no sooner starts to make sense when new finds upset it again and make it more confusing than ever. Important breakthroughs may be hoped for in the next few years in the light of current activity. From the other key Old World areas there are almost no data available. Only in the Americas are there glimpses of the process. Thus no coherent account of this crucial development in human history is yet possible. Certainly the shift to food production and village society ranks along with the emergence of man as the major unsolved problem in human history.

We may first consider why the beginnings of this process are localized in certain areas. It must be realized that only certain environments are suitable for initial efforts at farming, and that it required the development of special techniques and of special varieties of crops before farming could spread out of these favored environments into other habitats, such as regions of inadequate rainfall, dense forests, cold, damp climates, or heavy soils difficult to cultivate with hand tools. For example, the breadbaskets of the modern world, the prairie grasslands of the American Middle West, of southern Russia, Argentina, and Australia, were useless for agriculture until the development of effective steel plows not much more than 100 years ago.)

But a favorable environment for beginning farmers is not enough: Within such regions you must in addition have an area where plants and animals suitable for domestication exist naturally in the wild state in sufficient numbers. And it must be realized that there is only a limited number of species—especially of animals—that is both useful (or potentially useful) and domesticable, and that these species have restricted distributions that do not necessarily coincide with one another to any great extent. As a result of these natural controlling factors, it is possible with the help of natural scientists to identify in broad outline certain nuclear areas in various parts of the world where the beginnings of food production *could* have occurred. But this development was not automatic by any means and actually took place in only some of these nuclear areas. What factors caused it to occur in these certain places is of course the key question.

To better understand what may seem like a puzzling lack of knowledge of so important an event which took place not so long ago in readily accessible areas that have long been studied by archeologists, it is necessary to appreciate the recency of the study of the food-producing "revolution," that is, the recency of the search for concrete evidence to back up our theoretical concepts and to explain how the shift occurred. This is due to the fact that work in all these nuclear areas has concentrated on spectacular later remains. The small, inconspicuous earlier sites were overlooked or unexamined, so that knowledge of the prehistoric period in, for example, the Near East was previously limited to scraps from test pits sunk through the deep deposits of the big sites of later times. It is only in recent years that deliberate study of the crucial period has been undertaken, and even more recently that the interdisciplinary approach has been applied here, in an effort to recover all relevant information on ecology and life and not just a sequence of potsherds.

In general, the archeological picture in the Near East has been one of cave sites of the last hunters on the one hand or of well-established farming villages on the other, but nothing reflecting a transition between the two. Recent efforts have aimed at finding such a transition, on the assumption that the sites must be there awaiting discovery—that the hiatus in the record is more apparent than real. Also implicit is the assumption that the last hunters transformed themselves *in situ* into the first farmers in a rather surprisingly short space of time considering the extent of the changes necessary.

Research into the beginnings of food production is at best plagued by obstacles and in particular by the difficulties of recovering the earliest evidence of domestication. Without actual remains of the diagnostic portions of the animals or plants, we can speculate that a certain human group had begun to plant wild grains or to herd wild goats; but how to actually prove this at a particular site? Artifact evidence is not conclusive, since the same sickles and grinding stones that harvested and processed the first crops were previously used on their wild ancestors. And no special tools are used with sheep and goats. Equipment specifically for domestic animals (harness, ploughs, carts, saddles) is still a long way in the future. The presence and use in a site of grains and goats that later were domesticated is no evidence, although it would certainly suggest that the group involved was headed in the right direction. To be accepted as the result of farming, botanical study must demonstrate that the grain found has undergone change in the direction of the domestic form (as at Jarmo), or that it is genetically capable of giving rise to the domestic form.

Developments in the Near East–Aegean nuclear area had the most impact on the course of the overall cultural evolution of man, since they subsequently affected the widest area: Africa, Europe, all of western Asia, with important influence on eastern and southern Asia as well and, in modern times, extending to all the rest of the world. Because of these widespread effects and because of the large body of data available, more attention will be devoted to it.

The exact limits of this nuclear area are uncertain, and would be defined by the natural ranges of the potential domestic crops as they existed 9,000 to 10,000 years ago. The modern ranges of these species are fairly well known, but it cannot be assumed, although there has been a tendency to do so, that the ranges have remained unchanged for the last 10,000 to 15,000 years. Even though the climate is basically the same, the area has probably undergone alterations in soils and vegetation. The recently fashionable idea of a restricted nuclear area confined to the so-called "hilly flanks" zone of the foothills surrounding the Tigris–Euphrates Valley has now been abandoned even by its chief proponent. It is becoming evident that the whole process of domestication did not take place in any one area of the Near East and was not the achievement of any one group. Probably each crop and animal developed in a different part of the region and then eventually coalesced to form the standard farming complex when enough alteration had taken place genetically so that each crop could spread beyond its original habitat niche. This coalescence is indicated by the fact that the various components of this original farming complex do not all occur together in the same niche in the wild.

The mechanisms by which such a coalescence could easily take place are not hard to see. There is ample archeological evidence of widespread cultural diffusion within major areas of the Near East in this time range, but even more specific is the surviving evidence of actual trade in the form of obsidian, which was carried long distances from the two known sources in this part of the world. The scope of this trade is indicated by the fact that at sites 250 kilometers from the source, 80 percent of the chipped stone artifacts were of this material. Thus we know that different groups were in regular contact at least through the medium of certain individuals who traveled between them, and, assuming sufficient time depth, this same mechanism could transmit perishable items and ideas such as innovations in farming. Crops could even move unintentionally as food in a trader's pouch. In addition, it is evident that the very typical

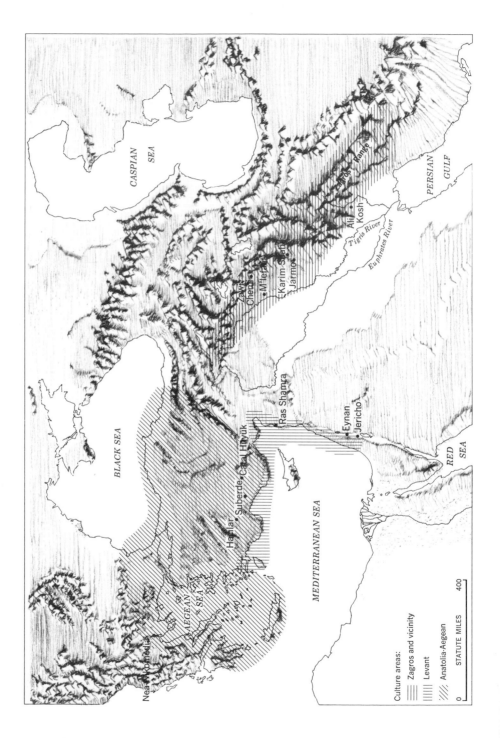

CASPIAN SEA

Zagros Range

Ali Kosh

Tigris River

Euphrates River

Zawi Chemi

M'lefaat

Karim Shahir

Jarmo

PERSIAN GULF

Ras Shamra

Eynan

Jericho

RED SEA

BLACK SEA

Hacilar

Suberde

Çatal Hüyük

AEGEAN SEA

MEDITERRANEAN SEA

Near Nomdella

Culture areas:

Zagros and vicinity

Levant

Anatolia-Aegean

0   400

STATUTE MILES

western Asian ecological pattern of seasonal transhumance goes far back into the past: the exploitation of different habitat zones at different times of the year when they become optimum by moving bodily from one to the other. People whose economy depends heavily on wild plants must generally do this, since outside of the tropics any particular vegetable food is available during only a relatively brief period of time. Again, it provides a mechanism through which food plants and/or animals could move into areas where they were not native and where incentive for artificial propagation would consequently arise.

It is evident that at least some of these same mechanisms must have been operative also in the New World, where the eventual effective farming complexes are composed of plants from a variety of sources transferred from their original habitats.

experiments with food production

What evidence is there at present of actual experiments with food production, with the deliberate propagation of plants and control of animals which led to domestication, a state in which marked changes have come about from the wild form as a consequence of man's interference?

There are at least three culturally distinct areas in the nuclear Near East. In one of these, Anatolia, no evidence of experimentation has been so far identified, but it is widely presumed that this will eventually come to light owing to the presence of substantial communities at a very early date, such as Suberde and the lowest level at Hacilar, which seem difficult to explain without some sort of food production. At any rate, this is a prime area for further research, and should be watched closely. The Aegean region may be thought of as primarily an offshoot of the Anatolian area. The evidence for possible experimentation comes from the other two areas: the Levant (the east coast of the Mediterranean) and the highlands lying east of the Tigris-Euphrates Valley (the Zagros Range and the immediately adjacent grassland).

The Natufian culture of the Levant, as we mentioned, was based on hunting but included sickles. These might have been used to cut reeds or grass, but if they were used to cut seed- or grain-bearing plants (as is commonly assumed) there are grounds for arguing that such plants must have been at least partially domesticated. The seeds of wild plants scatter easily, and cannot be harvested by reaping without losing most of them; wild seeds must be gathered by beating the heads into a container. One of the first changes under domestication is the development toward reten-

FIGURE   15–1.   *Near East-Aegean nuclear area.*

tion of seeds; mutations in this direction would be discouraged by natural selection in the wild, but under human cultivation would be encouraged because it would be just those plants which retained seeds during reaping which would end up in the grain bin and contribute most heavily to the next year's crop. Thus it is contended that the Natufian sickles are presumptive evidence of at least semidomesticated grain, although it was only a minor part of the economy.

That some at least of the Natufians lived in stone houses in long-term settlements of possibly 200 to 300 inhabitants like Eynan is a further hint of the direction in which life was moving; and then there is the cultural continuity between the Natufians and the earliest real village at the multilevel site of Jericho, the stage referred to as "Pre-Pottery Neolithic A," with a date of around 10,300 years ago. Here we have an impressive community eventually covering ten acres protected by imposing fortifications but with no clear evidence of its economic basis. The feeling that food production must be involved is inevitable.[2] And it should be pointed out that there is evidence of long-range trade in obsidian, indicating that earliest Jericho was in contact with large areas of the Near East and must have been open to whatever ideas and innovations may have been in the air at that time. Unfortunately, we have no idea as yet what these may have been elsewhere in the Levant, or in Anatolia from which the obsidian came, since we have no sites in these areas as old as earliest Jericho, and even those 2,000 years later lack evidence of the economic base, although again their size and complexity suggests food production (e.g., Muraibet, Bouqras, Ras Shamra).

There are a number of famous sites in the Zagros highlands that are frequently cited as reflecting experimental food production. At Karim Shahir and M'lefaat food-grinding equipment is a conspicuous feature, in marked contrast to the sites of hunting groups in this area at the close of the Pleistocene. However, the two types of sites might represent different traditions and not necessarily a shift in economy by the hunting groups, as is commonly claimed. The presence of a few ground stone artifacts and clay figurines is also cited as foreshadowing later developments.

Zawi Chemi shows the same general picture with the addition of baskets, storage pits, and house foundations. These, it is thought, are indications of a stable settlement pattern and argue against the shifting life characteristic of wild plant gatherers. What sort of plant foods were being ground up and stored is not known, but it must not be forgotten that acorns are used in this same area today and that California Indians maintained a fairly stable settlement pattern based on an acorn economy and rather similar grinding equipment. Of perhaps greater interest at Zawi Chemi is the possible evidence that sheep were being kept, though as yet they were morphologically indistinguishable from the wild form. This is

[2] Eynan and earliest Jericho are described and pictured in Mellaart, 1965, pp. 22–37.

inferred from the fact that the proportion of immature sheep bones relative to those of adults was far higher than is normal in a wild herd; man was interfering in the situation by evidently eating the young animals and saving the older breeding stock) The time horizon is indicated by the very similar level B1 at nearby Shanidar Cave, dated at almost 11,000 years ago.

The earliest actual remains of cultivated plants come from the lowest level at Ali Kosh, on the edge of the plain adjoining the Zagros uplands, which is at least 9,000 years old. Here were found charred kernels of domesticated barley and two early types of wheat. The people were evidently goat herders and wild plant collectors who were experimenting with cultivated grains brought down from their habitat at higher elevations in the Zagros.

Our only other examples of experiments in plant cultivation all come from the New World. Here the evidence is more abundant, primarily through the accident of preservation under arid conditions, and indicates a long period of such experimentation. The fullest picture is provided by a group of sites in the Tehuacan Valley near Puebla in the highlands of south central Mexico, representing over 9,000 years of human utilization of the area. The early inhabitants were hunters and gatherers of wild plant foods, but during the period roughly from 9,000 to 7,000 years ago they were growing a domesticated squash and avocados, and there are traces of other possible cultigens. However, such plants provided only an insignificant part of their diet. The people of the following stage (roughly 7,000 to 5,400 years ago) had ten kinds of domestic plants, including such future staples as maize and beans, but these are estimated to have supplied only 10 percent of their diet, which otherwise was obtained from hunting and from wild plants (available in great abundance), following a seasonal nomadic pattern of life. Only subsequently (approximately 5,400 to 4,300 years ago) did stable villages first appear and cultivated plants supply even 25 percent of the diet. Only two new species supplemented those previously known. Thus the early possession of a considerable variety of important domestic food plants actually had very little effect on the economy and way of life here, perhaps because of the ready availability of wild foods.

IMPT:

The earliest known populations on the arid northern coast of Peru, no more than 6,000 years ago, already led a fairly stable existence based on the resources of the sea and wild plants, but grew lima beans and gourds, the latter apparently only as containers or net floats and not as food. After about 4,500 years ago they were growing, in addition, cotton, chile, and two kinds of squash but still living primarily off the sea, which made fairly large villages possible. Full time agriculture arose only during approximately the last 750 years before the time of Christ, and was marked by the arrival from outside of a number of important staple crops including maize, potatoes, and manioc.

reference

Mellaart, James: *Earliest Civilizations of the Near East,* McGraw-Hill Book Company, New York, 1966.

suggested readings

Butzer, Karl W.: *Environment and Archeology: An Introduction to Pleistocene Geography,* Aldine Publishing Co., Chicago, 1964, pp. 416–437.
MacNeish, Richard S.: "Ancient Mesoamerican Civilization," *Science,* vol. 143, pp. 531–537, 1964.
Mellaart, James: *Earliest Civilizations of the Near East,* McGraw-Hill Book Company, New York, 1966, pp. 18–38.

domestication and concurrent advances

the process of domestication

It is appropriate at this point to discuss further just what was involved in the process of domesticating the plants and animals which formed the subsequent food supply of man as they still do today, and a little about the history of those of greatest importance, insofar as it is known.

Cultivated plants are valuable to man not just because he can grow them where and when he wants to and in whatever quantity desired, but primarily because they differ significantly from their wild ancestors and relatives in ways that greatly increase their usefulness. Many cultivated species are characterized by gigantism of certain parts or organs, as with our vegetables and fruits when contrasted with wild forms. These are precisely the edible parts. Wild grains, as already noted, are typically difficult to harvest because their seeds scatter easily. In addition, many are enclosed within tight hulls that must be removed before eating. Domestication has done away with these undesirable features, has increased yields, and has adapted the plants for growth outside their normal habitat. These useful characteristics can arise as natural variations through such genetic mechanisms as mutation, hybridization, and polyploidy. However, such variations have no survival advantage in the wild—often quite the opposite—and are eliminated through natural selection; it is only where man has interfered in the picture that they have become established and developed into the crops we know. The point of controversy is in what way early man interfered: whether by deliberate selective breeding as modern science does—or simply unintentionally by modifying the environment— weeding out competing growth, keeping livestock which added accidental fertilizer, and by generally messing up the natural habitats, as one botanist has put it, so that such variations survived, became established, and further developed. Man's unconscious tendency to utilize the most useful specimens, just like the greater likelihood of harvesting nonscattering grain mentioned earlier, introduces a certain element of human selection even if it is not deliberate.

Similarly, most domestic animals differ from wild forms in ways useful to man but with variations which would not survive in the wild. Domestication involves first of all the sexual isolation of portions of a wild species from the larger gene pool. In such smaller isolated groups, combinations of genes become different and characteristics may become frequent which are uncommon in the wild. Once in an artificial environment under human care, such mutations and changes in gene frequency could be perpetuated and, if perceived as desirable, might be less apt to be killed off for food and thus more or less unconsciously be selected for breeding. Since the processes of animal reproduction are so akin to those of man, unlike plants, we may suppose that far more deliberate selective breeding was apt to occur in the case of livestock, though in general this was probably a later development and not crucial in the earliest stages.

plant domestication

Cultivated plants are only a small fraction of the vegetable kingdom. What led to experiments in growing these certain few? In the case of seeds, it was only those wild cereal grasses or legumes with seeds large enough and borne in sufficient quantity to inspire harvesting, presumably precisely those that were customary sources of food in the wild form. The fact that seeds which fall on the ground will sprout and reproduce their kind must have been no mystery to men of this time. In the case of root crops and fruits, the use was self-evident, the problem being one of propagation. Some of the most important root crops do not grow readily from seed. It has been argued that knowledge of how to raise cereals would not equip or inspire anyone to cultivate bananas, which must be propagated by planting the side shoots, or yams, which grow from pieces of the tuber. It is partly on these grounds that an independent hearth of root- and fruit-crop cultivation has been postulated in Southeast Asia, and a possible separate development of yam cultivation suggested for the African rain forest. The major New World root crops such as manioc, peanuts, and potatoes also seem to have been independent inventions unconnected with seed crops, or even with each other.

In fact, we should avoid the mental picture, inspired by our own cultural values and attitudes, of some primitive Luther Burbank experimenting with every growing thing in his locality and presenting the world with a whole complex of domesticated plants. The domestication of each species is a problem in itself. To think of the domestication of plants per se as a general concept at this time, as we tend to do, is a modern illusion. The New World evidence certainly suggests that most domestications occurred separately in different places, and even that the same plant was independently brought under cultivation in more than one place. There can never have been any one localized hearth or even a few well-defined hearths of domestication. The wide extent of the Near East nuclear area, with its varying habitats, should convey the same impression. Another point to keep in mind is that it seems to have taken a very long time between the first domestication of a plant and its establishment as the primary basis of the economy. The obvious advantages apparent to us in hindsight were not apparent to the first cultivators.

Brief sketches of what is known of the history of certain major crops will serve as examples of what was involved in domestication.

Two species of wild wheat growing in the Near East were brought into cultivation at an early stage. Both are annual grasses of well-watered mountain areas. Wild emmer (*Triticum dicoccoides*), which is of restricted distribution, developed gradually under human control into the more satisfactory cultivated form (*T. dicoccon*), which was widely grown by early farmers. More widespread is the wild *T. boeoticum,* which tolerates cold and poor soil. This is believed to have given rise to einkorn (*T. monococcum*), also an important early crop, by a gene mutation which promoted retention of the seeds during harvesting and handling. Both of these early wheats more closely resemble the wild forms than do our modern ones. They are dark colored and hairy, and the kernels are enclosed in tight, stiff hulls, requiring roasting and grinding before the grain can be used. Emmer today is grown only in Ethiopia, and einkorn survives only in mountain regions where better wheats cannot yield a satisfactory crop. In at least one area (Anatolia), however, emmer underwent an important early genetic mutation, polyploidy (an increase in chromosome number), which over 8,000 years ago had produced new strains of wheat that could be threshed free of their hulls and were adapted to a wider range of growing conditions. From this group there eventually developed our modern bread wheat (*T. aestivum*).

Wild barley, though primarily a plant of slopes, has a much greater range areally and environmentally than the wild wheats and thus would have been available to a great many groups and more easily grown. In many areas of its range, however, no attention seems to have been paid to it. The wild form has two rows of kernels, the latter enclosed in tight hulls. Early in its association with man a genetic mutation produced six-row barley, which seems to have been better adapted to conditions differing from the original habitat: Hence this mutation got established in lowland areas and before long became the more common crop. A later development was the removal of the hulls and thus the production of naked barley more similar to our modern crop. Again, this was accomplished by mutation, since a single gene controls the difference between the two. The common modern form has been grown in northern Europe for probably 4,000 years.

Oats and rye were not early crops. Their wild ancestors are believed to have been weeds in wheat fields and to have spread in this way to northern Europe. Being hardier than wheat, they apparently came to be grown as separate crops in areas where wheat proved unsatisfactory and thus became established in their own right. It should be pointed out that weeds, even though not grown intentionally by man, are subject to the same environmental modifications, the same protection, and the same processes of selection for adaptability to cultivated conditions. Man has effected equivalent change in this large group of plants which has lived closely with him and traveled with him from the beginnings of cultivation. In some cases, as with oats and rye, economic use has been eventually or occasionally made of them. Many leguminous plants may have entered cultivation in this way. Indeed, since wild barley today is an inevitable weed of wheat fields in the Near East, it might well have been originally drawn into cultivation along with the first wheat through the same automatic selection for plants that retained their seeds during reaping rather than scattering at the touch as in the wild form.

Though no living wild plant can be identified with certainty as the original ancestor of maize, it is believed to have been a grass native to the highlands of Mesoamerica. In archeological sites in the Tehuacan valley maize first appears around 7,000 years ago in the form of tiny ears of a primitive, podlike variety. Authorities consider this to represent either a wild species or one in the very initial stages of domestication. These early forms would have been confined to the highlands, and may not even have been considered as grain, the entire ear being chewed green for its sweet juices. Subsequently, the ears became progressively larger as a result of cultivation, but extensive hybridization with the related grasses Teosinte and Tripsacum was required to produce a cereal of economic value, and in this form it was adapted for cultivation in lowland areas. Such strains then spread widely through the New World. The history of maize is one of the more complex and least understood chapters in the story of plant domestication.

animal domestication

The history of animal domestication presents a rather different picture in many ways. Although animals came to be an essential and integral part of the food-producing economy throughout the Old World, and virtually every animal profitable to domesticate (and capable of domestication) was brought under control, this was not the case in the New World. It is true that the American aborigines were severely handicapped by the lack

FIGURE   16–1.   *Stages in the evolution of maize, Tehuacan Valley, Mexico.* (Courtesy of Richard S. MacNeish.)

of suitable species, but still the very extensive experimentation with plants was not matched, as in the Old World, by a comparable interest in animals. The few species developed, such as the llama and turkey, were of very restricted distribution and failed to spread with their associated farming complexes. The familiar complex of Old World domestic animals took a long time to develop, while the earliest levels of effective farming are characterized in contrast by a variety of staple crops. Finally, while it is becoming clear that certain plants came into cultivation separately in more than one locality of the nuclear areas, this pattern can be demonstrated even more clearly in the case of Old World animals, with some domestications taking place outside of the nuclear areas, evidently as a consequence of stimulus diffusion: the spread of an idea and its application in a new situation.

The number of species of domestic animals is far smaller than that of plants and represents only a very small portion of the animal kingdom. Although hunting groups may exploit the animals of their habitat exhaustively, incipient food producers focus on those that are of maximum utility as food and, among these, those whose natural behavior patterns make them adaptable to (or preadapted for) a symbiotic relationship with man, which is not always the case. Animals capable of domestication are those that are naturally gregarious and able to reproduce freely in captivity. Viewed from the animal point of view, domestication could have occurred far earlier, but apparently had to await the attainment of a certain level by man: This would seem to be the level of stable settlement. Given the habits of man at this level on the one hand and the habits of certain animal species on the other, the appearance of domestication would seem almost inevitable. The actual process involved an interplay of biological processes and deliberate human interference.

Available evidence indicates that the animals originally domesticated were those commonly hunted in their respective areas and at the same time easily kept (such as wild sheep, wild goat, wild boar) as distinct from species that were often hunted but are hard to keep, like deer. A regular supply of meat seems therefore to have been the primary motivation. Other uses of animals which attained equal importance in human history not long after—for textiles, dairy products, traction, and transportation— were dependent on the subsequent development of special features through genetic change and on the discovery of castration as a means of making male animals tractable. None of these later uses would have been apparent in the wild form: Wild sheep have no wool, wild cows provide milk only for their offspring, wild chickens lay a minimum number of eggs. Nor do all peoples make use of these features: The Chinese, for example, never used wool or milked their livestock. Thus, the first domestic animals were easily fed herbivores whose main importance lay in their meat-producing qualities.

The presence of apparently domesticated sheep at Zawi Chemi some 11,000 years ago, previously mentioned, gives sheep priority at the moment as the oldest domestic animal. However, the goat must have come under human control in the Near East very soon after, if not equally early, since the goats found in the oldest levels at Jericho and Jarmo are already clearly recognizable as domestic forms and must reflect a considerable period of human management. Both animals are basic and ubiquitous elements of the food-producing economy over most of the Old World. The genetic changes leading to woolly fleece must have taken some time to develop, but there is possible evidence of woolen textiles at Catal Hüyük about 8,000 years ago. When the milking of sheep and goats arose is unknown, but it must go back at least 5,000 years. The ability of the goat to live on sparse vegetation opened up large areas of arid and mountainous terrain for human use. At the same time, the goat has unwittingly been one of man's major instruments for altering the landscape through destruction of vegetation and resultant erosion and soil loss. Both animals lend themselves to less settled or seasonal patterns of life such as transhumance, which also accounts for their ubiquitous association with man. The pig, on the other hand, requires a settled existence. Although it must have been domesticated in the Near East by 8,500 years ago, it is found only in permanent or long-term villages of sedentary farmers. Like cattle, the wild forms have a very wide distribution outside the nuclear areas and have clearly been domesticated at different times in several places (such as Europe, China, and possibly Southeast Asia) from more than one wild species. The latter cases may well represent independent cases of domestication.

It has been the traditional view, widely accepted as historical fact, that the dog was the first domestic animal and that he may have attached himself to man as a scavenger and become accepted as an aid in hunting. This was based on north European evidence, like so many other traditional "facts" of prehistory, and is not borne out elsewhere. The dog is not early in the Near East; it appears well after sheep, goat, and pig. All alleged early occurrences (e.g., in the Natufian) have now been discredited. The dog seems to have been domesticated at a number of places over a wide area from various types of wolves. Whether the local domestication in northern Europe was the result of stimulus diffusion or an independent invention is uncertain. At any rate, the dog was apparently domesticated in most cases as a food animal; this is especially clear in eastern and southeastern Asia. There is no evidence to support the view that he was domesticated, or voluntarily joined up with man, as a hunting companion. This role has developed only in fairly recent times. Primitive hunters do not use dogs in this way.

Domestic cattle are of more recent origin. It has been pointed out that sheep, goats, and pigs are relatively docile, whereas cattle are quite another matter, so that it is safe to assume that considerable prior experience with livestock would have been necessary before the familiar and widespread but dangerous wild bovines were successfully brought under human control. Cattle also require far more attention and thus involve organization of the community for this purpose. There are a number of hypotheses as to what led to this major undertaking. From the fact that many primitive cattle herders of modern times make no economic use of their animals but keep them at great effort solely as wealth or status symbols, plus the sacred status of cattle elsewhere (as in India) and their former widespread role as sacrificial animals, the view arose that cattle were domesticated initially for ritual and ceremonial reasons and that economic uses developed subsequently in certain areas. For example, they might have been captured and kept in confinement for sacrificial use on a permanent basis, thus creating a situation of breeding in isolation with the expectable genetic changes observable in other domesticates. Further encouragement has been given to this view in recent years by evidence of the religious symbolism attached to the bull in the Near East–Aegean area at this general time horizon and especially by the recent discoveries suggestive of this in the early levels at Catal Hüyük in Anatolia. Castration, essential to the historically most important function of cattle as the major source of tractive power, could have been inspired by the ritual human castration reflected in Near Eastern mythology; and inasmuch as its beneficial effects on bulls are not likely to have been foreseen, the origin of the practice is not otherwise easy to account for.

Another view, rejecting this approach, stresses that cultivated fields would have attracted wild cattle as "crop robbers" and thus have brought man and cattle together with overlapping but conflicting interests. Efforts to control such depredations might have resulted in capture of calves, and the rearing of captive young animals is a common phenomenon among primitive peoples. However, there is no evidence that such animal care or pet keeping has ever led to a more permanent relationship. A third view would see cattle as no different from the pattern of preceding animals: a common game animal, with the necessary attributes for thriving in captivity, eventually brought under control as a source of meat in a number of places by people accustomed to keeping domestic livestock for this purpose.

All domestic cattle were apparently derived from one or another local race or subspecies of the aurochs (*Bos primigenius*), which was very widespread in Eurasia at the time. Positive archeological evidence of domestic cattle at present dates back about 7,500 years, suggesting domestication in the Near East in the preceding centuries. Cattle remains in early farming villages are all of wild animals. Other domestications seem to have occurred in widely separate areas, such as India and Europe, the former giving rise to the zebu cattle, adapted to tropical conditions, which subsequently were introduced into Africa about 3,000 years ago. It is assumed that these cases of domestication outside of the Near East were more recent and resulted from stimulus diffusion, although the time when they occurred is unknown. Whatever its origin, cattle domestication was a very significant event in human history. The plow and the wheel follow soon after this acquisition of traction power, thus making the ox a major prerequisite for Old World civilization and technical progress. The absence of a comparable power source in the New World was a major handicap. Dairying, a less important (in the overall sense) use of cattle, goes back at least 5,000 years in the Near East.

The wild horse from which modern breeds derive was native to the great northern plain of Eurasia and was not present in any nuclear area. It is assumed to have been domesticated as a meat animal along the southern edge of its range by some group or groups of food producers who were present here by 6,000 years ago. It seems to have been introduced into the Near East around 4,500 years ago, where it was hitched to carts in imitation of the current use of oxen. Due no doubt to its greater speed but inferior strength, it came to be used with lighter vehicles; hence, though of limited economic use, its specialized value in warfare was soon recognized, and it was only in this role that the horse finally came into its own in the urban civilizations of the Near East. Horse-drawn chariots revolutionized warfare by providing a powerful and highly mobile striking force, which at the same time represented a very considerable investment (comparable to tanks and armored vehicles in modern war) which only wealthy chiefs and rulers or organized states could afford. This was a major factor in the development and centralization of political power, since ordinary citizens and "underdeveloped" neighbors could not hope to prevail against such a military advantage. And being in this way an important element of political power, the horse in the Near East–Aegean region had a special status through its primary association with the socially privileged classes. The same picture may be seen in China at a comparable stage.

In most of Europe, however, the horse was simply a work animal and a source of meat (as it still remains, for example, in France). This indicates that it was introduced there directly from the steppe and not via the Near East. There is no evidence that horses were ridden until around 3,500 years ago; again, this probably arose on the Eurasian plain (steppe) to the north, and it had two major consequences for human history. First, it made possible the development of a new economy and pattern of life, the specialized form of food production known as pastoral nomadism, based entirely on domestic animals, which made exploitation of the vast steppe grasslands possible for the first time since the Pleistocene big-game hunters. Secondly, it led to the development of mounted warriors who, from about 3,000 years ago, replaced the chariot as the decisive force and thus upset the balance and focus of military power with major consequences for human history in the Old World that lasted until the introduction of firearms. These developments will be discussed later on.

associated technological advances

Coinciding with the shift to food production, though not necessarily related to it in every case, are a number of the most important technological and behavioral developments in human history. This phenomenon creates the impression that a remarkable release of cultural potential followed this shift, as happened later in the wake of industrialization. And certainly there is an almost astronomical increase in the tempo of technical, social, and intellectual change in nuclear areas following the establishment of effective food production, with the key factors of civilization appearing within a few thousand years: the wheel, metallurgy, writing, city life, the state, organized religion. At any rate, the village farming stage is typically associated with such basic crafts as pottery, weaving, stoneworking by abrasion (grinding and polishing); with the presence of adequate houses, of equipment for the new economy, and (at least in some areas) of watercraft capable of crossing considerable distances of salt water; and with stable settlements and religious cults that suggest significant social and ideological reorientation. The roots of some at least of these developments can be seen prior to food production: stable settlements, houses, stone grinding, for instance, were not dependent on the ecological shift but certainly underwent improvement and intensification under the conditions of village life. (And the same could probably be said of most of the rest if we had better evidence of their history.)

The case of pottery is of particular interest. The mastery of this craft, which is no simple matter, has been called by Childe the beginning of science and perhaps man's first conscious utilization of a chemical change. It provided a fire-proof cooking vessel, a convenient container for liquids, and waterproof storage, and almost everywhere became an indispensable adjunct of human life when introduced. Almost universally it is also a major medium for aesthetic expression in form, surface treatment, and decoration.

Traditionally, it was viewed as the index fossil of Man the Farmer, and as probably a single invention that spread from the Near East over most of the world, which otherwise would have presumably remained innocent of this useful art. Evidence which has come to light in the last few years has shattered this traditional view beyond repair, although the realization of this has not yet taken hold. It is now known that pottery in the Near East postdates food production by a considerable time and lags behind other technological advances; that pottery in so remote and marginal an area as Japan goes back to the end of the Pleistocene and antedates food production by a good ten thousand years; and that the art most likely arose independently in several different places in both the Old and New Worlds.

Once established, the major ceramic traditions spread widely within continents. Individual styles, variations, and techniques within these also constituted culture traits that diffused readily and continually, which makes pottery the valuable tool that it is for the archeologist in tracing cultural relationships and influences. The factors involved in its invention—or more precisely in the experimentation necessary to evolve a successful ceramic technique—are unclear, though we can expect archeology to ultimately shed much light on the question. It should be recalled that clay figurines were being fired, apparently in a sort of kiln, back at the beginning of the final glaciation at Dolni Vestonice.

Generally speaking, pottery seems to be associated more with stable life than with a particular economy; while very typical of farmers, it is not confined to them. The sudden appearance of pottery in the Near East around 7,000 years ago is puzzling. In this case it cannot be correlated either with sedentary life, with a particular level of food production, or with the achievement of some higher degree of technological knowledge.

Though simple cordage of plant fibers or even human hair, often rolled on the thigh, is typical of virtually all hunters and gatherers, and woven basketry must go back to the Pleistocene over most of the world, the production of woven textiles had to await the invention of the loom and the large supplies of thread obtained from spinning with the aid of a rotating spindle which draws out and twists the fibers in efficient fashion. Neither of these devices is known to have existed before the village farming stage. And the major development of textiles must certainly have come with the availability of fibers from cultivated plants such as flax and cotton, and from wool.

Cutting tools and other small stone artifacts continued to be made by chipping—indeed, some of the finest workmanship is from this time— but the wide development now of grinding techniques brought the first really effective axes and other heavy woodworking tools, as well as stone vessels (which in parts of the Near East seem to have inhibited the development of pottery), a wide variety of beads and ornaments, and perforated objects such as mace heads, digging stick weights, and spindle whorls. Tough kinds of rock difficult or impossible to shape by chipping could now be used to produce sturdy tools less liable to break, and cutting edges could be resharpened. And stone could now be perforated for stringing or hafting by an abrasive such as sand activated by a rotating shaft. The new techniques of stoneworking were time-consuming and required ample leisure and patience. They could have become widespread only in a setting of stable life and ample food supply. But the new tools, especially the ax, greatly increased man's ability to cope with and alter the environment.

FIGURE 16–2. *Hafted ground-stone ax.* (Photo courtesy of National Museum, Copenhagen.)

Their effectiveness has been demonstrated by experiments with actual prehistoric stone axes. For example, in Denmark three men cleared 600 square yards of silver birch forest in four hours, over 100 trees being felled by one ax without any sharpening.

suggested readings

Brothwell, Don, and Eric Higgs: *Science in Archaeology*, Basic Books, Inc., Publishers, New York, 1963, pp. 235–274.

Cole, Sonia: *The Neolithic Revolution*, 3d ed., British Museum (Natural History), London, 1963.

Flannery, Kent V.: "The Ecology of Early Food Production in Mesopotamia," *Science*, vol. 147, pp. 1247–1256, 1965.

Harlan, Jack R., and Daniel Zohary: "Distribution of Wild Wheats and Barley," *Science*, vol. 153, pp. 1074–1080, 1966.

Mangelsdorf, Paul C., Richard S. MacNeish, and Walton C. Galinat: "Domestication of Corn," *Science*, vol. 143, pp. 538–545, 1964.

Zeuner, Frederick E.: *A History of Domesticated Animals*, Harper & Row, Publishers, Incorporated, New York, 1963.

the first farmers

some early village farming cultures

To present a representative sample of actual early farming villages from the various nuclear areas of food production around the world is surprisingly difficult. An attempt to do so brings home very forcibly just how little information is available on this important stage of development in the key areas. Few such sites have yet been excavated, and fewer still reported in any adequate fashion. All the well-studied "Neolithic" sites are of much later date and represent the subsequent spread of the food-producing way of life into outlying areas far from its source, undergoing adaptation and alteration in the process.

Nowhere is the situation more evident than in the Near East. Despite the burst of activity in field work in recent years, our knowledge is still mainly limited to generalizations of the type given in the preceding two chapters, and provides little towards a picture of human life and activities in a specific farming community during this period. Probably the most famous site of this type is Jarmo, excavated between 1947 and 1955 by Robert J. Braidwood of the University of Chicago, but still known to the world only through brief preliminary reports. Jarmo is located in the foothills of northern Iraq at an elevation of 2,500 feet; its date is placed by the excavator at around 6750 B.C. It represents either a fairly early stage of village farming or else a "backwoods" community that was marginal to the well-developed farming tradition of the nuclear Near East. The site has been partly eroded away and may originally have covered some four and a half acres. It seems to have consisted of twenty to twenty-five mud houses with an estimated useful life of 15 years, after which they would have been abandoned or razed and built anew. The population is thought to have numbered around 150. Sixteen stages of rebuilding have been identified in the site, but it cannot be said with assurance whether this represents continuous occupancy for several centuries or a succession of reoccupations of the same spot at intervals over a period of time. The former would require knowledge of techniques of soil renewal making possible the indefinite exploitation of the same plots of land, a level of sophistication that many are reluctant to accord such novice farmers if that, in fact, is what they were. Successive reuse of the same village site, on the other hand, is a familiar Near Eastern pattern, and would allow the community to move periodically to fresh land and subsequently return to a favored locality when the old fields had regained their fertility.

The houses, each containing several rectangular rooms, had walls of puddled mud, often resting on crude stone foundations. The technique, still in use today, consists in piling up a 3- to 6-inch course of mud stiff enough to stand by itself, allowing this to dry, and then adding further courses in the same fashion to the desired height. It is thought that the houses may have had low gabled roofs of brush or reeds plastered over with mud. Floors were of dirt spread over reeds. (This same type of architecture can be seen in the region at the present day.)

The farmers of Jarmo were growing barley, emmer, and einkorn that were genetically about midway between wild and fully domestic forms. Peas and lentils were also harvested, but are not surely cultivated. Goats were the only certain domestic animal, though figurines of dogs are adduced as evidence of the latter. Meat was primarily supplied by hunting, with pigs, sheep, and gazelle as the commonest quarry; cattle appeared only very rarely on the menu. Another major item of diet was snails, which seem to have been consumed in immense quantities.

Harvesting was done with sickles provided with a cutting edge of inserted flint blades, and grain was processed with mortars or querns. During the later period of the village's existence there were clay ovens probably for parching grain; clay basins set in the floor of each house may have served a similar function earlier or have been used as hearths. Pottery appears late and in such well-developed form that it is obviously borrowed from more advanced neighbors. The people of Jarmo seem to have preferred to grind bowls out of hard stone, mostly marble, in which they had achieved a high level of craftsmanship. Fragments of some 350 vessels have been recovered, and constitute a major category of the archeological finds. Another major category comprises the figurines of human females and of animals.

Stone was also fashioned by abrasion into numerous beads and other ornaments, as well as into such utilitarian items as celts, which may have been either hoes or axes. But for most cutting tools microblades and composite tools made therefrom were preferred, with completely unretouched blades as the commonest form. These continue to be produced by old techniques that seem out of place in association with pottery. Obsidian was the preferred material, and this had to be secured by trade from distant sources. The only other crafts evidenced at Jarmo are matting or basketry.

On the western edge of the Aegean–Near East nuclear area in northern Greece, near the city of Salonica (Thessaloniki), is the very interesting site of Nea Nikomedia which came to light in 1961. The earliest village here, radiocarbon dated at 6220 B.C., consisted of a number of detached, individual houses (two to five yards apart) on a slight rise near a body of water and surrounded by two concentric walls. This settlement pattern is in marked contrast to the solid rows of houses around courtyards so typical of the adjacent Near East. The houses were rectangular with a pole frame and mud walls, the basic unit apparently a 25-foot square. Some may have had more than one room. It is thought that these structures must have had peaked thatch roofs with overhanging eaves in order to protect the walls from rain. These walls were constructed with pole uprights 3 to 4 feet apart, the intervening space being filled with vertical bundles of reeds and the whole plastered on the inside with mud and on the outside with white clay. The walls rested on hard clay footings. Floors were of mud over reeds. One large building 40 feet on a side contained five female figurines; this fact, plus its size and central position, suggested some communal ritual use. The roof had been supported by very large posts, dividing the interior into a large central section and two side aisles.

Wheat, barley, and lentils were grown and harvested with composite sickles. Domestic goats and sheep were of significant importance. Wild pigs and cattle were being hunted, but the high proportion of immature animals among the remains suggests the possibility that some at least were already domesticated. If substantiated, this would represent by far the earliest instance of domestic cattle known. Small game, wildfowl, fish, and molluscs also figured in the diet. The sling (with clay sling stones) and less commonly the bow (using trapezoidal arrowheads) were the weapons used. Pottery is common from the beginning and is of good quality. The "fertility goddess" figurines, however, are reported to be all of sun-dried clay, not fired, the best examples being formed of separate parts pegged together. Stone was worked by both abrasion and chipping (blade technique). Clay stamps may have been used for decorating the body. Spindle whorls and loom weights attest textiles. The dead evidently were accorded scant attention, burials being scattered casually among the houses and nothing being placed in the grave with the deceased.

No really early farming villages are yet known in East Asia. The oldest studied at present, belonging to the so-called "Yangshao" or "painted-pottery" stage of the Chinese "Neolithic," already represent substantial villages and a well-established agricultural economy. The latter is evidently an East Asian development although its origins and history are unknown. The pattern of crops and domestic animals is distinctive, and it is only in the succeeding Lungshan stage, almost on the threshold of civilization, that evident western borrowings appear such as sheep, cattle, wheat, and the potter's wheel.

Pan-p'o-ts'un may be taken as an example of the numerous and widespread sites of the Yangshao stage in the Yellow River Valley of northern China which are usually located on river terraces. It was a fair-sized village of sedentary farmers and had evidently been occupied over a long period of time. Thus we may infer that intensive farming techniques, probably involving fertilization and crop rotation, had already been developed, enabling permanent exploitation of the same plots of land. Millet was the staple crop. Domestic animals were limited to dog (probably eaten) and pig, but the bulk of the meat supply was provided by the hunting of deer. A large communal structure with smaller dwellings clustered about it has been uncovered. During the earlier period of the village's existence, dwellings were semisubterranean pit houses; later they were built above ground. Storage pits, which may have been used for grain, are a common feature.

The village is surrounded by what is assumed to be a defensive ditch 6 meters deep, indicating a need for protection at this time, although there is no direct evidence of warfare. Six pottery kilns near the village suggest a certain degree of craft specialization. Although the bulk of the pottery found is coarse utility ware for household use, fancy painted pottery of high quality was produced for funeral purposes, being buried with the dead. This is decorated initially with zoomorphic designs, and later with geometric patterns. Infants and children were buried in urns within the village area, while adults were interred in a cemetery outside the village limits.

Early village farming communities in the New World are best known from the Valley of Mexico, a basin situated on a high plateau. In this general area of Mesoamerica, effective farming and sedentary village life seem to coincide with the appearance of hybrid strains of maize (corn)— a development which may have followed improved (moister) climatic conditions that facilitated the diffusion of crop plants between different regions. At any rate, other plants seem to have spread at the same general time, resulting in a widespread shared farming complex of species that had been genetically improved due to the crossing of a number of hitherto local strains. This complex included maize, grain amaranth, two squashes (grown primarily for the edible seeds), pumpkin, bean, chili pepper, bottle gourd, tobacco, avocado, tomato, and other fruits and vegetables. Cotton was also grown at lower elevations and traded into the Valley of Mexico.

FIGURE 17–1. *Foundations of a dwelling at Pan-p'o-ts'un* (bottom), *and reconstruction* (top). (From William Watson, *Early Civilization in China*, copyright © 1966 by Thames and Hudson Limited, London. U.S. edition by McGraw-Hill, Inc., New York. By permission of the publishers.)

Pulque, the fermented drink made from the sap of the maguey plant, may have already come into use; it was an important source of vitamins and minerals in the native diet of later times. Hunting of deer and waterfowl and fishing in the extensive lakes of the valley were also important aspects of the economy.

The thick deposits of refuse at the village sites—consisting mostly of corn husks—indicates occupancy of the same location over a long period of time and hence intensive farming techniques. It also indicates that rubbish was simply thrown out the door. These early villages lack any trace of a ceremonial center or public buildings so characteristic of later settlements. The dwellings were evidently built of poles, woven wattle plastered with clay, and topped with a thatch roof; they probably closely resembled the peasant houses of modern times, as was the case also in the Near East. Such structures leave no trace of a floor, foundations, or hearth in the archeological sites.

Farming was carried on with digging sticks; grains and seeds were processed for consumption on stone grinding equipment (metates). Simple types of pottery served as containers along, probably, with gourds. Cotton cloth was woven, the cotton being obtained by trade where it could not be grown, along with such luxury items as seashells and jade. Small un-retouched obsidian blades served as cutting tools, and the only weapons are represented by points for either darts or arrows. (The spear-thrower was the main weapon in this area in later times.) There is no trace of warfare at this time and no evidence of social differentiation. Burials are found scattered through the refuse deposits, and it is surmised that the dead may have originally been interred under the floor of the family dwelling. (It is impossible to tell where the houses once stood.) The most conspicuous and typical finds at these sites are clay figurines—all female. Since all are naked and have the sex organs emphasized, it is assumed that they are fetishes connected with human or agricultural fertility—or both. The figurines depict elaborate face and body painting and equally elaborate hairdos and headdresses. Their great variety and individuality suggests household fetishes. It is thought that any more generalized concept (e.g., "mother goddess") or community cult would result in more stereotyped depictions.

Other postulated independent farming complexes

Rice is historically one of the most important cereal crops domesticated by man. According to botanists, its origins lie in the Indonesia-Malaysia region. Many species and extensive hybridization are believed to have been involved in the development of the cultivated crop plant, and how it was moved such long distances and into such different environments is still an unsolved question. It must have had a long history of cultivation in island Southeast Asia to produce the present variety of systems employed. Furthermore, its cultivation is considered to be still developing and not yet to have reached the degree of perfection observed in other crops. Rice agriculture is the major feature of a farming complex that includes the domestic water buffalo and minimal use of any domestic animals for meat. The limits of its prehistoric diffusion were the coastal lowlands of Asia north to the Yellow River and west to India. Doubtless as a result of contact with Near Eastern farming traditions, we find dairying added in India; elsewhere, the absence of dairying and marked distaste for milk or milk products is a striking characteristic of the rice farming complex. These distinctively independent features, plus the tropical origin of both rice and the buffalo, make it necessary to postulate a major hearth of food production somewhere in the general Southeast Asia area, despite the lack of archeological evidence. Some time depth is indicated by occurrences of rice in the earlier farming villages of the Yangtze River Valley and southern China, although their age is unknown. Here is certainly one of the major mysteries of prehistory.

The essential differences between grain (seed) cultivation of cereal crops and the propagation of root and fruit crops, or vegeculture as it is sometimes known, have already been pointed out. It might be contrasted as sowing versus planting. In tropical areas of the Old World unsuited for the temperate zone cereal grains, and into which rice penetrated either later or not at all, there seems to have flourished a distinctive complex of vegeculture involving such food plants as yams, taro, bananas, breadfruit, sugar cane, and (in coastal areas) the coconut. Probably less is known about this than any other major food complex, but it is inferred that it must have arisen somewhere in Southeast Asia, from which it spread several thousand years ago into the Pacific islands (except Australia) and about 2,000 years ago crossed the Indian Ocean and spread across tropical Africa, where it had a major effect on the development and spread of food production, until then hampered by lack of suitable tropical crops. The domestication of the chicken, whose wild ancestor is native to Southeast Asia, is probably associated with this complex. (There is debate as to whether the chicken was initially domesticated for meat or for such non-utilitarian purposes as sacrifice or divination, which often seem to be its principal functions in the tropics.) Pigs and dogs (both as festive food animals, rather than serious contributors to the economy) everywhere accompany the complex, but might have been borrowed from China. The age, origin, and history of this important branch of human economy, and its relationship to the rice complex of the same general area, are major problems for the future. They point up the fact that less is known about the prehistory of Southeast Asia than any other area of equal significance.[1]

---

[1] A time depth on the order of 10,000 years for vegeculture in this area is suggested by recent field work on Taiwan.

A somewhat similar situation exists in the New World, where tropical forest farming based primarily on manioc is inferred to have originated independently in the Amazon basin, from which the crop plants diffused to all suitable environments. Again, the archeology of the area is still too little known to supply details. Certainly our lack of knowledge as to the origins of vegeculture in both hemispheres remains the most significant gap in any discussion of the transition from food gathering to food production as a universal process. Did stimulus diffusion from seed crop areas play a role, or is the practice of vegeculture so distinct that it must have sprung from separate roots, and with what motivation?

A few years ago G. P. Murdock advanced the hypothesis of an independent center of agriculture in West Africa. This has not yet been supported by archeological evidence, which indicates the opposite: namely, that West African agriculture arose as a result of experimentation with local plants (e.g., sorghums) after knowledge of the Near Eastern farming complex had penetrated from North Africa. The crops of the latter failed to spread since they were unsuited to conditions south of the Sahara. Although sub-Saharan Africa did not initiate food production by itself, it was quick to experiment and adapt the new potential to the locally available natural resources. It has been equally quick to adopt and distribute rapidly any suitable crop subsequently introduced from other tropical regions of the Old and New Worlds.

FIGURE 17–2. *Figurines from Tlatilco in the Valley of Mexico.* (By permission of the Museum of Primitive Art.)

the village farming stage: economy and life

Owing to the marked differences between the various regional farming patterns arising from the nature of the crops and animals as well as the environments, it is difficult to generalize about life at this stage. What follows will be understood to apply to the nuclear areas of the world.

The level of effective food production was perhaps reached most quickly by the mixed farming complex (plants and animals) of the Near East, which is directly ancestral to our own agriculture, though it took at least 3,000 years to evolve. Wheat and barley were fundamental to this complex. Like the millet of East Asia and the maize of the New World, they are very nutritious, easily stored, and yield a high return relative to the labor expended, which is typically seasonal and thus gives time for leisure. Rice has similar qualities, but the irrigated system of cultivation, which is by far the commonest, requires more continuous work. All of these regional staples were always accompanied by a variety of legumes, vegetables, fruits, fibers, and (usually) oil-producing plants. All these, including the cereals, were more like garden crops than field crops in our sense of the word, since they were grown in small plots by hand cultivation. All such farming by necessity was confined to areas of lighter soils. A crude plow and larger fields came later in those parts of the Old World where animal power became available. Experiments with growing the early Near Eastern crops using only the implements believed to have been employed suggest that yields at this stage were meager. Communities and individuals whose livestock were not numerous enough to slaughter depended on hunting and fishing for their meat supply, just as in pioneer America. The techniques employed remained identical with those of the postglacial hunters and do not reflect the advances in other fields of technology. In the New World, of course, hunting remained the only source of meat.

Harvesting of cereals in the Old World was with flint-bladed sickles of wood or bone, and the grain was parched (commonly in clay ovens in the Near East), ground to get rid of clinging hulls, and ground again into coarse meal. Grinding slabs (querns) or mortars are standard items of

FIGURE 17–3. *Flint sickle used by early village farmers.* (By permission from Sonia Cole, *The Neolithic Revolution,* copyright © 1959 by the Trustees of the British Museum–Natural History.)

equipment everywhere. The meal was cooked into mush or gruel, or else spread thin on hot stones to produce a sort of unleavened bread like Mexican tortillas. Gruel left standing in pots would soon ferment, and beer may have been one of the earliest discoveries of Man the Farmer. With pottery containers now typically available, it may be assumed that a greater variety of cookery than heretofore made its appearance.

Settlement was distributed in areas of suitable soil and adequate rainfall, or on occasion in situations with natural irrigation like Jericho which though situated in a desert area is watered by a natural spring. In the Near East at least, alluvial valleys were avoided at this early stage. The apparent stability of settlement in this region suggests early knowledge of techniques of intensive cultivation, permitting reuse of limited tracts of land. Fortified settlements are limited to a few instances (e.g., Jericho) in the Near East, and evidence of warfare is absent in most areas. Characteristically, it seems to have been a rare time of idyllic peace in human history.

Trade first becomes of importance to man at this stage, and patterns of communication develop. With people rooted to their own localities, trade was a crucial factor in culture contact and culture change. It also enabled communities to live more abundantly than they could do on their own resources of raw materials and skill, thus providing a means of surmounting ecological limitations and supplementing skills. The evidence for long-range obsidian trade in the Near East has already been cited.

With effective food production it is widely assumed that there would be food surpluses and considerable leisure for other activities; also that specialized craftsmen would begin to develop, supported by the community in exchange for their handiwork in more difficult crafts.

Villages are thought to have been self-sufficient communities, socially speaking, not forming part of any larger social grouping, each living in a world of its own. Economically they were also self sufficient; trade might make life better, but it was never necessary for survival. At this stage people still held their fate in their own hands.

summary and conclusions

The pattern of life reflected in the village farming community that had attained an effective level of food production was an end in itself and still persists over much of the world: the outstanding feature being the self-sufficiency of the local community and its ignorance of the outside world, which it does not have to take into account. Though we in the industrial west have largely departed from it in recent years, it was directly ancestral to our own rural life a few generations back before the mechanization of agriculture. The Near Eastern villager of 5,000 years ago was probably closer in his values and attitudes to the European peasant of modern times than he was to the city dweller of his own time a few miles away, so great is the contrast created by urban life. An admirable adjustment in its time, this "Neolithic" pattern is an anachronism in the modern world that has led some scholars to remark that "getting out of the Neolithic" may be one of the most serious problems that the modern world has to face. China has attempted to deal with the problem by forcible uprooting and reorganization; India and Africa are just beginning to face the problems created by their village and tribal societies.

But the village farming pattern also provided, initially, the essential base for higher sociotechnical development in a few areas as a result of factors which we do not yet comprehend. It was thus at one and the same time a dead end and the door to the future. The larger and more stable communities, the leisure, the possibility for specialization—all were prerequisites. Every food plant of major importance to the modern world was domesticated at this time, and it was through the coalescence of many separate domestications in each region that an effective level of food production was achieved.

The biological consequences of this ecological shift were no less significant than the cultural. In addition to population increase, to major changes in the numbers and distribution of racial groups, and to longer life span, with the elderly no longer a burden on society, the disease situations arising from food production have had no less decisive effects and have played perhaps the major role in subsequent human evolution. The primate-level sanitation notions of primitive man cause no problems in small groups that do not stay for long in any one place, but create health hazards when it comes to settled life in larger groups. The same situation of population increase and concentration must have been a very important factor in the proliferation of disease, since the ability of disease bacteria to establish themselves in man must have depended to a great extent on the degree of dispersion of the human population. The new way of life made malaria an important disease for the first time by bringing large populations into malaria areas where they had hitherto been scant. And as large numbers of people in more densely populated areas were reduced to a largely cereal diet, protein deficiency diseases have made their appearance. Garn (1963) believes that we may view much of recent human evolution as a series of local genetic adaptations to disease situations arising out of food production—situations for which man was not physiologically prepared.

reference

Garn, Stanley M.: "Culture and the Direction of Human Evolution," *Human Biology*, vol. 35, no. 3, pp. 221–236, 1963.

suggested readings

Chang, Kwang-chih: *The Archaeology of Ancient China,* rev. and enl. ed., Yale
    University Press, New Haven, Conn., 1968, pp. 78–120.
Coe, Michael D.: *Mexico,* Frederick A. Praeger, Inc., New York, 1962, pp. 64–78.
Cole, Sonia: *The Neolithic Revolution,* 3d ed., British Museum (Natural His-
    tory), London, 1963.
Mellaart, James: *Earliest Civilizations of the Near East,* McGraw-Hill Book Com-
    pany, New York, 1965, pp. 39–118.
Watson, William: *Early Civilization in China,* McGraw-Hill Book Company, New
    York, 1966, pp. 16–44. (Note: The author's views on the temporal and
    areal relationships of the Neolithic cultures are no longer accepted.)

urbanism

nature and significance of urbanism

The village farming stage represents the basic pattern of life of most of the human beings who have ever lived on earth. From the time that the new pattern became established and the human stock began to multiply beyond its previous limits, down to the present day, the vast bulk of the world's population has lived either as tribal societies or as peasant societies within the spheres of historic civilizations: peasants whose social patterns, economy, values, and outlook remain essentially those of the "Neolithic" and who do not participate in any real way in the urban civilization that controls them—a civilization to which they commonly feel alien and even hostile. The focus of peasant attention and loyalty is the kin group and the village; there is little identification with or loyalty to the nation of which they supposedly form a part. Each such village is basically self-sufficient—economically, socially, and politically.

In a few places, a totally new social and economic pattern arose: urban life, which is parasitic on the farming villages. It cannot feed itself; but it was the indispensable medium within which the arts of civilization arose. It also gave rise to, or was correlated with, the first appearance of political institutions. Urban life is more than merely much larger aggregations of population than the world had hitherto seen or than mastery of the art of living under such conditions in terms of social skills and discipline. More significant in the overall picture of cultural evolution is its symbiotic nature in contrast to the internal self-sufficiency of the village: a symbiosis implying a new and different pattern of human relationships, including the exercise of control over those outside the community and hence the beginning of larger territorial units. Through this political control and cultural dominance, the urban centers, a minority of mankind, came to dominate the majority and also to monopolize the historical record. Conventional history is the activities of this minority. The vast majority of mankind on whom their existence depends is ignored by historians as if it had never existed and remains as anonymous as the 40,000 preceding generations of prehistoric men.

Civilization, then—or any social or cultural advance over the village farming level with its seemingly innate conservatism—could only arise in an urban environment or something approaching it. And the village farming pattern was not bound to evolve urbanism, though it was certainly the prerequisite for it: obviously so in the economic sense and probably in other ways as well if only we knew more about it. On the contrary, the urban pattern arose in only a very few small localities around the world. Its occurrence anywhere else is the result of diffusion or colonization from these original centers.

At this point it would be well to consider just what is meant by the term "civilization." Although the word conveys a vague general notion to most of us, there is no real agreement among scholars on a precise definition. It is difficult to tell whether civilization is thought of as being synonymous with urbanism, that is, with the urban pattern of life, or whether it is regarded as something more. Some include the presence of cities among their criteria for civilization, implying the former view; others speak of the city as the cradle of civilization, implying the latter.

While there is no agreement on defining the concept of civilization, there is general acceptance of a purely arbitrary yardstick in the Old World: namely, the presence of a system of writing. Thus, any society capable of written records automatically qualifies as a civilization by a sort of tacit consent. Conversely, even a complex culture with impressive towns would be ineligible if no trace of writing was discovered. Probably there are few scholars who regard this yardstick without some misgivings and as other than an arbitrary convenience. Certainly it has little acceptance when applied to the New World, where elaborate societies could develop, as in Peru, with no system of writing whatsoever and apparently with only mnemonic devices for record keeping. We actually do not know the circumstances which brought writing systems into existence in a number of areas, and it is pure theorizing to claim that they are the inevitable outgrowth of a certain level of economic or social complexity. In fact, we may suspect that too often definitions of "civilization" reflect one's own as the ideal standard against which others are judged, generally to their detriment. It would be preferable, to avoid such ethnocentrism, to agree on a set of characteristics which have universal applicability and are designed to reflect a certain socioeconomic pattern or level of complexity.

Some characteristics often mentioned that might form the basis for such a definition of civilization are:

1. An urbanized society, with the emphasis not upon our image of a city (which is not present, for instance, in the early Chinese or early Mesoamerican civilizations or in Egypt), but rather upon the existence of social units of considerable size and complexity which evoked a whole series of new institutions and social patterns to make this way of life possible. Social stratification is commonly singled out as one distinctive feature.

2. A territorially based state (as opposed to kinship-based tribal units) exercising political and military authority through appropriate institutions and through a code of laws imposed from above, in contrast to the custom law and public opinion sanction of village societies.

3. A symbiotic economy based on centralized accumulation of capital and social surplus through tribute or taxation, in order to support an essentially parasitic social body, and also on extensive division of labor and numerous resultant full-time craft specialists which make the city a market center for the surrounding area. (Long-distance trade in luxury items is a consistent feature, though not a criterion, since it can occur at earlier levels though usually on a smaller scale.)

4. Advances toward exact and predictive sciences, usually involving a calendar, mathematics, and writing.

5. Impressive public works and monumental architecture are commonly cited as evidence of civilization, more specifically as symbolizing the presence of the less tangible criteria above, such as a concentration of capital, or new patterns of thought or of social organization. However, it can be demonstrated that extensive construction is not everywhere proof of complex sociopolitical organization, and thus should never be a sole criterion.

It should be stressed that these different proposed attributes of civilization take different forms in the various early experiments in urban life and by no means provide a uniform blueprint of the actual picture the world over.

Because the appearance of urban life constituted such a major change in human relationships; because it led to or was correlated with what is considered as "civilization"; and because in the Near East at least, the focus of Western attention, it has seemed to take form quite suddenly; so the concept of an "Urban Revolution" has gained some currency. It was originally proposed by the influential British prehistorian V. Gordon Childe as a counterpart to his "Neolithic Revolution" and presumably as an event equally decisive in human history. It does not, however, represent such a major reorientation of total human life as does food production, and certainly in the New World, where the rise of urbanism may have been a longer, slower process, the concept of a "revolution" would not likely have been formulated.

Nevertheless, the appearance of this new pattern of life was a development of major significance in the cultural evolution of man and had very profound consequences. Insofar as it was revolutionary, it should be thought of as a social revolution. Whereas the previous decisive shifts in human life had been primarily ecological and technological, with socio-cultural developments following as adjustments, urbanism is primarily a social and cultural change which led to technological and other consequences. The city, it has been well remarked, is a social invention. What we see, then, are basically changes in social institutions and a new pattern of relationships to other men rather than new relationships to the environment. The hallmarks of this new pattern, already mentioned, include such features as social complexity, new institutions, loss of self-sufficiency through dependence on a symbiotic economy characterized by specialization of labor, growth of trade, and the role of the city as a trade and manufacturing center. Increasingly, the new Urban Man came to be dependent on his social and cultural environment just as Man the Hunter had been at the mercy of his physical environment. Relative security has been a condition enjoyed only by the village farmers intermediate between the two. Under the urban pattern, the interdependence of society meant vulnerability to developments and events in the outside world over which one had no control, with the result that when the mechanism and delicate balance of urban life is upset by war, revolution, or other catastrophe, the effects on the city dweller can be catastrophic, unlike the situation in the self-sufficient rural village.

One of the most conspicuous features of this new pattern of life is the development of political institutions, including the emergence of the first states based on the total population of a defined territory, irrespective of kinship affiliations. Initially these took the form of "city-states": that is, a single city with the surrounding rural countryside from which it drew its economic support. Such states were in a sense the natural economic and social units under the new pattern of relationships They were also religious units, and the prominent role of organized religion in political life is another especially conspicuous feature of most early city-states the world over. Although religious institutions are not a consequence of urban life as are political institutions, and in fact some scholars would see religion as the catalytic agent in the initial formation of urban societies, still an elaborate development of organized religion is a characteristic of urbanism.

In the course of time, some at least of these city-states began to increase steadily in size, leading to growing political problems and clashes between them. Factors contributing to the rise of urban civilizations also increased the possibilities of conflict and warfare. With the more advanced societies reaching out beyond their own frontiers to distant markets and sources of raw materials, situations inevitably arose that led to wars of a colonial character (in modern parlance) with less advanced neighbors, or to conflicts with competing societies on the same level of cultural development. Thus, with the stage of urban civilization we see militarism becoming the characteristic feature of human life that it has been ever since. Simultaneously, then as in modern times, war proved to be a great impetus for further technological development. For example, wheeled vehicles and improved metallurgy were important primarily from the military standpoint. We can see a feedback relationship between war and cultural evolution as being both a consequence and a cause of cultural advance. Already we can discern a general pattern familiar to us: technological development creating a richer life but simultaneously creating important problems demanding solution—problems with which mankind has been wrestling ever since.

However, it would be erroneous to imply that all technical advance at this time was due to the appearance of militarism. On the contrary, the phenomenon most conspicuously discernible in the archeological record with the onset of urbanism is a major burst of creative energy as evidenced in very rapid stylistic and technical advances in arts and crafts. These must have been accompanied by equal ferment in the intellectual realm in order to account for the appearance soon after of writing, calendars, and the beginnings of science.

Urban life had important biological consequences as well, especially in providing a check on the growth of population. Urbanization brought with it problems of sanitation and contagious disease that were only minimal in the rural village and that have found adequate solution only in modern times. Generally speaking, cities maintained their populations through constant inflow from the countryside. It should particularly be pointed out that the large populations we associate with cities are by and large a phenomenon of the last hundred years. The great population growth in the early urban stage occurred in the countryside as a consequence of greater agricultural production stemming from such major improvements in farming as the plow and irrigation, which now appeared on the scene.

The birth of civilization poses two major problems which we might label *how* and *why*. There are those who believe that civilization may have arisen only once in the world and spread from there: that it resulted from the chance coincidence of a number of unrelated factors, a happenstance unlikely to have occurred more than once, the wonder being that it happened at all. Others feel that under favorable circumstances, given a certain level of development and the presence of some specific factors or phenomena, the ultimate emergence of civilization is inevitable or at least probable. Obviously, this controversy goes to the heart of the processes of culture and of what might be called "human nature." The question of multiple or unitary origins for civilization is therefore one of the basic problems in the study of man, and this accounts for the attention that is focused on the beginnings of urbanism. It is also a problem which archeologists should be able to solve eventually. At this point it seems highly probable that civilization arose independently in the Old and New Worlds, but whether at more than one locality in each is still hotly debated and cannot be settled on the body of evidence now available, although some cases appear stronger than others.

Why this development should have occurred where it did is another matter, and must involve explaining equally why it did *not* occur elsewhere. I think we can say flatly that there is no positive evidence that would help to answer this question. There are interpretations of available data that have been offered, but they are interpretations in support of one or another hypothesis and may be contradicted by other data, by new discoveries, or by alternative interpretations of the same data. And then there are theories which offer possible explanations for the end results. Probably no other area of prehistory has inspired so large a body of theoretical thinking.[1]

One famous example in recent years was the "irrigation theory" formulated by Karl A. Wittfogel, which held that the early civilized states were brought into being by the administrative requirements of managing large-scale irrigation systems, upon which effective exploitation of the arid alluvial valleys, cradles of a number of civilizations, was thought to be dependent (i.e., men submitted to higher authority as the price for life-giving water, which was only obtainable through extensive public works constructed, maintained, and controlled by a central administration). More recent studies demonstrate that the appearance of the first city-states antedates any such elaborate irrigation in these areas. Others have pointed out that very complex irrigation systems in modern times are operated successfully by village farming communities. And some civilizations arose in regions where irrigation is of little or no importance.

In commenting on such formulations, Robert Adams wisely observes that "Each of the early civilizations was the unique product of alternately conflicting and mutually reinforcing trends, and it is futile to hope that even their basic features will be explained in all cases as the predictable, predetermined outcome of some sort of general law" (Adams, 1960, p. 161).

The discovery in recent years of impressive towns such as Jericho in Palestine and Çatal Hüyük in Anatolia, all of them lying outside the pale of early urban civilization in Mesopotamia but evidently antedating the latter by several thousands of years, further complicates the picture.[2] It is hard not to consider these towns as representing at least experiments in urban living; yet lacking such conventional attributes of civilization, as writing, and without proof of the requisite socioeconomic complexity, no one is willing to call them cities. In all cases they seem to be dead-end developments: i.e., they did not lead directly to true urbanism and civilization, which only appeared in Palestine and Anatolia at a much later date and, presumably, in imitation of Mesopotamia. Thus at present we cannot explain or assess the overall significance of these early towns or say whether they, or something similar, formed an intermediate stage of development between the farming village and the true city.

---

[1] Some of the more significant discussions of the problem are listed at the end of this chapter under "Suggested Readings."

[2] Described in Mellaart, 1966, pp. 32–42, 81–101.

associated technical and intellectual advances

The urban pattern of life is generally associated with certain important technological and intellectual developments and achievements, some of them doubtless fostered by the new conditions and by the intellectual atmosphere they engendered, others appearing by coincidence at this time but certainly attaining full flower in the urban milieu or under urban stimulus. Because we place so much emphasis on these achievements and because we are accustomed to thinking of civilization as something shared in by all members of the community, it is important to realize that the major impact of early metallurgy or early writing systems lay 1,000 years or more in the future and that their overall effect on contemporary life was minimal. At best, they were of benefit to a small elite; the bulk of the urban population profited little, and the vast mass in the countryside remained untouched, if we except a few practical inventions such as plow and wheel.

Metallurgy arose independently in a number of areas, far from cities, where ores of easily worked metals were conspicuously available and where knowledge of heat control and the creation of relatively high temperatures had been mastered through the ability to fire good-quality pottery. Awareness of the distinct properties of metal among other natural substances has been evidenced by prehistoric or primitive peoples in many parts of the world where it occurs in suitable form to be shaped simply by hammering cold. The oldest metal artifacts are all of this type, and the products are sometimes surprisingly impressive. The process was a dead end in regions like Wisconsin, the Ohio Valley, or the Arctic, where a high level of pottery technology was lacking. But in others, such as portions of the western highlands of Iran and probably also of Anatolia, actual smelting and casting eventually developed. Ceramic technology has been called the beginnings of science, and we may surmise that the experimental attitudes and empirical knowledge involved, when transferred to already familiar metallic substances, led sooner or later to a grasp of the basic properties of ore and metal and of the processes involved in separating and working them. For example, the furnace necessary for smelting nonferrous metals is basically similar in principle to the potter's kiln, so that no major new invention was necessitated.

Metallurgy thus arose in a setting of village society and economy and presumably, like pottery, would have remained at the level of a local craft as ironworking, for example, was among so many primitive and peasant societies of recent times. In the Old World, it was only when the art spread to the developing cities, via itinerant craftsmen and traders, that major demand, and the wealth to back it up, led to the large-scale trade and mining enterprise that transformed metallurgy into a major industry and skilled craft and led to its highest development. Although too little is known about the history of metalworking in the New World, the association with urbanism is less close. Not only the earliest but the highest achievements of metallurgy are in nonurban regions, though in societies with an elite capable of affording luxury goods. In general, metallurgy is not a feature of the earlier and otherwise spectacular New World civilizations and is entirely lacking (except for traded metal objects) in one of the greatest, the Mayan.

Copper is everywhere the earliest important metal, due to its availability and ease of working, though small amounts of gold and silver also appear in early stages. Though satisfying ornamental needs, these metals were of limited value for more practical purposes, and it was only somewhat later, through a real invention, bronze, that metal may be said to have really come into its own as a utilitarian substance superior to any previous material. Bronze is an alloy of copper and tin; the difficulty of securing supplies of the latter in most areas was a further spur to the development of long-range trade. It also tended to make bronze metallurgy a monopoly of big-city industry or of a few metallurgical centers elsewhere and no longer a widespread village craft. The working of iron came much later, involving as it does a very different process—perhaps 2,000 years after the smelting of copper. It was iron, however, due to its ready availability and cheapness, that brought metal into general use.

As we have mentioned, early metallurgy (copper and bronze) had a very limited impact on the life of the time and its importance is easily exaggerated. Stone remained in general use for cutting tools and weapons. For a long time, metal was a luxury item that served no utilitarian purpose for the vast majority, although bronze came to play a role for military purposes for those who could afford it. Metal did not really become a significant attribute of human existence until iron, the "poor man's metal," came into general use and began to provide the implements and tools of everyday life and labor, as well as weapons that anyone could afford and any village could produce.

In fact, the most significant contribution of early metallurgy probably lay in the spurring of trade and in the developing of trade routes and trade networks. In addition, because persons involved in all phases of the metal industry—extraction, transportation, and manufacture—are characteristically full-time specialists, it played a further role in the developing division of labor.

A number of practical inventions seem to make their appearance with the beginnings of urbanism, although not all are universal. In the western half of the Old World, at least, where wheat and barley were the staple crops, the plow very greatly increased the productivity of agriculture and was thus doubtless a major factor in population growth and in the creation of economic surpluses essential for the viability and prosperity of the cities. Although the actual history of the plow is not known, there is no present evidence of its existence prior to this time. It seems to have come into use in the Near East–Egypt area, probably spread thence to India, and at a considerably later date diffused to China. Effective plowing depends on animal power and could not have developed before the availability of a suitable source, namely the castrated ox, which represented a considerable invention in itself. Similarly, the lack of any animal power in the New World condemned American Indian farming to hand methods. Beyond the zone of wheat agriculture, the plow was of minor importance to the rice growers of East Asia with their very different requirements and was useless to the slash-and-burn farmers of the tropical forests.

A parallel consequence of animal power, with a very similar history, was the wheel. Loads very likely were initially hauled on crude toboggan- or sledlike contraptions like the American farmer's stone boat, and we may surmise that the placing of rollers under very heavy loads might have led to the idea of wheels. Vehicles with crude, heavy, solid wheels—often of three planks fastened side by side—are present in the early urban civilization of the Near East and India and may still be seen in use, little changed, among the peasantry of these same areas today. A further development, or "invention," was the idea of using vehicles in warfare for mobility and striking power. This involved the development of the lightweight chariot with its spoked wheels, which became a decisive element of military power and spread as far as North China. Wheeled vehicles are absent or of limited importance in the regions where the same is true of the plow. The principle of the wheel was invented in Mexico, but probably due to the absence of draught animals, it remained only a toy. In addition to its function in transportation, the wheel came to serve another important purpose in the mass production of pottery, as the potter's wheel operating on the principle of the lathe. The concept involved represents a separate invention not inherent in the initial use of the wheel but generally speaking seems to follow upon it, and their distribution is roughly coterminous.

The moving of bulky or heavy loads for more than very short distances has depended on water transportation down to modern times: rafts, barges, and canal boats that could be floated down rivers or hauled by men and animals on the bank. These must have played a major role in such early river valley civilizations as Mesopotamia and Egypt, where heavy construction materials often had to be brought from considerable distances and the surplus crops transported to the urban repositories. Thus, although water transport can hardly be said to have been "invented" at this time, the new urban pattern was certainly an impetus for its major development. At this same time we have the first evidence of another important invention, the sail boat, although again we do not actually know its history. It must have been the major factor in creating long-distance trade by water routes, which on occasion had important historical consequences in effecting cultural diffusion and stimulation.

Large-scale public works of an economic or welfare character are also a general feature of the urban civilizations, the result of centralized control of organized manpower. Often these represent an intensification or elaboration of earlier small-scale activities. For example, an imposing city wall representing a tremendous investment of labor was characteristic of even the earliest Chinese urban centers but may be viewed as an elaboration of the smaller defensive walls typical of the later farming villages of preceding time. The growth and elaboration of irrigation systems, at least in arid Mesopotamia and Peru, was an immediate consequence of urbanization. In China, major irrigation works appear at a later stage of urban civilization and are probably correlated with a shift to rice as the economic staple. The tremendous yield per acre of irrigated rice may be assumed to be reflected in population growth at this time. Early urban China, in addition to defensive walls, was primarily concerned with flood control, doubtless a matter of interest also in the Indus Valley and in Egypt.

Archeologically, the most conspicuous feature of developing urbanism everywhere is monumental architecture: either a seemingly sudden flowering, or else a tremendous elaboration of earlier tendencies. In many centers this was initially overwhelmingly religious in nature, with structures reflecting secular power appearing later, although, as in Western civilization, religious edifices always remain a conspicuous feature everywhere. Like other public works, such monumental architecture was both a consequence of controlled, organized manpower and a reflection of the new values and idea systems involved in urbanization. It also embodied advances in engineering and aesthetic skills. The organized manpower was not necessarily the result of coercion by authority: It may in some cases have been inspired by religious zeal.

Closely associated, and equally apparent in the archeological record, is a great efflorescence of ornamental art and art objects, as well as the first appearance of representational or documentary art. The former are devoted almost entirely to the service of religion or to luxury goods, a situation strikingly reminiscent of recent Western civilization. Art was not for the masses, whose possessions were the products of mass-production industry with little aesthetic content. As in the case of metallurgy and other trappings of civilization, the benefits were highly restricted.

Representational art, depicting persons and activities, is especially characteristic of many urban centers and provides an important source of historical information, although generally speaking it is strongly biased toward religion, cult, and mythology.

Intellectual advances were no less striking than more technical ones. Most typically these were in the fields of mathematics and astronomy and led to such useful by-products as standardized weights and measures and calendars. Beyond this point, further advances in the direction of science were invariably halted. Perhaps because the intellectuals seem invariably to have been members of the priesthood, such intellectual activity became hopelessly entangled with ritualism and motivated by supernatural interests, such as divination. Astronomy degenerated into astrology, except for such observations as were necessary for calendrical purposes, and mathematical concepts remained frozen.

But the most important intellectual achievement was undoubtedly the invention of systems of writing in all but one of the early centers of urbanism—although again it had little effect on contemporary life and its real impact was yet to come. In Mesopotamia, writing is believed to have begun as bookkeeping, inspired by the need for records of this nature. Elsewhere, we simply do not know enough of its history to discuss its origin. We cannot even judge to what extent the early experiments in Mesopotamia may have sparked similar developments in Egypt, India, or even China, although the end products in each case were distinctively different. Certainly the appearance of writing in Mesoamerica is an independent phenomenon, although we know nothing of its beginnings.[3]

associated social and institutional developments

Unlike the technological and intellectual advances just discussed, the social and institutional developments associated with urbanism directly affected every city dweller, setting as they did the entire pattern of life, and exerted at least indirect effect on the surrounding countryside.

The prominence of religious structures in the earliest urban sites strengthens the hypothesis that religion functioned as the original political catalyst in the formation of urban societies and that the early states were strongly theocratic in character, with the priesthood in fact forming the ruling class. In Mesoamerica the whole pattern of settlement supports this view, with ceremonial centers as the nucleus and evident integrating factor of an otherwise dispersed community. In Mesopotamia, documentary evidence paints a picture of the city god and his temple as the center of economic as well as religious organization. The crucial supernatural role in agriculture, and hence in the national economy, of the priest-king of early China or the divine pharaoh of Egypt are well-known historical facts further attesting the widespread religious domination of society. The archeological picture from all early urban centers indicates that the social surplus went primarily to religious institutions and personnel. And as already noted the priesthood was universally the intellectual elite with a monopoly on knowledge and related skills such as writing. In general, the early urban stage seems to have been a time of local deities whose worship and jurisdiction were limited to one community or city-state, as contrasted with widespread cults and national deities of later times.

The first emergence of the state as a territorially based political institution has been mentioned as one of the most significant features of the urban stage. If initially under religious dominance, the general pattern subsequently in most centers was toward a gradual replacement by secular rulers, leading ultimately to political depotism. The conditions of city life, essentially an aggregate of strangers, made the old village patterns of

[3] The best concise, simple discussion of the history of writing and of the problems involved in developing writing systems will be found in Diringer, 1962.

social control by public opinion inoperable and created the necessity for control by law imposed from above, codified, and enforced through appropriate institutions.

Equally characteristic of urban society is social stratification, with institutionalized slavery as the lowest class. The subsequent growth of a commercial class, not initially in evidence, is noted at least for Mesopotamia, China, and Mexico. In general, there seems to have been a tendency for such stratification to become more rigid with time.

Specialization of labor has also been mentioned as a feature of urban society.

Certainly warfare and militarism everywhere increase with time, but the reality of an initial peaceful urban stage, as fashionably hypothesized, may be questioned. The ubiquitous defensive walls of early China were certainly not built just for exercise, and in desert Peru, where arable land was strictly limited, it is not surprising to find that expanding population was matched by increasing belligerence. On the other hand, Egypt after its initial unification faced no immediate rivals, there is no sign of warfare in the first towns of alluvial Mesopotamia, and the vulnerable settlement pattern of Mesoamerica would seem to betoken a relatively peaceful existence. In addition to the rivalries of growing states in most areas, their increasing wealth must have aroused the baser impulses of less civilized neighbors. The overthrow, or at least the plundering, of city states by "barbarians" is a perpetually recurring theme throughout history, most strikingly symbolized in the Great Wall of China. Any initially peaceful era was not for long, and large-scale militarism and empire building mark the later stages in every region of high civilization.

All external contacts were not hostile by any means, since long-distance trade is equally a hallmark of urban society. In alluvial valleys like Mesopotamia, even basic commodities such as timber and stone must be imported. Elsewhere, luxuries (such as metal) were the backbone of commerce, but it must be recalled that in the urban pattern such luxuries had become social necessities whose acquisition was no less compelling than that of the actual necessities of life.

six different experiments in civilization

Many standard textbooks and courses are apt to leave one with the impression that "prehistory" is the study of the prehistoric background of our own Western civilization. In part this is a function of the greater mass of information that has been available from this area until recently; but today this situation no longer holds. The overemphasis on the West seems to persist both through inertia and owing to an unfortunate ethnocentrism. Yet as anthropologists we should study Western prehistory not just out of curiosity about our own cultural origins, but rather in order to compare and contrast the phenomena involved with those involved in the formation of the other great civilizations, in the hope of arriving at a better understanding of basic culture processes—for this, and not the unraveling of history as such, is the business of the anthropologist. Thus, throughout this book we have attempted to view mankind as a whole and to maintain the thesis that no area or group is inherently more interesting or significant than any other. Cultural phenomena can as validly be demonstrated in Peru as in the Near East; the Maya of Yucatan can contribute as much to our understanding of man as can the ancient Greeks.

There are six areas of the world where urbanism and civilization developed apparently independently: Mesopotamia, Egypt, India, China, Mesoamerica, and Peru. All these hearths gave rise to great traditions and civilizations, and all seem to have developed more or less on their own. In other areas of the Old World, civilization and urbanism came later and largely as a result of diffusion from the primary hearths. In the New World, it never spread significantly beyond the nuclear areas. It should be one of the major tasks of prehistory to elucidate the similarities and the differences in the process of attaining the level of urban civilization in each separate case, with the ultimate aim, hopefully, of identifying the factors responsible and, perhaps, deducing generalizations. In these separate developments we have one of the better laboratory situations available to anthropology for the study of culture process.

references

Adams, Robert M.: "The Evolutionary Process in Early Civilizations," in Sol Tax (ed.), *The Evolution of Man*, University of Chicago Press, Chicago, 1960, pp. 153–168.

Diringer, David: *Writing*, Frederick A. Praeger, Inc., New York, 1962.

Mellaart, James: *Earliest Civilizations of the Near East*, McGraw-Hill Book Company, New York, 1966.

suggested readings

Adams, Robert M.: *The Evolution of Urban Society*, Aldine Publishing Co., Chicago, 1966.

Braidwood, Robert J., and Gordon R. Willey: *Courses toward Urban Life*, Aldine Publishing Co., Chicago, 1962, pp. 330–359.

Hole, Frank: "Investigating the Origins of Mesopotamian Civilization," *Science*, vol. 153, pp. 605–611, 1966.

Steward, Julian H.: *Theory of Culture Change*, University of Illinois Press, Urbana, 1955, pp. 178–209.

courses toward urban life:
the Near East

Mesopotamia

Disregarding the enigmatic early towns such as Jericho and Catal Hüyük, which as mentioned seem to have been dead-end developments and whose significance in any case we cannot assess as yet, the birth of urban civilization in the Near East occurred, on present evidence, in the lower part of the alluvial valley of the Tigris-Euphrates Rivers, the area known to ancient history as Sumer. This was not the type of environment favored by early farmers, being either swamp or arid desert, although it may well have held a small population of hunters and fishers. The first extensive settled communities seem to represent immigrants from the adjacent western highlands of Iran who may have appeared here sometime around 4750 B.C. Culturally, they were simply one of many local versions of the basically homogeneous village farming culture of the Near East, stretching from Greece to the borders of India. But after successfully establishing themselves in this alien and difficult environment—though potentially rich once the fertile soil had been reclaimed—they created the Ubaid culture which, for reasons we do not yet understand, was the embryo of the first civilization. With some assurance, we may see in these immigrants from the Iranian highlands the ancestors of the Sumerians of history.

It is hard not to view the Ubaid culture as a response to an extremely challenging environment and to wonder at the motivation of the first settlers, who could scarcely have envisioned the potentiality. The lower valley of the Tigris-Euphrates must have been in those days a maze of channels, lagoons, swamps, and canebrakes. To make it fit for farming

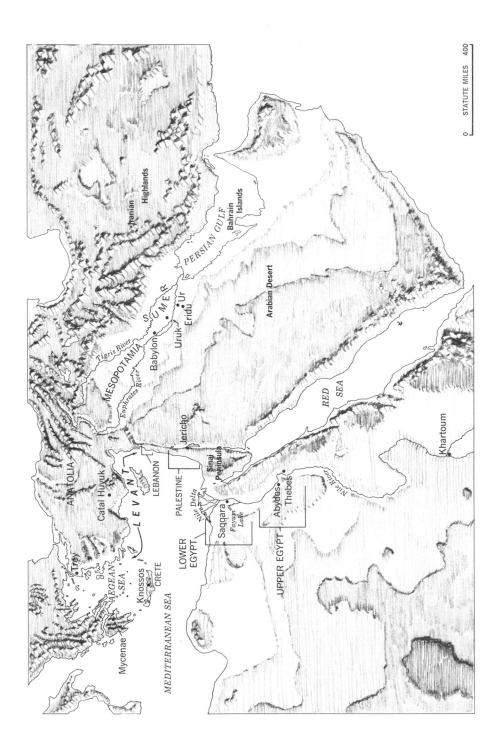

STATUTE MILES

0   400

ANATOLIA

Troy

MEDITERRANEAN SEA

AEGEAN SEA

Mycenae

Knossos

CRETE

Catal Huyuk

L E V A N T

LEBANON

PALESTINE

Jericho

LOWER EGYPT

Nile Delta

Saqqara

Fayum Lake

UPPER EGYPT

Abydos

Thebes

Sinai Peninsula

Nile River

RED SEA

Khartoum

MESOPOTAMIA

Tigris River

Euphrates River

Babylon

Uruk

S U M E R

Ur

Eridu

Iranian Highlands

PERSIAN GULF

Bahrain Islands

Arabian Desert

and settlement, arable land had to be created. This meant the draining of swamps, the protection of low-lying land from annual floods, and, equally, the supply of water to dry fields in a virtually rainless area, i.e., at least the beginnings of irrigation. It has always been the assumption that it would have required the intensive labor and organized cooperation of sizeable groups of men in order to construct the system of canals and dikes necessary to achieve this, not to mention the periodic maintenance required subsequently. Since political authority was surely nonexistent at this level, some have postulated that religion may have supplied the necessary social solidarity and priests the requisite direction and control. It is true that the earliest historical records from Mesopotamia—albeit 2,000 years later—reflect a picture of this sort, and the fact that the oldest Ubaid structure, at the famous site of Eridu, is a shrine, has also been noted in this connection. As a general rule, instances throughout the world of impressive public works in the absence of political control can be attributed to religious or cult zeal and direction; but one can also point to amazing constructions such as the Ifugao rice terraces in Luzon (Philippines) which represent no more than cooperation among kinsmen.

← why surely?

In addition to reclaiming the forbidding terrain, the settlers of the valley faced other unfamiliar problems. Alluvial soil is devoid of stone and the area lacks suitable timber: It offered only mud, reeds, and bitumen. For most of their needs, from buildings to tools, they had to make do with what was available. Bricks were invented: a very significant step which made possible the eventual construction of large buildings instead of just mud huts as previously. Smaller structures were doubtless of reeds, as in the swamps of this region today, either tied in bundles to form substitutes for timbers or woven into mats for the sides and roofs of quonset-like houses. Boats may have been of reeds lashed together and made watertight by caulking with bitumen. Even sickles were made of baked clay, although limited amounts of stone for artifacts were obtained by trade.

But the success of these settlers despite such handicaps is reflected in the growing prosperity of the Eridu community, where the original modest shrine underwent periodic reconstructions on an increasingly elaborate scale. By the seventh such reconstruction it was a spacious temple raised above flood level on an artificial platform and enclosing the remains of all the earlier shrines. Lacking, as far as we know, the plow or large-scale irrigation, their agricultural economy in this fertile, reclaimed region was still able to produce enough to support a growing population and to yield a surplus for the support of nonproductive activities such as organized religion, as well as for trade. With rising prosperity

FIGURE   19–1.   *The Near East-Aegean in the early stages of civilization.*

must have come increasing demand for commodities that the alluvial valley could not supply.

The Ubaid period seems to have spanned the time from approximately 4500 to 3500 B.C. In the latter part, a great expansion of population is indicated by the large cemeteries and extensive public works. This led to the reclaiming of additional land and the founding of new villages so that eventually the Ubaid people spread north to occupy the entire alluvial plain of Mesopotamia. They remained essentially village farmers, however, with probably only a limited number of specialized professions such as the priesthood. None of their settlements can be considered cities in either size or function.

The foundation for the future was being laid, however. Already we can see the typical historical Mesopotamian pattern of the community dominated by a monumental temple. And by the middle of the Ubaid period, as shown by the eighth reconstruction of the shrine at Eridu, the standard plan of the later Sumerian temple has been established. By this time at least it seems not unreasonable to infer that the temple probably played the central role in the community's economic life which we later find reflected in the earliest written records. If so, most of the land may have belonged to the temple and have been tilled on behalf of the deity by tenants, sharecroppers, or day laborers under the supervision of the priests—a system assuring maintenance of the canals and dikes and a rational utilization of the resources of land and water. The temple also served as the repository where the surplus of the group was concentrated. The network of waterways made it simple to transport produce to centers of settlement where it could be accumulated.

In the archeological sequence of southern Mesopotamia, the Ubaid period is succeeded by the stage labeled Uruk. Early Uruk is very poorly known as yet, but temples become increasingly elaborate, presumably reflecting a corresponding elaboration of society and culture. The appearance of various technological advances, such as the potter's wheel, has suggested the impact of outside stimulus, which would imply the contemporary existence of other centers of at least technical progress outside of Sumer. Certainly other regions of the Near East, such as Anatolia, were not standing still at this time, but we cannot say as yet what they may have contributed to the drama on center stage.

With the succeeding Late Uruk, which some prefer to call the "Proto-literate" period (around 3200 B.C.), the "urban revolution" is really under way. By its end we find real cities, truly monumental temples, an extensive division of labor, the first written records, and representational art. We can thus feel justified in saying that civilization has appeared. In the usual fashion, investigations in sites of this period have concentrated on the temples, with the result that little is known about everyday life.

Late Uruk temples are very elaborate architectural creations, often lavishly decorated, and built on top of imposing platforms so that they towered conspicuously over the flat alluvial plain. Sometimes these platforms were faced with limestone blocks which, of course, had to be brought from a great distance and testify to the resources of the society. The usual building materials, however, are brick and adobe. It has been estimated that the construction of one of these temples would have required the labor of 1,500 men for five years. As in earlier times, there is continual rebuilding and enlarging of these temples, as if each generation tried to outdo the preceding one. Thus each temple site consists of a long series of superimposed structures, which of course supply the archeologist with excellent stratigraphy and also with quite refined relative dating since each structure was comparatively short-lived.

The interiors of some of these temples were decorated with wall paintings (frescoes) in the new style of representational or narrative art that develops at this time. The same style of art is also engraved on seals and modeled on bas-reliefs and sculptured vases. It represents a complete break with the preceding art of Mesopotamia, which found its finest expression in geometric decorations on pottery. These narrative pictures are our chief source of information on the life and material culture of Sumer at this time, since few objects of daily use have been recovered.

In addition to the wall paintings, seals were an important art medium or are at least the one surviving most commonly in the archeological record. Seals used to make simple stamp impressions are in general use, but now begin to be replaced by the famous cylinder seals so characteristic of all subsequent periods in Mesopotamia. The latter have been likened to a short engraved rolling pin and operate in the same fashion as a rotary newspaper press: in this case being rolled over wet clay and leaving an extended impression. It has been suggested that these scenes may have been miniature reproductions of wall paintings and other major works of art.

In the latest Uruk temples clay tablets were discovered on which conventional signs—numerals and characters—had been scratched. These oldest known written documents represent temple accounts, and we must note again that anything worthy of being called a literary text was still far in the future. Early literacy was definitely "Proto-literate." It is generally thought that the priesthood who evidently administered the huge revenues received by the deity found it necessary to record their receipts and disbursements in symbols comprehensible at least to their fellow priests. Thus writing had its beginning in bookkeeping, at least in Sumer.

We find numbers from 1 to 9 represented by repeating a unit symbol. Another symbol stood for 10, and similar repetitions of this signified 20, 30, etc. There was a third symbol representing 60, which played a role comparable to 100 in our own decimal system. This "sexagesimal notation," already established now, was that used throughout historical times in Mesopotamia for all purposes, and still persists among us today for certain uses. Thus, our systems of dividing time and measuring angles are still based on Sumerian concepts; we have been unable to improve on them.

FIGURE   19–2.   *Examples of Mesopotamian cylinder seals with their impressions.* (By permission of The University Museum, Philadelphia.)

Aside from the numerals, most of the characters of the script are simplified depictions of objects; some, however, do not suggest anything (at least to the modern eye) and are assumed to have had purely arbitrary readings. And even the pictorial signs are rendered in such a conventionalized manner that many of them may well have had equally conventionalized meanings not necessarily connected with the object depicted. The script is believed to have been ideographic in nature, i.e., with each sign standing for an idea, or perhaps even for a word. In succeeding centuries this script undergoes a definite evolution. Although the signs remain largely pictorial, the temple scribes evidently agreed to use some of them with the phonetic value of the name of the object depicted; it thus became possible to spell out words instead of having to devise a new sign for each idea. The first phonetic use of these ideograms seems to have been for the writing of personal names, which would have been hard to render pictorially. As a result of this and other developments it thus became possible to greatly reduce the number of different signs used and hence to potentially expand the scope of what could be embodied in written form.

Although bronze had not yet been invented, metallurgy in copper, gold, and silver was already highly skilled. Coppersmiths had discovered that by alloying copper with lead they could lower the melting point; they had also mastered the complicated "lost wax" (*cire perdue*) method of casting, by which very elaborate forms can be produced.[1] All this indicates large-scale trade, with distant regions. Metallurgy, we will recall, was devoted only to luxury goods at this time.

Equipment, utensils, and other items for everyday use were mass-produced by specialist artisans. The pottery, for instance, has little aesthetic appeal as compared with earlier times. For luxury or religious purposes it was obviously unsuitable and was replaced by metal or stone vessels and containers. The skilled lapidaries of the time could carve out pots with spouts or handsome vases decorated with figures in relief.

But the appearance of civilization in Mesopotamia also brings the first direct evidence of organized warfare. Not only do we have actual weapons and the presence of walls around the city of Uruk, but some of the cylinder seals depict battle scenes or show war leaders, chariots, and bound captives. From the latter, the existence of slavery as an institution is inferred. The war chariots show that wheeled vehicles had already been

[1] A wax model is made of the object desired, and this is then coated with clay to form a mold, with holes left in top and bottom. Molten metal poured in at the top melts the wax, which runs out and is replaced by metal, and thus the wax model is exactly duplicated.

FIGURE 19–3. *Clay tablet with early Sumerian script.* (By permission of The University Museum, Philadelphia.)

adapted for military use, creating the decisive element of military power for the next 2,000 years.

The name Early Dynastic is applied to the succeeding period from the presence of a small group of very elaborate burials traditionally referred to as "royal tombs," which are assumed to represent an all-powerful ruling house. Nothing comparable is known before this time, and the contrast with the vast bulk of contemporary burials is striking. These royal tombs are underground vaulted chambers about 20 feet long, built of large slabs of imported stone. In addition to gold and silver jewelry, mirrors, metal weapons, and elaborate vases, the deceased is accompanied by anything from one to numerous attendants who had obviously been put to death as part of the funeral rites.

These burials reach their most spectacular form in the famous Royal Tombs of Ur, discovered in 1928 by Sir Leonard Woolley—one of the high points in the history of archeology.[2] They date from the final stage of the Early Dynastic and take the form of an underground house, sometimes of several chambers, at the bottom of a deep shaft. Access is provided by a sloping ramp. The first examples of the true arch, involving the principle of the keystone, a very important engineering achievement, can be seen in the construction. In addition to the funeral vehicles and draft animals, the deceased was accompanied by drivers, bodyguards, musicians, courtiers, and ladies of the harem. In one case, the remains of fifty-nine persons were found in the shaft outside the tomb, including six soldiers in full equipment and nine women adorned with elaborate jewelry. Subsequent rites, involving additional human sacrifices, appear to have been performed as the shaft was filled in by stages.

The rise of secular power, embodied in despotic kingship, in a society believed to have been hitherto dominated primarily by religious authority, is also indicated in Early Dynastic times by the presence of monumental structures that are not temples and are considered to have been palaces. Although we now know that there were actual earlier kings at Uruk, such as the once-legendary Gilgamesh, their powers were limited by an assembly of elders, and they may even have been elected. At best, they functioned as the chosen representative of the sovereign deity. What caused the shift in power is, of course, one of the basic problems in the history of human society. Organized religion remained a major and influential sector of life, with an ample share of the community's wealth, as is evident from the fact that temples and their rituals continued to get more elaborate. But ultimate authority, and the lion's share of taxation and tribute, had by now changed hands.

The Early Dynastic cities, covering a time span of approximately 2900 to 2450 B.C., were extensive, populous, and wealthy from all indications. They were all surrounded by walls, which betray the atmosphere of the times and remind us that growing political power seems inevitably to

---

[2] See illustrations in Mallowan, 1965, pp. 89–101.

foster militarism. In addition to the imposing public buildings, the houses of the population itself have come to light: one-story mud-brick structures of several rooms with small windows, grouped in compact blocks separated by narrow, winding alleys.

Bronze was in use by the last stage of the Early Dynastic; it may well have been discovered elsewhere in the Near East, and the art learned, but the skilled Sumerian metalworkers are probably as good candidates as any for the credit. Copper was imported from Iran, Anatolia, and Arabia; the source of their tin is uncertain. The upper class, the fighting men, and the artisans who supplied them were now well-equipped with adequate weapons and tools as well as purely luxury items, although the bulk of the population, especially outside the city, was little affected.

It has been argued that perhaps the major contribution of Early Dynastic Mesopotamia to Western civilization lay in the creation, or perfecting, of industrial and military equipment, portions of which were borrowed or copied by less advanced societies throughout the Near East and even in Europe. In this way, the material progress of a very considerable area can be seen as the direct result of these developments in Mesopotamia; it would probably not have taken the form it did, or occurred at the time it did, if it were not for the technical achievements of the Early Dynastic. The significance of this contribution is most easily seen in the realm of metallurgy since the standard tool types established at this time in Mesopotamia are subsequently found far and wide. But a parallel contribution probably lay in the perfection of a system of writing.

Egypt

Despite its geographical proximity to the Near East, Egypt belonged to another world—the world of Africa. Evidently the Sinai Desert was an effective barrier in early times. When trade contacts with the Near East developed, they were by sea and reflect the rise of maritime capabilities among other peoples. Again, the farming pattern of life had been well established in western Asia and the Aegean for at least 2,000 years before it seems to have appeared in the Nile Valley.

Farming and its associated technical arts spread to Egypt in much the same fashion as they did, for example, to central Europe: not as a transplanted culture or as a body of colonists, but as the basic materials and stimulus for the development of a local tradition that was distinctively different and reflected the local environment, values, and world view. As a result, the village farming societies of the Nile, though situated so close by, and with the same basic economic crops and animals, did not form part of the continuum of culture that we see stretching from the Aegean to the borders of India: They developed in a very different manner that was essentially African.

We have no evidence that the farming pattern was established in

Egypt very much before 4500 B.C. Any early sites in the valley itself are of course deeply buried under millennial accumulations of silt, and we must rely on remains from the valley margins and from adjacent lakes such as the Fayum. However, it would be hard to imagine simpler farming villages than those from Fayum, where the oldest radiocarbon date is 4450 B.C. There is no reason to think that the early cultures farther up the Nile are any older, and when one gets as far south as Khartoum, the population is practicing an essentially hunting-fishing economy as late as 3300 B.C. with only the first traces of domesticated goats and no crops.

The annual late summer flooding of the Nile deposits a layer of fertile silt over the valley floor, and primitive farmers have only to plant their seeds in this immediately for an abundant harvest. Neither cultivation nor fertilization was required, the soil retained sufficient moisture, and the same plot could be reused indefinitely. For agriculture on a larger scale, as population expanded, it was a question of controlling and directing the flood waters over the largest possible area, thus reclaiming and bringing into use tracts not otherwise suitable. However, it is likely that at least during the prehistoric ("predynastic") period these operations were relatively simple, in contrast to the reclamation work required in Mesopotamia, and easily handled by each village for itself. In consequence, predynastic Egypt was a land of independent villages, each primarily concerned with its own interests and with no need for interdependence. Even in historic times the pattern was basically the same. This, plus the total isolation, from the pool of ideas shared, via trade connections, by all the villagers of the Near East, makes it probable that they would have remained simple peasant communities. There was no reflection of the ferment going on in the world around them. Without eventual outside contact and stimulation, the emergence of conditions leading to civilization might have been long delayed.

Evidence of significant trade contacts both with the east coast of the Mediterranean and with Sumer itself appear in the last phase of the prehistoric period, the Gerzean. Some feel that the links with Sumer may have been directly by sea via the Persian Gulf and Red Sea. About 3100 B.C. the appearance of a series of innovations in Egypt reflects these contacts: Where only small, perishable structures had been known before, there is now monumental architecture of mud brick which even displays some Sumerian features; there are Sumerian art motifs, cylinder seals, and above all, the concept of ideographic writing, even though expressed in purely local signs. The development of Egyptian metallurgy may also be involved: Again, though it took local forms and used local materials, the techniques could well have been introduced. But despite all this, it would not be correct to say that civilization was transplanted into Egypt. What seems to have happened was that certain ideas and principles were introduced, grafted on to a strong native tradition, and then elaborated in distinctively local style. The process, in turn, must have sparked a burst of creative energy, and the end result was a truly Egyptian civilization.

We do not have sufficient archeological information from all parts of the Nile Valley to say just where this took place and hence to pinpoint the outside source or sources. If in the delta region, the Sumerian influence must have been indirect, via the Levant. If in Upper Egypt (i.e., the area of Thebes), this would support the view that there was direct sea contact between the Persian Gulf and the Red Sea coast of Egypt.

At any rate, the emergence of the essential pattern of Egyptian civilization was a rapid process, perhaps within a few generations, and coincides with the establishment of the absolute power of a single ruler over the entire length of Egypt who united the scattered villages into a single entity. This Pharaoh of Upper and Lower Egypt was a living god: not merely the earthly minister of a supernatural power, but divinity itself. Such a concept was alien to most of the rest of the world, but has had its echoes in Africa down to modern times. It was certainly the major factor in shaping the form of Egyptian civilization, which crystallized in the initial stage and underwent little basic change thereafter. This civilization was highly successful in its particular setting, as attested by its persistence for some 2,500 years, but had little to offer to the rest of the world. Its outstanding characteristic is extreme conservatism, an apparent aversion to any change. The proper way of doing things was formulated in the times of the early pharaohs and remained an ideal. Whenever the pattern was disrupted in later times, there was always a conscious attempt to restore the ideal.

Although this early Egyptian civilization—the period of Egypt's most spectacular flowering—is technically historical and capable of written records, these records are of a very limited sort and yield very little historical information. What was thought worth recording in those times is of scant interest and assistance to us. Our knowledge of ancient Egypt is overwhelmingly from archeology. Fortunately, its material culture has survived in abundance, partly because of the arid climate and partly because of the prescriptions of a religion which emphasized the necessity of providing for the welfare of the dead by equipping them in the style to which they were accustomed in life. In addition, art from the beginning was representational and concerned itself with depicting situations and events.

Our knowledge of the initial phase comes almost entirely from burials. What are assumed to be the royal tombs of the first pharaohs have been located at Abydos, the site of the capital during the first two dynasties. Although rifled in ancient times by grave robbers, like almost every royal tomb in Egypt, their surviving contents illustrate the rapid development of civilization on the Nile. Foreshadowed by the richer burials of the preceding Gerzean period, they are still from the very first outstanding in size and construction and become steadily larger and more complex. Midway through the first dynasty, the royal tombs already consisted of several chambers, and soon afterwards a stairway is added to provide access. In addition to the (originally) rich furnishings, the deceased sovereign was accompanied by a retinue of human victims who had presumably served him in life. Only 33 were reported found in the oldest tomb, but the third ruler is said to have been surrounded by subsidiary graves containing 275 female and 43 male attendants, while 269 others were interred around a memorial to the same monarch a mile away. As in the case with Sumer, where such practices were fashionable at roughly the same time, or early China, the custom seems to have fallen into disuse a few centuries later.

A further development in funerary architecture was the appearance of a large superstructure, the mastaba, erected over the underground tomb. This was a rectangular structure of mud brick, perhaps a reproduction in more durable material of the pharaoh's perishable palace, surrounded and concealed by several brick walls. The interior was divided into chambers crammed with offerings. These mastabas eventually evolved into the famous pyramids of Egypt. First the mastaba was filled in, becoming a solid mass of brickwork instead of containing interior rooms. The first real pyramid, the Step Pyramid at Saqqara from the third dynasty, could be viewed as six such mastabas of diminishing size, piled one on top of the other. It is also the first real stone structure in Egypt. Although, unlike alluvial Mesopotamia, stone was readily available along the banks of the Nile in Upper Egypt, no attempt had previously been made to use it more than incidentally. Brick was the accepted building material and continued to remain so, except for structures for the dead or temples for the gods. It is an amazing exhibition of Egyptian genius that this first experiment in stone construction should remain one of the most impressive structures ever built.

The social and economic results of the establishment of the kingdom were equally striking. There was an immense increase in wealth almost immediately. For example, some 10,000 stone vases were reported found in the tomb of one early ruler, representing a tremendous expenditure of man-hours of skilled craftsmanship as well as the expenditure for the often choice raw materials. A ruler's household would now contain more persons than an entire community in preceding predynastic times. The totalitarian centralized government, by enforcing internal peace and order and putting pressure on the peasantry, made intensive exploitation of the Nile bottomlands possible. It has been estimated that each farm family could produce three times more food than needed for its own consumption. The surplus, collected by an efficient tax system, was mostly devoted to the lavish living and colossal wealth of the rulers, although there was still plenty left over to support a whole new class of nonfarmers—servants, clerks, officials, priests, and craftsmen—and to pay for imported products. Any lumber worthy of the name, for example, had to come all the way from Lebanon.

There was nothing in Egypt analogous to the city-states of Mesopotamia, which formed natural economic units. Beyond the villages, there were only the market towns in each *nome* (administrative district or province). These towns were small and had no walls: Civil war was rare in Egypt and invasion rarer still, the surrounding deserts providing effective barriers. They were farmers' markets offering the products of simple crafts for humble needs plus the presence of local priests and officials.

Nowhere was there large-scale industry or commerce or a growing middle class as in Mesopotamia. Nothing demanded urban patterns of organization. When the central government on occasion collapsed, there were no local governments to take over: no focus of regional loyalties such as were provided by the local deities of Sumer. Religion in Egypt tended to promote the central authority: Since pharaoh was a god, his government was divine. Egypt was one and indivisible. The capital shifted arbitrarily with dynasties, and even in the capital there was no real civic life, no urban tradition: Everyone was dependent on the ruler and existed only for him. Such cities were merely unplanned, sprawling aggregations of buildings, with the moderately well-off aping the nobility on a small scale in dwellings and manner of life.

Egypt has been described as a court civilization rather than an urban civilization, and in fact it was never really urbanized. It was the regimentation of the entire population of the country, rather than the urban setting, which produced the conditions in which the arts of civilization could flourish. Egyptian civilization was inseparable from its political and social base and could not be exported.

Its contributions to the world were of a practical nature, such as the invention of a kind of paper made of the papyrus reed, widely used later in the classical world of the Mediterranean. Though a more sophisticated medium than the clumsy clay tablet, the latter at least ensured the survival of records for our benefits that were mostly doomed to disappear when written on a perishable substance. The method of tanning leather still used today is an Egyptian contribution, as are the techniques of cabinetmaking and joining. Egyptian jewelers were unsurpassed, and the striking blue glaze substance known as faience was widely exported in the form of beads.

Science, however, never passed beyond the first practical beginnings into intellectual inquiry. For example, the Egyptians had simple arithmetic, and this was adequate for even their impressive engineering feats, but they had no mathematics. Their calendar was based initially on the annual flood of the Nile rather than on astronomy.

It has been remarked that the study of Egyptian culture leaves one with the impression that the Egyptians were a clever and ingenious people whose progress was stultified by the development of one of the most rigid and highly centralized governmental systems which the world has seen. The complete union of church and state resulted in a correspondingly complete control over their subjects' minds and bodies. And such a system can function successfully only by very rigidly maintaining the status quo.

reference

Mallowan, M. E. L.: *Early Mesopotamia and Iran,* McGraw-Hill Book Company, New York, 1965.

suggested readings

Aldred, Cyril: *Egypt to the End of the Old Kingdom,* McGraw-Hill Book Company, New York, 1965.

Frankfort, Henri: *The Birth of Civilization in the Near East,* Anchor Books, Doubleday & Company, Inc., Garden City, N.Y., 1956.

Hole, Frank: "Investigating the Origins of Mesopotamian Civilization," *Science,* vol. 153, pp. 605–611, 1966.

Mallowan, M. E. L.: *Early Mesopotamia and Iran,* McGraw-Hill Book Company, New York, 1965.

Mellaart, James: *Earliest Civilizations of the Near East,* McGraw-Hill Book Company, New York, 1966, pp. 67–68, 129–132.

Trigger, Bruce G.: *Beyond History: The Methods of Prehistory,* Holt, Rinehart and Winston, Inc., New York, 1968, pp. 61–90. (Predynastic Egypt.)

Woolley, Sir Leonard: *The Beginnings of Civilization,* Mentor Books, New York, 1965.

courses toward urban life: South and East Asia

the Indian subcontinent

In contrast to the relatively restricted regions discussed hitherto, India and Pakistan should be thought of as constituting a subcontinent of varied and contrasting environments. For historical purposes, it falls into three main regions: the northwest (present West Pakistan), primarily the drainage of the great Indus River; the northeast, primarily the Ganges Valley; and southern India. Though these three regions had numerous cultural features in common, there were also distinct local differences.

The northwestern region was brought into the Persian empire in the sixth century B.C. and was subsequently conquered by Alexander the Great in 327 B.C., although it achieved political independence soon afterward in the indigenous Mauryan empire. The area thus had direct contact with Western civilization, at least from the sixth century; it was open to invasions and raids and formed the gateway through which outside groups periodically infiltrated the Indian subcontinent throughout its history. Environmentally, the Indus Valley is more or less an extension of the Near Eastern world.

The Ganges Valley presents a very different picture. Much less accessible to invasion, it was relatively isolated from outside influence, and any group entering this tropical environment found it necessary to adopt local ways of life in order to survive.

Southern India, about which we know the least and which is sharply divided by language from the Indo-European-speaking north in historic times, seems to have been free of any outside pressures. In general, what it borrowed from foreign sources it took selectively and shaped to its own patterns, and it exported far more than it took. It was from southern India that Indian civilization was later to spread to Southeast Asia and Indonesia.

The historic civilization of India had its origins in the seemingly sudden appearance of urban communities in the upper Ganges Valley sometime around 1000 B.C. In the present inadequate state of archeological knowledge, we know nothing of its antecedents or of the circumstances surrounding its emergence and very little of its nature. Whereas in other hearths of Old World civilization we can, by this relatively late date, call upon increasingly rich historical records to supplement the picture, India, in sharp contrast, has no comparable ancient history—owing primarily to the amazing lack of interest in history which traditionally characterized Indian thought. The past was mythological and was adequately reflected in the *vedas*, the Hindu "scriptures," oral traditions only set down in writing in much later times. From these arose the standard picture of the conquering Aryans introducing civilization into a savage India of aboriginal tribes, a picture that still dominates the scene. It should be stressed that it has proved impossible to identify the Aryans so far with any archeological culture in India. From the fact that Indo-European languages have been spoken by the majority of the population in historic times, we know that such an invasion must have taken place. It seems increasingly likely that they were a seminomadic Bronze Age group from what is now Soviet Central Asia. The invasion of this group is simply another example of the far-ranging movements of various warlike Indo-European-speaking peoples which are known to have taken place at this general time. They successfully imposed their speech over a wide area. But being far from civilized themselves, they were in no position to introduce civilization to anyone else. As with most later invaders of India, their holding of any initial political or military supremacy over the vast local population must have been followed by their absorption and by a resurgence of the older local cultural tradition. The "Aryan invasion," then, should be viewed as little more than an episode in the long evolution of a distinctive Indian civilization. But beyond this episode, Indian tradition is silent; there is no hint of an earlier civilized age, such as the Greeks had in Homer.

Archeology got off to a late start in the Indian subcontinent as compared with Mesopotamia, Egypt, or Greece and was for long primarily concerned with the spectacular monuments of later times. As late as 1920, Indian civilization was unique in the Old World in having almost no time depth. There was no prehistory in India and very little history.

The picture changed abruptly with the discovery of the Indus civilization in 1921 by Sir John Marshall and his colleagues. Thus at one stroke some 2,000 years were added to the history of the Indian subcontinent—although it must be borne in mind that this earlier civilization is essentially prehistoric, since we have no written sources that we can use to illuminate it. There is still a great deal that we do not know about the

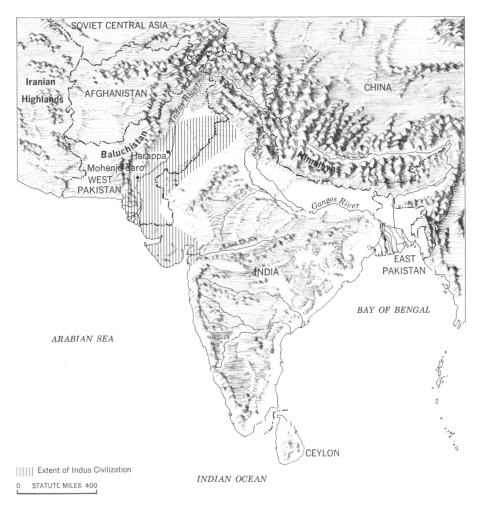

|||||| Extent of Indus Civilization

0 STATUTE MILES 400

FIGURE 20–1. *The Indus civilization.*

Indus (or Harappan, as some prefer to call it) civilization; research has been resumed, and a better understanding may certainly be expected. The great handicap is the almost unique lack of continuity of this civilization into historic times so that the light of history can help to interpret the prehistoric past. Elsewhere, only the Maya civilization approaches this situation. Even in the Valley of Mexico, or in Peru, we have far more to go on.

From the viewpoint of our interest in the history of man and in culture process, the Indus civilization poses three major problems. First, how did it arise, and more particularly, to what extent was it an independent development and to what extent due to outside borrowing or at least to outside stimulus. We are in a position to say with some assurance that it was sufficiently independent to be regarded as not just an offshoot of the Near East, and archeology confirms its distinctiveness. Second, what caused its collapse and virtual disappearance—the only example of such collapse with the possible exception of the classic Maya civilization. This aspect is of particular interest for an understanding of human culture. And third, how much, if indeed at all, did it contribute to the historic Indian civilization which arose considerably later in the Ganges Valley.

As to the immediate ancestry of the Indus civilization, there is still little that can be said. During the time when the formative processes were most probably taking place (i.e., roughly 4000 to 2000 B.C.), the Iranian Plateau, which lies between the Tigris-Euphrates and Indus Valleys, was occupied by a large number of settled village farming-herding communities, which, though differing in detail, represented essentially local variations on a basic pattern common to the entire Near East–Aegean area. All these communities were gradually verging on the beginnings of metal technology. As we have seen, the embryo of Mesopotamian urban civilization, the Ubaid culture, is thought to trace its origins to the western edge of this Iranian Plateau. The Indus civilization is too distinct to have stemmed from this same source. We now know enough about the archeology of central Asia and of India itself to know that Indus origins could not lie either to the north or to the east of the valley. By elimination, we are left with the eastern rim of the Plateau—modern Baluchistan and Afghanistan, bordering the Indus Valley on the west—as the most likely area in which to seek for ultimate ancestors.

It is assumed that the valley floor was as uninviting to early farmers, though in a somewhat different way, as was the Tigris-Euphrates Valley and that the first settlers must have also come from a highland area. If the western Iranian highlands could have spawned a group of immigrants capable of reclaiming the forbidding Tigris-Euphrates Plain and starting the ball rolling toward urban civilization, is it unreasonable to suppose that a comparable group on the eastern edge of this upland at the same general level of cultural ability and equipment might have done the same? And archeological evidence from early village communities in Baluchistan and Afghanistan is beginning to point in this direction. These communities already displayed a distinctive local flavor distinguishing them from those farther west (Fairservis, 1967).

The actual process of formation of urban civilization in the Indus Valley itself will doubtless be illuminated by excavating sites antedating the Indus civilization remains, and investigations along this line are currently under way. The weight of evidence so far suggests an indigenous development and no direct contacts with Mesopotamia until after civilization had been achieved.

The full time span covered by the Indus civilization and, in particular, when it began, is still uncertain. Radiocarbon dates from a series of sites run from approximately 2300 to 1750 B.C., but investigations have not yet reached the underlying earlier levels, which are below the present water table. Boring at one major site revealed a deposit 39 feet deep, the first 25 feet of which are under water.

The Indus civilization is best known from its two largest cities, Mohenjo-daro and Harappa, 400 miles apart but remarkably similar. Both are over 3 miles in circumference and are laid out in accordance with a highly developed city planning—the oldest example of this known and in marked contrast to the rabbit-warren cities of the Near East. The picture is one of a grid of oblong city blocks dominated by an artificial mound, presumably a citadel. At Mohenjo-daro, this mound is fortified by a fired brick (not mud brick) wall and solid towers, and contains a large granary as well as baths, pillared halls, and a palatial residence. Who occupied the latter—whether priest or secular ruler—and hence who held the reins of power in this society is one of the major unsolved questions. Since the citadel contains what are regarded as prototypes of both religious and secular structures, it would seem to have served as headquarters for both; in addition, the granary is interpreted as reflecting a governmental grain monopoly and hence the exercise of economic control as well.

The street plan was established in the earliest period yet known. Broad avenues 45 feet wide intersect at right angles to form blocks approximately 400 by 200 yards, and these are in turn subdivided by narrow lanes. Opening on to the latter are the well-made brick houses, originally plastered over with mud, typically composed of rooms around a courtyard with windowless outer walls. They are often substantial and sometimes quite large. Stairs led either to a flat roof or to an upper story: It is quite possible that the surviving brick structures may have had a more elaborate superstructure of wood. Houses were equipped with a bath, sometimes a well, and occasionally a latrine (also of brick). Public wells supplemented private water supplies.

The most characteristic feature of the Indus cities was the elaborate system of brick drains and sewers, complete with manholes for inspection—the most elaborate such system known in the ancient world, which elsewhere, except for Crete, paid scant attention to such problems. Shops can be recognized along main streets. Temples are not yet clearly identified, but there are structures that could have served the purpose. As Sir Mortimer Wheeler puts it, in its prime the whole city of Mohenjo-daro bespeaks middle-class prosperity with zealous municipal controls. Its population may have numbered as many as 40,000.

The site of Harappa was plundered a century ago to obtain materials for railroad construction, but the general picture seems to have been similar, with large granaries close to the citadel rather than within it. The standard city plan applied equally to smaller cities, which also reproduce the fortified citadel, grid streets, courtyard houses, and drains. In addition to the valley cities, a number of former seaports have been discovered in recent years.

As compared with other early civilizations, the Indus culture covered a truly enormous area, roughly triangular in shape with a base along 725 miles of coast, and stretching inland 1,000 miles. A major question is whether this represented a common culture shared by a number of more or less independent city-states or an actual political unity. If the latter, it would have been the first state in history to attain such proportions and a startling achievement in institutions and social control at such an early date.

Despite the superior living conditions, not to mention the impressive sewage systems, life expectancy must have been low in the Indus cities. Study of human remains shows that (for those that survived childhood) death most commonly occurred around age thirty; rarely did anyone live beyond forty. The racial type shows no essential difference from the modern population of the same area and was no more homogeneous. Evidently the subsequent invaders who entered this gateway to the subcontinent were either absorbed or of similar physical types to begin with, for they effected no significant genetic change.

The economy that supported the Indus civilization was basically the same as that of Mesopotamia and Egypt: wheat, barley, peas, sesame, and dates being the principal crops, plus the earliest cotton yet known. The domestic animals are somewhat different, the emphasis being on the humped zebu cattle and water buffaloes, which were better adapted to the local environment and may have been domesticated in the Indian subcontinent. However, shorthorn cattle, dogs, and cats were also kept, and possibly pigs, camels, horses, and donkeys. There was extensive trade, not only with adjacent India, but with Afghanistan, Iran, and the Persian Gulf. Around 2000 B.C. there was apparently an organized sea trade with Sumer in secondary and luxury goods, but no close contacts; it is suggested that the exchange took place at some intermediate trading center such as the Bahrain Islands. The long coastline of the Indus territory with its many seaports was naturally conducive to sea trade; these ports extended westward along part of the route, and others still farther west may yet be found. There was thus more reason for the Indus people to be seafarers than for the Mesopotamians with their relatively small seacoast at the head of the Persian Gulf.

It is curious that skilled metallurgy seems never really to have developed here, even at a relatively late date. Metal was used sparingly, and gives the impression of having been an expensive import. Although weapons were of copper and bronze, they were of rather primitive types;

and utilitarian cutting tools were merely stone blades, usually unretouched, in striking contrast to those of urban Mesopotamia.

Stamp (not cylinder) seals are the leading art medium in Indus cities and one of the commonest archeological finds: Over 1,200 have been found at Mohenjo-daro alone. Depicting mainly animals, most of them also have a short inscription in a pictographic script which, despite years of effort, has not yet been deciphered. The signs are completely different from those of either Mesopotamia or Egypt and are a significant barometer of the degree of independence and originality of the Indus civilization. Since there are rarely any duplicates, it is thought that these seals must in large part represent personal names. At least at one site they had been used to stamp clay sealing on bales and other commodities, but their full function remains uncertain. Other samples of the script have been found scrawled on potsherds, which suggests that literacy may have been rela-

FIGURE 20–2. *Indus Valley seals showing script.* (By permission of the Trustees of the British Museum.)

tively widespread and not, as in Egypt, the monopoly of a small professional group.

Another common art medium is the abundant terracotta figurines, especially of oxen, water buffaloes, and carts strikingly similar to those in the same region today. It is thought that the majority may have been toys. Actual sculpture is rare—only eleven examples among all the finds from Mohenjo-daro, plus a few small bronze figurines. The pottery suggests efficient mass production rather than an aesthetic medium.

The decline and fall of this impressive civilization is of course a problem of absorbing interest. Considering the vast area involved with its differing conditions, this can hardly have been a simultaneous event everywhere nor the result of identical causes. No single factor is ever responsible for such major phenomena in human history, despite our inevitable tendency to seek for simplistic causes. Many have been suggested or vigorously argued by one scholar or another: from the Aryan invasion or other attack to disease, floods, climatic change, destruction of the forests for building timber and for firing bricks, soil exhaustion, and geomorphological changes leading to lasting inundation of the valley. One or more may have been involved in each area of the Indus region although the evidence cited for hostile attack is increasingly discredited. But a combination of many unfavorable developments appears the more likely. In the case of Mohenjo-daro at least, it seems clear from the archeological evidence that the city was slowly dying before its ultimate end. According to Wheeler, economic decline is everywhere apparent: Trade petered out; civic pride seems to have been lost; slums of shoddy construction replace the substantial homes and orderly city plan. As he suggests, the city may well have been wearing out its landscape. However, at other sites, such as Harappa, the abandonment seems to have been more sudden and the same factors perhaps could not so easily be invoked unless the economy rested on a precarious ecological situation, easily upset. The question must remain unanswered for the present, though we may reasonably hope for ultimate understanding.

What has been described as a long phase of cultural fragmentation followed the downfall of this first civilization of southern Asia. At sites in the Indus Valley itself where there is any evidence of later occupation, the picture is one of local, poverty-stricken cultures deriving a little from the past but more from the highlands to the northwest, reinforcing the suspicion of an impoverished environment. Thus in the heartland there is no real continuity. But in the southeastern corner of the former Indus territory new finds show that the local provincial variant of the Indus civilization here shades off into successor cultures without a dramatic break. In these may be seen the roots of later village cultures of central and southern India, and in this respect there is some legacy. But with the subsequent decline of these post-Indus cities, civilization itself did in fact die out and did not reappear in this part of the world until much later and then from another source.

Historic Indian civilization seems not to have arisen in the Ganges Valley until some 500 or more years after the collapse of the major Indus Valley cities. Whether it owes anything to its predecessor is problematical and remains to be demonstrated, although as mentioned we know very little about the circumstances of its birth. This developing Ganges civilization was supplemented and stimulated by Persian influences from northwestern India in the sixth century B.C., and later spread to eventually embrace the subcontinent.

China

Our knowledge of the prehistory of China is unfortunately still as deficient as in the case of the Indian subcontinent. Prehistoric archeology in China only began in 1920, and large-scale archeological work has only come about under the Communist regime in the last two decades. Information is still scanty, and only a tentative interpretation of the formation of Chinese civilization can be attempted. Besides this brief span of activity, another major handicap to an understanding of the cultural process here is the lack of any chronology prior to 1500 B.C., and the prevalent assumption of a very late date for any cultural development above the hunting stage.

Stratigraphic evidence shows that the earlier Yangshao village farming stage evolved into the later Lungshan stage in the same nuclear area of the Yellow River Basin. Lungshan is characterized by considerably larger villages occupied over a longer time—in other words, by more permanent settlement patterns implying more intensive types of farming. These villages are sometimes surrounded by earthen walls, suggesting both an increased need for protection and also perhaps the presence now of a higher degree of community organization. Actually, there is no significant improvement in basic technology over the earlier Yangshao stage; the increasing productivity of the economy that led to a great expansion of population must therefore be due primarily to better organization and management. And increasing population density is perhaps the outstanding feature of Lungshan times, along with the greater elaboration of culture. Archeologically, Lungshan sites are readily identifiable by a very different type of pottery (polished black ware). Craft specialization by now is implied by the presence of the potter's wheel, and the existence of administrators and priests is suggested by the greater degree of community organization and the increased ritual activity. Differences in social status have been inferred from the evidence of burial practices. And there is clear indication of warfare, perhaps the consequence of overcrowding. But each village still remained a self-contained entity and not a part of a larger society and economy.

Another major development at this time was the colonization of vast new areas of present-day China hitherto unoccupied by farming or at least by cereal-growing peoples: In other words, this was the time when grain agriculture and its associated cultural patterns spread from the nuclear area over most of modern China. Until now, southern China had apparently been occupied by tropical root- and fruit-crop cultivators, and other areas only by hunters and gatherers. Cereal farming was introduced for the first time into these areas by Lungshan colonists from the north.

Geographically and environmentally, southern China is very different from the Yellow River Basin, and the many subregions of China also differ considerably from one another. Naturally, then, the dispersion of the Lungshan culture over such an extensive and varied area involved adaptation to a variety of different environments and the subsequent development of a number of regional traditions in the different parts of China, which were contemporary and basically of Lungshan type. In marginal areas like Manchuria, the Lungshan colonists mixed with the local postglacial hunting-fishing cultures. In south China, a land of jungles and hills, it was necessary to make important adaptive changes in the way of life. Here rice along with root crops came to predominate in the economy, and pile dwellings proved more practical than the northern house types. This whole process of the economic transformation of China affords a striking parallel to the picture in Europe.

Chinese civilization arose on the basis of that regional Lungshan tradition which occupied the old nuclear area in the Yellow River Basin. The first stage—the Bronze Age Shang civilization, the first historic dynasty, which began shortly before 1500 B.C.—has all the essential ingredients of a real civilization: writing, a calendar, highly developed bronze metallurgy, palaces, temples, a royal family and royal tombs, chariots, military organization, social classes, slavery, extensive trade, an organized and controlled economy, a population concentrated around administrative and ceremonial centers, and one of the world's great artistic traditions. This civilization seems to emerge suddenly, full-blown, in the archeological picture. Most scholars feel that there must have been a developmental stage, transitional from the Lungshan village farmers, which has not yet been discovered. Yet there is a strong continuity in many features from the one to the other: Much of Shang culture is at least foreshadowed in Lungshan. The gap between the two, then, may be more apparent than real. Rather, Shang culture may be thought of as being an intensification and elaboration of many previously existing features. There are unquestionably some completely new elements, like bronze metallurgy and writing. And settlements are no longer self-contained but interdependent parts of a larger whole. But the economic basis, the technology, the ritual life, warfare, social system, and architecture all represent, in essence, elaborations of what we can see in the Lungshan stage of village farming.

It has been the traditional Western view that civilization was introduced into backward China from the West. There have been two main arguments for this: the supposed greater age of the main elements of civilization in the Near East, and the lack of local antecedents in eastern Asia for these elements that seem to appear so suddenly. However, with the much larger body of archeological data now available, it is now possible to see local antecedents for many of them. And the complete lack of any chronological framework in China before 1500 B.C. makes arguments based on assumed temporal priority a risky business. It is perfectly possible that a few elements such as the war chariot and bronze metallurgy were borrowed from the West; but even so, they were developed from the beginning in a very distinctively Chinese way. This might suggest that stimulus diffusion rather than direct borrowing was the mechanism involved.

It should be emphasized that this apparent evolution from Lungshan to urban civilization occurred only in the nuclear area. Elsewhere in China, the other regional Lungshan village cultures persisted until brought to an end by acculturation with the steady expansion of the early Chinese civilization.

The exact nature of the transition from the Lungshan culture in the nuclear area to the Shang civilization still requires elucidation. Its new structure and configuration which clearly differentiate it from the village farming patterns must still be explained. These cannot be accounted for entirely in terms of technological advances, since agricultural techniques did not undergo any decisive and major change until very much later; nor is there any evidence that irrigation was a primary factor at this time. The causes must lie in the sociopolitical realm.

Parenthetically, it should be pointed out that all this concern with the nature of Shang origins, and the attention devoted to it, is warranted because we have here the most likely case for a completely independent development of urban civilization in the Old World outside of Mesopotamia. It therefore represents a prime laboratory situation for students of culture processes.

But the resultant Shang civilization is of very great interest and importance in its own right because it represents the birth of Chinese civilization as we know it historically: a civilization that shows an unbroken continuity down to the present day and that has played a major role in shaping the cultural development of all eastern Asia. No other civilization can boast of such a long, uninterrupted history. The other great nations of ancient times—Egypt, Mesopotamia, Greece, Rome, the Indus Valley, Mexico, Peru—all suffered eclipse, and their modern counterparts have little in common with the ancient culture.

In its initial phase, Chinese civilization occupied only a small part of the modern area of China, the lower Yellow River Valley. It exerted considerable influence on its immediate neighbors, who were regarded as non-Chinese barbarians, but the bulk of China remained in the realm of village farming culture. Until recent years, our knowledge of the Shang civilization was almost entirely derived from the excavations carried on near Anyang from 1929 to 1937 at the site of the last capital of the Shang

FIGURE 20–3. *Early Chinese civilization.*

rulers. This had been located in preceding decades by tracking down the source of the so-called "oracle bones," a standard remedy in Peking drug stores where they were regarded as a variety of dragon bone. Actually, they were divination records, a major necessity of Shang life, bearing signs that were finally recognized by scholars as archaic Chinese characters. (Until then, the Shang dynasty of Chinese traditional history had been considered mythological.) Thus there has been a tendency to view Anyang as synonymous with Shang civilization, whereas actually it represents only the final phase. This has naturally colored and shaped the picture, but excavations in recent years at the earlier Shang center of Cheng-chou now give a better perspective and understanding.

The cluster of sites in the vicinity of Cheng-chou has so far revealed five phases of Shang occupation overlying Lungshan remains. The earliest, unfortunately known only from a single site, gives the impression of being transitional from the village farming level. No metal has yet been found in association. The third and fourth phases may represent the traditional early Shang capital of Ao. Here we see a full-fledged city with the first example of a city wall, but it is already so imposing that it has been estimated that it must have required the labor of 10,000 men for 18 years. This is evidence that a high level of sociopolitical organization had been achieved. The locality was evidently a major political and ceremonial center with a very large population. The aristocracy lived within the walled portion and the craftsmen and farmers in the surrounding suburbs, the craftsmen grouped in specialized industrial quarters. Bronze foundries indicate a thriving metallurgical industry, but it is uncertain whether writing had yet appeared. In the light of the background afforded by the Cheng-chou sequence, the final Shang flowering at Anyang no longer appears suddenly out of nowhere. In particular, we now have antecedents for the late Shang bronzework, which at Anyang was carried to a peak of technical and aesthetic excellence hardly if ever equalled anywhere else at any time, so that Shang bronzes are prized possessions of Western art museums. At Cheng-chou it is less developed. A recent investigator who has made a study of early Chinese metallurgy believes that it shows little similarity to that of the West. In particular, the regular addition of lead to bronze is a Chinese peculiarity; the casting methods are also distinctive. The ready availability of copper and tin in the vicinity, plus the fact that bronze seems to have been regarded simply as a new medium for producing traditional forms previously made in pottery, wood, stone, and bone, could all be regarded as further increasing the likelihood of independent invention of bronze metallurgy in east Asia.

The group of settlements near modern Anyang formed a tightly organized unit around the administrative and ceremonial center of Hsiao-t'un and the Royal Cemetery at Hsi-pei-kang. The long excavations here are unsurpassed in scope and quality by anything in China, although the bulk of it unfortunately remains unpublished. The most spectacular

FIGURE 20–4. *Bronze ritual vessels of the Shang period.* (Courtesy of the Smithsonian Institution, Freer Gallery of Art, Washington, D.C.)

finds come from the great tombs in the Royal Cemetery (looted though it had been over many centuries), but it has been the thousands of inscribed oracle bones constituting in effect the Shang archives that have yielded the most information on Shang life and that are the outstanding feature of the Anyang sites.

It should be emphasized that early civilization in China, like early civilization elsewhere, was largely limited to the urban ruling class, and in the case of the finer achievements it was entirely so. Bronze metallurgy, which conferred a military advantage, and writing, in particular, were closely guarded monopolies. As in the Near East, the pattern is one of city rulers dominating a vast peasantry slowly emerging from primitiveness. The life of the rural population, then, remained almost unchanged.

Shang China ranks as an urban civilization, but urbanization and city life here assumed a rather different form. There are no physical counterparts to such cities as Ur, Mohenjo-daro, or Teotihuacán in the New World, yet the clusters of interdependent villages around a central nucleus that comprised the Shang capitals performed all the essential functions of a city and show a definite break from the village farming community pattern. This basic city pattern established at this time continued on into later historic periods, at least through the Han dynasty.

The city population was always divided into three groups: aristocracy, craftsmen, and farmers. Cities were rectangular or square in plan, carefully oriented to the four cardinal directions, and surrounded by a wall of rammed earth. This might be as much as 20 meters wide at the base, with an estimated original height of 15 meters, built up of 6-centimeter layers of pounded earth; most examples are not so massive. Initially, the wall enclosed only the central portion occupied by the aristocracy, with most of the population living in the "suburbs" outside; but with the passage of time, more and more came to be included inside the wall. The important structures in the center were erected on earthen platforms or mounds. And always these urban centers were composed of specialized quarters, reflecting the highly specialized organization of industrial crafts.

The traditional Chinese style of wooden architecture, which still survives in Japan and Korea as well as in China, seems to have made its first appearance at Anyang, insofar as we can infer from foundations. But the courtyard house—the standard ground plan for dwellings as far back as the time of Christ—had not yet appeared, nor had tile roofs or the use of bricks in construction, also so typical of historic China.

The chariot played a leading role in warfare, as in the West, and the resemblance between the Shang chariot and contemporary vehicles of the Near East is too close to be mere coincidence, in the opinion of many scholars. It should be pointed out that the remains of chariots date from late Shang times; they seem not to be part of the original picture. It has been suggested that the Shang first learned of chariots from their neighbors to the west and subsequent conquerors, the Chou, who were closer to the world of the steppe tribes and thus more open to Western ways. But we also hear of the Shang use of elephants for war and transportation, pointing to southern links as well. The chief fighting weapons were the halberd and the compound bow with bone- or bronze-tipped arrows. The early Chinese were especially fond of the halberd, a daggerlike axe on the end of a shaft, and elaborated many varieties. It is significant that the halberd was never one of the important weapons in the West in early times, nor are there Bronze Age parallels elsewhere in Asia to the Shang types or to their particular form of sacrificial axe.

The Shang civilization rested on an economic basis of purely "Neolithic" farming using hand techniques and with no apparent evidence of irrigation. Only the high level of organization effected by the Shang rulers could have enabled such primitive farming to produce a surplus adequate to support a civilization. We know that agricultural matters were the main concern of the ruler, though this referred largely to the all-important supernatural aspects; but there is also reason to believe that the actual control and management of agriculture was centralized to a considerable degree. The major preoccupation with ensuring adequate rainfall further suggests that irrigation was not yet of major importance in agriculture. This might also indicate that rice was not yet a staple crop.

Along with an urban type of organization, the use of writing is another basic patent of civilization which the Shang can claim. Actually, the script used on the famous oracle bones (which comprise the great bulk of our written sources from Shang times) is not the earliest form of Chinese writing, but had evolved from a still earlier stage when the characters were mere drawings of the things referred to. This initial type of writing was preserved for the inscriptions on the ritual bronze vessels, much in the same way that Egyptians clung to their clumsy hieroglyphics for official or sacred purposes, or "seal characters" remain in use for aesthetic reasons in Chinese and Japanese art of modern times. In comparison, the oracle bone script was already very advanced beyond the pictograph stage: The characters no longer resembled the objects represented but were ideographic in nature. This later script probably arose under the necessity of more record keeping in an increasingly complex administration. The principles of the script do not differ from those of the modern writing and are the same as those underlying the hieroglyphic and cuneiform writing of the Near East. And again it may be wondered whether the similarity in underlying principles is to be attributed to stimulus diffusion from the West or simply to convergence or the effects of the doctrine of limited possibilities.

The language used is the Chinese of historical records; the basic Chinese sentence structure is already present. It is true that only some 1,500 of the 5,000 known Shang characters can be interpreted with assurance, but this situation is reasonably explained by the reforms made in the Chinese writing system in the second century B.C. which largely obscured the meaning of the preexisting ideographs. Nevertheless, the principles of writing in China have remained basically unchanged.

The Shang kingdom appears to have been divided into a large number of feudal states, each headed by a lord appointed by the ruler, owing allegiance to him, and consisting of anything from two to forty towns with their attached farming lands. Our knowledge of the organization of the royal government is limited, but it seems to have been elaborate, with the king in direct and personal charge. There were several categories of officials: civil, military, and, most important of all, the group of councillors, chroniclers, diviners, and priests, who were closest to the king. The royal ancestors played a major role, and their advice was constantly sought through divination recorded in the archives of oracle bones. (These tortoise shell or bone tablets were the medium for written records.) In fact, it has been suggested that the Shang state was really a kind of theocracy, with the royal ancestors wielding the real power. It should be noted that theocratic political systems characterize at least several other early civilizations.

In the Shang social system we can see the dichotomy of the ruling

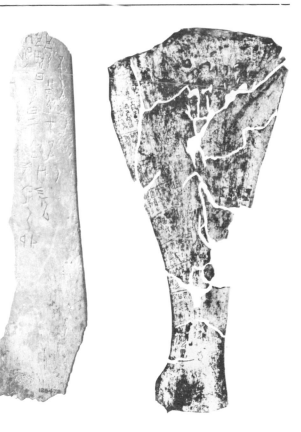

FIGURE 20–5. *Oracle bones showing Shang script.* (*Left:* by permission of Field Museum of Natural History, and Kenneth Starr; *right:* by permission from Sueji Umehara, *Yin Hsu,* copyright © 1964 by Asahi Shimbun.)

warrior-nobility and official class versus the great mass of peasant farmers which has characterized China ever since. This upper class, who were urban dwellers and monopolized the benefits of civilization, were divided into at least 200 "clans," each venerating their "clan" ancestor. In addition there was the small group of skilled craftsmen brought into the cities to serve the upper class. They were highly specialized in their occupations, which may have been organized by kinship groups, and probably enjoyed a higher status than the peasant farmers. The significance of slavery as a social institution is uncertain, although enslavement of war captives existed.

Women enjoyed a higher position than was the case in later Chinese history, judging by their influence in politics and government. Some of the rulers of feudal states are known to have been women, and queens were worshipped after death along with their kings. In fact three former queens had been especially deified as fertility goddesses to whom the Shang ruler sacrificed when he desired an heir. All this may be viewed as the survival of an earlier pattern once widespread in eastern Asia. It is only necessary to recall the predominant role of the Japanese sun goddess and the early historical references to female rulers in Japan—all so contrary to the historic subordination of women in the Far East.

Transitional from the social to the religious sphere is the practice of ancestor worship as it was institutionalized at Anyang, from which our information is derived (although it may have been confined at this stage to the upper class). Proper relationships with the ancestors required sacrifices: the more exalted the family, the more elaborate the sacrifices. Special sacrificial foods and libations of wine were the commonest, and it was for these purposes that the famous bronze ritual vessels were manufactured. These were of many different standardized forms: some for preparing and pouring libations, others for the ritual preparation and offering of the sacrificial foods. They were manufactured specially for each important sacrifice and also placed in graves as offerings. Special occasions called for blood sacrifices of animals and, for the royal ancestors, of humans—in this case, war captives.

Shang religious beliefs and practices were not confined to ancestor worship. There was a group of heavenly deities and another category of earthly deities. The heavenly gods were treated very differently from the ancestors and never received sacrifices. The earthly deities, on the other hand, received regular sacrifices and were entitled to sacrificial victims just like the ancestors. There was an elaborate calendar of official rituals, of which those for rain were the most important, being a major duty of the ruler, who in this way played a leading role in agriculture.

The most conspicuous examples of human sacrifice were in connection with royal funerals (reminiscent of early Mesopotamia and Egypt) and in laying the foundations of major public buildings, where victims were commonly buried. In the former case this was probably a matter of providing the deceased ruler with a suitable retinue for the afterworld rather than being a religious sacrifice.

Closely associated with the religious sphere was the practice of divination, which was one of the most important activities of the Shang government and exemplifies the dependence on the aid and advice of the ancestors and deities. The favorite method was what is often termed scapulimancy, the application of heat to a bone or tortoise shell and interpretation of the resulting cracks by an expert diviner. The question was inscribed on the material, and these "oracle bones" were then preserved as a permanent record in archives. The use of tortoise shell is characteristic of the late Shang period, but during the reign of certain kings ox bone was preferred.

Although Shang China can never have been completely insulated from the world of Western civilization, which reached out to it through the steppe tribes of central Asia, there is evidence of considerable isolation and of selectivity in the acceptance of what was made available. This is evident, for instance, in the very late adoption (as compared with the West) of such useful items as the plow, the use of brick in construction, and the sword; or by the adoption of cattle but not of dairying, of sheep with no use of wool. Distinctive preferences in everything from military weapons to textiles give the same picture.

reference

Fairservis, Walter A., Jr.: "The Origin, Character and Decline of an Early Civilization," *American Museum Novitates*, no. 2302, American Museum of Natural History, New York, 1967.

suggested readings

Chang, Kwang-chih. *The Archaeology of Ancient China*, rev. and enl. ed., Yale University Press, New Haven, Conn., 1968, pp. 121 160, 185 255.

Dales, George F.: "The Decline of the Harappans," *Scientific American*, vol. 214, no. 5, pp. 92–100, 1966.

Watson, William: *Early Civilization in China*, McGraw-Hill Book Company, New York, 1966, pp. 45–132.

Wheeler, Sir Mortimer: *Civilizations of the Indus Valley and Beyond*, McGraw-Hill Book Company, New York, 1966.

courses toward urban life:
the New World

Mesoamerica

In the New World, civilization developed in two separate areas: the region of southern Mexico, Guatemala, and vicinity that scholars refer to as Mesoamerica (see Figure 21–1); and the central Andes of South America, centering in Peru. Although a number of more or less distinctive traditions developed in the various parts of Mesoamerica with its differing environments, all seem to stem from a common source and show sufficient subsequent interaction or historical relationship to warrant treating them as an entity for our purposes here.

The initial steps toward food production were taken as early in the New World as in the Old, but it required a very long time to reach the level of effective village farming, the essential take-off point for any further sociocultural development. Chronologically, the Old World thus enjoyed a head start, and even though civilization, once under way, grew as rapidly in the New World, it had only had time to reach a stage roughly equivalent to the Old World "Bronze Age" when it was destroyed by European invasion. Yet even so, the Spanish conquerors were astonished at what they saw in Mexico and Peru, which in some respects were superior to contemporary Europe. For example, the Aztec capital, Tenochtitlan, may have been five times the size of London at that time. And we must realize

FIGURE 21–1. *Mesoamerica and Intermediate America.*

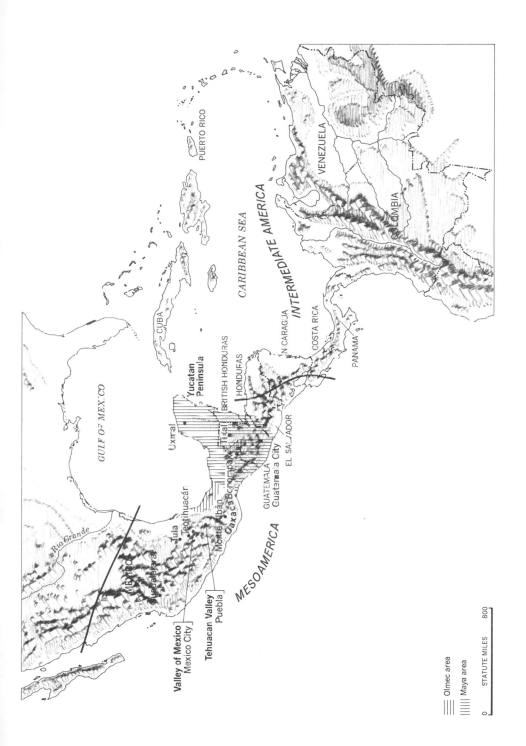

GULF OF MEXICO

Rio Grande

MEXICO

Guadalajara

Tula

Teotihuacán

Valley of Mexico
Mexico City

Tehuacan Valley
Puebla

Monte Alban

Oaxaca

MESOAMERICA

CUBA

CARIBBEAN SEA

PUERTO RICO

Yucatan
Peninsula

Uxmal

BRITISH HONDURAS

Tikal

Copán

GUATEMALA
Guatemala City

EL SALVADOR

HONDURAS

N CARAGUA

COSTA RICA

PANAMA

INTERMEDIATE AMERICA

VENEZUELA

COLOMBIA

||||| Olmec area

|||| Maya area

0   STATUTE MILES   800

that public works and other material achievements required far more effort in the New World than their counterparts in the Old, which had the advantage of animal power and the wheel. It is well for us to wonder what the American Indian civilizations might have developed had their isolation continued, and what contributions, other than staple economic crops, they might have made to the mainstream of world civilization.

There has been a long-standing reluctance in some minds to see the American Indian as being capable, unaided, of such achievements or to accept the possibility that civilization could have been created more than once in the world. Somehow, everything must be traced back to the Near East. In the last century, and continuing well into this one, this attitude was responsible for a long succession of crackpot theories.[1] It persists today even among some reputable scholars who champion extreme diffusionist views and invoke hypothetical trans-Pacific voyagers to kindle the torch of progress in the New World.

The evidence marshaled in support of such views, in the form of widely scattered individual cultural details having at least superficial similarity in the two hemispheres, ignores the many equally or even more striking similarities in different parts of the world which can be demonstrated to have no historical relationship with one another. In many areas or items of culture there is simply a limitation on the possible forms which human ingenuity can contrive: The end products in a certain number of cases are inevitably going to look more or less alike, for no other reason. There is also the phenomenon referred to as convergence, by which separate and unrelated developments in one way or another evolve similar forms, themes, or traits of culture. A convincing demonstration of Old World influence on the course of development in, say, Mesoamerica would involve the identification of an interrelated complex of traits at one point of origin in the Old World, the same complex contemporary in time at one point in Mesoamerica, a means of transporting the same and gaining it a foothold in its new home that is above reasonable criticism, and last but not least, proving that this particular complex of traits had actually played an essential role in the culture history of Mesoamerica and that without it things would not likely have turned out as they did. Despite their dedication, diligence, and exhaustive research, the diffusionist scholars have yet to demonstrate such a case or anything approaching it. It must therefore be concluded that there was no significant outside influence on the formative processes of New World civilization.

There are two striking contrasts in the pattern of development between the two hemispheres. Nowhere in the New World did civilization initially arise in an urban setting: The early centers were all simply ceremonial centers, the foci of interest of and support by the surrounding rural population. Religion seems to have been the initial catalytic agent,

[1] For a delightful account of these and their modern descendants by an eminent archeologist, see Wauchope, 1962.

though evidence of political power and warfare are not far behind. Urbanism developed at a later stage and not in every region. The second contrast lies in the minimal role played by metallurgy, and its lack of correlation with other achievements. For example, metal was unknown in Mesoamerica until after the "golden age" of early civilization, the so-called "Classic" stage. The highest intellectual achievements were attained by a people who never practiced metallurgy at all in any true sense, the Maya. And some of the finest metal work was done by groups that never approached civilization.

No small part of the secret of New World achievement lay in its primary economic basis, the intensive cultivation of maize. This crop provides one of the highest yields of any food source in terms of surplus, which gives leisure time for other activities. Even in the relatively poor forest soils of the tropical lowlands and with what seem rudimentary methods, it is claimed that a family can be supported with little more than 48 days of farm labor per year and that each farmer produces sufficient to support twelve nonfarming persons. It is a corresponding paradox, and a problem for students of culture, that more complex sociocultural levels should have been attained in only a small portion of the maize-growing area of the New World. This again points up the crucial role of factors other than economic and technological in the rise of civilization.

The methods of preparing and using maize are distinctive to Mesoamerica, and have remained unchanged to the present day. The day's supply is soaked overnight with lime to soften it, then pulverized on a grinding slab (*metate*) by rubbing a handstone over it. It may then be boiled or steamed (the familiar tamale) or spread thin on hot rocks and toasted into tortillas. Beans, squashes, and peppers made up most of the rest of the diet.

Environmentally, Mesoamerica divides basically into tropical lowlands, densely forested, and temperate highlands, much of them ranging from 5,000 to 8,000 feet, with numerous volcanoes soaring above. Within these major categories, however, there is tremendous diversity in conditions and resultant diversity in resources, crops, and harvest times. This has tended to minimize local self-sufficiency and to foster interdependence and exchange between regions and peoples, a pattern visible from very early times. Despite ethnic and linguistic heterogeneity, this has led to a sharing of ideas and new achievements and to repeated occasions for contact. Thus, although unaware of the common origin of their heritage in the distant past, the peoples of Mesoamerica broadly speaking continued to participate in a shared tradition through these mechanisms.

Patterns of farming vary with the region. The forested lowlands can only be cultivated by the shifting pattern of slash-and-burn, while the semiarid highlands permit more sedentary and intensive farming. A specialized technique, the *chinampas* (incorrectly popularized as "floating gardens"), was developed to exploit the swamps around the margin of the great lake that once filled much of the Valley of Mexico.

TIIE OLMEC CIVILIZATION

The age of civilization in Mesoamerica has been pushed back dramatically in recent years. It appears abruptly in the archeological record, without known antecedents, already full-fledged at least as early as 1200 B.C. according to radiocarbon dates. How much earlier it took form we do not know, but several centuries would seem minimal. This ancestral Mesoamerican civilization generally goes under the name Olmec, although we do not actually know the people responsible. Its heartland, in the sense of the area where remains are concentrated and the greatest elaboration of the culture is manifested, is the Mexican state of Tabasco and adjoining southern Vera Cruz, a territory only 125 miles long and 50 miles wide. The area is a swampy lowland covered with tropical rain forest: A less likely setting for the cradle of civilization can scarcely be imagined. Yet the present picture points to this as the birthplace of writing and of the incredibly complex and accurate calendar system which are the distinctive achievements of the Mesoamerican tradition. And the invention of. the calendar, of course, necessarily rests on prior achievements in mathematics and astronomy. Included here would be the concept of zero, which the European mind never fathomed and had ultimately to borrow from India via the Arabs, and position numeration of the sort familiar to us but unknown to the Romans, who had to struggle along with their clumsy "Roman numerals."

The standard Mesoamerican calendar positions any day precisely within a 52-year cycle. This was the system in common use in the highlands of Mexico. However, it is inadequate for long-term historical purposes beyond a 52-year period, since there would be no way of indicating in which of these endlessly repeating cycles the particular event had occurred: In the same way we speak of the "gay nineties" or the stock market crash of '29—which are firmly positioned in our mind but would baffle a historian of the future who did not know to which century they referred. What is needed is a continuous reckoning from some agreed point in time, as we use the birth of Christ, and this was provided for the lowland peoples of Mesoamerica by the so-called "long count" of elapsed time since a probably mythical date in the past corresponding to 3113 B.C. This elaborate system, undoubtedly developed long after the 52-year "calendar round," but probably also by Olmec genius, made it possible to record the absolute date of events in a manner familiar to us but otherwise rare in human history.

The most striking surviving feature of the Olmec culture is the colossal stone human heads and stelae (monuments). Some of these weigh 40 to 50 tons and must have been brought from sources as much as 80 miles away—which attests to a considerable level of social control and authority. Similarly, the impressive pyramid at the type site of La Venta, 110 feet high, must have required some 800,000 man-days of labor for its construction. The stone heads are stylistically perhaps the most sophisticated sculptures in the New World, yet they are the oldest.

FIGURE 21–2. *Olmec stone head.* (By permission of the Smithsonian Institution and M. W. Stirling.)

Of the everyday life of the people we know nothing. They must have been an essentially rural population scattered in hamlets and villages in those portions of the area around the centers that were suitable for cultivation, with the latter necessarily of the shifting slash-and-burn type. It has been estimated that a population of 18,000 would probably have been necessary to support such a center as La Venta. Though such a pattern of settlement and economy may seem a poor basis for civilization, we know for a fact that the impressive achievements of the later Maya civilization rested on nothing more elaborate.

By inference from the monuments and other art objects, the motivating force of this culture seems to have been a cult focused on the concept of a "were-jaguar": a supernatural being part human, part jaguar, or interchangeably one or the other, which was probably a rain god. And there is evidence to suggest the spread of this cult, or at least its outward manifestations, over larger areas of Mexico, perhaps by missionary activity. The great ceremonial centers are also presumed to reflect the predominant role of religion at this early stage. Nevertheless, there is evidence too of warfare and conquest, however motivated, and there are some who regard the Olmec as the first of a succession of empires that exercised control over considerable portions of Mesoamerica. Certainly their cultural influence was widespread, and in later Olmec times we can see the development of centers of derivative cultures in other regions, such as Monte Alban in the valley of Oaxaca, which, though distinctive in their own right, shared all the basic Olmec achievements.

The Mesoamerican tradition, thus launched, is characterized by a number of features inherited by the subsequent civilizations in each area, which betray their basic kinship, while at the same time set them off from other New World cultures. In addition to the hieroglyphic writing, the complex calendar, and the methods of preparing maize, already mentioned, these include ceremonial centers characterized by groupings of pyramids, often of impressive size, on which temples were situated and in which individuals of especial prominence were sometimes buried; books of deerskin or bark paper, folded like screens; a rubber ball game played in a special court; specialized markets; use of chocolate beans as money; religious attitudes emphasizing self-sacrifice and mutilation; a pantheon of deities including in particular the Feathered Serpent, a sort of culture hero, and a rain god; and a number of cosmological concepts.

THE MAYA CIVILIZATION

After the Olmec fade from the scene about 200 B.C. (their collapse as much a mystery as their birth,) the next great development of civilization in Mesoamerica occurred in the eastern portion—Yucatan and Guatemala. This is the Maya civilization, which from an intellectual and cultural standpoint was the outstanding achievement of the native inhabitants of the New World. Other peoples of ancient America surpassed them in technology (for instance, as we have noted, they lacked metal) and in political power (they were merely a group of independent city-states and not an empire), but on the basis of their art and science they well deserve the label of "the Greeks of the New World." At the same time it should be pointed out that in the light of our new knowledge of their Olmec predecessors, the Maya now appear as elaborators rather than as inventors and innovators. Furthermore, unlike other Mesoamericans, they exerted very little influence outside of their own area.

Maya civilization, at least in its material aspects, was taking form approximately during the span from 300 B.C. to A.D. 300. The abundance of easily available limestone in the area seems to have inspired experiments in increasingly elaborate public architecture. Although the motivation and impetus were predominantly religious, the forms in which they were expressed seem to reflect the particular interests of the Maya themselves. As one writer has put it, they were sitting on top of a gigantic erector set (their limestone habitat) and chose to play with it rather than to elaborate some other aspect of culture as another group might have done. In addition to quarrying, shaping, and carving limestone with only tools of local flint, the Maya early in the process learned to make an excellent plaster by burning limestone fragments and mixing the powder obtained with water, and also employed a concretelike substance of rubble and marl as a fill behind their masonry.

By the end of this formative period, Maya architecture had fully evolved: Sites are characterized by pyramid temples arranged around plazas and displaying all the typical structural features, including naturalistic frescoes and bas-reliefs in a sophisticated art style, and interior rooms built on the principle of the corbelled vault. The latter, so diagnostic of the Maya, was a substitute for the true arch, unknown in the New World: The successive courses of stone in the vaulted ceilings extended farther and farther out until they could be bridged by a single slab. This permitted the construction of only very narrow interior rooms and required very massive walls to offset the structural problems. Thus interior space constitutes only a small part of the bulk of any Maya building, and there results a style of architecture in marked contrast to the flat-beam roofs elsewhere in Mesoamerica.

Somewhere around A.D. 300, literacy and the elaborate long-count calendar came into use, borrowed, apparently, from contemporary cultures in the highlands and Pacific Coast to the west which had preserved the Olmec tradition; and with these developments, the classic period of Maya civilization may be said to have begun. It endured for 600 years. Its heartland was a vast forested lowland (see Figure 21–1), most of which is today almost uninhabited, but which in that period supported a large population and a prosperous economy. Although food was produced in abundance, it is likely that the actual wealth of this civilization came rather from industrial specialization and widespread trade. Textiles, for which the region was famous, made from the home-grown cotton, were a major export, other important products being honey, slaves, jungle products (such as brilliant feathers highly prized for headdresses), and, from certain regions, salt and cacao (chocolate) beans. There was heavy trade with centers as far distant as the Valley of Mexico; much of this went by sea along the coasts since overland travel in the lowlands is difficult.

But the traditional picture of the classic Maya civilization as a time of peace and tranquillity ruled over by intellectual priests has been shattered in recent years. There is increasing evidence that there was constant warfare between the rulers of the city-states, who set great store by military prowess and the subjugation of rivals and who visited torture and slavery upon the vanquished and death by sacrifice on their leaders. Rather than a theocratic system, these were secular states ruled by a hereditary elite wielding strong political power. The figures depicted on countless monuments are not, as we used to be told, gods and priests, but this elite and their retainers. Undoubtedly the most revealing insight into the highly stratified classic Maya society with its concern for warfare and slavery is provided by the mural paintings of Bonampak, discovered in 1946 in the heart of the jungle, certainly one of the outstanding archeological finds of the New World.

This is not to say that religion was not a major aspect of Maya life, as it was in all the ancient American civilizations. Learning as well as ritual was a monopoly of the priesthood. Since it is increasingly evident that the major breakthroughs must have been made by their Olmec

predecessors, it is hard to tell what achievements we may credit to the Maya intellectuals. As in the Old World, the study of astronomy degenerated into astrology and was pursued mainly for the sake of divination. Nor is there evidence of advances in mathematics beyond the amazing system which they inherited with the calendar. Maya ritual life was closely bound up with the latter and its prescribed succession of observances. Bloodletting from various parts of the body was the common act of devotion; human sacrifice, common in later times under Mexican influence, may have been rare in the classic period.

The Maya hieroglyphic writing cannot be deciphered, despite more than a century of effort, except for those portions dealing with the calendar and astronomical signs. There is a very considerable body of inscriptions on stone monuments, which were once thought merely to commemorate the passage of time, with which, we were assured, the Maya were obsessed

FIGURE 21–3. Left: *Cross-section of the Temple of the Cross, Palenque, Mexico, to illustrate Maya architectural and structural features. Note corbelled vaults, thick walls, and roof comb which provided additional surface for decoration, a primary concern.* (From *The Rise and Fall of Maya Civilization*, by J. Eric Thompson. Copyright © 1966 by The University of Oklahoma Press.) Right: *Artist's reconstruction of Temple II at Tikal, Guatemala.* (From Tatiana Proskouriakoff, *An Album of Maya Architecture*, by permission of the Peabody Museum, Harvard University.)

to the point of deifying it. We can now feel sure that these inscriptions are mainly historical and would provide a vital source of information if they could be understood. The monuments, it now seems certain, were erected to commemorate military victories and various events in the life and reign of the local ruler. In other words, they are quite like monuments elsewhere in the world instead of being incomprehensible reflections of a mentality and values totally divorced from our own. The Maya are turning out to be only human after all.

The great centers, which served both political and religious functions and are "ceremonial" only in the combined sense, were laid out according to no plan and grew by accretion, with continual rebuilding of the main structures. As in Mesopotamia, it is common to find a series of superimposed temple pyramids, the more recent covering and concealing the older. The largest Maya "city" and one of the greatest sites in the New

FIGURE 21–4. A *portion of the mural painting from about* A.D. *775 at Bonampak, Mexico.* Above, *a raid is depicted;* below, *judgment is passed on the captives.* (From *The Rise and Fall of Maya Civilization,* by J. Eric Thompson. Copyright © 1966 by The University of Oklahoma Press.)

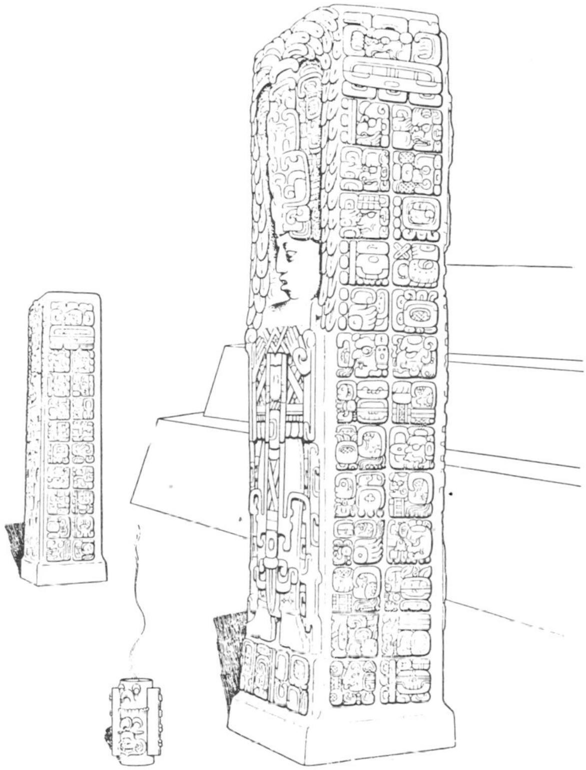

FIGURE 21–5. *Stelae at Quirigua, Guatemala, dedicated in* A.D. *775, showing hieroglyphic inscriptions.* (From *The Rise and Fall of Maya Civilization*, by J. Eric Thompson. Copyright © 1966 by The University of Oklahoma Press.)

World, is Tikal in Guatemala, now undergoing excavation by the University of Pennsylvania. Though smaller, Uxmal in northern Yucatan is certainly one of the triumphs of Maya civilization. In addition to the pyramid temples and the structures on low platform mounds that are generally called "palaces" (although their function is unknown), the material remains of Maya glory comprise the elaborate mural art, mostly in low relief, which adorns buildings and monuments, the fine polychrome pottery which provided another important art medium, the dated carved stelae (upright stone monuments), and the rich burials which have begun to be discovered in recent years within some of the mounds and pyramids. These are accompanied by human victims, usually adolescents or children.

The classic Maya civilization seems to have collapsed abruptly around A.D. 900. Not only were the great centers abandoned to the encroaching jungle, but the dense population of the lowlands disappears except for northern Yucatan, where it continued to flourish down to Spanish times as a peasant society. A vast area once teeming with activity and prosperity

FIGURE 21–6. *Artist's reconstruction of Copan, Honduras, a classic Maya ceremonial center.* (From Tatiana Proskouriakoff, *An Album of Maya Architecture,* by permission of the Peabody Museum, Harvard University.)

has remained virtually uninhabited to the present day. This phenomenon is probably the major enigma of New World prehistory and certainly one of the more significant problems posed by the history of man. Many theories have been proposed: disease, soil exhaustion, changing landscape, warfare, social revolution. But no single cause, or combination of causes, has yet been substantiated.

TEOTIHUACÁN

The third great regional civilization in the Mesoamerican tradition centered, by contrast, in the mile-and-a-half-high basin of the Valley of Mexico, at the prehistoric metropolis of Teotihuacán not far from modern Mexico City. Probably founded soon after the time of Christ and with no known local antecedents, Teotihuacán grew steadily in size, power, and degree of civilization, and was in its heyday from about A.D. 200 to 650, when it was overthrown by barbarian tribes from the north. It was thus

contemporary with the Maya efflorescence. From this metropolitan base—
the first and largest real city in the New World—the power of its rulers
spread as far west as modern Guadalajara and as far south as Guatemala
City, control of this vast territory being exercised through garrison centers.
Teotihuacán laid the foundations for the subsequent Mexican empires of
the Toltecs and the Aztecs, which were modeled after and built upon this
first highland empire. The military might and political effectiveness of
Teotihuacán—perhaps fostered, it has been suggested, by continual barbarian pressure—have earned its people the title of "the Romans of the
New World." Although they scored great achievements in architecture and
art, they never reached the level of culture attained by the Olmecs or,
especially, by the Maya.

With Teotihuacán we have an urban civilization quite comparable to
those of the Old World except for the total lack of metallurgy. But inasmuch as perhaps the chief role of metallurgy, as pointed out, was in

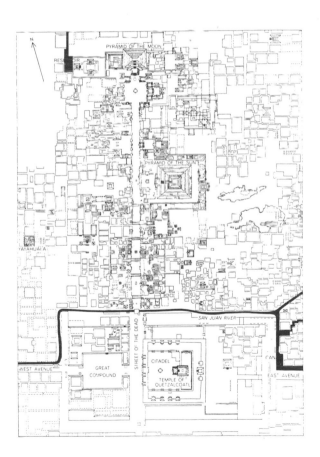

FIGURE 21–7. *Plan
of the central part of
the city of Teotihua-
cán.* (From *Teotihua-
cán* by René Millon.
Copyright © 1967 by
Scientific American,
Inc. All rights re-
served.)

the development of commerce, this same effect seems to have been achieved by the obsidian trade at Teotihuacán. The city itself is impressive by any standard, covering eight square miles of dense structural concentration, the entire area being laid out on a precise grid evidently established at the outset and subsequently adhered to. As an example of early city planning it is rivalled only in the Indus Valley.

The population has been variously estimated at between 50,000 and 100,000. The city contained over 4,000 buildings, mostly one-story apartments, each opening onto a patio, with windowless walls facing the street. Foundations and roofs were of a kind of concrete, walls were of stone and mortar or adobe brick, and both walls and floors were covered over with plaster. Evidence suggests that various crafts and industries each had their definite section. In addition, there are the ornate palaces of the elite, with their wall paintings, and the great ceremonial structures. Dominating the city is the huge Pyramid of the Sun, 200 feet high and 700 feet on a side—one of the great prehistoric monuments of the world and a reflection of the resources and labor controlled by those responsible. The exact nature of the ruling elite—whether secular, priestly, or combining both—is not known, but it can be assumed that they held an intellectual monopoly and were superimposed on a vast peasantry whose pattern of life remained that of the village farming stage. All over the Mexican highlands there is evidence of a great population expansion at this time, judging by the large number of sites. There seems to have been a great interest in building and in covering structures with frescoes and sculptures.

It seems unlikely that small, ill-equipped bands such as the barbarian tribes to the north must have been could overthrow the power of such a civilization in its prime. It is probable, therefore, that a decline must have set in previously, from causes unknown, although there is no obvious evidence of this. The final downfall of Teotihuacán was thus more of a coup de grâce at the hands of the barbarians who subsequently occupied the deserted city as squatters. When the unifying force of the empire vanished and with it the widespread trade network which it fostered, the highlands became fractionalized and civilization went into eclipse except for regional cultures in some of the outlying areas such as the valley of Oaxaca. But their downfall was only postponed until around A.D. 900, apparently coinciding with the collapse of the classic Maya civilization. It has been suggested that the agricultural economy of the highlands had been overexploited and exhausted, leaving the population ripe for revolution and the societies an easy mark for any invader.

The end of this classic period of Mexican highland civilization was followed by an upsurge of pure militarism, with an obvious glorification of war and corresponding eclipse of the former intellectual elite. It was a time of petty states and general disorder, symbolized by the fortifications which now appear for the first time. It was at this time that metallurgy was introduced, probably from the Andes region of South America.

Eventually, one of the warring groups, the Toltecs, achieved domi-

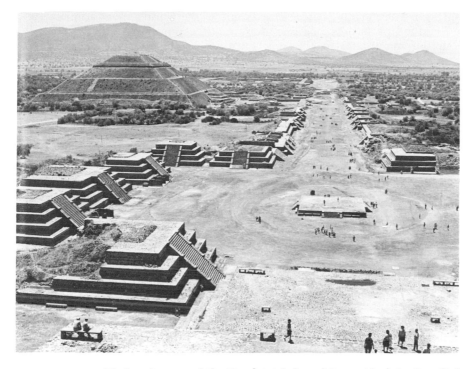

FIGURE 21–8. *Avenue of the Dead* (right) *and Pyramid of the Sun* (left middleground), *Teotihuacán*. (By permission of the Mexican National Tourist Council.)

nance for a short while and established an empire with its center at Tula. Anarchy again followed its overthrow, and after another period of warring petty states, the Aztecs rose to dominance about A.D. 1427, reestablishing a vast highland empire and commercial network and building another great urban center, Tenochtitlan, on the site of modern Mexico City. It was this last highland civilization that Cortez and his followers saw in full flower scarcely a century later and of which they have left us such vivid descriptions.

Peru

The arena of civilization in South America was that portion of the central Andes lying mainly within the boundaries of Peru, plus some contiguous highland areas of adjoining countries. It is a land of sharp environmental contrasts. The narrow coastal strip is one of the world's most arid deserts, and agriculture is only possible along a succession of rivers that cross it from the mountains to the sea. Farming is completely dependent on irrigation. At the same time, this same aridity has ensured the survival of the archeological record in a fashion equaled by few places elsewhere in the world. These river valleys are more or less isolated from each other by the terrain, which has tended to foster a remarkable number of distinctive localized cultural developments within a relatively small area. The bulk of the region is occupied by the foothills, slopes, and peaks of the Andes, with human occupancy mainly concentrated in intermontane valleys and basins, often lying at extremely high elevations. Rainfall is adequate for farming, though choice of crops is restricted at higher altitudes. Large areas otherwise unusable are suitable for grazing. Highland peoples have on several occasions in history invaded and controlled the coast, but the reverse has never occurred. The Andean region was to achieve the highest development of sociopolitical organization in the New World, culminating in the Inca empire.

General characteristics of the Andean civilizations include an economy based on very intensive hand cultivation with simple tools, use of fertilizers, irrigation on the coast, and terracing in areas of steep terrain; maize and cotton as staple lowland crops, and quinoa (a distinctive local cereal) and many kinds of potatoes at higher elevations; significant use of domestic animals such as the llama, alpaca (for wool), and guinea pig (an important meat source); a high development of weaving techniques and artistry, unsurpassed anywhere else in the world (much of which survives); outstanding ceramic art; skilled metallurgy; very impressive achievements in architecture, engineering, and public works; the late appearance of real urbanism; and, most striking among the world's civilizations, the complete absence of any system of writing or of a real calendar. In view of the many theories which posit the "necessity" of writing under certain circumstances or at given levels of social complexity, the ability of so highly developed an administrative system to function with only the aid of mnemonic records is of particular interest to students of culture.

When compared with the incredible abundance of prehistoric remains and the richness of the archeological record, the Peruvian area is still little known. Published scientific investigations have been relatively limited, and professional grave robbers (huaqueros) outnumber archeologists. Most of the picture as we know it has come from analysis of the abundant pottery, from the rich burials of the arid coast with their perishable materials, and from examination of the conspicuous major ruined structures. Chronology

FIGURE 21–9. *Area of Andean Civilizations.*

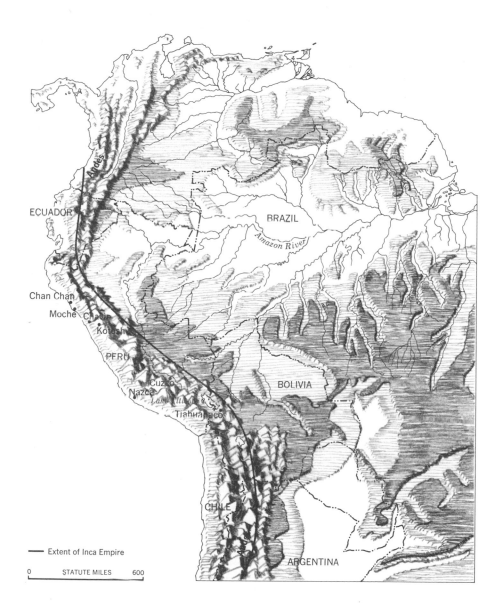

ECUADOR

Chan Chan
Moche
Chavín
Kotosh

PERÚ

Cuzco
Nazca
Lake Titicaca
Tiahuanaco

Andes

BRAZIL

Amazon River

BOLIVIA

CHILE

Andes

ARGENTINA

—— Extent of Inca Empire

0   STATUTE MILES   600

is unsatisfactory and approximate. A good deal could be said about art and crafts, but not much about prehistoric life, history, and culture process.

There had been a growing belief in recent years that the rudiments of civilization were introduced into Peru from Mesoamerica in the ninth century B.C., although subsequently developing along distinctive local lines and without apparent further contact with the north. This supposed first phase of Andean civilization was manifested in the appearance and spread of an initially highland cult associated with a feline deity and imposing structures which goes under the name of Chavin, from the type site. But new discoveries at the highland site of Kotosh by the University of Tokyo expedition throw the whole question open once more. An elaborate masonry temple excavated at Kotosh was evidently built at some time prior to 2000 B.C., and thus antedates anything comparable yet known in Mesoamerica by a good 800 years—(although we must point out that we do not know the date of the first appearance of the Olmec culture.) There is evidence of domesticated llamas at Kotosh, and agriculture must have been present in order to support such a society in this type of environment. Actual evidence of this may be forthcoming. In an interesting parallel with the Near East, pottery is not yet known; it first appears in 1800 B.C. and shows its closest affinities to wares in the Amazon basin to the east as well as to early wares on the southern part of the Peruvian coast. There is no suggestion of possible Mesoamerican influence until around 1000 B.C.

Peruvian agriculture seems to have been a blend of several complexes of domesticated plants having very different origins: the coast, the highlands, the Amazon lowland forest, plus apparent introductions from Mesoamerica such as maize. The ecological position of Kotosh, part way up the eastern slope of the Andes, could reflect a group of tropical cultivators adjusting to a colder climate in an area where some of their familiar lowland crops could still be grown but where new temperate-zone domesticates obviously needed to be developed.

The cult centers of the Chavin period, from the ninth century B.C., seem not to have been associated with large population concentrations; in fact, there are no known settlements of any size as yet. It has been suggested that only a small group of skilled craftsmen and builders was attached to each center and that for major manpower requirements reliance was placed on pilgrimages and gatherings for periodic festivals. The impressive stone temple at Chavin de Huantar is honeycombed with galleries and chambers on several levels, linked by stairways and ramps. A sculptured frieze originally encircled the exterior. The art style, depicting fantastic creatures, is very distinctive. Any animals appearing are supplied with feline features in some form, usually fangs and claws. It is the assumption that the jaguar was a major deity if not the center of attention. The culture associated with such centers spread over a wide area in the northern highlands and on the adjacent north and central portions of the coast, with influence visible still farther south. This spread is attested primarily by characteristic pottery and examples of the art style, and a certain amount of local variability is manifested. There is no evidence that the cult centers were united politically. There are no fortifications at this time and little indication of warfare. The period is considered to reflect theocratic control of society or at least the predominant role of religion.

Since the Chavin culture seems to appear suddenly in the archeological record without apparent antecedents for its distinctive features, an outside origin has often been postulated. The reported appearance of Mexican varieties of maize in Peru at approximately this time would suggest the existence of actual contact with the distant north, doubtless by sea, and lend weight to certain Mexican similarities with Chavin, especially in pottery. Thus it is possible that the stimulus for some features at least could be attributed to Mesoamerica; but there is much else that is alien to the latter.

The ensuing period in Peru, spanning the centuries around the time of Christ, saw a general fading out of the feline cult. It was a time of technological innovation and local variety in expression. Irrigation developed rapidly on the coast toward the end of the period, and the first terracing appears on steep slopes. Not surprisingly, this goes along with a great increase in population and larger settlements. The popularity of maize, the

FIGURE 21–10. *Feline figure in Chavin style.* (By permission of The University Museum, Philadelphia.)

first cereal to be grown in Peru, seems to have led now to the development of a local grain, quinoa, as a substitute at the higher elevations where maize will not ripen.

The period of approximately 500 years centering around A.D. 500 is termed the Classic, and saw the full flowering of the early civilizations. It was a time of highly organized and aggressive states, of full development of technical processes, and of flourishing art styles. Sites are marked by imposing buildings and public works, such as the vast adobe pyramids, the aqueducts and canals at Moche on the coast, or the stone structures and monuments of the highlands. Agriculture is now fully developed, with all the historic crops being grown in their great variety. Elaborate irrigation systems characterize the coastal valleys. All of the metallurgical processes and alloys known in the New World, with the exception of bronze, are now in use, although metal is primarily for ornaments, and only on the north coast are utilitarian objects manufactured. The south coast specialized in weaving and scored fantastic achievements. A similar technological level had been reached in all parts of Peru, but the picture is one of local traditions and local art styles.

A conspicuous representative of the Classic period is the Mochica culture of the north coast, known primarily from its famous pottery, which includes jars in the form of realistic modeled individual portrait heads and others with painted scenes depicting many aspects of contemporary life which provide a rich source of information. Like others of the Classic period, Mochica society was stratified and specialized, with wealthy and powerful political leaders who here at least seemed to play a dual religious-secular role.

Equally conspicuous in the southern highlands is the Tiahuanaco culture with its very distinctive art style, the type site a big center of stone structures and monolithic statues on the high bleak plateau of Bolivia near Lake Titicaca. During the 300 years after the Classic period, a culture partly derived from this underwent a great expansion and exerted wide influence over much of Peru. Whether it reflected the diffusion of cultural influence, the spread of a religious cult analogous to the earlier Chavin, or in some cases actual military conquest and control, is still an open question, but it forms a major unifying horizon marker in the archeological sequences of Peru.

The real urban phase in the Andean area was under way by A.D. 1300 or perhaps earlier. Although the highlands were temporarily in decline, three city-states appeared on the coast, and one (Chimu) became a real empire. It was a time of social and political development but little technological advance except for the invention or adoption of bronze. Large concentrations of population now appeared for the first time, living in walled cities with careful city planning that seems aimed at ensuring strict control. The impressive Chimu capital, Chan-Chan, covered 11 square miles and obviously required an extensive irrigation system for its

FIGURE 21–11. *Detail of prehistoric textile from Paracas on the south coast of Peru.* (Courtesy of The Brooklyn Museum.)

FIGURE   21–12.   Left: *Mochica portrait jar.* (Courtesy of Lee Boltin.)
Right: *Pottery beaker in Tiahuanaco style.* (By permission of The University Museum, Philadelphia.)

---

support. Highways facilitated internal communication in the Chimu empire, and fortresses and frontier walls were erected for external security.

The highland eclipse ended abruptly in 1438 with the beginning of the Inca expansion from a center in the area where they had been slowly consolidating power since the founding of the dynasty in A.D. 1200. Within 90 years their empire had reached its maximum extent, embracing the entire area of ancient Andean civilization, but only a few years later it fell to Pizarro. As an example of a totalitarian sociopolitical system, well documented by the Spanish chroniclers, it has had few equals in history, but its pyramidal structure, with all lines of authority running directly to the ruler at the apex, contained the seeds of its destruction when that apex was immobilized by the conquerors.

conclusions

This survey of the six initial experiments in civilization should point up the wide variety of circumstances and phenomena involved and the difficulty of making any generalizations about the process or of isolating causative factors that would apply even in individual cases. It would be premature to say that civilization is simply an accident, because certain areas of growing population, abundant economy, and, doubtless, increasing social complexity seem to have been predisposed, although it cannot be said, either, that the end result was inevitable and might not have been forestalled along the way if certain factors had failed to operate the way they did. It is equally important, for ultimate understanding, to learn why certain areas such as Anatolia, which seem to have been well on the way, never made the grade on their own.

It can be said with some assurance that civilization arose separately in two very different environments, the alluvial valley of Mesopotamia and the tropical forest of Mesoamerica: the former evolving directly to urbanism, the latter nonurban but later giving rise to true urbanism in a very different habitat and economic pattern, highland Mexico. In both cases it is suspected—but we really do not know—that religion was the initial social catalyst and source of authority, with political institutions and leadership, and conflict and expansion involving warfare, soon developing in a seemingly inevitable pattern.

In the case of Egypt, it seems highly probable that an initial stimulus from the Mesopotamian center was involved, although the subsequent development was independent and the end product distinctive of the area. But we cannot say that civilization would never have developed here without assistance, although it is probable that it would not have come when it did and perhaps not in quite the same form. In Egypt we again have a civilization lacking real urbanism, at least until very much later in history. The circumstances surrounding the birth of the Indus civilization are still uncertain. Here also we apparently have the sole case on record of a civilization that collapsed completely, in the sense that the tradition was effectively lost. In other areas, the fortunes of individual states and empires rose and fell, but the tradition continued and new groups built upon their predecessors. In India there seems to have been a 500-year hiatus, and it is an open question what role, if any, lingering survivals of the Indus tradition played in the rise of the later historic Indian civilization of the Ganges Valley.

China may be basically an independent case, although it was certainly not isolated from the West, and there were probable borrowings from time to time. Peru is in a somewhat similar situation. We do not yet know what initially started the ball rolling here. Peru is unique among civilizations in the absence of the supposed classic criterion of civilization, writing, and again points up the difficulty of making generalizations or of forcing human behavior into neat patterns to fit definitions. Urbanism came still later in Peru than in Mesoamerica, though it did develop; and the early Chinese civilization could not be called urban in the usual sense, although it increasingly became so.

Whatever its causes, the urban pattern of life was not an inevitable stage of cultural evolution for all mankind. It affected only a small portion, though this exerted a disproportionate influence on the history and development of the rest.

reference

Wauchope, Robert: *Lost Tribes and Sunken Continents*, The University of Chicago Press, Chicago, 1962.

suggested readings

Bushnell, G. H. S.: *Peru*, rev. ed., Frederick A. Praeger, Inc., New York, 1963.
Coe, Michael D.: *Mexico*, Frederick A. Praeger, Inc., New York, 1962.
Coe, Michael D.: *The Maya*, Frederick A. Praeger, Inc., New York, 1966.
Lanning, Edward P.: *Peru before the Incas*, Prentice-Hall, Inc., Englewood Cliffs, N.J., 1967.
Millon, René: "Teotihuacán," *Scientific American*, vol. 216, no. 6, pp. 38–48, 1967.
Sanders, William T., and Barbara J. Price: *Mesoamerica: The Evolution of a Civilization*, Random House, Inc., New York, 1968.
Thompson, J. Eric S.: *The Rise and Fall of Maya Civilization*, 2d ed., The University of Oklahoma Press, Norman, Okla., 1966.
Willey, Gordon R.: *An Introduction to American Archaeology*, vol. 1, Prentice-Hall, Inc., Englewood Cliffs, N.J., 1966, pp. 85–177.

the great transformation: Europe

introduction

The last seven chapters have dealt with cultural evolution in the dynamic, nuclear areas, an essentially vertical process through time within a limited region. Now it is time to consider what happened in the rest of the world: And this will prove to have been largely a process of *transformation*—transformation of the population over vast areas from the status of post-glacial hunters (where we left mankind in Chapter 14) to that of village food production—and in a few areas, to town and even city life—as a consequence of the *horizontal* spread of these new patterns from their points of origin.

As will be seen, this process of horizontal spread was by no means a uniform one that followed essentially the same form and course in the various regions of the world. Over most of Europe new patterns seem to have spread in a revolutionally rapid manner by contagion, and some-times by actual colonization from the southeast, which was adjacent to and perhaps formed part of the nuclear Aegean–Near East region. In con-trast, the transformation of other areas (for example, North America) was a protracted process whose full effect was ultimately realized only in the ecological zones best suited to the crops involved.

Any further generalizations are best postponed until the course of events in each major region has been described and the factors involved have been evaluated.

The later prehistory of Europe—that is, from around 7000 B.C. to the time of Christ—is of particular interest and significance from two points of view. First, it provides what is at present the best-documented laboratory for the study of culture change and culture process through time. Examples of this are the introduction and spread of the food-producing way of life over almost all of Europe and its adaptation to suit new and varied conditions; the diffusion of the religious cult represented by the practice of collective burial and its incorporation into a wide variety of cultural settings; the rise of a European metallurgical industry and its effects; and the varied changes that took place in an originally uniform Indo-European culture as it became established over large parts of the continent. Owing to the intensive study to which the small area of Europe has been subjected by a large body of archeologists, there is a mass of information, unparalleled elsewhere as yet, through which to observe processes such as these at work over long spans of time.

Second, the major role of prehistoric Europe in shaping modern Western civilization is only beginning to be appreciated. Just as our long preoccupation with the classical civilizations obscured the debt that they, and the West, owed to the ancient Near East, so also it has led us to regard ourselves as the modern heirs of Greece and Rome. Yet as Linton pointed out, the modern mechanized civilization of Europe (and America) owes more to the cultures of northern Europe and to their "barbarian" roots, than to either Greece or Rome. And it is during this later prehistoric period that these roots developed and the foundations of modern Europe were laid.

Following the Pleistocene, with the appearance of climatic and environmental conditions essentially like the present, the population of Europe had, as we have seen, achieved an efficient adjustment comparable in many ways to that of the Archaic stage in the New World. This way of life might have persisted indefinitely had not a different economic system, with a potential for radical cultural (and biological) change, been introduced into Europe from outside and accepted by at least some of the population. It is doubtful that such a change would have occurred had Europe been as isolated as, say, Australia and left completely to its own devices. For one thing, the necessary domesticable plants and animals were, with a few exceptions, not readily available. For another, the apparent efficiency of the European postglacial cultures in exploiting their resources suggests little, if any, pressure for change.

Yet, though outside influence played a vital part in launching further cultural evolution in Europe, it must not be assumed that the prehistoric populations of Europe were merely borrowers and imitators. The "Neolithic" and metal age cultures of Europe are in no case replicas of those of the Near East. They are distinctively European—new creations by Europeans, locally developed to meet the very different conditions of Europe. And this phenomenon set the pattern out of which could grow the distinctive civilization of historic Europe.

The course of cultural development in Europe during this later prehistoric period can be viewed in terms of ten stages or episodes for purposes of this discussion. The first four of these are not time periods but rather are phases of cultural development whose chronological placement usually varies from region to region, in rough proportion to the distance from the Near East. In these earlier stages, the process of transformation can be visualized in a very general way as a series of concentric shock waves spreading out from the point of initial impact in the southeast corner of Europe. Later on, when the processes of change act more rapidly and affect large areas in relatively short order, the stages become time periods as well.

FIRST STAGE   Although hypothetical in terms of archeological evidence, we must postulate an initial stage during which the fundamental elements of the village farming pattern were introduced into southeastern Europe from Greece,[1] Anatolia, or both, sometime between 9000 and 6000 B.c., perhaps in some cases by actual immigrant groups and otherwise by diffusion. The oldest known farming sites, belonging to the following period, are already so distinctive that they cannot represent transplanted alien groups, but must already have a respectable local history behind them. The process was not as simple as might appear from arrows drawn on a map. Crops and techniques were originally developed to suit Near Eastern conditions. Not only is Europe as a whole markedly different from the Near East, but it comprises three equally different ecological zones from the standpoint of farming. The Mediterranean zone is distinct climatically from the rest of Europe, while at its eastern end it merges with the coastal portion of the Near East. Hence farming could penetrate the Mediterranean coasts with the least necessity for major changes, and since access is necessarily by water, there is maximum opportunity for direct transplantation of colonists from the Aegean and Near East. In the temperate zone which includes the bulk of Europe, however, Near Eastern farming could penetrate only selectively and at times with difficulty, involving substantial adaptation. Any direct colonization from the Near East would have been limited to the initial implantation on the southeastern margin. Lastly, northernmost Europe was off limits to early farmers, and only certain elements of their culture were eventually able to penetrate the region.

SECOND STAGE   The archeological record provides clear evidence at this time of the development of distinctively European farming cultures representing successful adaptations to local conditions and the colonization of considerable parts of Europe by such groups.

Three extensive and clearly recognizable culture areas or major traditions are apparent at this time: the "tell" settlements of the southeast, the Danubian or "long house" farmers of the loess regions of central Europe, and the settlers of the coasts and islands of the central and

---

[1] Greece and the Aegean region, having their closest ties with Anatolia, are considered here as part of the Near East nuclear area. But there is a growing feeling that much of the rest of southeastern Europe may have to be considered equally nuclear.

western Mediterranean. Each of these culture areas displays remarkable internal homogeneity despite their extent, and this homogeneity is a distinctive feature of the second stage and presents a marked contrast to the great variety of local cultures in subsequent times. Much of Europe, however, especially the western half, was still unaffected by these developments, and here the hunting patterns established in early postglacial times continued to exist (see Figure 22–1).

The farmers of the southeast practiced what was essentially a variant of the Near Eastern food-producing economy, with intensive agricultural techniques enabling permanent occupation of the same spot. As a result, their settlements, like those of the Near East, are typically characterized by deep stratified midden deposits or "tells." Such a settlement pattern never developed anywhere else in Europe, as conditions were not suitable. The lower levels of such famous sites as Vinča near Belgrade and Karanovo in Bulgaria reflect this second stage; the cultural tradition is sometimes referred to as Starčevo or Starčevo-Körös. The Karanovo settlement, approximately 800 by 600 feet in area, consisted of fifty to sixty small, square, one-room houses with hearth inside, indicating occupation of each by a nuclear family and suggesting a total population of perhaps 300 for the village community. Construction was of mud, reinforced inside with woven saplings. Cereals were grown, and sheep, goats, pigs, and cattle raised. There is evidence of the usual technology associated with such an economy. Pottery is well made and thoroughly European, indicating a long local development. Trade is evidenced by obsidian from northern Hungary and shells from the Mediterranean. Ideology is reflected only in female figurines.

Since central Europe is so climatically and geographically dissimilar to the Near East, different agricultural techniques and a different way of life were required to adapt the village farming pattern to this new environment before it could become established and spread. This adaptation seems to have occurred on the northern margins of the southeastern tell area at a late stage in the Starčevo tradition. The sites of central Europe lack the deep deposits and hence indicate shorter occupancy, although the same spot might be reoccupied after an interval of time. This suggests a shifting settlement pattern usually associated with slash-and-burn agriculture or some comparable system that exhausts the soil in any locality after a period of use because of lack of adequate techniques for restoring fertility. Equally characteristic, and shared only by the analogous Tripolye farmers of the Russian-Romanian border area, is the dwelling pattern of "long houses"—large structures probably housing a number of related families under one roof. This suggests patterns of social organization very different from anything hitherto observed.

FIGURE   22–1.   *Europe in Stage Two.*

STATUTE MILES 400

Tell settlements

Tripolye Farmers

Danub an

Mediterranean Coast

Caucasus Mountains

BLACK SEA

ANATOLIA

AEGEAN SEA

Karanovo

Vinca

Save

MEDITERRANEAN SEA

Pyrenees

Whatever their origin, these first farmers of central Europe (whose cultural tradition has been labeled "Danubian I") colonized a vast area with amazing rapidity, judging by the uniformity of cultural remains between distant points: Over a longer period of time, local differences would have been bound to develop. However, their occupation of this extensive territory was only scattered and not continuous and is almost entirely confined to areas with loess soils. Thus they seem to have sought out the patches of good land easily tilled by hand with stone hoes and digging sticks and to have bypassed the remainder. The rapidity of their spread, plus the absence of any trace of military equipment or defensive measures, indicates that their colonization encountered no resistance. Either the central European area was only very thinly populated by hunting groups at this time, or else the latter occupied a different ecological habitat, the areas of no interest to the Danubian farmers (who, significantly, seem to have done no hunting), thus allowing peaceful coexistence in the absence of competition. Danubian I sites, readily identifiable by the distinctive type of pottery used, have yielded radiocarbon dates ranging from about 4600 B.C. to about 3800 B.C.

The Danubian farmers cultivated barley and bread wheat in addition to more primitive cereals such as einkorn and emmer, and flax for oil and (probably) for textiles. These crops would have rapidly depleted the soil in central Europe, where they are not native, had the nitrogen not been restored to some extent by the leguminous plants which were also grown— peas, beans, and lentils. The solid construction of Danubian I houses certainly suggests that the people expected to use them for more than just a few years, and this may have been the factor that made it possible. To what extent this effect was purely accidental and to what extent the Danubians understood the problem and consciously attempted to cope with it, we cannot say. Domestic sheep, cattle, and pigs were kept in small numbers, but were definitely secondary in the economy. The latter two may have represented, at least in some cases, local domestications of European wild forms by groups already familiar with stock raising.

Typical Danubian I villages were composed of twenty or more rectangular "long houses" averaging about 100 by 25 feet in size. These were substantial gable-type buildings having a heavy frame of posts and timbers and walls of woven saplings (wattle) plastered with clay. No more impressive architecture was developed subsequently in prehistoric Europe north of the Mediterranean region, and it even compares favorably with much of the housing in early medieval times. It is generally thought that a dwelling of this size must have been occupied by a small clan or comparable group of kinsmen. The total population of such a village has been estimated as possibly about 600. This, of course, was a very dramatic jump in population for a region previously occupied only by scattered groups of hunters. Probably 600 to 800 acres of land under cultivation at one time would have been required to support such a community.

The definite plan of the Danubian I villages indicates some degree of community organization, but there is no indication of chiefs or other social distinctions among the inhabitants. It is thought that the primary social and economic role was played by the kin groups reflected in the "long houses" and that this would have provided a more mobile and adaptable system to account for the rapid Danubian spread (such units could readily move and function independently of the rest). These kinds of groups would be in contrast to the static communities of the southeast which are presumed to have been complexly organized village cooperatives, no segment of which could effectively break away and function on its own.

The times, as well as the people, were peaceful, as judged by the absence of anything that could be identified as a weapon and by the vulnerability of the unprotected villages. If the colonists had contact with the previous occupants of central Europe, it must have been slight, with little exchange. This is in contrast to the succeeding stage in this area when microliths came into use, indicating borrowing and influence from indigenous hunting groups if not actual amalgamation. All in all, Danubian I represented a very successful adaptation to the environment of central Europe so long as there was unlimited suitable land available for the needs of this type of economy. Its importance lies in the fact that it formed the first foundations for the whole future cultural and economic aspect of the area.

Far less well-known than the preceding two culture areas in the second stage is the third area, comprising the coasts and islands of the central and western Mediterranean. The food producers who colonized this region are known primarily from their style of pottery with impressed decorations. The affinities of the pottery, and its distribution on islands and coasts never more than fifty miles inland, indicate that these people were capable seafarers coming originally from somewhere in the eastern end of the Mediterranean. This, of course, also attests to well-developed navigational abilities and seaworthy ships by at least 5000 B.C. Unfortunately, little information is yet available about the houses and settlement patterns of these colonists or about their economy, other than that they apparently had domestic animals but also did considerable hunting. Typically, they seem to have mixed with or borrowed from the indigenous hunting population wherever they settled, as indicated by their adoption of the latter's microlithic stone technology. Their culture would seem to represent an adaptation by some eastern Mediterranean population to the particular environment of the central and western Mediterranean.

THIRD STAGE   During this stage, the areas of primary colonization described above expand until all parts of Europe suitable for primitive farming have been occupied. At the same time, the rather uniform, homogeneous primary cultural traditions of the preceding stage now break up into a large number of smaller and more or less distinct regional cultures. This process, to be repeated in later stages of European prehistory, was brought about by divergent adaptations to a wide variety of local conditions and was accelerated, especially in southeastern Europe, by the penetration of new influences from the Near East. Also contributing to the diversification process was the formation of what might be called "secondary farming cultures," resulting from the adoption of the new economy, along with its equipment, by various groups of indigenous hunters who had hitherto remained outside of the village farming sphere.

By the close of this stage, the adaptation of food production to European conditions had been completed, and the acculturation of the older hunting population to the new way of life had been effected. The successful nature of the adaptation is indicated by the greatly expanded population apparent. At this point, then, we see Europe occupied by a large number of distinct societies that were self-sufficient, independent, probably speaking distinct languages, and perhaps hostile to one another. Trade existed, but was limited in many areas to luxuries. The economic base was still shifting cultivation over much of Europe, with permanent villages only in the southeastern "tell" area. And with the growing farming population, the available fresh land for clearing became more and more limited and the possibilities for conflict between groups increased.

Because of the confusing number of local cultures from now on, reference to them will be avoided as much as possible and attention concentrated rather upon trends and major developments. In the Mediterranean region a new wave of cultural influences, coming from the Aegean area, is reflected in the appearance of painted pottery which eventually replaces the impressed wares. Southeastern Europe, with the advantage of maximum exposure to the higher cultures of Anatolia, naturally shows the most accelerated development, and some astonishingly rich and complex cultures now flourished here. It should be emphasized that Anatolian–Near Eastern influence on Europe was a continuing process throughout the later prehistoric period and not merely an occasional event. Europe was at all times part of a larger world and shared, in an attenuated fashion, in the general advance of civilization. The prehistoric cultures of southeastern Europe played, in these early stages, an important role as transmitters of these external influences to the bulk of Europe, foreshadowing their future role as middlemen in the metal trade which was to prove so crucial a factor in the further rise of European culture.

The middle levels of the stratified Karanovo site in Bulgaria reflect a typical southeastern culture of our third stage. The earlier small square dwellings have been replaced by larger rectangular ones with an entrance and sometimes a porch at one end, but still evidently accommodating only a single nuclear family. The overall size of the village apparently remained essentially the same. Houses continued to be of wattle and clay construction, but the interior plaster walls and perhaps the exterior as well were adorned with gaily painted decorations. Life must have been far from drab in these times and even quite comfortable, as suggested by clay models of remarkably modern-looking couches, chairs, and benches that seem to have been padded or upholstered. Although European peoples of this time have always been considered lacking in aesthetic expression, striking naturalistic seated figures recently unearthed in Romania indicate that artistic talent was not always absent.

In central Europe at this stage the Danubian farmers have expanded their original territory and undergone cultural change. There is now a greater emphasis on stock raising than before and more evidence of hunting and fishing. The latter in particular suggests influence from increased contact with the indigenous hunting population. These second-generation Danubians are surrounded by a variety of what we might call "secondary Danubian" cultures, representing the acculturation of neighboring hunting groups to the new economy. The fact that villages are fortified shows that life was no longer peaceful as heretofore. Social patterns have also changed, the former communal "long houses" being typically replaced by smaller (about 20 by 12 feet) two-room dwellings, with a small room in front containing a clay oven. The village at Aichbühl consisted of twenty-four such dwellings and had an estimated population of 120 persons, probably implying 170 acres of crops under cultivation. But villages of up to seventy-five houses are also known.

The spread of the new economy to the north European plain, an area offering difficult conditions for farming, took place at this stage. This probably resulted from a combination of northward movement by expanding Danubian settlers and acculturation of the dense local hunting-fishing population, descendants of the postglacial Maglemosian peoples. Successful adaptation to the regional conditions is reflected in what is termed the

FIGURE 22–2. *Clay statuettes, Hamangia culture, Romania.* (From Dumitru Berciu, *Romania*, copyright © 1967 by Thames and Hudson Limited, London. By permission of the publishers and the Institute of Archaeology, Bucharest.)

FIGURE 22–3. *Reconstruction of the village at Aichbühl.* (By permission from J. G. D. Clark, *Prehistoric Europe,* copyright © 1952 by Philosophical Library, Inc.)

First Northern Culture, the outcome of these processes. By the end of the stage the area from the Rhine to the Vistula was occupied by a number of warlike groups representing varying adjustments of this culture to local conditions; they extended their influence as far as Austria on the south and Britain on the west.

The increasing shift to a largely pastoral economy which seems under way now over much of north central Europe among the later Danubians and their neighbors to the north may have been caused primarily by ecological change in the habitat of the region. There is reason to think that excessive slash-and-burn farming over many centuries by an expanding population would have altered the vegetation cover in the direction of a lighter type, as well as have impoverished the soil. This would result in large areas of lighter forest available for pasturing livestock while at the same time returns from cultivating the soil dwindled. Barley, which is better suited to such changed conditions, evidently replaced wheat as the main crop at this time, and increasingly larger herds of animals are in evidence. It has been suggested that these larger herds may have resulted in the manuring and eventual restoration of the exhausted soils of abandoned crop lands, a beneficial development for the future. At any rate, this shift to a more pastoral life undoubtedly had major social consequences. It has been pointed out that it would have led to competition for grazing land and to opportunities for individual enrichment through cattle stealing—something new in European society, where no means of personal wealth had hitherto been available. The shift from communal long houses to single family dwellings perhaps reflects a fragmentation in social structure resulting from this more individualistic pattern of life.

In our third stage we also see the transformation of western Europe to food production. The cultures that develop as a result are strongly regionalized from the start, and survivals from the old local hunting traditions they replaced are conspicuous in all. The conversion resulted from influences from a number of directions, but most importantly from the village farming communities that had been evolving in the western Mediterranean culture area, end products of the tradition launched by the first settlers. The most famous of these local west European cultures of this stage is that of the Swiss "Lake Dwellers," technically termed the Cortaillod culture. The settlements, long thought to have been built on piles over the water (presumably for protection), are now known to have been situated on the shores of lakes which have since risen. Owing to the waterlogged conditions, an abundance of perishable materials has been preserved, and we have a far fuller and more vivid picture of early European farming life here than is available elsewhere. Complex basketry and the earliest linen textiles known from Europe are among the remains as well as wooden bows and utensils. Three types of wheat were grown as well as legumes and flax, There was a marked preponderance of cattle and pigs among the animal remains.

At some time shortly before 3000 B.C. the first farmers migrated across the channel to southern England, drawn from the regional cultures of France and Belgium but also showing signs of influences from the north European plain as far east as Poland. Europe was becoming increasingly cosmopolitan and culturally complex, it is evident, and no group lived in isolation from the larger scene. The first British farming culture, known as Windmill Hill from the type site, practiced an economy generally similar to that of the Swiss Cortaillod, but is characterized by large enclosures formed by earthworks and ditches that may have served as cattle corrals; they do not seem to have been fortified villages. Another group of immigrants from the continent settled in Ireland at about the same time.

FOURTH STAGE Bronze metallurgy had been introduced into the Aegean area from its centers in Anatolia, launching the Early Bronze Age of the Aegean which is represented by the Early Minoan period on Crete and the Early Helladic cultures of mainland Greece. Bronze metallurgy was also established in the Balkans by 4000 B.C. This in turn brought about a quest for sources of copper to sustain the new industries since the Aegean area had none, resulting in the development of the first copper metallurgy in central Europe in those localities where copper ore was available—namely, the eastern Alps and central Germany. The concept of metallurgy and the techniques employed were originally introduced from the Aegean or from Anatolia, but they were applied to European raw materials by local craftsmen almost from the beginning. Outside of these limited centers of ore production, however, the bulk of Europe north of the Mediterranean continued to follow and elaborate its existing patterns of life.

During this same time the Aegean-Anatolian area was exerting another major influence of a very different sort on Europe, in the form of the religious cult of collective burial and megalithic tombs, which was associated with concepts of ancestor worship and the Mother Goddess. Evidences of this religion or series of religions begin to appear in Spain and western Europe around 3000 B.C. Archeologically it is characterized by the occurrence of large collective tombs used over a period of centuries for repeated multiple burials and for ceremonies venerating these dead ancestors. These structures were thus not only sepulchers but temples as well. The actual use of very large stones ("megaliths") in the construction of many of these tombs did not in itself have any religious significance, although the term "megalithic" has come to be widely used as a name for this cult.

The distinctive form in which this cult spread from the western Mediterranean area through France, the British Isles, and beyond to northern Germany and Scandinavia is actually a Spanish invention in the sense that it represents a crystallization in the new environment of Spain of preexisting religious beliefs brought from the eastern Mediterranean by colonists familiar with such concepts as ancestor worship, collective burial, and the Mother Goddess. Prehistoric Spain, then, took over various ideas borrowed from the Aegean-Anatolian colonies which were being planted along its shores and shaped these into a new cult which was then exported to the rest of western Europe. Its rapid spread may be traced by a series of related monuments in different regions but built in each case by the local people of the region. These monuments show many similarities in architecture, in the religious symbolism employed, and in the remains of ritual practices; but in each case the associated artifacts are entirely those of the local culture, and thus they differ from one area to another. In the course of time, the cult underwent changes and local developments in each area. The archeological record therefore reflects a classic example of the indirect influence of foreign religious ideas on a variety of native cultures in northern Europe.

The question immediately arises as to how and why this religion should have spread so rapidly and so widely at a time of limited and difficult communications. Conquest or invasion is ruled out, since there is no evidence of any change in population and the associated artifacts in every case are no different from those previously in use in the same region. Clearly, the monuments and the cult were assimilated by the existing local cultures. However, some of the sites do suggest the arrival of small intrusive groups by sea—perhaps trading colonies, whence the cult spread to the local population. The idea of actual missionaries propagating a new faith is harder to visualize, whereas far-flung movements motivated by trade were a common picture in the Mediterranean by this time. Certainly the general distribution of the megalithic remains in northwestern Europe demonstrates conclusively that the spread could only have been by sea, whatever the motive. This, of course, presupposes seaworthy sailing vessels and the ability to undertake long voyages in the stormy Atlantic, a far cry from conditions in the Mediterranean where typically only oar-propelled craft were used.

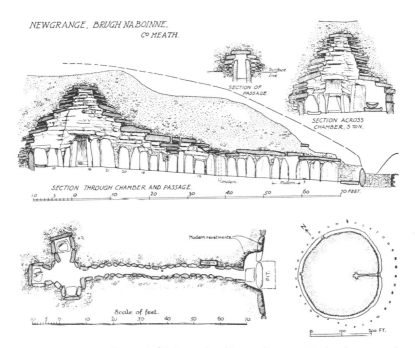

NEWGRANGE, BRUGH NABOINNE, CO MEATH.

FIGURE 22–4. "Megalithic" tomb at New Grange, Ireland, covered by a mound. (From Proceedings of the Prehistoric Society, courtesy of J. G. D. Clark.)

It must be borne in mind that northernmost Europe, beyond the limit of effective primitive farming formed by the northern edge of the deciduous forest (see Figure 22–5), had remained relatively untouched by these crucial changes in the life of the continent. Here in Scandinavia and northern Russia the old hunting-fishing economy continued to hold sway, essentially a survival of the postglacial Maglemosian tradition of northern Europe. While a few items of new equipment (such as pottery and the ground-stone technique for making heavy woodworking tools) were accepted from the farming cultures, there was no incentive for further change since the existing pattern enabled exploitation of the northern habitat with maximum efficiency. Economic emphasis varied according to the resources of the particular area: sealing and deep-sea fishing along the coasts, moose hunting and fresh-water fish in the coniferous forests of the interior. The population was always concentrated along lakes, rivers, and seashores, clear evidence of the basic role of fishing. The essential mobility for this way of life under northern conditions was provided by skis, sleds, and boats, some of which may have been skin-covered. They also made possible long-distance trade in luxury items

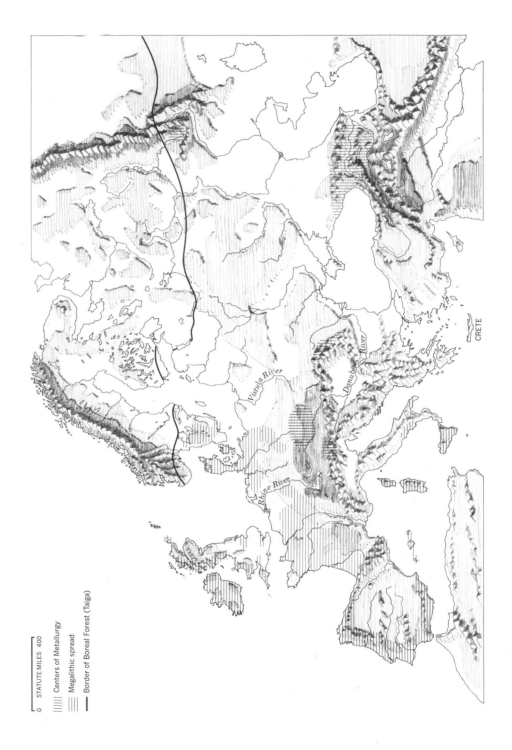

STATUTE MILES 400
0

||||| Centers of Metallurgy

≡ Megalithic spread

── Border of Boreal Forest (Taiga)

Vistula River

Rhine River

Danube River

CRETE

and superior forms of stone axes, which explains in part the relative cultural homogeneity of these northernmost Europeans over a vast area. They may doubtless be regarded as the ancestors of the Lapps and Finno-Ugrian peoples of today. Their culture is especially characterized by the use of polished slate for many artifacts and by the naturalistic art in the form of carvings and of engravings on rocks, mostly depicting game animals.

FIFTH STAGE   The brief but eventful fifth stage saw the "Neolithic" of Europe and the Early Bronze Age of the Aegean area brought to an end by widespread invasions and ethnic movements. In central Europe and around the Aegean this was due to the invasion about 2300 to 2200 B.C. of the warlike bearers of the Kurgan culture from the steppe region north of the Black Sea where they had already been established for some time. Their most characteristic feature was the practice of burying their chiefs and important persons under conspicuous mounds of earth, commonly called "kurgans" in Russia. A primarily stock-raising people of considerable mobility with a technology transitional between stone and metal, they were almost certainly speakers of an Indo-European language or languages, now appearing in Europe for the first time, from which the speech of nearly all the modern peoples of Europe has developed. (A branch of them entered Anatolia and became the Hittites; another destroyed Troy about 2300 B.C.) The Kurgan invaders are thus the linguistic ancestors of most of the living population of Europe or of those of European descent elsewhere in the world today. Under their impact the existing cultures of Europe were either destroyed or soon faded out, and new patterns were established, so that by about 2000 B.C. the map of Europe had been completely changed.

The archeological evidence from this time is consistent with the view that a uniform language and social organization had been imposed on this vast area from northwestern Europe to central Russia and south to the Aegean in the span of a few centuries by a powerful conquering minority. This picture meets the requirements of linguists deduced from the study of the evolution of the forms of Indo-European speech and is also corroborated by the known history of the Hittites and Kassites in the Near East. Their success in conquering two-thirds of Europe was probably due to their patriarchal, stratified social organization as opposed to the loosely organized village communities of Europe, and to the mobility provided by their possession of wheeled vehicles. The identification of the Kurgan people as being the original Indo-Europeans is further strengthened by the fact that the oldest stratum of the vocabulary in Indo-European languages (those terms shared by all modern languages that relate to economy, re-

FIGURE   22–5. *Europe in Stage Four.*

ligion, society, dwellings, and settlement patterns and are hence assumed to reflect the life of the ancestral Indo-Europeans) correspond closely to the archeological traits of the Kurgan culture. There is no such close correspondence with the traits of any other archeological culture of this time or with the preceding indigenous cultures of Europe. This disposes of the theory advanced by some scholars that Indo-European speech is indigenous to Europe and has a very long history there.

It must be emphasized that we are dealing here not with the colonization of Europe by the Kurgan people but with the conquest of the existing population by a single comparatively small but militarily superior group, a process entirely analogous to a number of subsequent conquests of Europe that are accepted as historical fact. There is thus nothing inherently improbable in this interpretation of the archeological evidence.

Only southwestern Europe and Crete were unaffected by this conquest. Crete, still safely isolated by water, achieved the flowering of its Middle Minoan civilization without interference. Southwestern Europe was affected by the movements of a different group, the so-called "Bell Beaker" people, known from their distinctive pottery, who now appear in many areas from an original homeland in Spain and seem to have blocked further westward expansion of the Indo-Europeans. Believed to have been to some extent in search of new sources of metal ores, the Bell Beaker people were prospectors and entrepreneurs interested in exploiting the metallurgical resources of western Europe. They played an important part in opening up trade routes that were later among the vital arteries of the European bronze industry and in initiating ore mining in the British Isles.

SIXTH STAGE   The sixth stage is represented by the formation of regional Indo-European cultures, differentiated from the initial homogeneous Kurgan culture that had spread so rapidly over much of Europe. During the first centuries after the conquest, a process of hybridization took place. Although the older European population survived to form a definite majority, their cultures faded out. Enough of the previous ways of life remained, however, to give a local cast to each of the new Indo-European cultures that developed in the various parts of Europe. Evidence at this time, then, suggests the formation of a number of separate groups which probably reflect linguistic differentiation into local dialects of Indo-European that subsequently gave rise to the modern languages. The results of this process were the Early Bronze Age cultures of Europe north of the Mediterranean (c. 1800 to 1500 B.C.) and the Mycenaean civilization of Greece and vicinity.

Economically, metallurgy had little initial effect on the mass of the

FIGURE   22–6.   *Bronze Age Europe.*

STATUTE MILES 400

Metallurgy centers

Trade routes

Bell Beaker culture

Limits of Indo-European spread

Expansion of Aunjetitz

Regional Cultures

NORTHERN HUNTER-FISHERS

TURBINO

TIMBER GRAVE

BALTIC

NORTHERN CULTURES

AUNJETITZ

NORTH CARPATHIAN

MONTEORU

NORTH PONTIC.

TEI

Hittites

Troy

Mycenae

Crete

population. Metal was an expensive commodity used only for the weapons and ornaments of those who could afford it. Except for the introduction of the plow and the wagon at this time, the life of the farmer and herder went on much as before. Aside from itinerant metalsmiths in the west, metallurgy was concentrated in a few central European centers, which supplied products for the surrounding areas and increasingly for export to the Aegean along well-established trade routes. In fact, the Mycenaean demand for bronze was undoubtedly the primary factor responsible for expanding and intensifying this initially limited metallurgical industry of central Europe, and this demand increased steadily as Mycenaean technology continued to advance.

The bronze exports followed the route already established earlier by the trade from the Baltic area in amber, a commodity much prized by the Mediterranean peoples for its supposed magical properties. Its value in relation to size and weight and the restricted source of amber in northern Europe explain its important role in launching early trade activity north from the Mediterranean and pioneering the routes and mechanism of the subsequent commercial flow of the Bronze Age.

Expectably, the warrior overlords of central Europe, descendants of the Kurgan invaders, played a leading role in this process as the patrons of the copper smelter and the bronze smith and as traders of their products. Gradually, their wealth and power began to grow, as symbolized conspicuously by their burial mounds. They are represented by the Aunjetitz (Unetice) culture of the Early Bronze Age which shows such a unity over a large area of central Europe that it suggests a possible political unity as well. The power of these Aunjetitz chieftains continued to increase as the metal industry grew and flourished, and finally expressed itself in expansionist tendencies. Around 1400 B.C., for instance, they overran the Danube valley and destroyed a number of earlier cultures. This process was accentuated by their descendants, who are called the Urnfield people because they adopted the custom of cremating the dead and burying the remains in urns, forming large cemeteries. At the same time, the eastern (Indo-Iranian) branch of the Indo-Europeans, who had remained in the original steppe homeland east of the Volga, invaded and occupied Iran (Persia) and northern India, imposing their languages, as in Europe. In India they are known to history as the Aryans.

Although retention of the term "Bronze Age" for the span of time between 1800 and 750 B.C. in Europe may seem like a quaint anachronism or the dead hand of the "Three Ages" tradition, the label is fully justified here for it was the bronze trade that was responsible for the cultural advances, for the prosperity, and for the external influences that primarily shaped the life of this time, as well as for the spread of ideas throughout Europe to an extent not hitherto possible. The resultant cultures achieved a level that is only now beginning to be realized and appreciated: not only a high level of craftsmanship in their metal work, both from the technical and artistic standpoints, or a sheer volume of manufactured output that surpassed even that of the Mycenaeans of Greece or the Minoans of Crete, but a governmental and social structure that seems to have been essentially similar to that of the Mycenaean Greeks and the Hittites. There is no need to wonder any longer why they were soon to shake the civilized world to its foundations.

SEVENTH STAGE Despite the surprisingly high level of culture, the Bronze and Iron Ages in Europe were times of great instability and ethnic flux: Populations were always on the move—often with destructive consequences. This reached its apogee in the seventh stage with the great migrations and invasions in the decades between 1240 and 1200 B.C. At this time the Urnfield peoples of central Europe (the latter-day Aunjetitz warriors) and their allies in the northern Balkans (such peoples as the Phrygians, Armenians, and Dorians of history) swept down into the Mediterranean world, destroying the Mycenaean and Hittite empires, putting an abrupt end for a time to urban civilization in Greece and the Aegean and throwing the whole eastern Mediterranean into a turmoil. They also caused major ethnic and cultural changes in Italy, the Balkans, and Anatolia.

EIGHTH STAGE The Late Bronze Age of central Europe (the eighth stage) which emerged from this process holds the limelight owing to the temporary eclipse of the brilliant civilizations of the eastern Mediterranean. It was also important, however, as a period of significant economic and technological change with lasting consequences, to the extent that Childe has spoken in terms of an "industrial revolution" at this time. For example, metal technology became widespread instead of primarily a luxury industry. With the downfall of Mycenae, the export market for the booming central European metal industry collapsed and their products became cheaply available for the first time to the mass of Europeans for everyday purposes. A variety of bronze tools came into use and were widely traded throughout Europe, making possible, among other things, notable advances in the art of woodworking which has played a major role in the technology of northern Europe ever since. A more productive economic system than before, with resultant population increase, was developed by the Urnfield cultures in central Europe, who seem to have consolidated a system of settled mixed farming that was to prevail over extensive parts of Europe down to the Roman period—a stepping-up of agriculture, capable of supporting larger settlements. No further significant economic change occurred in European life until the Roman conquest. The Urnfield cultures thus laid the economic foundations for the subsequent Iron Age, as well as forming the cultural basis on which the Iron Age culture of Europe arose under Greek, Etruscan, and Scythian influence.

The Indo-Europeanization of Europe was finally completed towards the close of the Bronze Age. Increasing population, greater mobility due to the fuller use of horsedrawn chariots, and the military advantage conferred by the new slashing type of sword led to a major westward expansion of the Urnfield peoples, swamping weaker peoples, displacing others, and causing widespread secondary population movements in distant regions. This process is reflected in the spread of the Celtic languages to Spain (eighth century) and Britain (c. 500 B.C.). This ethnic instability was not confined to the west: Eastern Europe in the eighth century suffered another major invasion from the steppes, this time by the Scythians, the first pastoral nomads to appear on the scene, whose mounted warriors overran all opposition and penetrated as far as eastern Germany in the fifth century. They left a strong imprint of Asiatic culture on all of eastern Europe, conquered the early Slavs (who became the "Scythian farmers" of Herodotus' report), and ruled southern Russia for many centuries. This serves as a reminder that peoples and ideas from the steppe played a major role in later prehistoric Europe at all times. It is easier to understand how this occurred when we realize that the steppe zone at its western end merges with the north European Plain and thus provides a highway for any mobile group directly into the heart of temperate Europe.

In the Mediterranean area at this time, iron made its first appearance following the fall of the Hittites who had held a jealous monopoly, and about 700 B.C. the beginnings of the famous Etruscans are discernible. The Etruscans are now regarded as a local development in northern Italy with outside stimulus rather than as an alien intrusion from Anatolia, which had been the traditional view.

NINTH STAGE   The Early Iron Age of central Europe (700 to 400 B.C.) came into being with the penetration of ironworking northward from the Mediterranean and its establishment north of the Alps as a major local industry supplanting bronze in the old centers of metallurgy. Iron was not completely unknown here in the preceding centuries, but as yet it had played no significant role. This stage, commonly labeled the Hallstatt period after a famous cemetery, saw the rise of a series of new local cultures based on the Urnfield tradition. The adoption of horseback riding and iron weapons created a revolution in the art of war and a new aristocracy of mounted warriors, perhaps replacing or displacing a previous military aristocracy of charioteers. At any rate, it was a warlike period characterized by wide-ranging conquests but with little shift in population. All settlements were fortified. Iron, in this initial stage, did little for the common people. Its role as the proletarian metal was still in the future. There was, consequently, no fundamental alteration in European patterns of life at this time. Rather, the basis of European life revolved about an intensified concentration of economic and political power in a few hands, leading to the establishment of larger political units ruled by petty kings.

TENTH STAGE   The final stage north of the Alps, the Late Iron Age, represents the culture of the historic Celts and has been labeled "La Tene," the term referring primarily to a rather distinctive art style that grew out of Hallstatt under the influence of increasing contact with the classical civilizations of the Mediterranean. This developed in the area north of the Alps and spread widely in the fourth century B.C., carried by Celtic groups to the Balkans, Asia Minor, and all over western Europe. In Germany, the contemporary Teutonic tribes, being more remote from outside influences, continued in their old ways. The Celts of France are known to us as the Gauls; other Celtic tribes lived in Belgium and the British Isles. The Roman conquest of these Celts, and their incorporation into the Roman civilization, terminates the prehistoric period in western Europe. Northern Europe, and Europe east of the Rhine, however, remained prehistoric for some time longer, the term Roman Iron Age often being applied to this period. In general, prehistory ended in these extensive regions of Europe with the introduction of Christianity, often not until the tenth or eleventh centuries or even later.

suggested readings

Clark, J. G. D.: *Prehistoric Europe: The Economic Basis*, Philosophical Library, Inc., New York, 1952.

Gimbutas, Marija: "The Indo-Europeans: Archeological Problems," *American Anthropologist,* vol. 65, no. 4, pp. 815–836, 1963.

Hood, Sinclair: *The Home of the Heroes: The Aegean before the Greeks,* McGraw-Hill Book Company, New York, 1967.

Müller-Beck, Hansjürgen: "Prehistoric Swiss Lake Dwellers," *Scientific American,* vol. 205, no. 6, pp. 138–147, 1961.

Piggott, Stuart: *Ancient Europe*, Aldine Publishing Co., Chicago, 1965.

Sieveking, Gale: "The Migration of the Megaliths," in Edward Bacon (ed.), *Vanished Civilizations of the Ancient World,* McGraw-Hill Book Company, New York, 1963, pp. 299–322.

Taylour, Lord William: *The Mycenaeans,* Frederick A. Praeger, Inc., New York, 1964.

the great transformation:
Asia, Oceania, and Africa

the steppe zone of central Eurasia

Between the northern forest, where the hunting way of life persisted into
historic times as the most effective pattern of exploitation, and the agricultural civilizations of the Near East, India and East Asia, lies a belt of
grassland stretching from southern Russia to Manchuria which is environmentally similar in many ways to the American Great Plains. Because the
tough grass sod can only be broken with a steel plow, this vast area had
little appeal for early farmers, who could utilize only the river valleys or
the patches of forest in the intermediate "forest-steppe" along its northern
edge where the soil could be worked by hand. It was not until the development of economic patterns based primarily or entirely on livestock that
this steppe grassland could be effectively exploited and became a culturally
dynamic and politically powerful area. But this development came late.

Archeological evidence from the steppe zone is still very inadequate
as compared with Europe, especially with respect to the earlier periods and
the ecological transformations which are our particular interest. Food production was evidently introduced into the area in the form of the basic
Near Eastern pattern of mixed farming and stock raising. This process
could have occurred at either or both of the two points on the northern
margin of the nuclear Near East where there is contact with the steppe:

FIGURE   23–1.   *The Steppe zone of Eurasia.*

312

MANCHURIA

MONGOLIA

Steppe

CHINA

Yellow River

Altai Mountains

Steppe

Boreal Forest Taiga

Yenisei River

Forest Steppe

Boreal Forest Taiga

Forest Steppe

Volga River

Steppe

ARAL SEA

CASPIAN SEA

TURKMENISTAN

IRAN

Caucasus Mountains

ANATOLIA

MESOPOTAMIA

STATUTE MILES 400

0

the Caucasus, and the foothills of Turkmenistan. It must have occurred at some time prior to 3000 B.C. Whether this introduction involved actual colonization of suitable portions of the adjacent steppe zone by Near Eastern groups or merely the spread of crops and domestic animals and their adoption by indigenous hunting-fishing populations, is not clear. Since one manifestation of the earliest food-producing culture of central Eurasia is a late stage of the Kel'teminar tradition of the Aral Sea region, previously based entirely on hunting and fishing, the latter process is suggested. This earliest known food-producing culture is also manifested in the lower Volga area as the initial phase of the Kurgan tradition, which we have already encountered, and far to the east on the upper Yenisei River as the Afanasievo culture. We thus know it as yet only from the extreme margins of central Eurasia, and assume its existence over the vast territory inbetween. The similarity of these widely separated manifestations indicates the spread of this pattern by actual movements of peoples and also leads us to suppose that, like the Kurgan people, all were speakers of an ancestral Indo-European language or languages.

The pattern represented an adaptation to local conditions in that primary emphasis was placed on livestock, and hunting and fishing retained varying degrees of importance. We may suppose that these people, or some of them, were responsible for the domestication of the horse, which was native to this area, in imitation of their existing livestock. Domestic horses were valued for meat and milk, as they have been into modern times in this same area. No other use seems to have been made of them until they were introduced into the Near East around 2500 B.C., where they began to be hitched to chariots. Domestication of the camel may also have occurred along the arid southern fringe of the area. We know that the westernmost of these steppe food producers, the Kurgan people, had ox carts at the time of their explosion westward into Europe and that this mobility was an important factor in their success. However, they were in no sense nomadic, normally living a fairly sedentary life in fixed settlements; they were simply equipped for long-range movement if need be. We have no proof as yet that this same pattern held true for their eastern cousins in central Asia and Siberia, but we suspect that the latter at least had a capability for distant migrations. Similarly, we may postulate throughout the steppe the same patriarchal, stratified society that seems typical of the early Indo-Europeans. Technologically, the steppe was still dependent on stone tools, though small amounts of copper come into use as time goes on.

After 2000 B.C., contemporary with the Bronze Age cultures of Europe that developed in the aftermath of the Indo-European conquest, the steppe was occupied by the ancestors of the Indo-Iranian branch of the Indo-European language family. Their steppe Bronze Age cultural pattern is exemplified by the Andronovo culture from the Urals to the Yenisei and the closely related Timber Grave culture of the lower Volga, the ancestors of the later Scythians of history. Major sources of metal ores and centers of metallurgy existed at three points on the margin of the steppe (the Caucasus, the southern Urals, and the Altai) so that these peoples were advantageously situated from the viewpoint of bronze technology. Unlike Europe, metallurgy here did not arise as a response to demand from outside markets or play a comparably dynamic role in subsequent culture history. The Ural and Altai metal centers served only local needs, and the dynamic factors in steppe history were of a different sort.

The economy and pattern of life on the steppe during the Bronze Age shows no essential change over the preceding period, but there was increasing emphasis on the horse both economically and ritually. It was during this time—perhaps about 1600 B.C.—that some of the central Asian steppe peoples moved southward into Iran and northern India, imposing the Indo-European languages whose descendants are spoken there today. (In India, these are the Aryans of Hindu tradition.) By this time also, stock raising had spread east of the Altai mountains to the steppes of Mongolia, but farming did not go with it. Here we see an apparent case of an interesting phenomenon: the transformation of hunters directly into pastoralists, with no intermediate stage of even partial farming.

Around 1000 B.C. or slightly before, the second transformation of the steppe zone occurred. In a relatively short space of time, a new economic pattern took shape that made possible full exploitation of the grasslands themselves for the first time—pastoral nomadism. Representing one of the major adaptations in human history, it was a way of life based entirely upon the grasslands and upon possession of herds of cattle, horses, and sheep of adequate size to provide all the necessities of life. Pasturage for herds of this size requires continual movement and hence maximum mobility. Evidently, this had not been available previously, in spite of the migratory capabilities displayed on occasion by the early Indo-Europeans. The only innovation known to have occurred at about this time in the area and which could have provided the extra mobility, was horseback riding. It therefore seems likely that this was the catalyst in the sudden transformation of the steppes. Where it first arose is still unknown, but both riding and the new pastoral nomad pattern must have spread like wildfire from one end of the grassland zone to the other.

The mobility provided and required by nomadism led to population movements on a scale hitherto unknown in terms of distance and rapidity. Also, the mounted warrior, like any major military innovation, conferred an advantage militarily on the nomad peoples. Between these two factors and spurred to motion by intergroup pressures and quest for pastures, the steppe peoples for the next 2,500 years, from the Scythians to the Mongols, exerted an impact on world history out of all proportion to their actual numbers or their level of cultural development. On the one hand a continuous threat to the major Old World civilizations and to settled populations anywhere within reach (Europe, for example), they also served as a transmission belt across the vast expanse of Eurasia between the cultures of West and East, otherwise isolated from each other. Thus they were carriers of culture as well as destroyers and were often notably receptive to influence from any direction. The striking "animal style" art tradition of the steppe nomads of the last millennium B.C., one of the great art styles of the world, is as much a reflection of their tastes and capabilities as are their better-known military conquests.

Unfortunately, very little is known as yet about the processes involved in the two transformations of the central Eurasian steppe zone which were to have such repercussions on the course of human history in the Old World: the first leading to the expansion of the Indo-European speaking peoples and the second to the impact of the nomads. It is possible to sketch only the broad outlines, and the space devoted here to the subject is not commensurate with its overall significance to our subject. Certainly it is a prime area for future research.

East Asia and the Pacific

As already indicated, the cereal-growing agricultural pattern that was developed in the Chinese nuclear area spread eventually (by around 2500 B.C.) to all parts of modern China that were suitable for farming, including the island of Taiwan and the middle Amur valley. Yet it never passed these frontiers, and of all the world's nuclear areas, China seems to have exerted the least influence on the outside world.

For instance, adjacent central Asia and Mongolia were more influenced economically by the distant Near East: obviously, in this case, because China had nothing to offer that was suited to the steppe environment. But a more anomalous situation exists in the case of Korea and Japan, which lie next door to the major center of Chinese dynamism (North China) and at the same latitude, and which display today agricultural patterns that seem very similar to those of China. Yet these two areas seemingly resisted the spread of food production for many thousands of years. In Japan it is not known to have come until around 600 B.C., in the form of rice agriculture; and this may well have come to both Japan and Korea not from adjacent China, but from Southeast Asia. If a still earlier phase of vegeculture ever existed in Japan (as some have suggested), this would also point toward Taiwan and Southeast Asia, not toward China.

Some factors which help to explain this paradox in the case of Japan are geographical isolation (although island groups far more isolated were subject to mainland influence) and the efficiency of the existing gathering economy (a situation known or suspected to have inhibited enthusiasm for farming in Africa and North America). These factors would seem far less pertinent in the case of Korea, with Chinese settlers just across the border in Manchuria. But it is true that northern Korea is not an inviting area for agriculture and seems to have served as a barrier to any significant Chinese cultural influence for some time. Even so, as compared with

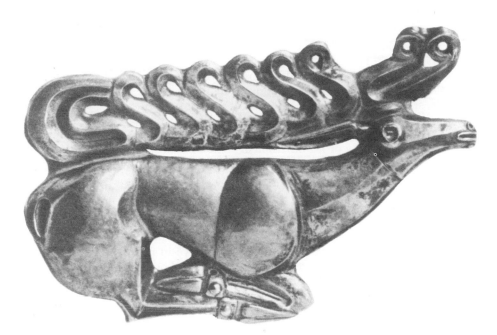

FIGURE 23–2. *Examples of animal-style art.* (From E. D. Phillips, *The Royal Hordes: Nomad People of the Steppes*, copyright © 1965 by Thames and Hudson Limited, London. U.S. edition by McGraw-Hill Book Company, New York. By permission of the publishers.)

other areas of the world, the limited dynamic impact of the Chinese nuclear area on the outside world presents an interesting problem.

In Chapter 17, reference was made to the apparent role of Southeast Asia as a hearth of food production at two different time levels: a rice complex, which spread west to India and north to the Yellow River (as well as, much later, to Korea and Japan); and an earlier level of vegeculture (root and fruit crops) with a possible time depth on the order of 10,000 years (on new evidence from Taiwan), which contributed eventually to the economy of far-off tropical Africa (as will be noted presently), and also provided the entire farming (or rather, gardening) economy for the Pacific Islands.

The evidence for Southeast Asia's role in the transformation of these considerable areas is largely botanical so far, and the attempt to reconstruct the process has leaned heavily on hypothesis and speculation. Only in respect to the Pacific Islands do we have some idea of what occurred. Here, archeological research has been very active in recent years, and the outlines of the story are beginning to emerge, although many basic problems still remain.

It will be recalled that late Pleistocene hunters were able to reach New Guinea and Australia and perhaps also some of the larger adjacent islands of Melanesia where a fishing-gathering economy would have been feasible. Settlement of the remaining Pacific Islands had to await adequate watercraft and a food-production complex which, combined with fishing, could support life on these smaller islands where pure gathering was impossible. This combination of events seems to have occurred between 2000 and 1500 B.C. on present evidence; and the process of settlement extends from that time until the occupation of New Zealand about 1000 A.D. Only then was the secondary expansion of man finally completed. However, with the exception of such distant islands as Hawaii, Easter Island, and New Zealand, the settlement of the Pacific seems to have been essentially accomplished perhaps as early as 500 B.C.

This expansion was carried out by peoples speaking languages of the Austronesian (Malayo-Polynesian) family and stemming originally from Southeast Asia—possibly from the South China-Taiwan area, perhaps some via the Philippines. Certainly the whole process was a far more complex phenomenon than the standard migration theories have hitherto visualized.

These peoples, in addition to adequate watercraft and an efficient fishing complex, had pottery, bark cloth instead of textiles, ground-stone woodworking tools for skilled carpentry, and a root-fruit crop (vegeculture) complex well suited to island conditions that included yams, taro, breadfruit, sugarcane, and coconut. Depending on the locality, some were eventually more important than others. Yams, for instance, are characteristic of Melanesia; taro, breadfruit, and coconut are the staples that make life possible on many a Polynesian coral atoll. Pigs, dogs, and chickens were valued as festive foods, but were not basic to the Pacific Island economy.

Prehistory in this part of the world lasted effectively until the voyages of Captain Cook (1768 to 1779), although isolated groups still living in the "Stone Age" have been discovered in recent years in New Guinea and Australia.

Africa

The spread of food production from the nuclear Near East area to northern Africa was a process roughly parallel to what occurred in Europe and roughly contemporary, except that the environment of North Africa was very similar to that of the Near East and hence there was need for little change or adaptation of the original farming pattern. Involved in the process were both actual movements of farmer colonists and adoption of the new economy by fairly sedentary food-gathering populations already resident in the area.

The transformation of Egypt (i.e., the Nile Valley) had taken place by at least 5000 B.C.; in the remainder of North Africa, including the northern margins of the Sahara, the process had been completed by 3500 B.C. at the latest. However, as we noted earlier, the southern Sahara region was characterized at this time by such an efficient pattern of food gathering that there was little incentive to change, especially when the Near Eastern crops were not well suited to sub-Saharan conditions. Thus, although at this time of favorable Saharan climate these food gatherers were in close proximity to farmers on the upper Nile and elsewhere, with no insuperable barrier between, the further spread of the new way of life into Africa was halted for some time. In this case, then, the spread was not irresistible or immediately revolutionizing, and we can see the factors capable of hindering the process.

Climatic change bringing increasing aridity had recreated the Sahara barrier between north and south about 2500 B.C. From that time on, sub-Saharan Africa was a separate world effectively cut off from the major developments taking place in the Mediterranean and the Near East which kept continually stimulating and enriching the course of history in Europe and central Asia. We can observe the effects of this isolation and speculate what European culture history might have been like under equal isolation by examining the subsequent history of sub-Saharan Africa and the manner and timing by which food production and metallurgy eventually spread over this area and transformed both its way of life and its population to those known in historic times. It must also be pointed out that human and animal disease has, in addition, been a severe limiting factor in African cultural development, acting to keep the economy at a simple and relatively primitive level. This factor plus poor soils, uncertain rain-

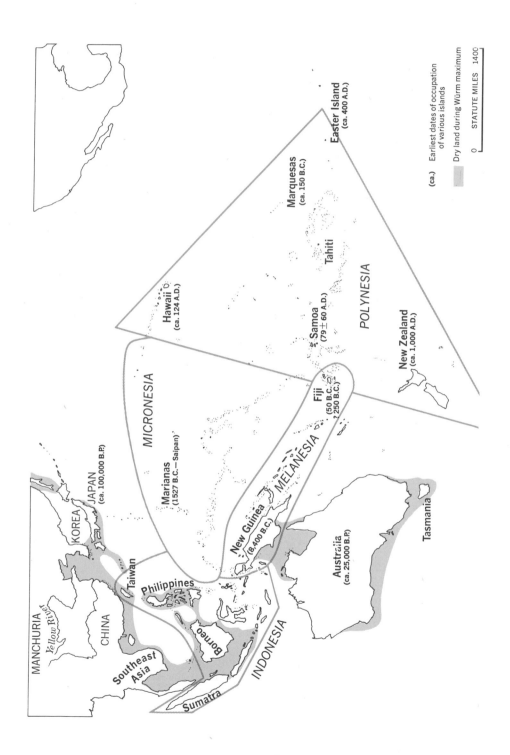

MANCHURIA

Yellow River

CHINA

KOREA

JAPAN
(ca. 100,000 B.P.)

Southeast
Asia

Taiwan

Philippines

Borneo

Sumatra

INDONESIA

New Guinea
(8,400 B.C.)

MELANESIA

Australia
(ca. 25,000 B.P.)

Tasmania

MICRONESIA

Marianas
(1527 B.C.— Saipan)

Fiji
(50 B.C.–
1,250 B.C.)

Samoa
(79 ± 60 A.D.)

Hawaii
(ca. 124 A.D.)

Tahiti

Marquesas
(ca. 150 B.C.)

POLYNESIA

New Zealand
(ca. 1,000 A.D.)

Easter Island
(ca. 400 A.D.)

(ca.)   Earliest dates of occupation
         of various islands

         Dry land during Würm maximum

0   1400
        STATUTE MILES

fall, and abundance of natural foods have all combined to discourage specialization and more intensive farming methods. However, sub-Saharan Africa has always been very receptive to new ideas that would tend to improve the economy and make subsistence easier and has proved quite capable of experimenting with such innovations and adapting them to local needs, even though the area made no major contribution to overall human advancement. Also, like the New World, sub-Saharan Africa was handicapped by lack of wheeled vehicles and pack or draft animals. Manpower was the only available source of energy, and farming techniques were limited to what could be done by hand.

By force of circumstance, Africa thus pursued its own course, as unrelated to that of the bulk of mankind as was that of the American Indians. Even so, it merits attention, not only for an understanding of the historical background of the emerging nations of the continent, but also because it provides an outstanding laboratory situation for studying the effects of isolation and environment on cultural evolution.

Unfortunately we cannot present the story of the transformation of Africa in anything approaching the detail possible for Europe or North America since the evidence available from Africa for this period is as yet totally inadequate and permits sketching only the broad outlines of the process. The limited space devoted to the subject here is a reflection of this regrettable situation and not an indication of any lesser interest or importance of the area. We may hope that it will be possible before long to afford much fuller treatment to this chapter of the human story.

At the outset of the transformation process, two major habitats and ecological patterns are discernible in sub-Saharan Africa: the grasslands of eastern and southern Africa, occupied by scattered hunting groups carrying on the pattern established in postglacial times; and the forest margins and savannah of western and central Africa, where the population was already sedentary, in fairly sizable concentrations, and was subsisting on starchy wild vegetable foods and fish. It is not impossible that some incipient vegeculture was even under way—i.e., deliberate efforts to improve and propagate staple root and fruit plants, which, as explained earlier, is a totally different concept from the sowing of seeds on which Near Eastern farming was based. The dense rain forests occupying the rest of the region were doomed to remain at a primitive level until the advent at a much later date of metal tools and special crop plants suited to this environment.

The first establishment of self-sufficient food production was a slow and gradual process that seems to have occurred among two different populations: the Negroes in the savannah belt stretching west from the

FIGURE 23–3. *Settlement of the Pacific Islands.*

Nile; and the Afro-Mediterraneans in the Horn of Africa, as a result of influences from Egypt via the upper Nile in the fourth millennium B.C. Experimentation with food production took place in both areas, and it is possible that village-tribal social patterns were already in existence before this occurred and were not an outgrowth of economic change as was the usual picture elsewhere. It appears to have been only after some time (just prior to the birth of Christ) that the new economies spread farther south, carried by the southward expansion of these two racial groups as they spread over the bulk of sub-Saharan Africa. By this time, both peoples may have possessed a metal technology, though perhaps not initially; it is possible that it spread subsequently.

The expansion was a relatively rapid movement, and the transformation was primarily a process of colonization rather than acculturation, although there is evidence in some areas of the absorption and hybridization of the previous hunting population, and some groups are obviously the product of acculturation. The Hottentots, a pastoral group of Bushman type, are a classic example of the latter. In other areas, many hunting groups persisted in peaceful coexistence with the newcomers, the two ways of life apparently exploiting sufficiently different habitats. The transformation of Africa, despite its rapidity, had not been completed by the time of European contact: The Dutch reached South Africa before the Negro food producers, and found a population still culturally in the Pleistocene.

The two original farming complexes differed in their nature and history. In the case of the savannah Negroes, crop experimentation must have been going on from at least 2500 B.C., with effective farming achieved around 500 B.C. There must have been local domestication of wild yam species, perhaps in a number of areas, and this could hardly have been inspired by knowledge of North African cereal cultivation. The domestication of sorghum, apparently in the central part of the savannah belt, is, however, generally assumed to have been an application of the concept to a local species. Millet, an important staple of the Negro complex, may have come in from Ethiopia. Sheep and goats were of secondary importance, borrowed either from the Nile or the north.

The Afro-Mediterraneans of the Horn (Ethiopia and vicinity) received cereals from the Nile which apparently inspired them to experiment with local seed-bearing plants in this botanically rich area. They produced a cereal (teff) that never achieved importance outside of Ethiopia (where it is still grown) and a type of millet of more widespread utility, among others. Livestock was acquired from those portions of the Sahara and Nubia bordering on the Nile, perhaps as these areas became unsuitable for grazing, along with the herding pattern. In the last few centuries B.C. zebu cattle of ultimate Indian origin reached the Horn from southern Arabia. Far better suited to African conditions, these may have sparked the shift to a purely pastoral economy by some Afro-Mediterranean groups. Others developed a mixed economy of farming and stock raising. Both

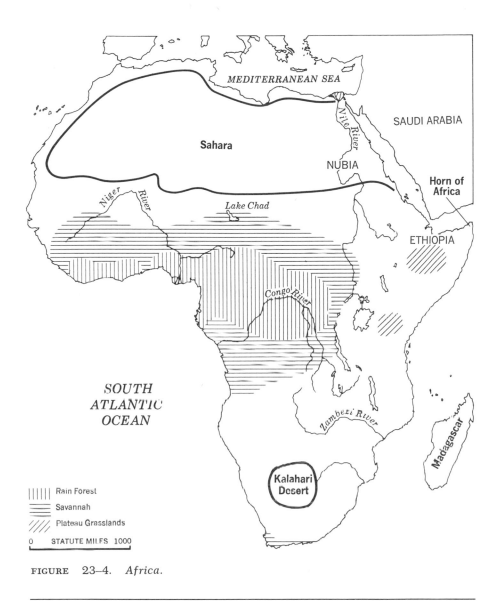

FIGURE 23–4. *Africa.*

types moved south when the expansion started, but the mixed economy pattern was to become the more widespread.

In the early centuries A.D., southeast Asian food plants reached the east African coast, evidently brought by the Indonesians who were to settle

Madagascar, and were introduced into the interior, spreading rapidly across the tropics to west Africa. The most important of these were taro, bananas, and sugarcane. The acquisition of these tropical crops greatly facilitated the spread of farming into the humid forest region, and a distinctive pattern developed here in which domestic animals were of little significance, in contrast to the picture elsewhere in Africa.

suggested readings

Jettmar, Karl: *Art of the Steppes,* Crown Publishers, Inc., New York, 1967.
Phillips, E. D.: *The Royal Hordes: Peoples of the Steppes,* McGraw-Hill Book Company, New York, 1966.
Solheim, Wilhelm G.: "Southeast Asia and the West," *Science,* vol. 157, pp. 896–902, 1967.
Suggs, Robert C.: *The Island Civilizations of Polynesia,* Mentor Books, New York, 1960.

the great transformation: the New World

North America

Very extensive areas of North America remained in the Food-gathering Stage until their occupation and absorption by European civilization in recent times, either due to environmental factors or to their isolation from the main centers of cultural development. These areas include the Arctic, the northern boreal forest, the West Coast, and much of the arid or mountainous interior stretching east across the Rockies to approximately the 100th meridian. Here the patterns and adaptations developed in postglacial times persisted. But in two major regions—the Southwest and the East—these patterns were altered by the spread of farming from the Mesoamerican nuclear area and later by the diffusion of some elements of higher civilization from the same source, initiating new cycles of cultural development. The whole way of life in these two regions was not necessarily transformed immediately, however, and in this respect North America contrasts with the usual picture in the Old World.

The region commonly referred to as the Southwest centers in the states of Arizona and New Mexico with portions of adjacent states and northwestern Mexico (see Figure 24–1). It is characterized by an arid environment, and, except on the south, was effectively isolated from other human populations of any significance. Influences diffusing from Mesoamerica into the local desert cultures of postglacial type gave birth to the Southwestern cultural tradition and pattern of life during the period from 100 B.C. to A.D. 400. Further diffusion from the same source continued to influence the subsequent developments in the region almost into historic times, especially in the southern portion.

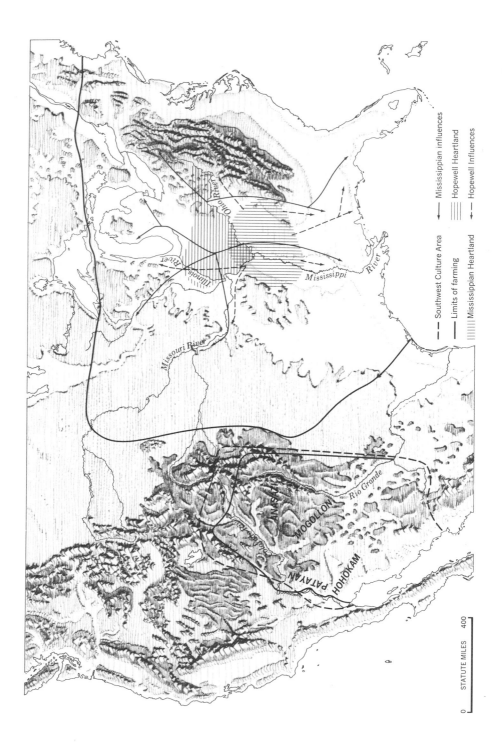

Mississippian influences
Hopewell Heartland
Hopewell Influences
Southwest Culture Area
Limits of farming
Mississippian Heartland

Ohio River

Illinois River

Mississippi River

Missouri River

Rio Grande

MOGOLLON

PATAYAN

HOHOKAM

STATUTE MILES
0   400

The beginnings of farming in the Southwest can be traced back to a much earlier time, though its initial cultural impact was slight. A primitive form of maize was being grown in a restricted area of the Mogollon Mountains about 2500 B.C., and probably squash and gourds also. Beans and improved varieties of maize appear about 1000 B.C. All these crops evidently diffused northward along the slopes of the mountain ranges from central Mexico. Farming apparently spread to the rest of the Southwest from this Mogollon area, although the details of the process are not known. This spread is associated with the appearance of the first settled village life. The earliest Southwestern pottery does not appear until around 100 B.C. and is probably also to be attributed to Mexican influence. During the ensuing 500 years, the pattern of village farming with associated technologies was established all over the Southwest. At this stage, the region was in the process of creating a new way of life by synthesizing elements from Mesoamerica and from the old local desert cultures. By A.D. 400 the Southwestern tradition had emerged and begun to develop its distinctive features. Thus the transformation of the Southwest from its postglacial food-gathering pattern was not a process of introducing a new way of life in toto as an effectively functioning whole, although the environment was essentially the same as that of highland nuclear Mexico and no adaptation of crops or techniques would have been required. The process was rather that of the successive diffusion of individual elements that eventually, over a long span of time, were combined by some Southwestern groups into a distinctive local version of village-farming economy and society.

The subsequent development of the Southwestern cultural tradition took the form of four regional variants: the Anasazi of the northern plateau, ancestors of the modern Pueblo Indians; the Mogollon of the central mountains; the Hohokam of the southern deserts, probably the ancestors of the modern Papago; and the Patayan of the Colorado River Valley, ancestors of the modern Yuman tribes. These regional variants represent separate ethnic groups as well as reflecting environmental and ecological differences within the larger region. The highest cultural development was reached by the Anasazi and Hohokam, around A.D. 1000 as reflected in the great Anasazi towns, and continuing in subsequent centuries. After A.D. 1300 to 1400 a general decline set in over the entire Southwest from its peak climax, the cause of which has not been ascertained, although such factors as climatic change or the invasion of hostile Athabascan tribes have been suggested. Unlike the situation in so many other parts of the New World, the first Europeans did not interrupt Southwestern culture at its peak.

FIGURE   24–1.   *Farming cultures of North America north of Mexico.*

The prehistoric Southwest supported a dense and sedentary population as compared to surrounding regions, on an economic basis of intensive agriculture. This frequently involved irrigation and the construction of quite impressive irrigation systems, especially in the desert south. Villages were the social and settlement units from the start and later large towns. Society was fundamentally democratic, with emphasis on community action. Sociopolitical organization was limited to the community or at most to a small area. This of course is a very different pattern from contemporary Mesoamerica. It is interesting to note that eastern North America took on much more of a Mesoamerican flavor in these respects, despite the much stronger Mexican influence on the Southwest.

Architecture is probably the most striking feature of the Southwestern tradition, especially the apartment house structures of masonry or adobe; examples familiar to many are the prehistoric "cliff dwellings" and the essentially unchanged modern Indian pueblos. Other distinctive elements are the specialized ceremonial structure (kiva) and (in some localities) courts for playing team games with a rubber ball on the familiar Meso-

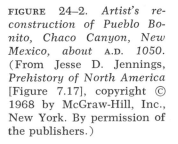

FIGURE 24–2. Artist's reconstruction of Pueblo Bonito, Chaco Canyon, New Mexico, about A.D. 1050. (From Jesse D. Jennings, Prehistory of North America [Figure 7.17], copyright © 1968 by McGraw-Hill, Inc., New York. By permission of the publishers.)

american pattern. The Southwest also became one of the major centers of ceramic technology in the Western Hemisphere, featuring fancy wares with painted decoration that also reflected a highly developed aesthetic tradition. This has survived to the present day.

Eastern North America provides an interesting comparison to the transformation of Europe since the two areas are rather similar environmentally and in terms of the cultural-economic patterns that had emerged from the adaptation to this habitat in postglacial times. However, in marked contrast to Europe, there were no major intrusions by migrants or invaders after 10,000 B.C., nor was eastern North America directly contiguous, as was Europe, to a nuclear area: It is separated from Mesoamerica by a long stretch of inhospitable country with scanty population.

The postglacial adaptation and resulting cycle of cultural development in the East—usually referred to by the label "Archaic"—reached a culmination of achievement just prior to the appearance of farming that some have termed the "Archaic climax." There is a wealth of archeological information on the life of this time. The concept of a climax implies that many elements of this life first appeared at this time and were not characteristic of earlier stages; however, some may well have a greater time depth. This climax was a time of considerable population growth, of relatively stable settlement, and of regional adaptations to a variety of particular local conditions. It was also marked by trade in raw materials between such regions, and may have been in advance of contemporary Europe in this respect. In areas where copper ore was readily available, it was worked by cold hammering (as in the earliest stage of Old World metallurgy), and the manufactured objects were spread by trade. Over most of the East there was no pottery at this time, in marked contrast to Japan with its otherwise quite comparable level of cultural and economic development. In the period 2500 to 2000 B.C., pottery characterized by the use of fibers as tempering material appeared in the southeastern region of the East, but whether as an independent invention or as an introduction from northern South America (Colombia) where pottery is slightly older, cannot yet be established. The rarity of instances of independent invention of major technological innovations in human history makes this possible case of particular interest.

New cultural patterns made their appearance in eastern North America around 1000 B.C., launching the stage often known as "Early Woodland." Most conspicuous were the Woodland pottery of the northern part of the area and the practice of constructing mounds over burials. The origin of both is obscure. Some relationship has been postulated between the Woodland pottery and that of Siberia, which shows general resemblances in techniques of manufacture and decoration. This pottery was introduced into western Alaska, but there is a gap of several thousand miles from here to the nearest occurrence of Woodland pottery. If a relationship exists, it must represent a case of "stimulus diffusion"—the spread of an idea which takes root only upon eventually reaching fertile soil.

At about the same time or shortly after (1000 to 500 B.C.) the first trace of cultivation appeared in the form of gourds and squash, evidently from Mexico, followed by efforts to domesticate some local seed-bearing plants. Maize was a later addition and perhaps spread from the Southwest rather than directly from Mexico. However, these cultivated plants played initially only a minor role in the economy and had no real impact on culture or way of life. The differentiation of what must be regional ethnic groupings or "tribes" is visible in the archeological record. The center of cultural activity was clearly east of the Mississippi River at this time, and the whole pattern is particularly characterized by accentuated attention to burial ceremonialism.

The ensuing period (200 B.C. to A.D. 400), often termed "Middle Wood-

FIGURE 24–3. *Prehistoric Indians of the Hopewell period as reconstructed from figurines and grave finds:* left: *woman dancer;* right: *dignitary.* (Modified from *Archaeology of Eastern United States*, edited by James B. Griffin, by permission of The University of Chicago Press. Copyright © 1952 by The University of Chicago.)

land," is more appropriately labeled Hopewellian, since the tradition known as Hopewell (from the type site) dominated most of the East at this time. It reached its climax in southern Ohio, as reflected in the large, spectacular sites that were the dominant religious, political, and population centers. These sites consist of sizable, complex burial mounds and geometric earthworks enclosing anywhere from ten to hundreds of acres and laid out with amazing accuracy. In our grandparents' day these constructions were considered to be beyond the capabilities of the local American Indian tribes and were commonly ascribed to a mysterious vanished race, the "Mound Builders." Another major Hopewellian development occurred in the Illinois River Valley, while many contemporary groups elsewhere shared many features of this pattern, and still others were at least slightly influenced. The economy underlying this efflorescence was still primarily based on hunting and gathering, the previous highly efficient "Archaic" system which had proven itself capable of supporting a considerable population, with the addition of maize cultivation. These were the first known maize growers in the American Middle West, and it seems highly probable that this was a factor in the cultural climax which occurred at this time.

Some authorities feel that Hopewell is best viewed as a religious cult which a number of different groups adopted and grafted on to their own cultures. But whether a cult or a cultural tradition, Hopewell was certainly

FIGURE 24–4. *Hopewell earthworks at the Newark site, Ohio. The long, parallel walls at the top extend for two and a half miles.* (From *The Hopewell Cult,* by Olaf H. Prufer. Copyright © 1964 by Scientific American, Inc. All rights reserved.)

characterized above all by a tremendous emphasis on burial ritual, which J. B. Griffin describes as being a climactic expression of a central theme of their way of life. It evidently was sufficient to motivate the enormous amount of labor and organization reflected in the mounds and earthworks, since there is no reason to suppose a level of sociopolitical organization sufficient to achieve this by coercion, although differentiation of status in the society is evident. The large mounds contain the remains of hundreds of individuals and may represent successive interments over a long period of time.

Hopewell is also characterized by a highly developed, varied art, both naturalistic and conventionalized, executed by sculpturing and carving, and by intensified trade. The latter imported copper, silver, meteoric iron, mica, and quartz crystals from various points in the Middle West; marine shells and sharks' teeth from the Gulf of Mexico; and obsidian from the Yellowstone Park area. It is thought that these were obtained by actual trading parties and not by simply passing from hand to hand. In return, manufactured objects of copper, flint, and pipestone were exported. All of this activity centered in southern Ohio. Both art and the acquisition of prized materials through trade were part of the religious ceremonialism that permeated all aspects of life.

FIGURE   24–5.   *Examples of Hopewell art:* left: *platform pipe in the form of a duck hawk;* right: *pottery vessel.* (Modified from *Archaeology of Eastern United States,* edited by James B. Griffin, by permission of The University of Chicago Press. Copyright © 1952 by The University of Chicago.)

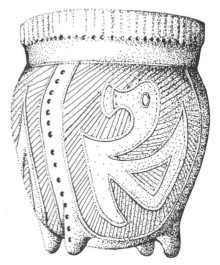

The widespread cultural dominance demonstrated by Hopewell was achieved both through actual expansion by population movement and by diffusion of influences. Groups situated farthest from the centers of highest development show only slight Hopewell influence, and their cultures are much less rich.

After A.D. 400 there is a period of decline and fading out of Hopewell in the central area that had been the main arena. Around the northern and eastern margins of this, the general pattern of life that had now been established continued into historic times, and a number of local cultures (such as the famous Iroquois) underwent their own limited development. The term "Late Woodland" has been applied to these traditions. In these marginal areas farming was important but never became the sole basis of the economy.

The shift to basic dependence on agriculture in eastern North America took place in the central Mississippi Valley (St. Louis to Vicksburg) between A.D. 700 and 900. Societies of this type go under the label of Mississippian. Owing to the new and different economic base and orientation, these societies were tied to specific localities and emphasized territoriality and land ownership. The large supplies of storable food produced brought a marked increase in population, specialization of labor, and elaborate agricultural ceremonialism of a community nature. This ceremonialism subsequently spread widely through the area of the southeastern United States. As the result of a climate ideally suited to growing maize, it was the Mississippi Valley and the Southeast that enjoyed cultural dominance during the last thousand years of Indian history in eastern North America, in contrast to the earlier Hopewell dominance centered farther north. The fertile alluvial river bottomlands were the centers of population.

Between approximately A.D. 1000 and 1500, increasing population brought about an expansion of the Mississippian territory by migration up river valleys from the original heartland. However, the latter continued to be the scene of the major development of Mississippian culture. Here we find the remains of large towns, such as Cahokia, covering 10 to 40 acres and fortified with stockades and bastions. These were tribal capitals and also the main population centers. Typically they consisted of a central plaza bordered by flat-topped pyramids, often of impressive size, on which were situated the major civic and religious structures. These, along with the hundreds of dwellings, were constructed of wattle plastered with clay. In these towns was to be found an organized priesthood, hereditary chiefs, and a stratified society. The overall picture is strikingly reminiscent of Mesoamerica.

The Mississippian cultural climax occurred between A.D. 1200 and 1500 and was seen in full bloom by early explorers like De Soto. There were, of course, many local variations, styles, and traditions reflecting the different tribal groupings following this pattern of life. Religious symbolism, always a conspicuous feature, spread widely and provided a unify-

FIGURE   24–6.   *Reconstruction of Mississippian mound group at the Anna site near Natchez, Mississippi. The large mound is about 60 feet high.* (From Jesse D. Jennings, *Prehistory of North America* [Figure 6.33B], copyright © 1968 by McGraw-Hill, Inc., New York. By permission of the publishers.)

ing element. Some of this was probably derived from Mexico. What has been called the "Pan-Southeastern Ceremonial Complex" appears around A.D. 1000, and by the period A.D. 1300 to 1500 many fundamentally similar religious attitudes and practices were to be seen over a large part of the Mississippian culture area.

To summarize the transformation of eastern North America: We see an initial introduction of farming spread by diffusion, grafted on to existing cultures, and simply enhancing the productivity of an existing highly efficient "Archaic" gathering economy which was already supporting fairly large stable populations and quite rich cultures, without basically altering the pattern of life or changing the economy. Farming, therefore, simply supplemented, rather than changed, the existing situation. This enhanced productivity aided the culmination of ongoing cultural traditions that climaxed in the remarkable Hopewellian period, one of the major achievements of the prehistoric populations of eastern North America. The subsequent growth, in the most favorable farming area farther south, of true agricultural societies with towns and temples brought a major change in life and also a population expansion. This Mississippian pattern spread largely by actual migration and colonization, though the associated cult ideas spread more widely by diffusion. This pattern remained centered in the area of the southeastern United States and did not affect the continuation of older ways of life in the north and northeast of eastern North America. The Mississippian development resulted in the final climax of prehistoric culture in the East.

Intermediate America

Lying between the area of Mesoamerican civilization on the north and Andean civilization on the south is a considerable territory embracing Central America and northwestern South America. Since it forms a portion of the rim of the Caribbean, and the remaining lands around that sea are in some respects a cultural outlyer, the designation "Circum-Caribbean" has sometimes been applied to the total region for anthropological purposes. Viewed from the standpoint of this chapter, however, Central America and northwestern South America are best understood and have the greatest significance as an intermediate zone between the two centers of high civilization, and the label "Intermediate America" is suggested as appropriate. The eastern rim of the Caribbean, formed by the island chain of the West Indies, was influenced and colonized from a different hearth, the tropical forest area of South America (see map Figure 21-1).

Although this intermediate zone has sometimes been dismissed as merely a passive recipient of developments elsewhere, its strategic geographical position dictates a significant role as an intermediary and transmitter of cultural stimuli. It is true that the area lacks any evidence of empires, cities, temples, forts, tombs, or irrigation works and seems to have produced only small chiefdoms or incipient states leaving scanty remains for the archeologist, yet their chiefs and priests possessed considerable power and wealth. And it must not be forgotten that the highest development of gold working in the New World is found in this same area.

Owing to the nature of the material remains left by the prehistoric cultures of the intermediate zone—largely restricted to potsherds and looted gold objects devoid of context—the task of attempting to reconstruct the prehistory of the area is beset with difficulties, quite aside from the lack of attention it has received from researchers whose interests are understandably drawn to the high civilizations. We will focus on Colombia, from which the best information is available.

Prior to 1000 B.C., sedentary life seems already to have had a long history in Colombia, based on abundant river and lake resources. The earliest pottery yet found in the New World occurs in shell mound sites of this general type. Around 1000 B.C. manioc appeared in the lowland areas, having spread from the Amazon basin where it was presumably first domesticated. Initially, the cultivation of this root crop was no more than a supplement, though it gained in importance.

The cultural phase in Colombia known as Momil reflects the transition from roots to maize as a staple crop. Maize was introduced from Mesoamerica at this time as a fully developed economic complex along with other cultural items. (A parallel situation is visible in neighboring Venezuela.) This would seem to represent an actual incursion of a Mesoamerican group accustomed to dependence on maize. Under the previous economy, even though sedentary life was possible, there was no surplus since roots and fish cannot be stored under local conditions. The advent of maize seems to have had immediate social consequences since the beginnings of stratified society and the rise of specialists is suggested now by the archeological remains. It is probable that gold metallurgy had its beginnings at this time.

Maize farming provided the basis for all future cultural development in Colombia; in particular, it made possible the settlement of the extensive highland areas for the first time. The variety of habitats provided by the rugged terrain and consequent range of climates plus the botanical richness of the region made it an ideal laboratory for experimentation with new food plants, which occurred as the population expanded. This same rugged terrain also promoted decentralization of settlement in the highlands, in contrast to the centralized lowland riverine sites; the resultant isolation of local groups acted to break down any initial cultural homogeneity and gave rise to many local cultural traditions.

At the same time, repeated colonization of the Pacific Coast of Colombia by Mesoamerican seafarers was an important factor in the cultural development of much of the region. Influences from these outsiders spread far inland and were responsible for a much greater complexity and richness of culture than would otherwise have been the case. The first phase of this seaborne contact began as early as 1200 B.C. with the introduction of the jaguar cult; a second phase, around 500 B.C., brought many new traits and resulted in the development of the priest-temple-idol complex in Colombia, increased social stratification and craft specialization, and high technological development.

The peak of political and social development in this part of South America, represented by groups like the Chibcha, was simply a village federation united under the control of a single powerful chief who also functioned as high priest. But this was the exception and not the rule.

The islands of the West Indies lay beyond the zone of direct Mesoamerican or Andean cultural influence; they were settled by groups from the tropical forest of northeastern South America whose cultures reflected some echoes of the more complex life to the west of them in the Inter-

FIGURE 24–7. *Gold pendant representing an anthropomorphic Crocodile God. Tairona culture, 1000–1500* A.D. (Courtesy of Robert Woods Bliss Collection, Dumbarton Oaks, Washington, D.C.)

mediate Zone. Farming and pottery had spread north as far as Puerto Rico by about A.D. 200 and had reached Cuba by A.D. 1000. In this area manioc was the staple food crop, with maize frequently in a secondary role. There was some rather poor metallurgy in contrast to the high level of craftsmanship in the Intermediate Zone, but the general level of social and religious development was rather similar, as exemplified by chiefs, priests, and the "zemi" religious cult, though lacking the benefits of direct Mesoamerican influence in these respects.

conclusions

We have seen that the process of transformation of the world outside of the nuclear areas by the horizontal spread of food production had a very different aspect from region to region.

In Europe, some initial colonization from the Aegean–Near East nuclear area was perhaps involved, though very little is known about this stage. For the most part, however, the transformation was brought about by colonization on the part of Europeans who had already developed distinctive farming patterns suited to European conditions, and by acculturation of indigenous hunting populations who came in contact with the new way of life. A significant amount of adaptation was involved, owing to environmental conditions differing from those of the nuclear area, and distinctive local cultural developments were typical. Relatively speaking, the transformation was a rapid and revolutionary process. A subsequent and somewhat parallel phenomenon was the spread of metallurgy: initially introduced from outside, but immediately giving rise to local centers of development from which, eventually, it spread to the rest of Europe with important effects on technology.

The transformation of the steppe zone of central Asia may have been launched by diffusion of the new pattern to sedentary gathering groups near the margin of the Near East (again, we know almost nothing about this stage), but the major spread must have been accomplished by subsequent rapid migration of populations that had developed a complex satisfactory for the area, with a considerable emphasis on livestock. Quite early in this process the domestication of the native horse and camel of the region must have occurred in imitation of the existing livestock. Thus the central Asian steppe served as a secondary nuclear area which made significant contributions to the original Near Eastern pattern. And eventually there was the very sudden development here of pastoral nomadism, one of the major economic patterns of mankind, which was to enable the steppe peoples to exert an impact on human history out of all proportion to their numbers.

In East Asia, the influence of the Chinese farming pattern is very curiously limited to the area of modern China. Yet the Southeast Asian rice complex spread west to India and north to the Yellow River and eventually to Korea and Japan, though it failed to penetrate the latter until a very late date, raising some interesting problems. This rice complex, it should be pointed out, undergoes no essential change or adaptation when exported from its tropical homeland to areas, like Japan, of quite different environment. How it may have been spread, or when, we do not know. The older Southeast Asian vegeculture complex is closely tied to the tropics, within which it spread widely from Africa on the west to Polynesia on the east, carried by sea by far-ranging colonists. Only with the aid of this economic base was it possible for man to occupy the islands of the Pacific. Other than varying emphasis on particular crops in some localities, the complex underwent no essential changes over this vast area.

The mechanics of the spread of food production to North Africa from the Near East are not clear; it may have been a rapid process, and some actual colonization was doubtless involved. The resulting patterns varied with the particular habitat: intensive farming in the Nile Valley, a close facsimile to the Near East in northwestern Africa, and an emphasis on cattle in the Sahara. After the transformation of North Africa, there was a considerable delay before the process was repeated south of the Sahara. This may probably be explained both by the efficiency of the fishing-gathering economy characteristic of the zone immediately below the Sahara at this time and also by the unsuitability of the Near Eastern crops. It took a while before a satisfactory local farming pattern could be developed, inspired by awareness of cultivation elsewhere, but when this occurred, the transformation of southern Africa was quite rapid and was perhaps coincident with the spread of metallurgy. The process was greatly facilitated by the introduction of Indian zebu cattle, better suited to local conditions than others were, and by the acquisition of certain tropical crops from Indonesia. The transformation was primarily accomplished by actual southward migration of populations practicing the new economies, with some instances of acculturation of local hunting groups either to farming or herding. It has taken place since the time of Christ and had not been completed at first European contact in South Africa. Subsequently, a number of New World staple crops such as maize, manioc, and peanuts were introduced, readily adopted, and spread very rapidly over large areas by diffusion, demonstrating that African farmers have been quick to improve their economy whenever opportunities have arisen.

Eastern North America was an area characterized by a very efficient gathering economy capable of supporting a fairly dense and relatively sedentary population. Agriculture was initially introduced and spread by the separate diffusion of certain crop plants; it did not arrive either as an integrated farming complex or as a socioeconomic pattern. These crops were simply grafted on to the existing way of life as a supplement and seem to have wrought no basic changes, although the first great culture climax in the area (Hopewell) does seem to immediately follow the introduction of maize. This initial role of agriculture persisted until historic times in the north and northeast; only in the milder climate of the southeastern United States did a full commitment to a farming economy subsequently take place, with important social consequences, and give rise to the second (Mississippian) culture climax. This was a complete and irreversible transformation of the sort familiar in most of the rest of the world. The pattern expanded its area by colonization.

In the Southwest there was also a total commitment to the new way of life and hence a complete transformation. Here again it seems to have been a question of the separate diffusion of various elements over a period of time from the nuclear area which were reworked into a distinctive Southwestern socioeconomic pattern by the local population.

In the Intermediate Zone, there was apparently initial diffusion of manioc from the Amazon Basin, but it was maize and accompanying cultural influences from Mesoamerica that actually changed the way of life and sparked cultural development. These seem to have been brought by actual migrants and colonists from the north, who came by sea in some cases. Influence from the Andean nuclear area to the south would seem to have been minimal.

Viewing the world as a whole, it will be seen that the process of transformation by horizontal spread runs the gamut from actual spread of social patterns or of economic complexes by migration or colonization to spread of individual crop plants by diffusion. Similarly the impact of this transformation may range from total commitment to a new way of life to an economic supplement grafted on to an existing efficient system. In many regions the spread seems to have been irresistible in that the hunting pattern could not survive in competition; hunting groups had to assimilate or retreat to a marginal refuge area (if this were possible) or face extinction. In other regions the spread seems to have encountered resistance or disinterest, resulting in delay or in only selective acceptance of some elements of the new pattern. There are areas, such as Europe, transformed so rapidly that the term "revolution" would seem entirely appropriate, and others where it would be a patent misnomer. And always there are the limits to this spread and transformation set by environmental factors: Unlike hunting, food production is not a pattern of universal applicability to which all mankind might ultimately aspire. Often it had to be adapted to local conditions before the transformation could be accomplished. We must not lose sight, either, of the racial, demographic, and biological effects on mankind resulting from the great transformation, the nature of which was outlined in the chapters on the first farmers. These effects are now virtually worldwide.

suggested readings

Griffin, James B.: "Eastern North American Archaeology: A Summary," *Science*, vol. 156, pp. 175–191, 1967.

Prufer, Olaf H.: "The Hopewell Cult," *Scientific American*, vol. 211, no. 6, pp. 90–102, 1964.

Reichel-Dolmatoff, G.: *Colombia*, Frederick A. Praeger, Inc., New York, 1965.

Willey, Gordon R.: *An Introduction to American Archaeology*, vol. 1, Prentice-Hall, Inc., Englewood Cliffs, N.J., 1966, pp. 178–341.

index